THE ZONDERVAN 2011

PASTOR'S ANNUAL

An Idea & Resource Book

T. T. Crabtree

ZONDERVAN®

ZONDERVAN.com/
AUTHORTRACKER
follow your favorite authors

ZONDERVAN

The Zondervan 2011 Pastor's Annual
Copyright © 1970, 1990, 2010 by Zondervan

Requests for information should be addressed to:
Zondervan, *Grand Rapids, Michigan 49530*

Much of the contents of this book was previously published in *Pastor's Annual 1971* and *Pastor's Annual 1991*.

ISBN 978-0-310-27590-9

10 11 12 13 14 15 16 17 18 19 /DCI/ 23 22 21 20 19 18 17 16 15 14 13 12 11 10 9 8 7 6 5 4 3 2 1

CONTENTS

MISCELLANEOUS HELPS

Messages on the Lord's Supper

Themes for Wedding Ceremonies

CONTRIBUTING AUTHORS

Tal D. Bonham		Sunday evening messages
H. C. Chiles	A.M.:	August 7, 14, 21, 28
T. T. Crabtree		All sermons not attributed to others
R. B. Culbreth	A.M.:	September 4, 11, 18, 25
William T. Flynt	A.M.:	January 9 April 24 May 1, 15 June 5
James G. Harris	A.M.:	November 6, 13, 20
David G. Hause	A.M.:	November 27 December 4, 11, 18, 25
Furman Kenney	A.M.:	May 8 June 12, 19, 26 July 10, 17, 24
Howard S. Kolb	Wed.:	June 1, 8, 15, 22, 29
C. J. Lawrence		Messages for Children and Young People
Jerold R. McBride	A.M.:	July 3 February 13, 20, 27 October 2, 9, 16, 23, 30
Roy D. Moody	Wed.:	January 5, 12, 19, 26
R. Trevis Otey	A.M.:	March 6, 13, 20, 27 April 3, 10, 17 God's Masterpiece Sunday evening messages

PREFACE

Favorable comments from ministers who serve in many different types of churches have encouraged me to believe that the *Pastor's Annual* provides valuable assistance to many busy pastors as they seek to improve the quality, freshness, and variety of their pulpit ministry. To be of service to fellow pastors in their continuing quest to obey our Lord's command to Peter, "Feed my sheep," is a privilege to which I respond with gratitude.

I pray that this issue of the *Pastor's Annual* can be blessed by our Lord in helping pastors to plan and produce a preaching program that will better meet the spiritual needs of the congregation to which they are called to minister.

This issue contains series of sermons by eleven contributing authors who have been effective contemporary preachers and successful pastors. Each of these authors is listed with his sermons in the acknowledgments. I accept responsibility for those not listed there.

This issue of the *Pastor's Annual* is dedicated to the Lord with a prayer that he will bless these efforts to let the Holy Spirit lead us in preparing "A Planned Preaching Program for the Year."

—*T. T. Crabtree*
Formerly pastor,
First Baptist Church
Springfield, Missouri

JANUARY

■ **Sunday Mornings**

The suggested theme for the first morning messages of the year is "Responsible Christian Living."

■ **Sunday Evenings**

The Sermon on the Mount will serve as the basis for the fifty-two Sunday evening messages for the year. In the Sermon on the Mount, Jesus portrays the ideal inner spirit, influence, conduct, motives, faith, and ministry of those who become his followers and his servants.

■ **Wednesday Evenings**

The suggested theme for the first Wednesday evenings of the year is "Counsel for Christians." These messages are designed to encourage and strengthen the people of God.

SUNDAY MORNING, JANUARY 2

Title: The Door of Opportunity

Text: "But I will tarry at Ephesus until Pentecost. For a great door and effectual is opened unto me, and there are many adversaries" (**1 Cor. 16:8–9**).

Scripture Reading: 1 Corinthians 16:1–9

Hymns: "Lead On, O King Eternal," Shurtleff

"Ring Out the Old, Bring in the New," Tennyson

"Another Year Is Dawning," Havergal

Offertory Prayer: Heavenly Father, we thank you for the joyous blessing of life and opportunity as we enter our journey through another year. We look to the past with gratitude and to the future with faith. We thank you for that which you have bestowed upon us. We come this morning to offer not only our tithes and offerings but also our time and our talents. We offer ourselves to you that our lives might reflect your glory. Accept these offerings of our love as indications of our devotion to you and as symbols of our desire to be a blessing to the world in which you have placed us as your servants. In Jesus' name we pray. Amen.

Introduction

The poet Louise Fletcher Tarkington spoke for most of us when she said:

I wish that there were some wonderful place
Called the Land of Beginning Again
Where all our mistakes and all of our heartaches
And all of our poor, selfish grief
Could be dropped like a shabby coat at the door,
And never put on again.

Our desire as children of God is to do better in the future than we have in the past.

The new year presents us with the opportunity of finding a "Land of Beginning Again." We will be using a new calendar, and we will be facing new challenges and new responsibilities, but we are deceiving ourselves if we believe that the new year will be completely different from the old year. For we will be confronted with many of the struggles, problems, and heartaches we knew during the past year.

While we may have a deep inward desire for some fantasy land, a land of beginning again, we will be much more realistic if we recognize that our present position is really our door of opportunity for significant achievement and worthwhile service. Paul probably would have liked to have found some land of beginning again during those days when he labored for our Lord and for a needy people in the city of Ephesus. Instead of fleeing or fainting because of difficulty, he said, "But I will tarry at Ephesus until Pentecost. For a great door and effectual is opened unto me, and there are many adversaries" (1 Cor. 16:8–9). In spite of difficulties, disappointments, and outright opposition, the apostle Paul determined that he would seize this opportunity for significant service and busy himself with doing what needed to be done at the moment. You and I can make the coming year a significant one if we make a similar decision. At times all of us have unrealistic, romantic ideas about the golden door of opportunity that will open for us tomorrow. We must confess that we are looking for the goose that will lay golden eggs. We face the peril of dividing time up into only two periods—the past and the future. The past has gone into the tomb of time. The future is yet in the womb of time. The only part of time that we have is today.

I. Today is our day of opportunity for effective service (John 9:4; 2 Cor. 6:2).

To stress the importance of making the right choices, Shakespeare had Brutus say:

There is a tide in the affairs of men,
Which, taken at the flood, leads on to fortune;
Omitted, all the voyage of their life
Is bound in shallows and in miseries.
We must take the current when it serves,
Or lose our ventures.

The absolute necessity of recognizing the importance of the present, in contrast to the past or the future, is emphasized by John Oxenham:

> *But once I pass this way,*
> *And then — no more.*
> *But once — and then, the Silent Door*
> *Swings on its hinges —*
> *Opens . . . Closes —*
> *And no more I pass this way.*
> *So while I may,*
> *With all my might,*
> *I will assay*
> *Sweet comfort and delight,*
> *To all I meet upon the Pilgrim way.*
> *For no man travels twice*
> *The Great Highway*
> *That climbs through Darkness up to Light —*
> *Through Night*
> *To Day.*

A. *It is foolish to weep over lost opportunities.*
B. *It is foolish to wait for the future.* The future is but a dream. It may be nothing more than a mirage. The only thing that we can be certain of is the present.

II. We will always face many adversaries.

It is romantic fantasy for one to wish for a life of ease and comfort in which success can be achieved without struggle. Significant success will always involve struggle against hardships, difficulties, and disappointments.

A. *Paul was confronted with many adversaries.* He was opposed by the Jewish leaders who violently disagreed with his ideas about the kingdom of God. Paul believed that the kingdom of God was wide enough and large enough to include the Gentiles. He believed that the love of God was all-inclusive and that God was just as concerned about redeeming the Gentiles as he was the sons of Abraham. In preaching salvation through faith in Jesus Christ, he was confronted with violent opposition that led to his imprisonment and eventually to his death. In spite of his external opposition from religious leaders, Paul continued his faithful service.

Paul experienced hostile opposition from the pagans whose financial security was threatened by the conversion of those who contributed to their business in Ephesus. Those who profited because of the temple of Diana were agitated to the extent that they rioted (Acts 19:23–29).

B. *Our Lord was confronted with many adversaries.* On one occasion even Christ's family sought to dissuade him from the direction in which his life was pointing. Once when he returned to his hometown of Nazareth, the people were so enraged by his message that they sought to thrust him over a cliff (Luke 4:28–29). Almost from the beginning he experienced hostility and opposition on the part of the religious establishment who saw him as a threat to the laws and traditions as they interpreted them. This conflict eventually led to his death.

At the beginning of his ministry, our Lord was violently opposed by the Devil, who sought to tempt him to deny his redemptive purpose. There were times during Jesus' ministry when even the disciples opposed him (Matt. 16:22–23; John 11:8).

We may worry about external opposition, but perhaps our greatest danger will be the internal hindrances that keep us from doing God's will for our lives. These inward adversaries can be conquered only as we enter the doorways of opportunity for worship, study, and prayer in which we let God work within us so that his will might be accomplished through us.

Each of us has a built-in tendency to avoid obligations, burdens, or difficulties. We have an inborn love of the easy life. It is natural for us to be selfish and self-centered. Unless we are alert and determined to do otherwise, we will find ourselves drifting through this coming year, adding days to our lives instead of filling those days with significance and meaning.

III. Seizing our opportunities for service.

God has granted to us the privilege of being alive in this year of 2011. Before us is a road that offers many doors of opportunity. Each of us would be exceedingly wise to enter each door of opportunity that God opens for us.

A. *The door to divine sonship is open to all who will receive Jesus Christ as the Savior from sin (John 1:12).* Some have already seized the opportunity to enter this door. We can rejoice that the door is still open for others to enter. Some, like the rich young ruler, have declined to enter this door and consequently remain in the darkness of spiritual destitution outside the family of God.

B. *The door of faith is open.* Paul rejoiced that God opened the door of faith to the Gentiles (Acts 14:27). He was delighted that Gentiles could trust God and walk by faith and enjoy his favor. To each of us is given the privilege of walking by faith (Prov. 3:5–6). To walk by faith is to enjoy the presence of God as did Enoch and Abraham and others (see Heb. 11).

C. *The door to the closet of prayer is always open (Matt. 6:6).* Jesus instructed us that once we enter the closet of prayer, we are to close the door that we might enjoy the intimacy of personal communion and fellowship with the heavenly Father. Once we are in the closet of prayer, we are invited to shut out that which would distract and hinder us from hearing what the heavenly Father would communicate to us.

D. *The door to Christian witnessing is open.* Paul speaks of a door being open to preach Christ's gospel in the city of Troas. The door will be open for us to announce the good news of God's love in our community and in our city during this coming year. We, like the apostle Paul, should be praying that "God would open unto us a door of utterance, to speak the mystery of Christ" (Col. 4:3). If we know Jesus Christ, we have the message that God can use to bring forgiveness and new life to those about us. Let us pray for each other that we will be able to speak as our Lord would have us to speak to those who need the message of his love and grace.

Conclusion

Jesus said, "I am the door: by me if any man enter in, he shall be saved, and shall go in and out, and find pasture" (John 10:9). Jesus is the door to forgiveness. He is the door into new life, eternal life, the very life of God. He is the door to new spiritual power and energy. He is the door to hope for the future as we seek to live lives of significant achievement and service. He is the door to the eternal home of God at the end of the way.

On this first Sunday of the New Year, let each of us determine that we will be alert to seize every opportunity for worship and service to our God and to those about us. By so doing we will discover that we have already found the land of beginning again.

SUNDAY EVENING, JANUARY 2

Title: Introducing the Sermon on the Mount

Text: "And seeing the multitudes, he went up into a mountain: and when he was set, his disciples came unto him: And he opened his mouth, and taught them, saying" (**Matt. 5:1–2**).

Scripture Reading: Matthew 5:1–12

Introduction

One of the most appalling judgments against Christendom today is ignorance of the demands of Christ in the Sermon on the Mount. On May 26, 1961, the Reverend Paul Brooks Leath preached an unusual sermon at the 104th annual meeting of the Southern Baptist Convention in St. Louis, Missouri. The large crowd in Kiel Auditorium that morning listened attentively for almost half an hour as Leath quoted the Sermon on the Mount from Matthew 5–7. When he had finished, many convention messengers rushed to the public relations booth to purchase a copy of the message.

I. Critics of the sermon.

A. *The Sermon on the Mount has attracted its critics.* Along with praise from the greatest minds both inside and outside of Christendom, the Sermon on the Mount has received more opposition, distortion, and dilution than any other piece of literature, yet it has outlived all the accusations. For instance, the German philosopher Nietzsche concluded that it has a "debasing effect on man." But his plea for a "master morality" and the evolution of the "superman" lost its popularity when the world saw in Hitler the result of such a philosophy.

B. *The Sermon on the Mount is still judged out of date, however, by those who would relegate its relevance to the past and those who would postpone its relevance to the future.* Albert Schweitzer, the most outspoken proponent of the former view, believed that the Sermon on the Mount is a part of Jesus' "interim ethic," which was relevant only during the interim between the time it was delivered and Jesus' death. The dispensational view of the sermon, on the other hand, assumes that Matthew 5–7 constitutes the "law" that will not be in effect until the period before the millennium.

II. Ignorance of the sermon.

A. *The greatest opposition to the Sermon on the Mount continues to be the neglect of its teachings in the lives of Christians.* The sermon has become the flag under which the lives of many Christians sail instead of the rudder that steers their course. If the proverbial visitor from Mars landed in a typical Christian community, having read the Sermon on the Mount en route, he would conclude that he had landed in the wrong place.

B. *At a Christian summer assembly, some simple questions on the Sermon on the Mount were asked of a group of students between the ages of seventeen and twenty-four.* Only 37 percent knew that the Sermon on the Mount is recorded in Matthew 5–7; 35 percent merely indicated that it is found in the book of Matthew; 21 percent gave the wrong chapters in Matthew; 7 percent left the question unanswered; none of them indicated that the shorter form of the sermon is also found in Luke 6. Most of them (91 percent) knew that Jesus preached the Sermon on the Mount; only 8 percent indicated that they did not know; 1 percent said that James preached the sermon. Almost half (48 percent) could not quote a beatitude. Typical beatitudes listed were "Blessed are the poor in heart" and "Blessed are the peacemakers, for they shall obtain peace." More than 20 percent could not quote the Golden Rule. Such answers as "Be ye kind to one another" and "Love thy neighbor as thyself" were common.

III. Importance of the sermon.

The Sermon on the Mount in Matthew 5–7 has been more widely discussed than any other piece of literature of equal length. Some Christian scholars have emphatically asserted that the best-known fact about Jesus is that he gave the Sermon on the Mount. Mahatma Gandhi, a great leader outside the ranks of Christianity, praised the sermon as the unadulterated message of

Jesus. Parts of the sermon have even been taught in the name of science and psychology.

A. *"Into a mountain."* Our Lord had spent the night on a mountain in prayer. He came down out of the mountain to call out the Twelve. Matthew indicates that he went up into a "mountain" (*oros*) to deliver the sermon. On the other hand, Luke pictures the scene as a "plain" (*pedinos*). Even though there is no relationship between the Greek words *oros* and *pedinos*, there is reason to believe that both of them speak of the same locality. In Isaiah 13:2 of the Septuagint, *oros* and *pedinos* are combined (*epi orous pedinos*) to denote a level, flat mountain. Thus, Jesus and the disciples probably gathered on a plateau while the multitudes gathered on the outskirts of it. Even though the exact location cannot be identified, it is not unreasonable to believe that such a place can be found in the mountain range between Tiberias and Nazareth.

B. *"When he was set."* The Jewish rabbi often preached while walking around or standing, but when he wanted to teach his class something of utmost importance, he sat down to speak. Jesus was getting ready to say something to which all disciples should pay attention.

C. *"His disciples came."* It has been said that the Sermon on the Mount "was spoken into the ear of the church and overheard by the world." The Sermon on the Mount is addressed primarily to the disciples of Jesus Christ. However, the conclusion of the sermon (Matt. 7:28) indicates that the multitudes were present at least at the end of the sermon. The sermon, therefore, is the description of how one should live after becoming a Christian; it does not describe entrance into the Christian life. The cross, the resurrection, the Second Coming, the Lord's Supper, baptism, and other basic doctrines of Christianity are not even mentioned in the sermon. When people accept the challenge to follow Christ, they take upon themselves the demands of discipleship set forth in Matthew 5–7.

D. *"He opened his mouth."* The Greek phrase used here is not just a fancy way of saying "he said" or "he spoke"; it is used to describe solemn, dignified utterances. It signifies that what one is about to hear is of paramount importance. The same Greek phrase is used to describe one who pours out of his mind and heart truths that are central and dear.

Conclusion

History reveals that when Christians have taken seriously the demands of the Sermon on the Mount, spiritual revival has resulted. When Christians apply the teachings to their lives, unsaved people will flock to church to see what they are missing. Jesus' teachings in Matthew 5–7 are intended to be the rudder that steers the course of Christians rather than the flag under which they sail.

WEDNESDAY EVENING, JANUARY 5

Title: Why God Loves You

Text: "For God so loved the world, that he gave his only begotten Son, that whosoever believeth in him should not perish, but have everlasting life" (**John 3:16**).

Scripture Reading: John 3:1–17

Introduction

One of the great mysteries that people seek to understand is the love of God. Every definition fails to fully define it. John 3:16–17 overwhelms us with its meaning. We wonder why God would love a world that is in revolt against him. And many individuals wonder why God loves them.

I. God loves you because you are his creation.

The Bible tells us that people are a special creation of God. Although we do not know the method God used to create man, we do know that man did not just happen. Genesis 2:7 says, "And the LORD God formed man of the dust of the ground, and breathed into his nostrils the breath of life; and man became a living soul."

A. *God showed his love for you by creating you in his image.* This is not a physical image but a spiritual image. God gave you:
   1. The power to think (Isa. 1:18).
   2. The power to choose (Josh. 24:15).
   3. The power to love (Mark 12:30–31).
   4. The sense of right and wrong (James 1:13–14).
B. *God showed his love for you by creating you to know him.* People are never complete until they know God in a personal relationship through Jesus Christ. Because people were created to know God, God through love has revealed himself to them:
   1. To know him through Jesus Christ. God chose for people to know him through his Son, Jesus Christ. Jesus said during his earthly ministry, "He that hath seen me hath seen the Father" (John 14:9).
   2. To know him through a study of the Bible. The Bible is God's message to humans. By studying the Bible, we can know the nature, holiness, love, judgment, grace, work, and will of God.
   3. To know him through observing nature. If we are willing to observe nature, we can know God better. The psalmist said, "The heavens declare the glory of God; and the firmament sheweth his handiwork" (Ps. 19:1).

II. God loves you because you need him.

If you were to search the pages of history, both secular and biblical, you would discover fact after fact that proves that people cannot get along without God.

A. *You need God to redeem you from sin.* No person is able to redeem himself or herself from sin. Redemption is the work of God through his Son, Jesus Christ. The apostle Peter said, "You know that it was not with perishable things such as silver or gold that you were redeemed from the empty way of life handed down to you from your forefathers, but with the precious blood of Christ, a lamb without blemish or defect" (1 Peter 1:18 – 19 NIV).

   1. Your redemption cost God his Son (John 3:16).

   2. Your redemption cost Jesus Christ his love (Mark 10:45).

   3. Your redemption cost others their prayers, their time, and sometimes their lives (2 Cor. 5:18 – 20).

B. *You need God to help you live for him.* One of the privileges of being a Christian is the opportunity to make your life count for God. You cannot do this alone; you can do it only through God's help.

   1. God gives help for growing in spiritual knowledge (2 Peter 3:18).

   2. God gives help for effective Christian service (Phil. 4:13).

   3. God gives help for overcoming temptations (1 Cor. 10:13).

   4. God gives help for knowing and following his will (Rom. 12:1 – 2).

   5. God gives help for the loving of others (1 Thess. 3:12).

   6. God gives help for the meeting of life's needs (Phil. 4:19).

Conclusion

You may never fully understand why God loves you. This fact should cause you to think about your responsibility to God. Where would you be if it were not for the wonderful love of God? Have you recently expressed your gratitude to God for his love?

SUNDAY MORNING, JANUARY 9

Title: The Devil Wants You

Text: "And the Lord said, Simon, Simon, behold, Satan hath desired to have you, that he may sift you as wheat" **(Luke 22:31)**.

Scripture Reading: Luke 22:31 – 34

Hymns: "Guide Me, O Thou Great Jehovah," Williams

           "I Love Thy Kingdom, Lord," Dwight

           "Take My Life and Let It Be," Havergal

Offertory Prayer: Heavenly Father, we rejoice in this day that you have made. We worship you and praise you with all of our hearts, for out of the abundance of your unwasted fullness you have blessed us. We bring our tithes and offerings that others might hear the story of your love, grace, and mercy. Accept these tithes and offerings and bless them for your purposes. In Christ's name. Amen.

Introduction

While I was a pastor in Kentucky, during my seminary days, I picked up one of my members walking along the road. When he got in my car, he asked me if I had heard about him seeing the Devil the other night. I told him that I had not but that I would be interested in hearing about it. He told me that it happened on the way to his home in Happy Hollow. The Devil suddenly appeared in the path ahead of him, and his car lights gave him a good view. I asked what he looked like, and he said, "He had feet like a horse, a body like a calf, a long neck, and a gash down his side. And he wouldn't get out of my way."

When I asked him what he did next, he replied that he jumped out of his car and ran to his brother's house. With guns and flashlights they came back looking for the Devil. The man said, "We didn't find him, but we did see his tracks."

Whether my church member actually saw the Devil or had been sampling some of the stuff they make up in the hills of Kentucky, I couldn't say, but I can testify that it frightened him so that he attended church the next three Sundays, which was a record for him!

The study of the Devil has fascinated people through the years, and in this message I want to sum up some biblical teachings on the Devil.

I. There is a Devil.

A. *Isaiah 14 and Ezekiel 28 talk about the fall of Lucifer.*

B. *Jesus said that there is a Devil.*
   1. He saw him in the temptations.
   2. In the parable in Matthew 13, Jesus said that the enemy that sowed evil seeds was the Devil.

C. *He is called by several names — Beelzebub, prince of the world, Satan, Dragon, and others.*

D. *Other passages.* Peter told Ananias that Satan had filled his heart (Acts 5:3). Paul spoke of the power of Satan in his sermon to Agrippa (26:18). He further told the Corinthians to deliver the immoral member to Satan for the destruction of the flesh (1 Cor. 5:5). And again he warns in 2 Corinthians 2:11 against letting Satan get the advantage. First John 3:8 states that "he who does what is sinful is of the devil" (NIV).

E. *How does the Devil look?* Satan wishes that we would picture him as the comical character dressed in red with pointed ears, a tail, and a pitchfork, but the Bible does not describe him like that. Instead, he can make himself like a man or any other being.

   If you have never met the Devil, it is because you and the Devil are going in the same direction. You remember the Devil in the case of Job? He had been walking up and down, seeking whom he might devour (1 Peter 5:8). He is always on the job.

F. *Back to the text.* You may ask, "Why didn't the Devil go after Judas Iscariot instead of Peter?" He already had Judas, and now he wanted Peter, because he knew that Peter would be the future leader of the disciples.

II. What does the Devil want with me?

He wants to "sift you as wheat." He wants to expose everything that could bring shame and accuse you before God.

A. *He wants to paralyze your life.* Satan is the author of confusion and fear, and he will try to use both to keep you from living a victorious life.

B. *He wants us to be lukewarm concerning certain subjects — divorce, desecration of the Lord's Day, drinking, gambling, fornication, homosexuality, etc.*

C. *He tries to disrupt our convictions.* The Devil wants to still your tongue in religious matters yet loosen it in other things.

D. *He gets angry when you are true to Christ.* The Devil cannot throw your soul into hell unless you allow him to, but he can cause you trouble here if you do not combat him with the Word of God, our mighty sword.

E. *He wants you to stir up trouble with your pastor, in your church, and in your home.* Satan does not concern himself with the carousing party crowd, because he has them. He wants to trouble God's people.

F. *The Devil wants you to have a feeling of self-sufficiency.* This is where Peter was. He said, "Lord, I am ready to go with thee, both into prison, and to death" (Luke 22:33). Peter was sleeping while his Master was praying, and he was not prepared for what was coming. He was resisting while his Master was submitting. He followed afar off and sat down among his Lord's enemies and denied his Lord and faith.

You must beware of compromising with the Devil. If you do, he will beat you every time, for he is more skilled at the business.

G. *The Devil does not want you to pray things through.* He will tell you there is nothing to prayer. If Jesus had not prayed for Simon Peter, we do not know what would have happened to him. What a wonderful thing it is to have someone praying for you. Jesus is praying for us and will not fail us. Samuel said to his people, "God forbid that I should sin against the LORD in ceasing to pray for you" (1 Sam. 12:23).

III. How can we get rid of the Devil?

James says, "Resist the devil, and he will flee from you" (James 4:7).

A. *Jesus defeated him by using Scripture and refusing to compromise or yield in the least.* The Devil must back off from Jesus, for Jesus has defeated the Devil every time they have met.

B. *We can defeat the Devil in Jesus' name.* The Seventy said, "Lord, even the devils are subject unto us through thy name" (Luke 10:17). Jesus tells us to pray "in his name."

C. *In Revelation 12:11 we find the secret of defeating Satan.* "And they overcame him. ..."

1. By the blood of the Lamb.
2. By the word of their testimony.
3. And they loved not their own lives unto death.

Jesus told Peter that he was praying for him and that, when Peter returned to the Lord, he should "strengthen the brethren."

Conclusion

People say, "I am just like Simon Peter." It is wonderful if they are, but it is doubtful. Look at him after he "turned back" to Jesus. He said such things as, "We must obey God rather than men." And at the time of his death, he asked to be crucified head down because he felt unworthy to face death in the same manner as his Lord.

The Devil will tell you right now to postpone trusting Christ, because he wants you. Now is your opportunity to show him that he has no authority over you.

SUNDAY EVENING, JANUARY 9

Title: Happiness Is ...

Text: "Rejoice, and be exceeding glad: for great is your reward in heaven" (**Matt. 5:12**).

Scripture Reading: Matthew 5:3–12

Introduction

The ancient island of Cyprus was given the Greek name *He Makaria*. It was called "The Blessed Island" because it was self-contained. The climate was perfect, the soil was fertile, and natural resources were so abundant that those who lived on the island needed never to look elsewhere for provisions. The Beatitudes paint the picture of the self-contained individual. Our Lord's use of the word "blessed" (*makarias*) is the most complete definition of true happiness. Happiness is what "happens in us" instead of what "happens to us." The Beatitudes describe happiness that is not caused or touched by outward circumstances.

I. An unhappy world.

Some of the world's unhappiest people are Christians. Many Christians have just enough religion to make them miserable but not enough to make them happy! Peter Marshall described many modern saints when he said, "Some Christians are too Christian to enjoy sinning and too sinful to enjoy Christianity." Some Christians have enough religion to keep them out of a tavern on Saturday night but not enough to keep them off the golf course on Sunday morning. Some Christians have enough religion to recognize their need for prayer but not enough religion to take them to their church's weekly prayer meeting. Some Christians have enough religion to keep them from reading obscene literature but not enough to read their Bibles daily.

II. Why so many unhappy people?

A. *They do not know the meaning of real happiness.* The English word *happiness* comes from the root *hap*, which means "chance." To many people, true happiness depends on the chances of life. As far as they are concerned, the circumstances of their lives give and take away happiness. *Contentment, satisfaction, fun, pleasure, delight, fortune,* and *luck* are their synonyms for happiness.

B. *Many fail to realize that God intends for them to be happy.* The Greek philosopher Epictetus said, "God made all men to be happy." It is noteworthy that in the first words of the Sermon on the Mount our Lord congratulates Christians on their attainment of true happiness. God intends for everyone to be happy, or "blessed."

C. *They are seeking happiness in things.* Real happiness is not found in a newer car, a larger bank account, a fast boat, a new house built on mortgage row, or any other material thing.

III. God's formula for happiness.

A. *Congratulations Christian!* You have found the secret of happiness in realizing your spiritual helplessness. Like the beggar who depends on others for his needs, you have realized that all your needs are met in Christ: you are "poor in spirit."

B. *Congratulations Christian!* You are sincerely sorry for your sins. You cannot sin and enjoy it. You are among those who "mourn."

C. *Congratulations Christian!* You are God-controlled. Like a wild animal that is brought under the control of its master, you have let your impulses, passions, instincts, thoughts, and actions come under the control of Jesus Christ. You are not weak but "meek."

D. *Congratulations Christian!* The closer you get to God, the more sinful you feel; and the further you get from God, the more dissatisfied you are. You maintain a holy dissatisfaction with yourself because you are one who "hungers and thirsts after righteousness."

E. *Congratulations Christian!* You have had a personal encounter with Jesus Christ known as the new birth, in which the Holy Spirit has cleansed you and made you "pure in heart."

F. *Congratulations Christian!* You have learned to put love into words and actions. You have learned the opposite of being self-centered. You have learned to be "merciful" toward your fellow humans.

G. *Congratulations Christian!* You are actively engaged in the most important project on earth — making peace between rebellious men and our loving heavenly Father! You are not just a peace lover; you are a "peacemaker."

H. *Congratulations Christian!* You are living the Christian life without compromise, for "all that will live godly in Christ Jesus shall suffer persecution"

(2 Tim. 3:12). What a joy to be numbered among those who are "persecuted for righteousness' sake."

Conclusion

Five of the Beatitudes deal with a person's vertical relationship with God—poor in spirit, those who mourn, the meek, those who hunger and thirst after righteousness, and the pure in heart. Three of the Beatitudes deal with a person's horizontal relationship with others—the merciful, the peacemakers, and those who are persecuted for righteousness' sake. Just as the first five of the Ten Commandments deal with a person's relationship with God and the last five with a person's relationship with others, the Beatitudes also possess the same vertical and horizontal relationships. True happiness is found when one gets right with God and fellow humans.

WEDNESDAY EVENING, JANUARY 12

Title: When You Pray

Text: "But thou, when thou prayest, enter into thy closet, and when thou hast shut thy door, pray ..." **(Matt. 6:6)**.

Scripture Reading: Matthew 6:5–8

Introduction

If prayer is every Christian's vital breath, how would you describe your prayer life? Is it strong or weak? Do you really pray as you should and as you would like? Most of us are not happy with the way we pray. We are aware that real joy and peace cannot be ours until prayer becomes a vital part of our lives.

From the teachings of Jesus on prayer, we can find the help we need in learning to pray. He taught his followers:

I. When you pray, pray sincerely (Matt. 6:5).

Jesus was aware that many had problems in learning to pray because they did not pray sincerely. They were making a stage production out of prayer, praying to be seen by others. As a result they knew nothing of true prayer.

A. *Be truthful in prayer.* There is no place for untruthfulness in prayer. Paul urged Christians, "Stand therefore, having your loins girt about with truth" (Eph. 6:14). We do not pray to fool God but to have communion with him.

B. *Be thankful in prayer.* As Christians, we are to give thanks always for all things. The psalmist said, "Enter into his gates with thanksgiving, and into his courts with praise: be thankful unto him, and bless his name" (Ps. 100:4).

C. *Confess your sins in prayer.* "If we confess our sins, he is faithful and just to forgive us our sins, and to cleanse us from all unrighteousness" (1 John 1:9).

    1. Open sins are those known by others.

    2. Hidden sins are those known only by God and ourselves.

D. *Ask of God in prayer.* James 4:2 says, "Ye have not, because ye ask not." In prayer we are to let our requests be made known to God.

    1. We are to ask of God in behalf of others.

    2. We are to ask of God for ourselves.

II. When you pray, pray secretly (Matt. 6:6).

Jesus taught us to pray in secret, or solitude, that we would:

A. *Keep prayer from becoming a show.* Prayer can be reduced to a mere show. This is what happened to the praying of the hypocrites. Prayer can become:

    1. A show of false piety.

    2. A show of false concern.

B. *Shut out the thoughts of the world.* Every Christian has to face the problem of shutting the thoughts of the world out of his prayer time.

    1. Thoughts of the world cause distractions in our praying.

    2. Thoughts of the world destroy the urgency of our praying.

C. *Have communion with God—*

    1. Communion that helps us know God better.

    2. Communion that gives us spiritual knowledge.

    3. Communion that enables us to do Christian service.

III. When you pray, pray simply (Matt. 6:7–8).

The hypocrites of Jesus' day tried to make prayer complex and difficult. Jesus taught that we are to pray simply.

A. *In words.* Prayer is not the grouping of idle words that impress others; it is simple language that comes from the soul. We are to talk with the Lord in words that:

    1. Reveal love.

    2. Reveal need.

    3. Reveal commitment.

B. *In faith.* Without faith, prayer is meaningless.

    1. In faith, we believe God.

    2. In faith, we obey God.

    3. In faith, we serve God.

Conclusion

Through prayer we will be able to gain the spiritual strength and wisdom we need for living and serving. As Jesus taught others to pray, so will he teach us. May we like the disciples say, "Lord, teach us to pray."

SUNDAY MORNING, JANUARY 16

Title: The Peril of Idolatry

Text: "Little children, keep yourselves from idols. Amen" **(1 John 5:21)**.

Scripture Reading: 1 John 5:18–21

Hymns: "All Hail the Power," Perronet

            "O Worship the King," Grant

            "Follow On," Cushing

Offertory Prayer: Holy heavenly Father, we bring our best gifts to you. In addition to our tithes and offerings as expressions of our gratitude for your blessings upon the work of our hands, we bring you the adoration of our hearts and the praise of our lips. We pray your blessings upon all the agencies, institutions, and ministries that are made possible by these tithes and offerings. Bless those who will be assisted by these contributions. Relieve the suffering and bless those who preach the gospel around the world. Through Jesus Christ, our Lord, we pray. Amen.

Introduction

John, the beloved apostle, closed his epistle to those whom he addressed as "my little children" with a strong warning against the peril of idolatry. This warning follows three bold affirmations of faith.

First, he asserted that true children of God do not live in sin (5:18). While it is possible for the child of God to fall into sin, it is not a believer's nature or practice to continue to live in sin.

Second, he affirmed his faith and their faith in their own divine sonship (5:19). He had no doubt that they had experienced the new birth. He warned these twice-born people that the world in which they lived was under the power of the Evil One.

Third, he affirmed his own faith and that of the recipients of this letter in the incarnation (5:20). He was writing to those who believed that Jesus Christ was the Son of God and that he had come into this world from his Father.

Following these three bold affirmations, John issued a warning against the peril of worshiping false gods: "Dear children, keep yourselves from idols" (5:21 NIV).

Those to whom John wrote were surrounded by idolaters. They were confronted with the possibility of switching their affections and giving their love and loyalty to something or someone less than the true God. If they were exposed to this danger, we can be assured that this is a peril that also confronts each of us. Therefore we must be alert as we walk through this new year.

I. Idolatry is deceptive in nature.

Idols can be either external or internal. Before we realize it, we can be worshiping a substitute for the true God.

A. In what do you trust for security and meaning for your life?
　1. Is your trust for security in self alone?
　2. Do you find security in the things that can be placed in a safe-deposit box?
B. What do you consider to be of supreme worth to your life?
　1. Is your family your object of supreme value?
　2. Do your friends occupy the place of supreme worth?
C. What is the supreme love of your heart?
　1. Have you given to your spouse the place that belongs only to God?
　2. Have you been guilty of making idols out of your children?
　3. Do you make a god out of your work or your profession?
D. To what do you give your highest loyalty?
　1. Your country?
　2. Your company?
　3. The crowd?

II. False gods cannot satisfy the deepest needs of life.

In the law of Moses, God forbade the worship of idols and the making of images. An image always limits, restricts, and misrepresents. It can never portray a true representation of God.

A. *Every idol is a poor substitute for the real thing.*
B. *False gods are helpless in our time of need.*
C. *False gods are human creations.*
D. *False gods will usurp the place that belongs to God alone.*

III. Idolatry may take many forms.

A. *Nature worship.*
B. *Hero worship.*
C. *Pleasure worship.*
D. *Mammon worship.*
E. *Self-worship.*

IV. Christ should be the object of our worship.

A. *Christ alone is trustworthy to be with us in our times of deepest need.*
B. *Christ alone is worthy of the supreme love and loyalty of the human heart.* Family, country, and business will take the proper place as we put Christ first.
C. *Christ alone is of supreme value.*

V. How can we escape the peril of idolatry?

A. *We need to prayerfully reexamine our hearts and lives.* We need to look at our loyalties and our priorities.
B. *We need to draw close to God and seek his divine assistance as we put forth an effort to worship in spirit and in truth.*
C. *We need to rededicate ourselves to the true God deliberately and definitely.*

Conclusion

Have you let some false god usurp the place that belongs to God alone?

The history of Israel is the history of a people who not only worshiped the true God but who also from time to time drifted into idolatry. The prophets came to call them to repentance and held out before them the promise of forgiveness. Let us thank God that we still have an opportunity to return to him and to give to him the supreme love and loyalty of our heart. Let us heed the warning of the beloved apostle, "Little children, keep yourselves from idols."

SUNDAY EVENING, JANUARY 16

Title: "Poor in Spirit"

Text: "Blessed are the poor in spirit: for theirs is the kingdom of heaven" (**Matt. 5:3**).

Scripture Reading: Psalm 32

Introduction

Said a blind man as he felt of an elephant's tail, "It feels very much like a rope."

"It is very much like a tree," said another blind man as he felt of the elephant's leg.

A third blind man felt of the elephant's side and exclaimed, "It is like a wall."

Many people are just about this blind to the meaning of real happiness. They pursue happiness in things and with other people only to learn that they are not really happy.

There is a logical spiritual sequence throughout the Beatitudes. As is the case with the first of the Ten Commandments, the first beatitude is the key to understanding the other seven. All other Christian characteristics grow out of being "poor in spirit."

I. Happy are those who realize their spiritual helplessness.

    A. *The Greek word for "poor" is derived from the root that means to "crouch."* It carries the idea of a beggar crouching on the street to beg from those who pass by. It is the picture of one who realizes that he needs help and throws himself at the mercy of his benefactors. The Christian recognizes his spiritual needs and sees himself as he really is.

    B. *In the parable of the prodigal son, the younger son left his father and brother because he felt that his father was no longer capable of telling him what to do.* But "when he came to himself" he returned to the waiting arms of his loving father (Luke 15:17).

    C. *We are helpless to answer the three greatest questions of life: Where did I come from? What am I doing here? Where do I go from here?* Only when one recognizes his spiritual helplessness in answering these questions can he find real happiness.

II. Happy are those who see themselves as God sees them.

A. *As a sinner.* "All have sinned" (Rom. 3:23). "All we like sheep have gone astray" (Isa. 53:6).

B. *As an object of God's love and concern.* Every person is made in the image of God and is capable of fellowship with God (Gen. 1:26–27).

C. *Pride is the opposite of this beatitude.*
   1. Religious pride. Some believe that they are saved by their own good works. God's plan of salvation, however, is completely "by grace ... through faith" (Eph. 2:8–9).
   2. Intellectual pride. Many are proud of what they know. How sad that some have never realized that "knowledge puffs up.... The man who thinks he knows something does not yet know as he ought to know" (1 Cor. 8:1–2 NIV).
   3. Material pride. Pride in material things keeps many people busy trying to keep up with the Joneses only to learn that when they have caught them they have refinanced and started again! How sad that some have never realized that "a man's life does not consist in the abundance of his possessions" (Luke 12:15 NIV).

III. Happy are those who accept the will of God as the goal for their lives.

A. *The promise of this beatitude is "theirs is the kingdom of heaven."* The kingdom of heaven comes in a person's life when the will of God is being done. God's will is being done when God is reigning in the heart and life of the Christian. Our Lord taught us to pray, "Thy kingdom come. Thy will be done" (Matt. 6:10). He challenged us to "seek ... first the kingdom of God, and his righteousness" (Matt. 6:33).

B. When people realize their spiritual helplessness and see themselves as God sees them, the will of God can be done in their lives.

Conclusion

Benjamin Franklin once drew up a list of twelve virtues that he thought embodied the essential traits of a good life. He carefully kept a little book with a page allotted to each trait. He concentrated on one of these each week and recorded his violations in the book. Upon showing his list to a Christian friend, he was reminded that he had omitted humility. He immediately added humility to the end of his list, and it read like this: temperance, silence, order, resolution, frugality, industry, sincerity, justice, moderation, cleanliness, tranquility, chastity, and *humility.*

WEDNESDAY EVENING, JANUARY 19

Title: What Causes a Christian to Sin?

Text: "He denied before them all, saying, I know not what thou sayest"
(Matt. 26:70).

Scripture Reading: Luke 22:54–62

Introduction

It does not take long for a new Christian to find out that a Christian still sins. We older Christians know that sin is still a problem in our lives. Many of us ask, "What causes a Christian to sin?"

One of the best ways to find an answer for the perplexing problem of a Christian's sinning is to look closely at the life of the apostle Peter. He was one of the first of the apostles to follow Christ, but being one of the Twelve did not keep him from sinning. All of the gospel writers tell of Peter's denial of Christ. From their account of his life, we find three things that will cause a Christian to sin.

I. Pride causes a Christian to sin.

It was with pride that Peter said to Jesus, "Though all men shall be offended because of thee, yet will I never be offended." Then Jesus replied, "Verily I say unto thee, That this night, before the cock crow, thou shalt deny me thrice." Peter said, "Though I should die with thee, yet will I not deny thee" (Matt. 26:33–35). Peter, like many of us, failed to see that his pride would be his downfall.

A. *Pride causes one to feel spiritually superior to others.*
　1. Superior to others in knowledge.
　2. Superior to others in ability.
　3. Superior to others in dedication.
　4. Superior to others in results gained.

B. *Pride causes a person to fail to understand the power of temptation.* The Christian, filled with arrogant pride, is an easy victim for the power of temptation.
　1. Temptation has the power to deceive.
　2. Temptation has the power to cause disobedience. Proverbs 11:2 says, "When pride cometh, then cometh shame."

C. *Pride causes a person to trust in himself.*
　1. To trust in himself for wisdom to meet any problem.
　2. To trust in himself for strength to meet any problem. Many Christians have trusted in themselves as being able to meet any problem only to discover later that "pride goes before destruction, a haughty spirit before a fall" (Prov. 16:18 NIV).

II. A fear of others causes a Christian to sin.

Peter, who was going to be so brave, found himself controlled by a fear of others.

A. *A fear of others causes a person to deny his Savior by his words (Matt. 26:69–75).*
   1. Words that are untrue. Although Peter said he did not know Christ, no amount of lying words could convince others that he was not with the Galilean.
   2. Words that are painful. Nothing could have been more painful to Christ than the words of Peter, "I know him not."

B. *A fear of others causes a person to deny his Savior by his actions (Luke 22:54–62).* He who, a few minutes before, had tried to fight the mob single-handedly, capitulated to a woman's sneer. Peter's weak, compromising actions led to one denial after another.

   Under the control of the fear of others, we sometimes find ourselves denying Christ. The words of Proverbs 29:25, "Fear of man will prove to be a snare, but whoever trusts in the LORD is kept safe" (NIV), should help all of us with the problem of fearing others.

III. Neglect of fellowship with God causes a Christian to sin.

Peter was with Jesus in the garden of Gethsemane when Jesus went to pray, but he neglected to pray as Jesus had instructed him. In this he neglected fellowship with God.

A. *Neglect of fellowship with God brings a loss of spiritual power.*
   1. Spiritual power that allows a person to remain courageous in the face of an enemy.
   2. Spiritual power that enables a person to remain faithful to the assigned tasks.

B. *Neglect of fellowship with God leads to open disobedience.*
   1. Open disobedience is the result of secret disobedience.
   2. Open disobedience brings shame. Peter was never the same; he lived forever with a sense of shame for his sin. Through prayer, Bible study, and worship, we have fellowship with God. We dare not neglect our fellowship with him.

Conclusion

We know that Christians sin, but many of us fail to see the causes for sin. In the life of Peter we have seen the causes for sin, but also in his life we find forgiveness of sin. As Peter confessed his sin and found God's forgiveness, we can confess our sins and be forgiven (1 John 1:9).

SUNDAY MORNING, JANUARY 23

Title: The Peril of Becoming a Spiritual Dropout

Text: "And let us not be weary in well-doing: for in due season we shall reap, if we faint not" **(Gal. 6:9)**.

Scripture Reading: Galatians 6:1–10

Hymns: "Take Time to Be Holy," Longstaff

"Have Thine Own Way, Lord," Pollard

"Where He Leads Me," Blandy

Offertory Prayer: Holy Father, as we worship today we bring our tithes and offerings that your kingdom's work might have proper financial support. We thank you for both the privilege and the power to acquire wealth. We rejoice in the opportunity of showing our love for you and our concern for a needy world by our offerings. Accept these gifts and bless them with your grace and power as they minister to the needs of our world, for in the name of Christ we pray. Amen.

Introduction

A high school dropout is a student who leaves school before graduation or completion of a program of study. Could we define a spiritual dropout as one who for some reason ceases to participate in the ministry of the church?

I. The peril of becoming a spiritual dropout.

The Bible gives many examples of persons who became spiritual dropouts, at least for a while. The book of Jonah describes a prophet who became a spiritual dropout. Jeremiah became so depressed and exhausted that he wanted to become a prophetic dropout (Jer. 20:7–9). Elijah became a spiritual dropout because of a combination of exhaustion, loneliness, and fear (1 Kings 19). John Mark was a spiritual dropout who later returned to his task and became a profitable and efficient servant of the Lord (Acts 12:25; 13:13; 15:37–41; 2 Tim. 4:11).

II. The multiple or mingled causes for spiritual dropout.

A complete list of causes for dropping out spiritually is not possible. Our text mentions only one of the factors that contribute to a person becoming a spiritual dropout.

A. *Weariness (Gal. 6:9).*
B. *The difficulty of the struggle (Eph. 6:10–11).*
C. *An improper desire for financial success (1 Tim. 6:5–10).*
D. *An unwillingness to forgive those who have mistreated us (Matt. 6:14–15).*
E. *The neglect of either private or public worship (Heb. 10:24–25).*
F. *An incomplete response to the total will of God.*
G. *The deliberate toleration of known sin.*

H. *Unrealistic expectations concerning the perfection of others.* Unless we are on guard, we will always be tempted by excuses for falling by the wayside and becoming spiritual dropouts.

III. The high cost of becoming a spiritual dropout.

A. *Have you considered the high cost to you personally of becoming a spiritual dropout?* You suffer when you neglect to be or to do that which God has willed for you.

B. *Have you considered the high cost to others who could be blessed by your life and by the ministry that you could render?* Consider how your family will be deprived and even robbed by your neglect to be the person you are capable of being with God's help.

C. *Consider the high cost to God, who is busy trying to redeem a lost world.*

The cost of becoming a spiritual dropout is entirely too great to pay. We cannot afford to drop out and fail to finish our course for the Lord.

IV. A prescription for preventing spiritual dropout.

A. *Recognize that salvation is something more than a ticket on a train that carries you to heaven.*

B. *Accept personal responsibility for yourself, for your decisions, and for your destiny.*

C. *Accept some responsibility for others.* Recognize that God has saved you that you might be of service to others.

D. *Respond to the continuing inward encouragement provided by the Holy Spirit as he seeks to lead you toward spiritual maturity.*

Conclusion

Christ Jesus is interested in helping each of us become mature, competent, and productive persons. He came that we might have life and that we might have it more abundantly (John 10:10). This rich, full, significant life is possible only to those who continue to trust him and who cooperate with him as he seeks to lead us upward and onward. The responsibility and the opportunity face each of us.

SUNDAY EVENING, JANUARY 23

Title: "They That Mourn"

Text: "Blessed are they that mourn: for they shall be comforted" (**Matt. 5:4**).

Scripture Reading: Psalm 51

Introduction

"Laugh and the world laughs with you; cry and you cry alone" is the philosophy of our day. To many this is the age of laughter; the last thing anyone wants to do is to cry or mourn.

What a bombshell drops on us in the second beatitude! Our Lord tells us that there is happiness in sorrow, comfort in crying, gladness in grief, and bliss in being brokenhearted.

I. The wrong kind of mourning.

Does Jesus place a premium on crybabies, sad sacks, lemon faces, and sob sisters? Certainly not! The best way to arrive at the meaning of this beatitude is to eliminate the ideas it does *not* teach.

A. *Depression because of the world situation.* It is easy to get depressed in any age, particularly in this day of advanced communication. There has never been a day when people have been so well informed about each other's sorrows.

B. *Disappointment because of material failure.* The apostle Paul said that the "sorrow of the world worketh death" (2 Cor. 7:10). Disappointment because of material failure has driven many to despair. This is not blessedness.

C. *Bitterness because of injured pride.* Many Christians are wearing spiritual chips on their shoulders that have sapped them of spiritual power and made them more and more bitter each day.

D. *Grief because of discovered sin.* It is said that Judas "repented himself" when his sins were discovered. There is no blessedness in this sort of grief.

E. *Self-pity.* The person who pities himself bores other people with the repeated story of his troubles until he is left more and more to himself.

The second beatitude is speaking of something deeper and more meaningful than depression, bitterness, disappointment, grief, and self-pity.

II. The right kind of mourning.

A. *Happy is the person who is sorry for his sins.*

1. This kind of sorrow precedes repentance, because "godly sorrow brings repentance" (2 Cor. 7:10 NIV). The psalmist wrote that "the LORD is close to the brokenhearted and saves those who are crushed in spirit" (Ps. 34:18 NIV).

2. As Peter was preaching the gospel on the day of Pentecost, the Holy Spirit was doing his work. The people who were "pricked in their heart" cried, "Men and brethren, what shall we do?" (Acts 2:37). Peter replied, "Repent, and be baptized every one of you in the name of Jesus Christ for the remission of sins" (v. 38).

3. Sorrow for sin is a continual trait in the Christian's life. The genuine Christian not only expresses sorrow for sin at the time of his conversion but also throughout his life. One of the outstanding marks of being a Christian is that the Christian cannot sin and enjoy it. The Christian's battle with sin and Satan is not won on the day of conversion nor on this side of eternity (Rom. 7:18–25).

B. *Happy is the person who is sorry for the sins of others.* Abraham Lincoln said, "I am sorry for the man who cannot feel the whip when it is laid on the other man's back."

34

1. Our Lord is the prime example of sorrow for the sins of others. Because he cared for our sins, "he [was] despised and rejected of men; a man of sorrows, and acquainted with grief" (Isa. 53:3). The shortest verse in the Bible is "Jesus wept" (John 11:35). But do not let the length of that verse hide its meaning. As Jesus stood at the grave of Lazarus, his tears were not shed for Mary and Martha. He was not crying because his good friend Lazarus was dead, for he was planning to raise him from the dead. Jesus cried because of that ugly, foul thing called *sin* that had introduced death to man. He knew that "the wages of sin is death" (Rom. 6:23). Jesus also wept over the city of Jerusalem because of the inhabitants' spiritual blindness caused by sin (Luke 19:41–42).
2. If this trait could be recovered in our churches, revival would result. "As soon as Zion travailed, she brought forth her children" (Isa. 66:8). John Knox travailed, and the Church of Scotland was revived. John Wesley travailed, and the Methodist movement was born. Martin Luther travailed, and the Reformation broke out like a wildfire.

III. The true mourner's reward.

The promise of this beatitude is "they shall be comforted."

A. *Comfort of the Holy Spirit.* It is significant that the word "comforted" (*parakaleo*) is the same root from which *paraclete*, Jesus' word for the Holy Spirit, is derived.

B. *Comfort of knowing that one's sins have been forgiven.* Sorrow for sin leads to repentance, which removes from the back of the sinner the heavy load of sin.

C. *Comfort of knowing that one has been saved by God's grace, not by his own works.* Years ago a communist orator in Hyde Park pointed to a bum across the street and cried, "Communism can put new clothes on that man." A Christian shouted from the crowd, "But Christ can put a new man in those clothes." When a person turns his sins over to God in Christ instead of trying to atone for them himself, he receives immediate comfort and lives at peace with himself.

D. *Comfort of anticipating the second coming of Christ.* His coming is the Christian's "blessed hope" (Titus 2:13). Those who are found faithful when he comes and who have been watching for his coming are called "blessed" (Matt. 24:46; Luke 12:37–38, 43; Rev. 16:15).

E. *Comfort of heaven forever.* Only when people are sorry for their sins and repent of them can they expect to go to heaven when they die. There are several comforting things about heaven.
   1. Heaven is a place for the saved of all ages (John 14:2).
   2. Heaven is a place of rest (Heb. 4:9–11; Rev. 14:13).
   3. Heaven is a safe place (Matt. 6:19–20).
   4. Heaven is a place where sorrow cannot enter (Rev. 21:4).
   5. In heaven we see Jesus (1 John 3:2).

Conclusion

An unfortunate explorer caught in the bitter cold in the far North had many things to tell about his grueling experience. He said that as long as his feet pained him, he was happy. When the pain was gone, his feet were doomed. So it is with the conviction of the Holy Spirit. When a person is sensitive to the Holy Spirit and is sorry for his sins, he can truly be happy. But when he has lost his sensitivity to the convicting power of the Holy Spirit, he is doomed to a spiritual freeze-out.

WEDNESDAY EVENING, JANUARY 26

Title: Why a Christian Must Share Christ

Text: "Then Peter said, Silver and gold have I none; but such as I have give I thee" **(Acts 3:6).**

Scripture Reading: Acts 3:1–10

Introduction

Have Jesus' words in Matthew 28:19–20 and Acts 1:8 lost their meaning to you? As you remember, he said here: "Therefore go and make disciples of all nations, baptizing them in the name of the Father and of the Son and of the Holy Spirit, and teaching them to obey everything I have commanded you. And surely I am with you always, to the very end of the age"; and "You will receive power when the Holy Spirit comes on you; and you will be my witnesses in Jerusalem, and in all Judea and Samaria, and to the ends of the earth" (NIV). These words of Jesus were given as a commission to his followers to share him with the rest of the world.

Most of us have failed in the sharing of Christ with others. We have made the "Great Commission" our "Great Omission." Because of this fact, we need to look at why a Christian must share Christ.

From a study of Acts 3:1–10, we find three reasons to share him.

I. Christians must share Christ because they know the spiritual needs of others (vv. 1–5).

Although Peter and John were on their way to the temple to pray, they could not help but see the lame man at the gate of the temple. They knew that this man had a great need, but it was a need for the saving knowledge of Christ, not for money.

As Christians, we know the spiritual needs of others.

    A. *From personal experience.*

        1. The experience of being separated from God.

        2. The experience of being troubled by guilt caused by sins.

        3. The experience of being uncomfortable around others because of our lack of spiritual understanding and knowledge.

B. *From the teachings of the Bible. The Bible teaches that:*
   1. All people are sinners (Rom. 3:23).
   2. Sin brings death (Rom. 6:23).

There are great numbers of people who need Christ. They may be our friends, loved ones, or someone we do not know. As a Christian, do the spiritual needs of others trouble you?

II. Christians must share Christ because of what Christ has done for them (v. 6).

Peter said, "Silver and gold have I none; but such as I have give I thee." Like Peter and John, we must share Christ with others because of what he has done for us. He has given us:
   A. *Everlasting life:* "For God so loved the world, that he gave his only begotten Son, that whosoever believeth in him should not perish, but have everlasting life" (John 3:16).
   B. *Forgiveness of sins:* "In whom we have redemption through his blood, the forgiveness of sins" (Eph. 1:7).
   C. *Peace with God:* "Therefore being justified by faith, we have peace with God through our Lord Jesus Christ" (Rom. 5:1).
   D. *Joy:* "Ye rejoice with joy unspeakable and full of glory" (1 Peter 1:8).
   E. *A purpose for living:* "But seek ye first the kingdom of God, and his righteousness" (Matt. 6:33).

III. Christians must share Christ because they know that Christ is the only hope for others (v. 6).

   A. *Christ is the only way of salvation (Acts 4:12).*
   B. *Christ is the only mediator between God and man (1 Tim. 2:5).*
   C. *Christ is the only way to real life (John 14:6).*
   D. *Christ is the only sacrifice for humankind's sins (Gal. 1:4).*

Since Christ is the only hope for a world lost in sin, we as Christians must share him with others now.

Conclusion

Far up the Amazon River a missionary was using a flannelgraph to aid her in telling a group of school children about Jesus. As she talked, an elderly man, with stooped shoulders and gray hair, joined the children. He sat with rapt attention as the missionary told the story of God's grace as it is revealed in Christ.

After the children were dismissed, the old man came up to the missionary with this question: "May I ask, madam, if this interesting and intriguing story is true?"

"Of course," the missionary said. "It is the Word of God."

With countenance and voice revealing his doubt, the old gentleman said, "This is the first time in my life that I have ever heard that one must give his life to Jesus to have forgiveness from sin and to have life with God forever."

Then with a note of finality he concluded: "This story cannot be true or someone would have come before now to tell it. I am an old man. My parents lived their lives and died without having ever heard this message. It cannot be true, or someone would have come sooner."

Although she tried hard, the missionary could not convince the old gentleman of this truth from God's Word. Turning to make his way back into the denseness of the jungle and the darkness of sin, he kept repeating the words: "It cannot be true. It cannot be true or someone would have come sooner" (from R. L. Middleton, *My Cup Runneth Over* [Nashville: Broadman, 1960], 86).

SUNDAY MORNING, JANUARY 30

Title: Christ and the Multitudes

Text: "To proclaim the year of the Lord's favor" (**Luke 4:19 NIV**).

Scripture Reading: Matthew 9:35–38

Hymns: "God, Our Father, We Adore Thee," Frazer

"He Included Me," Oatman

"Tell Me the Old, Old Story," Hankey

Offertory Prayer: Holy, heavenly Father, help us to give ourselves completely to you. Help us to dedicate our minds, our wills, and our emotions to you. Today we bring to you our tithes and offerings. Help us to bring our best gifts in a true spirit of worship as did the wise men of old. In Christ's name we pray. Amen.

Introduction

When Jesus came to Nazareth, he went into the synagogue on the Sabbath as was his custom. He read a passage from the scroll of the prophet Isaiah and declared that this passage was being fulfilled in the day in which they were living. This was a bold declaration of his messiahship.

The words that Jesus read provided for his listeners a blueprint of his mission on earth. There is in these words from the prophet Isaiah a plan for the modern church to follow. They provide a sketch of the ministry that every Christian should render in today's world.

We need to understand the life and ministry of Jesus as well as properly relating ourselves to his death for us on the cross. He is the Redeemer who came to save the world from sin by dying on the cross. He is the Teacher who came from heaven to instruct his followers in the way that they should think, act, and serve. He is the Physician who came to heal the brokenhearted and to minister to all who suffer.

In Jesus' life and ministry we have a model for holy living and for effective service to God and others. Our Lord's ministry was determined by his knowledge of the will of God and his awareness of the needs of the people. He came announcing that his mission was "to proclaim the Lord's favor." He came on the scene, not to relate facts about an absentee God who dwelt in the past, but rather to announce the glad tidings that God is at work in the present doing wonderful things for those who will trust him.

The peril that many of us face is the danger of thinking of God as being at work in the past or in the future without recognizing that he is concerned about the present. We continue to live in the year of the Lord's favor. God is vitally interested in today's world, and he depends on his people to cooperate with him in a ministry to the world's multitudes today.

I. Christ Jesus took the initiative with the multitudes.

A. *Christ might have fixed his residence in a central location and invited the population to come where he was, but he did not do this.* Some congregations have made the fatal mistake of assuming that if they erect a building and invite people to come, they are fulfilling the mission that Christ committed to his followers. They could not be further from the truth.

B. *Jesus took the initiative in ministering to the multitudes.* He would have his people go where the multitudes are today. He ministered:
1. In homes.
2. On the streets.
3. In synagogues.
4. By the seaside.
5. On the mountaintop.
6. In open fields.

C. *His was a threefold ministry.*
1. To the spirit he was the Preacher with a message from God.
2. To the mind he was the Teacher come from God.
3. To the body he was the great Physician who brought relief from suffering.

D. *His was a positive, aggressive ministry of mercy.* If we would truly be his people in today's world, we must likewise take the initiative in a total ministry of mercy to the needs of our world.

II. Christ really saw the multitudes.

When Christ saw the multitudes, he was moved with compassion for them. He suffered with them and for them. He saw behind the mask that people wore, and his heart was moved by their deep inward needs. Today's multitudes are very similar to what they were during Jesus' days on earth. He is moved with compassion for the multitudes today. Today's multitudes are:

A. *Afraid. Fear rules in the hearts of many.*
B. *Insecure.*
C. *Uncertain.*
D. *Pessimistic.*
E. *Shortsighted.*
F. *Materialistic.*
G. *Disappointed.*
H. *Objects of God's redemptive love.*

Christ would have each of his followers really see the needy multitudes in the modern world. He assures us that the eternal God of our fathers is concerned about the people who live in this day. He encourages us to trust in the goodness and grace of God.

III. Christ had hope for the multitudes.

A. *His hope was based on his knowledge of the will and purpose of God.* Jesus was motivated by the conviction that the eternal God was concerned about the multitudes (Luke 4:18–19). This divine concern with persons touched their total needs.

B. *Christ encouraged his disciples to pray concerning the multitudes (Matt. 9:37–38).* We are not to tell God what he should do for the multitudes. Prayer is to be a dialogue, and we are to listen to what the Father would relate to us about meeting the needs of those around us.

Conclusion

Christ came to proclaim that we live in the year of the Lord's favor, that God is at work in the world. He encourages his disciples to become proclaimers of this wonderful truth. He saw in the action of God and in the proclamation of God's gracious purpose hope for a world that was in desperate need.

If we would cooperate with our Lord in a ministry to the multitudes, we must do something more than just be learners and listeners. We must become laborers. We need to labor in the study, in the school, in the office, in the factory, in the home, in the pulpit—anywhere and everywhere there is need.

This is the year of the Lord's favor. Laborers who are diligent, skillful, faithful, and devout are needed. Laborers who are joyous, optimistic, and articulate are needed. Let each of us go out into our individual world to announce the good news of God's favor to every person, whatever the need might be, to bring sight to the blind, to set at liberty those who are captives of sin, and to preach the acceptable year of the Lord.

SUNDAY EVENING, JANUARY 30

Title: "The Meek"

Text: "Blessed are the meek: for they shall inherit the earth" (**Matt. 5:5**).

Scripture Reading: Psalm 37:1–11

Introduction

St. Paul's Cathedral was finished in 1710 after thirty-five years of construction. The architect waited attentively for Queen Anne's reaction. He was elated when she said that the cathedral was "awful, amusing, and artificial." If someone said this of an American structure in the twenty-first century, the architect would not be elated. However, the queen's words in 1710 did not mean what they mean today. *Awful* meant "awe inspiring," *amusing* meant "amazing," and *artificial* meant "artistic."

"He is as meek as a mouse," we often say, because we do not like mice. The meaning of the word *meek* is much misunderstood today. Many think of a meek person as a weak, flabby, milquetoast, spineless creature who is unable to stand up for himself or for anyone else. Many easygoing, lazy people are thought to be meek when they are really indolent. Many peace-at-any-price people, who would rather compromise their convictions than take a stand, are called "meek." But none of these describe the meekness of which Jesus spoke.

I. Happy is the God-controlled person.

A. *The Greek word for "meek" (*praus*) is the standard word used to describe a domesticated animal.* The picture is that of a young colt broken to harness. It implies purpose in control; the colt is harnessed to something. The Christian is really happy because his impulses, instincts, passion, thoughts, and actions have been brought under God's control. This God-controlled person lives a disciplined life of service.

B. *God controls everything in the committed Christian's life.* His affections, conscience, will, temper, motives, conduct, and speech have been brought under God's control because Christ holds the reins of his life.

C. *An animal is controlled when it is in the presence of its master.* The same is the case with the committed Christian. He lets God take the reins of his life each day because he realizes that he lives in God's presence.

II. Happy is the teachable person.

A. *The meek person can be told something; he does not do all the talking.* He is ready to listen and learn. Someone has paraphrased the words of our text as "Blessed are they who can be told something, for they shall learn enough to get by in the world."

B. *A sign hanging over the machines in a factory admonished the employees: "When the threads get tangled, send for the foreman."* But on one occasion a workman tried desperately to untangle the threads on his machine. When the foreman finally came, he asked, "Didn't you read the sign?"

"Yes, but I was doing my best to take care of it myself."

"Doing the best you can," said the foreman, "always means sending for the foreman."

C. *The teachable person is humble.* If one is really humble, he does not even know it. A humble person never asks for more than his due; he already feels overpaid.

The story is told of a little watch that looked up at Big Ben and said, "I wish I was as high as Big Ben so that everyone could notice me too." The owner of the watch suspended it on the face of the tall clock tower next to Big Ben, but no one could see it. Elevation became annihilation. Those who long to be elevated for their talents and to be noticed by others are only asking for annihilation. "Everyone who exalts himself will be humbled, and he who humbles himself will be exalted" (Luke 14:11 NIV).

D. *The teachable person is trusting.* Instead of worrying about his provisions, he trusts God for them. Life's greatest question for him is "Lord, what wilt thou have me to do?" (Acts 9:6). Job asserted, "The LORD gave, and the LORD hath taken away; blessed be the name of the LORD.... Though he slay me, yet will I trust in him" (Job 1:21; 13:15). What trust! What meekness!

III. Happy is the person who has fellowship with God.

The promise of this beatitude is "They shall inherit the earth." Certainly our Lord is not speaking of a physical inheritance at some future day.

A. *The Christian inherits the purpose for which God created the earth.* God created Adam and Eve for fellowship with him. When one has been born again and lets God control his life in Christ, he inherits fellowship with God. Until one has been born again, he is merely inhabiting the earth; when Christ takes the reins of his life, he inherits the earth!

B. *When a person comes to Christ for salvation, he takes upon himself the spirit of true meekness (Phil. 2:5–8).*

Conclusion

A girl bound with duct tape and in a trance was found in a Las Vegas hotel. She was unable to remember her past. Her purse contained a tiny notebook with only one page, on which was written a cryptic inscription. This led the police to a Los Angeles hospital, but no one at the hospital knew the girl. When they asked for her name, she said, "Eno Onmai." Someone took the time to unscramble the name and found that, when turned backward, it said, "I am no one." There is no better description of a person who has not let Christ take the reins of her or his life.

FEBRUARY

■ Sunday Mornings

On the first Sunday of the month, complete the series "Responsible Christian Living." The theme for the three remaining messages in the month is "Proclaiming the Gospel."

■ Sunday Evenings

Continue the series on the Sermon on the Mount.

■ Wednesday Evenings

Begin the series "The Commands of Jesus Christ."

WEDNESDAY EVENING, FEBRUARY 2

Title: The Command to Repent

Text: "The kingdom of God is near. Repent and believe the good news!" **(Mark 1:15 NIV).**

Scripture Reading: Mark 1:15

Introduction

Our Lord declared that his disciples could prove their love for him by keeping his commandments. His commandments are not burdensome and restricting; obedience to the commandments of the Lord of love makes abundant life possible.

It is interesting to note the emphasis on which our Lord began his public ministry. According to Mark, his message came to a climax in the call for repentance and faith. If we would understand the mind and mission of Jesus, we must clearly understand the meaning of this primary command, this initial invitation.

Some have considered the call to repentance in terms of its being a threat. One could easily get this impression from Jesus' comments about repentance as recorded in Luke 13:1–5. In reality our Lord was inviting his listeners to change their basic fundamental viewpoint and attitude in such a manner as would make it possible for them to participate in the kingdom of God.

I. Repentance makes forgiveness possible.

Throughout the Scriptures repentance and remission of sin are tied together. There can be no remission of the guilt of sin apart from repentance. In Luke's account of the Great Commission, we hear Jesus saying, "This is what is written: The Christ will suffer and rise from the dead on the third day, and repentance and forgiveness of sins will be preached in his name to all nations, beginning at Jerusalem" (Luke 24:46–47 NIV). Paul summarized his ministry in the city of Ephesus in terms of preaching "repentance toward God, and faith toward our Lord Jesus Christ" (Acts 20:21). Apart from repentance there can be no forgiveness, no salvation, no eternal life.

II. Continuing repentance makes spiritual growth possible.

Some make the fatal mistake of thinking of repentance as being associated only with the initial spiritual experience of conversion. Repeatedly we hear our Lord urging the churches in Asia Minor to repent. He was addressing himself to those who entered into the family of God by repentance and faith.

To repent means to "change the mind." To repent is to reverse your thoughts, to completely change your mental outlook. The call to repentance is the call to accept the viewpoint of God. The call to repent is the call to look at things as God looks at them and to evaluate them as God evaluates them. Repentance results in a mental transfiguration, in a spiritual reorientation of your total personality.

Real repentance touches the springs of our actions. It goes to the source of our motives. If we would be obedient to our Lord's command to repent, we would be seeking continually to have a proper attitude toward God. We need to reverse our thoughts concerning the nature of sin. Instead of loving sin and clinging to sin, we must look at sin as Christ looked at sin. We must see it in all of its deadly destructiveness.

To genuinely repent is to change your attitude toward yourself. Instead of living a life of self-assertion, we will live a life of self-giving. He who genuinely repents experiences a change of attitude in relationship toward others.

Conclusion

Repentance has been described as a journey from the mind of the flesh to the mind of the spirit. It is that openness of mind and heart to God that makes it possible for us to be more than just natural persons and to become spiritual persons. If we would be genuinely Christian, we must take seriously our Lord's command to repent.

SUNDAY MORNING, FEBRUARY 6

Title: To Be Continued

Text: "As thou hast sent me into the world, even so have I also sent them into the world" (**John 17:18**).

Scripture Reading: Luke 4:14–21

Hymns: "This Is My Father's World," Babcock

"The King's Business," Cassel

"Serve the Lord with Gladness," McKinney

Offertory Prayer: Heavenly Father, out of the abundance of your grace you have ministered to us in a most lavish manner. We thank you for the good gifts that you have sent into our hearts and into our homes. We thank you for forgiveness and for eternal life. We thank you for the privilege of being able to work and earn a living. We thank you for your blessings on the work of our hands. Today we come bringing tithes and offerings that we might cooperate with your great kingdom's work here in our own community and to the ends of the earth. Bless and multiply these offerings for the preaching of the gospel and for the relief of suffering. Through Jesus Christ, our Lord. Amen.

Introduction

The prayer that is commonly called "The Lord's Prayer" is in reality the disciples' prayer. Jesus gave it to his disciples so that they might know how to communicate more effectively with their heavenly Father. If there is a prayer in the New Testament that can be called "The Lord's Prayer," surely it is the one recorded in John 17. This chapter contains the prayer that Jesus prayed shortly before his betrayal and crucifixion. In this prayer he speaks to the Father about his disciples continuing the ministry for which he came into the world. He declares, "As thou hast sent me into the world, even so have I also sent them into the world."

Perhaps the most comprehensive description of Jesus' reason for coming into the world is found in a quotation from the book of Isaiah that he read upon his return to the synagogue in Nazareth following his baptism and his temptation experience (Luke 4:16–19). In these words Jesus reveals his concept of his ministry. He sets before us the meaning, the method, the movement, the message, and the motive behind his ministry.

In these words Christ speaks not only concerning his ministry to us as individuals but he also reveals the ministry that he would have us to continue in the world. Often in reading magazines we discover that the editor or the printer has placed a note at the bottom of the page, "Continued on page...." This indicates that we have not reached the end of the article or story and tells us where we can find the balance of the article. When Jesus came to the end of his earthly ministry, he declared, "To be continued." The rest of the story is to be completed by his followers. In his description of his own ministry, we can find a description of the ministry that he would have us to be continuing in the modern world.

I. To preach the gospel to the poor.

It is interesting to note that at the top of the list of the Messiah's functions is that of announcing the good news of God to sinners. This was primary with him and should be primary in the activity of the modern church as well as the individual Christian.

    A. *The pinch of poverty. Jesus knew what it was like to be poor as far as material things were concerned (Matt. 8:20).* There are many types of poverty—material or economic, social, cultural, and others.

    B. *Spiritual poverty is perhaps the most depriving and impoverishing form of poverty*

45

that people can know. Christ came to announce the good news of God's grace, forgiveness, and love to those who were suffering because of the poverty of sin. Humankind's greatest poverty does not relate to stomachs or clothes or houses. Our greatest poverty is in the realm of the spirit.

The nature of sin is such that people often are blind to their own spiritual poverty. Only as our eyes become open to our spiritual poverty can we begin to be enriched by the greatest blessings that God has to offer (Matt. 5:3). In every nation, even affluent ones, there are pockets of poverty that create problems of national significance. In less affluent nations, many people starve to death for lack of an adequate diet. As great as are the problems created by economic poverty, we need to recognize that our spiritual poverty is our greatest problem. Christ came that he might reverse this spiritual poverty problem that has plagued the human race from the beginning of time. "For you know the grace of our Lord Jesus Christ, that though he was rich, yet for your sakes he became poor, so that you through his poverty might become rich" (2 Cor. 8:9 NIV).

II. To heal the brokenhearted.

In our modern day we have stood in amazement before the technical accomplishments of medical science. Many never dreamed that the day would come when a heart transplant could be a reality. Christ came to give people new hearts and to heal the brokenhearted.

A. *Hearts are often broken by errors of judgment.* All of us have made mistakes. We have made decisions or followed policies that led to heartbreak.

B. *Hearts often are broken by the cruelty of others.* A husband can break the heart of his wife. A wife can break the heart of her husband. Children can break the hearts of their parents. Parents can so treat their children as to break their hearts and cripple their spirits. In mercy Christ ministers to those who are brokenhearted because of the cruelty of others.

C. *Hearts often are broken by the tragedies of life.* We live in a world ruled by the law of cause and effect. Most of us know someone who lives with a broken heart because of some tragic accident.

D. *Many hearts are broken by the complexities of our present secular society.* Christ would have his church minister to the brokenhearted in today's world. If we want to be true followers of Christ, we must seek to bind up and to heal the broken hearts of those about us.

III. To proclaim deliverance to the captives.

Captives are those who have been captured and restricted by some alien power, deprived of their freedom to be and to do. Jesus was referring to those who find themselves taken captive and deprived by sin.

A. *Some are restricted by the sins of others.* Children often suffer because of the sins and failures of their parents. Others may be greatly influenced by companions and discover that they have chosen a destructive way of life that leads to slavery.

B. *Most people are restricted by the sins of self.* In the final analysis, no individual can hold someone else responsible for his own decisions and failures. If a man finds himself enslaved by sin and crushed by evil, he needs to recognize and accept the fact that his is a self-imposed slavery.

C. *Many are restricted by the customs, laws, and traditions of our society.* Some are hindered and restricted and handicapped because of prejudice. Minority groups are discriminated against by the majority. Jesus Christ would be identified solidly with the needs of any group that was wrongly restricted and deprived by the society that surrounded them. He came to liberate people from every form of slavery. He came to set people free to become the children of God and the servants of God. He came that people of all classes might be adopted into God's family.

IV. To restore sight to the blind.

A. *The ability to see is one of the greatest privileges and joys that one can possess.* To be blind is a tragedy of indescribable proportions. However, physical blindness is not as serious in its consequences as is spiritual blindness. To be blind to spiritual reality is to miss life at its best. Vast multitudes are blind to the love of God and to the spiritual reality of his concern for them.

B. *Many are blind to the destructive nature of sin and to the awful results of a life of sin (Rom. 6:23).*

C. *Many are blind to the joys of a living faith that makes God real in the present.*

D. *Many are blind to the only way of salvation through Jesus Christ.*

E. *Many are blind to the greatness of our salvation through Jesus Christ.*

Jesus Christ came to give sight to the blind. He would open our eyes and help us to see the things that are of supreme importance.

V. To set at liberty those who are bruised.

People have experienced a wreck on the road of life. The life of no faith and a life of sin have shattered them. People are but fractions of what God meant for them to be. They are like pieces of a puzzle that need to be put back together again, and Jesus Christ came to do just that. With Jesus as our Savior, Teacher, Friend, and Guide, life can take on new meaning and significance. Life can be blessed with new health and vitality.

VI. To proclaim the acceptable year of the Lord.

Christ came as a worker because he believed that God was at work (John 5:17; 9:4). Jesus did not teach that God had finished his work and that there was nothing left to be done. He taught rather that God was at work in the present and that God wanted to bless the hearts and lives of those who would respond to him by faith and obedience.

Conclusion

Paul sought to impress upon the Corinthians the urgency of the present.

"Behold, now is the accepted time; behold, now is the day of salvation" (2 Cor. 6:2). Paul was urging upon the followers of Christ at Corinth to believe that God was ready at that moment to do wonderful things for them and through them. When God is ready, we should make it a point to be ready.

We live in the acceptable year of the Lord. This is the year in which God is at work in the world. He would have the church continue the ministry that was inaugurated by Jesus Christ. He would have each of us engage in the various ministries that our Lord engaged in. This is our opportunity and responsibility.

SUNDAY EVENING, FEBRUARY 6

Title: "They Which Do Hunger and Thirst"

Text: "Blessed are they which do hunger and thirst after righteousness: for they shall be filled" **(Matt. 5:6)**.

Scripture Reading: Isaiah 55

Introduction

It was a hot, sultry day. No doubt the wind was blowing and there was dust in the air. The sun was beating down on those who were gathered around Jesus on a flat plateau between two small mountains. Those who heard the Sermon on the Mount could well identify with the first three beatitudes. They were certainly acquainted with poverty, and they knew what it meant to mourn. The Roman government had taught them the meaning of control. If some were beginning to lose interest by now, Jesus regained their interest with the fourth beatitude. Perhaps at the very time that Jesus spoke these words, the stomachs of many growled with hunger and their mouths were parched with thirst.

I. The challenge: righteousness.

A. *Many are seeking happiness when they should seek righteousness.* Those who make happiness the goal of their lives seldom find real happiness. A religious sect in Hungary had as its chief tenet that salvation was gained by laughing, so they practiced their religion by laughing all of the time. They laughed long and loud. In fact, they laughed so loudly and boisterously that they were brought into court for disturbing the peace. They were not really happy, because they were too busy doing things that they thought would bring happiness. Instead of seeking happiness, one should seek righteousness. Our Lord challenges us to "seek ... first the kingdom of God, and his righteousness" (Matt. 6:33).

B. *Righteousness means getting right with God through Christ.*
1. In the Old Testament, righteousness and salvation are thought of as the same thing (Isa. 46:13; 51:8; 61:10).
2. In the New Testament we are told that righteousness and salvation come through Jesus Christ: "Righteousness from God comes through

48

faith in Jesus Christ to all who believe" (Rom. 3:22 NIV). Through Christ we are made "the righteousness of God" (2 Cor. 5:21). "Christ is the end of the law so that there may be righteousness for everyone who believes" (Rom. 10:4 NIV).

3. Christ never becomes a reality to anyone to whom he does not first become a necessity. We hunger, and he is the Bread of Life (John 6:35). We thirst, and he is the "water springing up into everlasting life" (John 4:14).

C. *Righteousness means living right with God.* The verbs used in this beatitude describe the hunger of one who is starving for food and the thirst of one who will die unless he drinks. The hungry person hungers for the whole loaf and for the whole pitcher of water. The Christian takes seriously the admonition, "Be ye therefore perfect" (Matt. 5:48). The closer one gets to God, the more sinful he feels. The further he gets from God, the more self-righteous he feels. True happiness is found in living right with God.

II. The comfort.

This beatitude is considered by many to be the most challenging and the most comforting of all the Beatitudes. The challenge is righteousness. The comfort is that blessedness is promised to those who hunger and thirst after righteousness — not to those who attain it.

A. *The reason that people reject Christ is that they do not desire enough to become a Christian.* When one is truly saved, he maintains this holy dissatisfaction with himself. There is a holy tension between what he is and what he ought to be. His is the spirit of the psalmist who said, "As the hart panteth after the water brooks, so panteth my soul after thee, O God. My soul thirsteth for God, for the living God" (Ps. 42:1–2).

B. *Many people hunger and thirst for pleasure, prestige, position, possessions, and wealth.* Some people actually join a church because they are seeking these things instead of seeking righteousness. But the true Christian's attitude is much different.

C. *The Christian does not say, "I am interested in Christ"; he says, "For me to live is Christ."* The Christian does not say, "I would like to come to terms with Christ"; he says, "I surrender all to Jesus Christ."

III. The promise.

The Christian who hungers and thirsts for righteousness shall be filled (*chortadzo*). This word was used to describe the feeding and fattening of cattle with fodder and grain. Just as the animal is fattened a little bit more at each feeding, the Christian who hungers and thirsts for complete righteousness gradually grows in the Christian life.

A. *The Christian with a spiritual appetite grows in the Christian life.*

B. *The Christian with a spiritual appetite receives peace of mind.* The Lord is his Shepherd who makes him lie down in green pastures and leads him beside still waters (Ps. 23:2). The pasture and the water correspond to hunger and thirst.

C. *The paradox of this beatitude is that the Christian is filled yet continues to hunger and thirst.* The more he is filled, the more he hungers and thirsts. It goes on and on, yet the Christian is filled and fully satisfied in Christ.

Conclusion

Do you have a spiritual appetite? Is your appetite being spoiled because you are gorging yourself at Satan's table, or are you hungering and thirsting for righteousness?

WEDNESDAY EVENING, FEBRUARY 9

Title: The Command to Believe the Gospel

Text: "The time is fulfilled, and the kingdom of God is at hand: repent ye, and believe the gospel" **(Mark 1:15).**

Scripture Reading: Romans 10:1–17

Introduction

Our Lord issued an invitation—or was it a warning?—for his listeners to repent and believe the gospel. Surely we can believe that it was a gracious command by which he intended to bless those who responded. To hear the gospel, the good news of God's love, makes it possible for people to repent, that is, to change their minds about God, about life, about themselves, and about others.

I. What is the gospel?

Paul defined the gospel in terms of the good news about how Christ Jesus died for our sins, how he was buried, and how he arose from the dead on the third day. People need to understand the significance of these events if they are to obey the command of the Lord to believe.

The gospel is the good news about the unselfishness of the eternal God, who seeks to save sinners, who loves his creatures and wants to be their heavenly Father.

II. How does a person believe?

If we would be obedient to our Lord's command to believe, we must first hear the gospel (Rom. 10:17). When we hear the gospel, we must accept it as the truth. We must not only give the consent of our minds to the truthfulness of the Word of God as it is contained in the Bible, but we also must put our confidence and trust in this good news that God loves us.

Can you believe the truth about God as it is declared in John 3:16? This verse tells us what God is like. He is the God who so loved that he gave his Son to die on the cross for each of us. We must respond to this truth with confidence, trust, and obedience if we want to receive the grace, mercy, and love of God. We must place our name in the center of John 3:16 and believe that it is talking about us.

Conclusion

Jesus invited his listeners to believe. If we refuse to believe, we shut him out of our lives. We rob ourselves of the blessings that God has for us.

SUNDAY MORNING, FEBRUARY 13

Title: The Theological Foundations for Proclamation

Text: "This is the word that came to Jeremiah from the LORD: 'Stand at the gate of the LORD's house and there proclaim this message'" (**Jer. 7:1–2 NIV**).

Scripture Reading: 1 Corinthians 9:1–16

Hymns: "We've a Story to Tell," Nichol

"O Zion, Haste," Thomson

"I Love to Tell the Story," Hankey

Offertory Prayer: Our Father in heaven, may your name be honored and glorified through song, sermon, prayer, confession, and thanksgiving this day. Unworthy though we are, we are grateful for the countless good things you have showered on us. May we be faithful proclaimers of your truth, not keeping it to ourselves, but sharing its riches with all humankind. Grant that our theology be right, our hearts warm, and our compassion real as we proclaim your Word. In the name of Christ we pray. Amen.

Introduction

Whether Jeremiah's calling God's people back or Paul's preaching the truths of Christ, the proclamation is one of certainty and unwavering authority. There appears to be some solid rock, some common foundation undergirding and prompting their proclamation. What is this foundation?

As the early Christians went everywhere proclaiming the gospel, what imparted such a ring of authority to their message in the face of all sorts of adversities and refutations? What compelled them to proclaim the story of Christ again and again?

Upon what foundation do we find a sure footing as we proclaim the gospel to a world flooded with lost souls? That foundation is the same as that on which Jeremiah, Paul, and the early Christians stood. It is the foundation of great and abiding theological truths that time and eternity shall never change.

I. The unchanging authority of God's Word.

"Therefore go and make disciples of all nations, baptizing them in the name of the Father and of the Son and of the Holy Spirit, and teaching them to obey everything I have commanded you. And surely I am with you always, to the very end of the age" (Matt. 28:19–20). Changing times, changing emphases, changing interests, and changing theologies have not changed this authoritative command of God's Word. It still stands as a theological foundation for proclamation.

    A. *God's Word makes proclamation mandatory.* Jesus said, "As my Father hath sent me, even so send I you" (John 20:21). Christ is saying that even as he has received a mandate from his Father, so he hands a mandate to us.

        1. Because of the clarity of the Bible's teaching, proclamation is mandatory. There may be some things in the Bible that are not clear, but the command to witness is not one of them. Jesus states as a fact, "You *will be* my witnesses" (Acts 1:8 NIV, emphasis added).

        2. Because of the responsibility that the Bible places on us, proclamation becomes mandatory. The responsibility that is ours to proclaim God's truths could be no more clearly stated than in Ezekiel 33:6: "But if the watchman see the sword come, and blow not the trumpet, and the people be not warned; if the sword come, and take any person from among them, he is taken away in his iniquity; but his blood will I require at the watchman's hand."

    B. *The unchanging authority of God's Word assures the proclaimer of success.* "He that goeth forth and weepeth, bearing precious seed, shall doubtless come again with rejoicing, bringing his sheaves with him" (Ps. 126:6).

        1. Because of the power of God's Word, success is promised (Heb. 4:12; Rom. 1:16).

        2. Because of the purpose of God's will, we are assured of success: "The Lord is not ... willing that any should perish, but that all should come to repentance" (2 Peter 3:9).

II. The unregenerate condition of the world.

The events and spirit of our day would lead none of us to question John's assertion that "the whole world lieth in wickedness" (1 John 5:19). A rather detailed and relevant listing of prominent sins that substantiate John's claim is found in 2 Timothy 3:1–7. Some of the sins mentioned are selfishness, greed, arrogance, blasphemy, sexual perversion, and religious sham.

III. The unalterable condemnation of sin.

Time has not caused God to go soft on sin; his condemnation of sin still stands. The wages of sin is still death, and the soul that sins may be assured of death.

    A. *The condemnation that rests on sin cannot be ignored or denied.* Both the righteousness of God and the nature of sin make impossible our escaping condemnation. But there is a way out: "He who conceals his sins does not prosper, but whoever confesses and renounces them finds mercy" (Prov. 28:13 NIV).

B. *Why this condemnation? It arises from a basic unbelief: "Whoever does not believe stands condemned already because he has not believed in the name of God's one and only Son" (John 3:18 NIV).* Since unbelief both refuses to acknowledge personal need and rejects God's only remedy, nothing but condemnation can follow.

IV. The unavoidable life beyond.

"It is appointed unto men once to die, but after this the judgment" (Heb. 9:27). A question that has plagued people from generation to generation from the earliest pages of human history until today is that question raised by Job: "If a man die, shall he live again?" This is such a life-shaking question that it tugs at the foundation of every branch of human knowledge and learning.

A. *Death is only a doorway to the unavoidable life beyond.* The first Christian missionaries to England went as far north as the kingdom of Northumberland. King Ethelbert questioned the wisdom of another religion being thrust upon his already overly religious and superstitious people. To decide the fate of this new faith in his kingdom, the king called a meeting of all his lords. As they met late into the night in a large room with open beams and open windows, a sparrow flew out of the darkness through a window, and winging his way through the lighted hall, he flew out another window back into the darkness of the night. Silence fell on the convocation, and a respected lord stood and said, "Sirs, that sparrow symbolizes all I know about the soul of man. It comes through the window of birth into the lighted halls of life to wing its brief way, alas, through the window of death and again into the darkness of night whence we know not. I say if this new faith can tell us whence the soul cometh and whither it goeth, let it be preached!" Christianity soon spread throughout Northumberland.

B. *In this life beyond, eternal destinies will be sealed (Luke 16:26).* These destinies shall be sealed on the basis of belief (John 3:16). You can be certain of your destiny because of the promise, "Whosoever shall call upon the name of the Lord shall be saved" (Rom. 10:13).

V. The unconquerable Christ among us.

"This Jesus hath God raised up, whereof we all are witnesses" (Acts 2:32). The enemies of Jesus thought they had conquered him on the cross, but his resurrection proved him to be the unconquerable Christ. At Pentecost the key idea in Peter's sermon was "Christ is alive—he remains unconquerable!"

This same unconquerable Christ is with us today, urging us to proclaim his message. He still possesses all power (Matt. 28:18) and imparts power to those who will do his work (Luke 10:19).

Beyond this, the unconquerable Christ promises victory. " 'I tell you the truth, anyone who has faith in me will do what I have been doing. He will do even greater things than these, because I am going to the Father' " (John 14:12 NIV).

Conclusion

As we stand and proclaim the gospel of Christ, we stand on a solid theological foundation. The unchanging authority of God's Word, the unregenerate condition of the world, the unalterable condemnation of sin, the unavoidable life beyond, and the unconquerable Christ among us make even more mandatory our proclamation of the gospel.

SUNDAY EVENING, FEBRUARY 13

Title: "The Merciful"

Text: "Blessed are the merciful: for they shall obtain mercy" (**Matt. 5:7**).

Scripture Reading: Luke 10:30–37

Introduction

Christians are the only genuinely happy people on earth. They are happy because they realize their spiritual helplessness, because they cannot sin and enjoy it, because God controls their lives. Thus far in the Beatitudes, Jesus has dealt only with humankind's relationship to God. We come now to the first beatitude that deals with a person's relationship to others.

I. A world without mercy.

A. *In Jesus' day there was a lack of respect for human life.*
   1. Jesus taught that there is joy in heaven when a sinner repents; the Jews taught that there is joy in heaven when God's enemies are exterminated.
   2. Roman slaves were considered tools of their masters. They could be beaten, killed, or sold. It was said of many Roman masters that they delighted more in the sound of a cruel flogging than the sound of birds singing.
   3. Aristotle said, "Let there be a law that no deformed child shall be reared." It was a common practice for the unwanted child simply to be thrown in the garbage can. The professional beggar often retrieved the child from the garbage, maimed him, and used him to awaken sympathy from those who gave alms.

B. *In our day there is a lack of respect for human rights.*
   1. Our laws indicate that we respect human life. During the industrial revolution children where forced to work long hours chained to looms to keep them from running about the mills and factories. Laws were enacted to forbid child labor. When human lives were threatened by automobiles, traffic laws were passed to protect innocent people from drunken and careless drivers. Various types of alcohol and narcotic regulations have been enacted because of our respect for human life.

54

2. Every human being has a right to become a Christian, but only a small percentage of evangelical Christians ever even attempt to witness to their unsaved friends.
3. Every human being has a right to fair treatment, for each is created in the image of God. We are equal, and that means we should have equal rights!
4. The lack of respect for human rights ultimately leads to a lack of respect for human life.
5. The bitter, critical, unhappy, despondent people of today are those who have no respect for the rights of others.

II. The meaning of mercy.

A. *Mercy is usually used in the Bible to describe God and his relationship to people.*
   1. The earth is full of God's mercy (Ps. 119:64).
   2. God's mercy reaches to the heavens (Ps. 36:5; 57:10).
   3. God's mercy endures forever (Ps. 100:5).
   4. God is rich in mercy (Eph. 2:4).
   5. God's mercy is the ground for a person's appeal to God in times of trouble (Ps. 59:16).
   6. People have hope because of God's mercy (1 Peter 1:3).
   7. God hears a person's prayers because of his mercy (Ps. 66:20).
   8. Salvation in Christ is available to all people because of God's mercy (Titus 3:5).

B. *To be merciful is to have the same attitude toward people that God has.* It means to think of others as God thinks of them, to feel for others as God feels for them, to act toward others as God acts toward them.

C. *Above everything else, God demands mercy of us.* In God's sight, mercy is superior to religious activities (Hos. 6:6). The prophet Micah said that God requires us to "do justly, and to love mercy, and to walk humbly with thy God" (Mic. 6:8).

D. *Mercy is love in action.* It is not a vague, general benevolence but a love that shows compassion in deed as well as word.

   The neighbors crowded about their friend whose horse had just been killed in an accident. One well-meaning friend kept saying, "I'm sorry; I'm sorry!"

   "I am sorry fourteen dollars' worth," said another friend. "How much are you sorry?" They passed the hat, and enough money was taken to buy the man another horse. This is love in action.

E. *To be merciful toward our fellow humans means to have compassion on those who are at our mercy.* Jesus said to the woman caught in adultery, "Go, and sin no more."

III. The promise for mercy: "They shall obtain mercy."

A. *Our Lord is speaking of the mercy that God bestows on his children in the day of judgment (2 Tim. 1:16–18).*

55

B. *This promise does not mean that God will be merciful to us if we are merciful to other people.* If this were the meaning of this beatitude, it would be inconsistent with the teaching that salvation is by grace through faith (Eph. 2:8–9).

C. *This beatitude teaches that if we are truly saved, we will be merciful.* Our Lord is saying that the merciful person is the kind of person who will receive the mercy of God in the day of judgment.

Conclusion

The supreme example of mercy is found not only in the words of our Lord, but also in his actions. One sees him hanging on the cross—one who never sinned, one who did no harm to anyone, one who came preaching the truth, one who came to seek and to save that which was lost. He could have complained about the nails in his feet or the crown of thorns on his head, but he chose to say, "Father, forgive them, for they know not what they do." The circle of God's love became large enough to include the thief who hung on a nearby cross. That circle reaches even to us. To refuse to step inside that circle is to know hate, revenge, and bitterness. But to step inside is to know mercy.

WEDNESDAY EVENING, FEBRUARY 16

Title: The Command to Worship God Only

Text: "Then saith Jesus unto him, Get thee hence, Satan: for it is written, Thou shalt worship the Lord thy God, and him only shalt thou serve" (**Matt. 4:10**).

Scripture Reading: Deuteronomy 6:1–15

Introduction

In our Scripture text, Satan was tempting Christ to avoid the suffering of the cross. He offered to give Christ the kingdoms of the world if he would but fall down and worship at his feet. Christ had come into the world in order that the kingdoms of the world might become the kingdom of God. The pathway to this achievement was by the way of the suffering of the cross. Satan was suggesting that this suffering was unnecessary, that there was a much easier way to redeem the world than suffering the humiliation of death by crucifixion. The Savior resisted this temptation in the power of the Holy Spirit and with the help of the Word of God that he had stored away in his heart and mind. Our text is not only a quotation from the book of Deuteronomy; it was also a guiding principle in Jesus' life. It comes to us as a gracious command. We are to worship the Lord only, and we are to give to him our undivided loyalty and service.

I. The genuine worship of the true God saves us from idolatry.

People are spiritual creatures. There is within us a nature that causes us to want to worship either the true God or something less than the true God.

A. *Some people worship a god no bigger than themselves.* They place themselves at the center of the universe.

B. *Some people worship material things.* They give their undivided loyalty and energy to the pursuit of that which can be purchased with money.

C. *Some people worship pleasure.* They are on a perpetual quest for fun, excitement, and adventure.

D. *Some people worship science and technology.* They believe that education and progress will solve the deepest needs of life. To worship anything other than the true and living God is to be guilty of idolatry.

II. The value of true worship.

To fasten one's heart and mind on loving God and giving him supreme love and loyalty is to experience life in its richest form.

A. *Real worship brings to the heart of the worshiper a peace that passes all understanding.* To come face-to-face with the holiness of God can be unpleasant and painful as we see our own sinfulness. However, if the worship experience is complete, the feeling of guilt will be followed by confession and repentance, which will result in forgiveness and cleansing. The God who forgives and cleanses imparts the gift of peace to those who come to him in genuine worship.

B. *Real worship enables a person to rise above the temporal and the transitory.* It gives us a vision of God on the throne of the universe, sovereign and supreme, majestic and holy, in control of world events. To see God in this manner can stabilize a person in a time of uncertainty.

C. *Real worship brings strength for victory in the struggles of life (Isa. 40:28–31).*

D. *Real worship aids us greatly in solving the problems of life.* To go apart into a private place for worship or into the house of the Lord with God's people with a hungry, reverent, receptive heart makes it possible for God to break into our thoughts and give us the guidance we need.

III. The conditions of real worship.

A. *We must have faith to believe that God draws near to those who draw near to him (James 4:8).* The God who seeks to bless and the sinner who seeks God's presence will not be kept apart.

B. *We must believe that the God who has revealed himself through Jesus Christ will work within us as we seek him sincerely and steadfastly (Heb. 11:6).*

C. *We must somehow recognize the many opportunities that come to us for experiences of worship.* The Savior comes repeatedly for experiences of communion and communication with those who listen and are willing to receive him (Rev. 3:20; Matt. 18:20).

Conclusion

Genuine worship of the true God is the deepest need of our lives. We need to place worship in the right place in our lives. Worship and service are never separated; the quality of our service will be no greater than the quality of our worship. We prove our love for our Lord as we worship the true God sincerely and steadfastly.

SUNDAY MORNING, FEBRUARY 20

Title: Twenty-First-Century Needs for Proclamation

Text: " 'Do you not say, "Four months more and then the harvest"? I tell you, open your eyes and look at the fields! They are ripe for harvest' " (**John 4:35 NIV**).

Scripture Reading: John 4:31–37

Hymns: "A Mighty Fortress," Luther

"Onward Christian Soldiers," Baring-Gould

"I Will Sing the Wondrous Story," Rowley

Offertory Prayer: As we look upon your world, O God, we would be overwhelmed by its need for your truth were it not for your grace that sustains us. Grant, our Lord, not merely that we see these needs, but that we also feel them. May the compassion that flooded your heart as you looked upon the multitudes fill us and prompt us to share your message with our needy world. Take now our gifts of love and bless them. Use them as means of conveying your story to lost humanity. In the name of our Lord we pray. Amen.

Introduction

Evangelical Christianity has always been marked by a strong sense of urgency. But this characteristic may be felt in an intensified manner today. Never before has there been such a strong feeling that the cause of Christ must either make its impact on the world today or forever forfeit its chance of survival.

If ever there was such a time, the day has long since passed when Christianity can aimlessly drift along, taking its own good time. For the sake of both the salvation of the lost and the survival of the Christian faith, the church today must become aware of the twenty-first-century needs for proclamation. Such an awareness will inject a new sense of urgency into the proclamation of the gospel.

I. A directive purpose in life.

"But when he saw the multitudes, he was moved with compassion on them, because they fainted, and were scattered abroad, as sheep having no shepherd" (Matt. 9:36).

Much of the prevailing restlessness and wretchedness of our day is born of sheer aimlessness. Many have the joyrider's attitude toward life. They are unconcerned as to both direction and destination. They have as much reason to be at one place as at another. Thus they not only burn up their energies without going anywhere, but also miss the joy of the ride.

A. *A directive purpose in life is not found in the alternatives of the world.* "Why spend money on what is not bread, and your labor on what does not satisfy?" (Isa. 55:2 NIV).

1. Humanitarianism is one alternative the world has to offer. It issues the call to lose oneself in service to others. We are warned by Paul against making a god of humanitarianism: "If I give all I possess to the poor and surrender by body to the flames, but have not love, I gain nothing" (1 Cor. 13:3 NIV).

2. Intellectualism is another inadequate alternative. Too often the attitude reflected in Ecclesiastes 1:16–17 is typical of scores of people today. "I thought to myself, 'Look, I have grown and increased in wisdom more than anyone who has ruled over Jerusalem before me; I have experienced much of wisdom and knowledge.' Then I applied myself to the understanding of wisdom, and also of madness and folly, but I learned that this, too, is a chasing after the wind" (NIV).

3. Existentialism is often offered as a way of life. This *ism* says, "The way to know is to experience." Godless existentialism says, "Because life is an illusion, the only thing you really know is the essence of self." The Christian existentialist responds, "Because God is real, the way to know life is through a vital experience with him."

B. *A directive purpose in life is not found in the religion of veneer.* "When you spread out your hands in prayer, I will hide my eyes from you; even if you offer many prayers, I will not listen. Your hands are full of blood" (Isa. 1:15 NIV).

Israel's religion of perfunctory deeds had degenerated to a religion of veneer. Never has religion or spirituality been as popular as it is today. But a religion of veneer is a poor alternative through which youth can see and from which they will turn.

C. *A directive purpose in life is found only in a saving encounter with Jesus Christ.* As Paul rehearses his saving encounter before King Agrippa, he states that Christ said, "I have appeared to you to appoint you as a servant and as a witness of what you have seen of me and what I will show you" (Acts 26:16 NIV).

Saul of Tarsus already had a purpose and goal in life—that of being one of the most influential Pharisees in Israel—and he was well on his way. But he had no real directive purpose until he had a saving encounter with Christ.

A directive purpose imparts happiness and power. In an acre of sunshine there is enough heat to melt rocks into liquid if the rays are focused. A saving encounter with Christ provides the divine lens that draws our scattered rays into one dominant purpose.

II. A clear statement of the gospel.

"For if the trumpet give an uncertain sound, who will prepare himself for battle?" (1 Cor. 14:8).

A. *A clear statement of the gospel makes the way of salvation plain.* A young man sat in my office with his fiancée and said, "I have been in church all my life, but I never heard how to be saved until you told me." This young man then made a clear-cut decision to trust Christ as his Savior. For someone such as this young man to attend church and Sunday school all his life and never hear in simple words how to be saved is a tragedy — one that is repeated more often than we would like to think. This is a twenty-first-century need for proclamation.

B. *A clear statement of the gospel calls people back to Christian morality.* "For what fellowship hath righteousness with unrighteousness? and what communion hath light with darkness? . . . Wherefore come out from among them, and be ye separate, saith the Lord, and touch not the unclean thing; and I will receive you" (2 Cor. 6:14, 17).

1. There is the need for a morality that marks a Christian as distinctly different. We are to be a "peculiar" people (Titus 2:14). This does not mean "odd," but rather different in that a Christian has a special relationship to Christ that expresses itself in a different kind of conduct. Our lives should be different, not because we have a "superiority complex," but because we follow a "superior code of ethics."

2. Christian morality relates the gospel to the whole of life. John warns us, "My little children, let us not love in word, neither in tongue, but in deed and truth" (1 John 3:18). The priest and the Levite on the Jericho road failed to relate God's truths to life. Perhaps the beaten Jew said later, "I needed no sermon on the love of God as I lay beaten on the road; I needed a practical demonstration of the love of God. I did not need a discourse on ethics; I needed a display of ethics."

III. A mandate for missions.

The proclamation of the gospel engenders spiritual enthusiasm for spreading the gospel abroad. "I know your eagerness to help, and I have been boasting about it to the Macedonians, telling them that since last year you in Achaia were ready to give; and your enthusiasm has stirred most of them to action" (2 Cor. 9:2). What accounted for such enthusiasm for the Lord's work? The proclamation of the gospel! We need to become excited about witnessing and about missions.

William Hordern relates that during the Second World War, a writer said that the Nazis believed all the wrong things with fanatical zeal while the Western world believed all the right things with great enthusiasm. This is the problem that haunts modern Christianity as it faces the forces of political change in the world.

Can we at this late hour discover again the springs of motivation that prompted Christians again and again to overcome the world? If we can, all the misguided ideologies will have met their match.

Conclusion

The time has come for Christians to cease apologizing for their gospel and to start proclaiming it. The fanaticism of evil and wrong ideas must be met by the enthusiasm of the gospel.

SUNDAY EVENING, FEBRUARY 20

Title: "The Pure in Heart"

Text: "Blessed are the pure in heart: for they shall see God" **(Matt. 5:8)**.

Scripture Reading: Philippians 4:1–9

Introduction

Unsaved people are not interested in the Beatitudes because they convict unbelievers of sin. They have no use for the first beatitude because it leads them to admit that they are helpless. And, as if this were not enough, Jesus tells unbelievers in the second and third beatitudes that they must be sorry for their sins and must let Christ control their lives. But this is not all. Unsaved people find in the fourth beatitude that the goals of their lives must be changed. They must no longer hunger and thirst after wealth, prestige, and power, but after righteousness. This way of life results in their being merciful in dealing with others. The Beatitudes are not well received by unsaved people who are not interested in the demands of Christian discipleship.

The sixth beatitude is no more popular than the first five. It demands a trait often thought to be "old fashioned"—purity. In this age of playboy philosophy and new morality, purity is often thought to be out of place.

I. God is known only through the heart cleansing of the Holy Spirit.

A. *No doubt this beatitude reminded Jesus' listeners of the Middle-Eastern custom of preparing for a king's visit.* The streets of the city through which the king was to pass were carefully cleansed and prepared for his visit. Only those who took part in the cleanup campaign were allowed to gaze upon their king as he passed their way. Jesus indicates in this beatitude that God demands an internal cleansing. Emphasis is not to be placed on external whitewashing but on internal spirit cleansing.

B. *Salvation is not a secondhand matter.* The daughter of a prominent minister found Christ at a Billy Graham Crusade. "The only religion I have ever known is an inherited religion," she said. Many who are traveling on the spiritual momentum of righteous ancestors have not yet awakened to the fact that God demands an individual cleansing of the heart.

C. *When a person is saved, he or she experiences this inward cleansing.* It is by "the washing of rebirth and renewal by the Holy Spirit" that one truly becomes pure in heart (Titus 3:5 NIV). This beatitude speaks of the new birth

61

(John 3:3) and the new creation (2 Cor. 5:17) by which one is genuinely converted to Jesus Christ.

D. *Purity of heart is the prerequisite for entrance into heaven.* Without holiness "no man shall see the Lord" (Heb. 12:14). "He that hath clean hands, and a pure heart" will stand in God's presence (Ps. 24:3–4).

II. Jesus Christ demands a cleansing of heart because sin is basically a disease of the heart.

A. *The scribes and Pharisees of Jesus' day acted religious without being religious.* They extracted twelve hundred rules and regulations from just one of the Ten Commandments. They even went so far as to forbid the eating of eggs laid on the Sabbath. A woman was forbidden to look in a mirror on the Sabbath because she might see a gray hair and pluck it out. A man was forbidden to use his cane on the Sabbath for fear that dragging his cane in the dust might constitute plowing. The modern counterpart of the Pharisees is the person who says, "If I do good, I will be good!"

B. *The heart must be cleansed before the life can be cleansed.* David's life was cleansed only when he asked of God, "Wash me thoroughly from mine iniquity, and cleanse me from my sin" (Ps. 51:2).

C. *A person's actions are changed when his or her heart is changed.* Character is not the result of conduct; conduct is the result of character. Martin Luther was fond of saying, "Good pious works do not produce good pious men. But good pious men produce good pious works."

D. *Our Lord had much to say about the need for cleansing the heart to cleanse the life (Matt. 15:18–20).*

III. How does one become pure in heart?

A. *The Holy Spirit enlightens the eyes of the heart (Eph. 1:18), and God, "who commanded the light to shine out of darkness, hath shined in our hearts" (2 Cor. 4:6).*

B. *Sin darkens the eyes of the heart (2 Cor. 4:4).* When Jesus comes into the heart, the Holy Spirit is allowed to do his cleansing work (1 John 1:9).

Conclusion

The promise of this beatitude is consummated in the future. Tennyson, in later years, asked his son (the executor of his estate) to see that the publishers of his poems placed "Crossing the Bar" at the end of the book. When asked on one occasion to reveal his dearest wish, he said, "A clearer vision of God." It is no wonder then that these are the last words of his poem:

> *For tho' from out our bourne of Time and Place*
> *The flood may bear me far,*
> *I hope to see my Pilot face to face*
> *When I have crossed the bar.*

The pure in heart will someday see their Pilot face-to-face.

WEDNESDAY EVENING, FEBRUARY 23

Title: The Command to Follow Jesus

Text: "And as Jesus passed forth from thence, he saw a man, named Matthew, sitting at the receipt of custom: and he saith unto him, Follow me. And he arose, and followed him" (**Matt. 9:9**).

Scripture Reading: Matthew 9:9–13

Introduction

Some people have heard the "call of the wild" and have given their lives to living on the frontier of human progress. Others have heard the call of the field and spend their lives out in the open among growing things. Others—at times all of us—hear the beckoning call of gold, and we find ourselves chasing dollars. To find the greatest thrill that life can know, we need to respond to the call of Christ. The highest happiness, the greatest sense of satisfaction, is found in a day-by-day response to our Lord's command, "Follow me."

I. Jesus gave the command "Follow me" to many.

A. *He gave this command to Philip, the spiritual seeker (John 1:43).*

B. *He gave this command to Peter, Andrew, James, and John, who were fishermen (Matt. 4:19).*

C. *He gave this command to Matthew, the hated and traitorous tax collector (Matt. 9:9).* In responding to this command, Matthew gave up a comfortable job but found a destiny. He lost a good income but found honor and self-respect. He lost financial security but found spiritual security.

D. *He gave this command to the rich young ruler (Matt. 19:21).* Because he had great riches, and because they had first place in his heart and life, he declined our Lord's invitation and went away lost.

II. How can we follow Christ today?

A. *To follow Christ today, we must accept his attitudes.* We consent to do this when we make the response of repentance toward God. To repent is to change the mind, to express the deep inward desire to discover the mind of Christ and to accept his perspective as our perspective. We can follow him by accepting his attitude toward God and toward life, toward time and eternity, and toward sin and judgment.

B. *To follow Christ today, we must identify with his ambitions.*
  1. He came to do the will of God in all things (John 4:34; 5:30).
  2. He came to serve the needs of others rather than himself (Mark 10:45).
  3. He came to make known the good news of God's love for all people.

C. *To follow Christ today, we must adopt his affections.*
  1. He loves God supremely.
  2. He loves people sincerely, steadfastly, and sacrificially.

63

D. *To follow Christ today, we must imitate his actions.* Perhaps the best biography of Jesus is to be found in the five words, "He went about doing good."

Conclusion

Every call in life promises something—knowledge, power, wealth, or something else. But the only truly satisfying call is Christ's call, "Follow me," for he promises fellowship and souls saved for the glory of God as our reward.

SUNDAY MORNING, FEBRUARY 27

Title: Your Role in Proclamation

Text: "Ask the Lord of the harvest, therefore, to send out workers into his harvest field" (**Matt. 9:38**).

Scripture Reading: Matthew 9:36–10:1

Hymns: "Throw Out the Lifeline," Ufford

"Let the Lower Lights Be Burning," Bliss

"Seal Us, O Holy Spirit," Meredith

Offertory Prayer: Heavenly Father, we pray that you will send forth laborers into the harvest. As you send us, we will gladly go. As you call our children, we dedicate them to your service. As you use a portion of the material goods committed to us, we give it freely. In loving response for every good and perfect gift that you have sent our way, we offer our prayers, our gifts, and ourselves today. In our Lord's name we pray. Amen.

Introduction

The gospel message may be indelibly inscribed on your mind. You may have a keen awareness of the needs that surround you and know well the New Testament plan for proclamation. But until you become involved in personal proclamation, all of your knowledge is of no avail. You stand beneath the stern judgment of God—knowing the truth but not sharing it.

Eight out of ten experiences of our Lord as recorded by John are experiences with individuals. One by one he witnessed, made plain the way of salvation, and urged people to follow him.

The modern church has tended to emphasize mass evangelism to the neglect of this simple and personal New Testament approach. Time has now forced the church either to return to the dominant New Testament method of proclamation or to abandon any serious hopes of winning numbers of people to Christ.

I. Your role in proclamation calls for compassion.

"But when he saw the multitudes, he was moved with compassion on them, because they fainted, and were scattered abroad, as sheep having no shepherd" (Matt. 9:36).

    A. *Because of distress, your role calls for compassion.* Those whom Jesus saw were distressed, harassed, and worried. The normal reaction when one sees a multitude is wonder and awe, but not so with Christ. His was one of pity and compassion. He saw the wolf as well as the sheep, Satan as well as humans.

        1. Sin gives birth to distress. Cain was distressed because of sin. The rich young ruler went away "sorrowfully" because of sin.

        2. Distress develops mental agony. "And the king was much moved, and went up to the chamber over the gate, and wept: and as he went, thus he said, O my son Absalom, my son, my son Absalom! would God I had died for thee, O Absalom, my son, my son!" (2 Sam. 18:33).

        3. Distress, if unchecked by the grace and power of Christ, ends in frustration. Many who have not known the healing power of the Lord have succumbed to the cynical philosophy of life expressed in Ecclesiastes 12:8: "Vanity of vanities ... all is vanity."

    B. *Because of instability, your role calls for compassion.* The multitudes today are as "scattered" as they were when Christ looked upon them. This word means "thrown or tossed about."

        1. False teachings encourage much of the instability that plagues people (Eph. 4:14). The Jews heard every kind of doctrine. They did not know which way to turn, and this brought compassion to the heart of Christ, and so it should to us.

        2. Spiritual and emotional instability expresses itself in endless pursuits. Sometimes it is the pursuit of physical pleasure. "Why spend money on what is not bread, and your labor on what does not satisfy?" (Isa. 55:2 NIV). Others pursue intellectual satisfaction, "ever learning, and never able to come to the knowledge of the truth" (2 Tim. 3:7).

          A statesman told of his youthful ambition to become a U.S. senator. After years of hard work and waiting, his state sent him to Congress. He entered with fear and trembling, so awesome was his responsibility. He soon began to wonder how many of the others had been elected. They seemed to care so little for their people and even less for their place of service. He had attained his goal, but now it seemed dull and commonplace.

II. Your role in proclamation urges immediate action.

    "Then he said to his disciples, 'The harvest is plentiful but the workers are few'" (Matt. 9:37 NIV). Christ is saying, "There is much to be done but few to do it. Whatever we are to do, we must do it now!"

    A. *Your role in proclamation urges immediate action because of the scarcity of laborers — "the workers are few."*

1. The scarcity of laborers is accentuated by the multitudes to be won. Years ago a pastor asked twenty-nine adults on the street in a town in Missouri how a person is saved, and only seven could answer. One wonders what the result would be today!
2. The scarcity of laborers can be solved by prayer. "Ask the Lord of the harvest, therefore, to send out workers into his harvest field" (Matt. 9:38 NIV). Such prayer will not only call others forth, but it will thrust you forth into the fields as well.

B. *Your role in proclamation urges immediate action because of the urgency of the hour.* In John's account, Christ says, "Open your eyes and look at the fields! They are ripe for harvest" (John 4:35 NIV). For a farmer to wait beyond harvesttime to do the harvesting would mean losing most of the crop. The harvest of souls cannot wait either.

1. The urgency of the hour is emphasized by the numbers already dying without Christ. Many are characterized by Jeremiah 8:20: "The harvest is past, the summer is ended, and we are not saved." How many who died in your town last year died without Christ? And how many of these did you even try to tell about Christ?
2. The urgency of the hour is seen in the brevity of our lives. "What is your life? You are a mist that appears for a little while and then vanishes" (James 4:14 NIV).
3. The urgency of the hour is heightened by the imminence of Christ's return (Matt. 24:42).

C. *Your role in proclamation urges immediate action because of the tragedy of a lost soul.* "The rich man also died and was buried. In hell, where he was in torment, he looked up and saw Abraham far away" (Luke 16:22–23 NIV). The tragedy of a lost soul is the hopelessness of his or her condition. Between the saved and the lost, between heaven and hell, there is "a great gulf fixed" (Luke 16:26).

III. Your role in proclamation requires an empowering.

"And when he had called unto him his twelve disciples, he gave them *power* against unclean spirits" (Matt. 10:1, emphasis added).

A. *Because of the futility of human effort, your role in proclamation requires an empowering.* This truth is dramatically illustrated in the powerless disciples at the foot of the mountain on which Christ was transfigured. In the face of human need, they had no power to meet that need because, as Christ pointed out, they had neglected their own spiritual lives (Mark 9:28–29).

1. Human effort is no match for Satan's powers, "for we wrestle not against flesh and blood" (Eph. 6:12).
2. The futility of human effort is transformed when divinely empowered. The same men who were powerless at the Mount of Transfiguration became men of great spiritual power and healed "all manner of disease" (Matt. 10:1). Why? Because of the transforming power of God.

3. The futility of our human effort keeps us mindful of our dependence on Christ. "But we have this treasure in earthen vessels, that the excellency of the power may be of God, and not of us" (2 Cor. 4:7).

B. *Because of the magnitude of the task, your role demands an empowering.* Matthew 9:37 reminds us that "the harvest is plentiful" (NIV). Only a supernatural empowering can prepare us for such an overwhelming task.
   1. There is the magnitude of the souls to be won (Matt. 7:13).
   2. There is the magnitude of the time to be spent. "Then said I, Lord, how long? And he answered, Until the cities be wasted without inhabitant, and the houses without man, and the land be utterly desolate" (Isa. 6:11).
   3. There is the magnitude of the effort to be expended. Christ tells us to "go out into the highways and hedges, and *compel* them to come in, that my house may be filled" (Luke 14:23, emphasis added).

C. *Because of the miraculousness of salvation, you need an empowering.* The disciples in Matthew 10:1 were sent out to perform miraculous deeds and thus needed a miraculous empowering.

Conclusion

Only you can fill your role in proclamation—not your pastor and not your Christian friends. You play the major role in the eternal welfare of certain souls. By the grace of God, in the power of God, and for the sake of God, play your role as an ambassador of Christ.

SUNDAY EVENING, FEBRUARY 27

Title: "The Peacemakers"

Text: "Blessed are the peacemakers: for they shall be called the children of God" (**Matt. 5:9**).

Scripture Reading: Ephesians 4:17–32

Introduction

A painting that once hung in a Florence, Italy, gallery was named *Peace*. It pictured the sea tossed by a fierce storm with dark clouds, wild waves, and fierce lightning. Out in the water there was a huge rock against which the waves dashed in vain. In the cleft of the rock was a small bit of green vegetation surrounded by beautiful flowers. Nestled among the greenery was a dove sitting calmly on her nest undisturbed by the wild fury of the storm.

I. Our quest for peace.

Everyone wants the peace and serenity exemplified by the dove in the cleft of the rock.

A. *We seek peace in a world of strife.* In the past 4,000 years there have been fewer than 300 years of peace in our world. In Quincy Wright's *A Study of*

War, we learn that, in the 461 years between 1480 and 1941, the following countries were involved in the number of wars as listed: Great Britain, 78; France, 71; Spain, 64; Russia, 61; Austria, 52; Germany, 23; China, 11; Japan, 9; the United States, 13.

In recent years there have been more than 80 wars occurring in the world within a year's time.

B. *Why some do not find lasting peace.* They misunderstand the meaning of peace.
1. Peace is no vague dream or pleasant hope. It is the reality of which Isaiah spoke: "Thou wilt keep him in perfect peace, whose mind is stayed on thee" (Isa. 26:3).
2. Peace is not just the removal of our problems nor just the absence of strife. When Jesus preached, there was strife between the Jews and Romans and between his followers and the Jewish leaders. The Roman Empire had forced the world to its knees.
3. Peace overcomes our problems even in the midst of strife (Phil. 4:7).
4. Peace is from within, not from without. Paul said, "The peace of God, which passeth all understanding, shall keep your hearts and minds through Christ Jesus" (Phil. 4:7). The Greek word for "keep your hearts and minds" is a military term that pictures the sentry who walks back and forth guarding his camp during the night. While he is there, the camp is safe. So, in the same manner, God guards our hearts and minds through Christ Jesus, and therefore we are at peace.

II. Our peace in Christ.

The only true and lasting peace to be found in this world is found in Jesus Christ.

A. *Even before Jesus was born, it was prophesied that he would bring peace (Isa. 9:6; Ps. 72:7).*
B. *At Jesus' birth the heavenly host announced that he would bring peace to earth (Luke 2:14).*
C. *Throughout Jesus' ministry he brought peace to others.*
1. He interpreted his preaching as a mission of peace (Luke 4:18).
2. He taught his disciples that they could know peace in a world of tribulation (John 16:33).
3. He instructed his disciples to spread peace (Luke 10:5).
4. In times of despair, he brought peace to his disciples (John 14:1–2).
5. He promised his disciples that the Holy Spirit would continue to bring them peace even after his departure (John 14:1–2).
D. *Only those who are justified by faith in Christ possess everlasting peace (Rom. 5:1; Isa. 48:22).*

III. The role of the peacemaker.

It is only logical that Jesus would assign the role of peacemaking to those who have found true and lasting peace in him.

A. *The peacemaker is not merely a peaceable person, a peace lover, or a peacekeeper.* The peace-at-any-price person who just does not want to get involved is not the person of which our Lord speaks in this beatitude. Neither is he the peace lover, for even some warmongers are peace lovers.

B. *The peacemaker is an active, positive force in the world.*

1. He makes peace with himself. Every person is challenged with the decision to do right or wrong. Some are never at peace because they are doubleminded; they have not given Christ control of their lives, and therefore they battle with their wrong desires. When one can say, "I live; yet not I, but Christ liveth in me" (Gal. 2:20), he has made peace with himself.

2. He makes peace with others. In many areas the peacemaker is actively engaged in his Christian task—in the home, in the community, in the church, or maybe even in international affairs. The peacemaker goes out of his way to find new ways of making peace with others. By what he does not say or do, by what he does say or do, and by how he says or does it, the peacemaker makes peace. He goes the second mile, turns the other cheek, and loves his enemies.

3. The most important task of the peacemaker is the task of witnessing to the unsaved. Herein the peacemaker makes peace between rebellious humans and the God of peace. As the Christian shares his faith in Jesus Christ with those who are unsaved, he becomes the peacemaker in the best sense of the word, fulfilling the promise of this beatitude, for the peacemakers are "children of God." One is never more like God than when he is making peace.

Conclusion

Billy Graham often told the story of a man who had fallen from a high scaffolding. A preacher was called to the scene to witness to the man. He said, "My dear man, I am afraid you are dying. I exhort you to make your peace with God!" The injured man replied, "Why that was made nineteen hundred years ago when my glorious Savior paid all my debt on the cruel tree. Christ *is* my peace and I *do* know God!"

MARCH

■ **Sunday Mornings**

Begin a series on the theme "The Seven Words from the Cross" and continue it through Palm Sunday. These sermons should help people to understand the nature of our Lord's sacrificial death for us.

■ **Sunday Evenings**

Continue the series on the Sermon on the Mount.

■ **Wednesday Evenings**

Continue the series "The Commands of Jesus Christ."

WEDNESDAY EVENING, MARCH 2

Title: The Command to Hear

Text: "And he said unto them, He that hath ears to hear, let him hear" (**Mark 4:9**).

Scripture Reading: Mark 4:1–12

Introduction

Repeatedly our Lord told his disciples to use their ears to really hear. Later on in Mark 4 we hear Christ again say, "If any man have ears to hear, let him hear" (Mark 4:23). Then he says, "Take heed what ye hear: with what measure ye mete, it shall be measured to you: and unto you that hear shall more be given" (v. 24). Without question our Lord is declaring that people are to be spiritual receiving stations, hearing and responding to the voice of God.

How well do you hear? Some animals can hear much better than people. And people can hear better than some animals. An alligator can hear only one-fifth as well as man, a minnow one-fourth, and a frog only one-half. Yet a dog can hear twice as well as man, a cat two and one-half times, and bats five times as well.

I. The ability to hear is to be treasured.

A. *Only one in approximately six thousand children is born without the ability to hear.*

B. *The ability to hear often declines as we grow older.*

C. *The ability to hear can be lost by disease or accident.*

D. *Some who have lost the ability to hear have this ability restored by hearing aids, surgery, or cochlear implants.*

II. The invitation to hear.

A. *God spoke through Moses to encourage the people to hear (Deut. 31:11 – 13).*

B. *God spoke through Isaiah to encourage the people to hear (Isa. 55:3).*

C. *Jesus repeatedly encouraged his disciples to use their ears to hear and to heed the message of God (Matt. 11:15; 13:9, 16).*

D. *Christ repeatedly encouraged the churches of Asia Minor to hear the message that he was proclaiming to them.* In Revelation 2 and 3 the refrain that concludes each of the seven letters to the churches of Asia Minor is, "He that hath an ear, let him hear what the Spirit saith unto the churches."

III. Each of us is responsible for hearing:

A. *God's commandments.*

B. *God's warnings.*

C. *God's invitation.*

Conclusion

When God speaks we should give the most careful and reverent attention. It is not enough merely to hear what God says; we must heed what he says. He who hears and heeds the voice of the Lord will find strength and stability for living (Matt. 7:24 – 27).

SUNDAY MORNING, MARCH 6

Title: The Word of Forgiveness

Text: "Jesus said, 'Father, forgive them, for they do not know what they are doing.' And they divided up his clothes by casting lots" (**Luke 23:34 NIV**).

Scripture Reading: Luke 23:34 – 48

Hymns: "Christ Receiveth Sinful Men," Neumeister

"Blessed Redeemer," Christiansen

"My Faith Looks Up to Thee," Palmer

Offertory Prayer: Our heavenly Father, today we thank you for all your rich gifts to us. We praise you for forgiveness and for eternal life. Because your love has come to us, we have been caused to love you. Accept our tithes and offerings as tokens of our love for you and as indications of our faith in your work in this world. Bless the use of these tithes and offerings to the salvation of souls. May your kingdom come on earth and your will be done as it is in heaven. In Jesus' name. Amen.

Introduction

Christ stood in the hall of the high priest's palace, being mocked by the men who crowded about him. He was struck, cursed, and reviled by them. But the Son of God patiently submitted and uttered no rebuke.

Christ was placed before the council of the high priest. Men gave false witness against him; he was condemned as worthy of death; men spat on him and struck him with rods. Nevertheless, he made no murmur nor complaint.

Christ was then brought before the profligate Herod and the vacillating Pilate; he was mocked with a royal robe and a crown of thorns. But still the Son of God patiently submitted.

Christ was hurried away amid jeers and curses to the hill of Calvary outside Jerusalem. He was flung to the ground upon the rough wooden cross; the nails were driven into his hands and feet; the cross was raised to an upright position. But in that awful agony the Son of God had so far uttered no cry.

The soldiers were unconcerned as they gambled for his clothes. The Jews standing around the cross hurled their jeers at him who called himself the Son of God. They taunted him with words that had more truth in them than they ever dreamed: "He saved others; himself he cannot save" (Matt. 27:42).

It was only then that Christ spoke. What did he say? Words of condemnation? Words of reproof against those who had seen his deeds of mercy and love? Words of bitter disappointment because men exchanged hatred and death for his words of life?

No, they were none of these. They were a prayer: "Father, forgive them; for they know not what they do." How can we understand this? How can we fathom such a love? Let us allow Christ's words to speak to us today.

I. The prayer Jesus offered.

Christ began to pray. He might have called legions of angels to his side. He might have called down fire and brimstone to destroy the mockers as with Sodom and Gomorrah. He might have spoken the word for the earth to open and swallow them as in the days of Korah's rebellion. He might have, but instead he prayed, "Father, forgive them."

A. *For whom did he pray?* He prayed for those who were crucifying him—the soldiers who drove nails into his hands and feet. He prayed for the mob who cried, "Crucify him! Crucify him!" He prayed for the chief priests who mocked him and said, "He saved others; himself he cannot save." He prayed for Judas who betrayed him and for Peter who denied him. And certainly he prayed for us, for it was our sins that crucified him: "He was wounded for our transgressions, he was bruised for our iniquities" (Isa. 53:5).

B. *For what did he pray?* He prayed for forgiveness! Forgiveness for Peter's cowardice, for Pilate's compromise, for Judas's greed, for the Pharisees' hypocrisy, and for our sin.

There are many things we can do about our sins. We can try to make reparation for the harm caused by them. We can seek to counterbalance them by good works. We can say we are sorry for them. We can weep over them. We can regret them. But the one thing we cannot do is forgive them. Only God can forgive sins (Luke 5:21).

C. *On what basis did Jesus pray?* How could God forgive such sin and wickedness? How could he and still be a God of holiness? The implication here is clear. He was saying, "Father, *forgive them* and *condemn me.*" He who did not know sin was, on the cross, becoming a sin offering for all sin. The writer of Hebrews says, "Without shedding of blood is no remission" (Heb. 9:22). Jesus was shedding his blood that there might be forgiveness.

Moses prayed for his people, "Forgive their sin" (Ex. 32:32). But this intercession was not adequate, for Moses himself needed his sins forgiven. Paul prayed, "I could wish that myself were accursed from Christ for my brethren" (Rom. 9:3). But this was not adequate, for Paul needed his own sins cleansed. Christ offered himself as a sinless sacrifice that all might be forgiven.

II. The plea Jesus made.

"Forgive them; for *they know not what they do.*" This was the plea of Christ.

A. *Was Christ excusing their actions?* Of course not! He was not implying their innocence. God did not deal with them as if they had committed no crime. The very prayer, "Father, forgive them," shows that the Lord held them guilty.

B. *Did they not know?* They did not know the enormity of their crime. They did not know the far-reaching effect of their sin.

Men have never known. Neither do we! Adam and Eve did not know in the garden. Samson did not know with Delilah. David did not know with Bathsheba. And today men do not know the consequences of their sin. They do not know how much their sin cost God. They do not know how much their sin will cost them. They do not know how much their sin will cost those who love them. They do not know how much their sin will cost the church of Christ.

C. *One day they will know.* When the unsaved stand before the judgment seat of Christ, they will realize the result of their rejection of Christ. They will see the far-reaching effect of their evil and will be judged accordingly.

D. *Was Christ's prayer answered?* Yes! Even before he died, a thief on the cross next to his turned to him in faith, saying, "Remember me when thou comest into thy kingdom." On the day of Pentecost Jesus' prayer was answered when the multitude was saved. And today it is answered when people accept his offer of forgiveness.

III. The precedent Jesus set.

In our Scripture text we see Christ setting a precedent for all time. He illustrated by his death all that he had proclaimed in his life. Some people say that the ethic of Christ is idealistic and cannot be practiced, but here we see him showing that it can and must be practiced if we are to be his disciples.

A. *Christ loved instead of retaliating.* You and I would have been ready to blast those beneath the cross from the face of the earth. We would have consigned them to the lowest regions of hell. But not our Christ. He had come "to seek and to save that which was lost," not to destroy. He had told his disciples, "Love your enemies, bless them that curse you, do good to them that hate you" (Matt. 5:44). Here he embodied the precept we must practice as Christians.

B. *Christ prayed rather than condemned.* Christ had begun his ministry in prayer and had continued his ministry in the power of prayer. He had taught his disciples to "pray for them which despitefully use you, and persecute you" (Matt. 5:44).

C. *Christ hoped rather than despaired.* These were evil and sinful people whose hearts had become hardened. They were cold, calloused, and indifferent. We would have considered them beyond the reach of God. But Christ never gave up on any person. Thus, if these people should be prayed for, we should never give up hope and stop praying for anyone.

D. *Christ forgave because he loved.* The implication here is clear. Jesus was willing to forgive all these people—even those crucifying him and Judas who betrayed him. He expects us to do the same. He taught us to pray, "Forgive us our debts, as we forgive our debtors" (Matt. 6:12). Peter asked how many times one should forgive, and Jesus told him to forgive without limit (Matt. 18:21–22). He also said, "If ye do not forgive, neither will your Father which is in heaven forgive your trespasses" (Mark 11:26). We must forgive in like manner.

Conclusion

When artist Leonardo da Vinci was painting his masterpiece *The Last Supper,* he had a furious quarrel with a friend. In anger and malice he made up his mind to draw this man's face as the portrait of Judas, the traitor, and he did so. But then he found that he simply could not paint the face of Jesus to his satisfaction. Time after time he tried and failed and almost gave up the task in despair. At last he regretted his harsh treatment of his former friend, and he wiped the features of Judas from the canvas. On the following night, it is said, da Vinci had a dream in which he saw more vividly than ever before the form and face of the Savior, and on the next day he began to transfer the vision swiftly and joyfully to his picture. And that, so the tale runs, is the secret of the beauty of his representation of Christ in the greatest of his works.

We shall never be able to reproduce, in heart and life, any recognizable likeness of our Lord as long as we cherish resentment, hatred, and revenge. To be his disciples, we must love as he loved.

SUNDAY EVENING, MARCH 6

Title: "Persecuted for Righteousness' Sake"

Text: "Blessed are they which are persecuted for righteousness' sake: for theirs is the kingdom of heaven. Blessed are ye, when men shall revile you, and persecute you, and shall say all manner of evil against you falsely, for my sake. Rejoice, and be exceeding glad: for great is your reward in heaven: for so persecuted they the prophets which were before you" **(Matt. 5:10–12)**.

Scripture Reading: John 15:17–27

Introduction

The eighth beatitude seems to be out of place until we see the logical order of the Beatitudes:

1. Recognition of need: the poor in spirit, they who mourn, and the meek.
2. Satisfaction of need: they who hunger and thirst after righteousness.
3. Indications of satisfaction: the merciful, the pure in heart, and the peacemakers. The poor in spirit are the most likely to be merciful, they who mourn become pure in heart, and the meek are the peacemakers.
4. Outcome: living the Christian life without compromise, and therefore being persecuted.

The first seven beatitudes describe the Christian directly, and the eighth describes the Christian indirectly. The eighth indicates what is sure to happen to the Christian in whose life the other seven are evident. The same promise is given for the first and the last beatitude: "for theirs is the kingdom of heaven." From the first to the last, they describe the kingdom citizen.

I. Only persecution for righteousness is blessed.

A. *Different kinds of persecution that are not blessed.*
1. Some suffer persecution because they are difficult. They are, so to speak, born in the "objective mood and the kickative case."
2. Some are persecuted because they are foolish. They lack the ability to manage, and they have poor judgment.
3. Others are persecuted because of self-righteousness. "Praise God! I haven't sinned in fifty years," cried the self-righteous saint in a testimony meeting. No wonder she suffered persecution! There is a vast difference between being offensive by self-righteousness and causing an offense because of righteousness.
4. Some are persecuted for wrongdoing. Peter admonished us not to suffer persecution "as a murderer, or as a thief, or as an evildoer, or as a busybody in other men's matters" (1 Peter 4:15). Many dedicated Christians suffer persecution because they are "busybodies." No one

suffers more than the person who cannot seem to keep his nose out of other people's business. The person from whose mouth the venom of criticism flows freely is usually persecuted by the world.

B. *Persecution for righteousness*. But what kind of persecution is blessed?

1. When a person is persecuted for being like Christ. "If they have persecuted me, they will also persecute you," said Jesus to his followers (John 15:20). Paul said, "All that will live godly in Christ Jesus shall suffer persecution" (2 Tim. 3:12).

   a. Jesus was reviled. Some said he was mad (John 8:48; 10:20). He was mocked on the cross, but he did not retaliate (1 Peter 2:23).

   b. Jesus was persecuted. Even as a child he suffered persecution from Herod. Throughout his public ministry, the Pharisees, scribes, Herodians, and Sadducees caused him much persecution. At his crucifixion they scourged him, spit on him, slapped him, and cursed him.

   c. All manner of evil was said against Jesus falsely. Throughout Jesus' ministry the Pharisees accused him falsely, even to the point of claiming that he had cast out demons by the prince of the demons. Before his crucifixion he endured illegal trials by both Jews and Romans. False witnesses testified against him.

2. When a person is persecuted because he is willing to live by his faith. Paul spoke of the apostles' persecution in these terms: "we are made a spectacle unto the world.... We are fools for Christ ... despised.... we both hunger, and thirst, and are naked, and are buffeted, and have no certain dwellingplace ... being reviled.... we are made as the filth of the world, and are the offscouring of all things" (1 Cor. 4:9–13). When reading the early accounts of persecution, we are prone to ask, "Does the modern Christian suffer persecution at all?" In the first century, Christians were flung to the lions or burned at the stake. Nero wrapped some Christians in pitch and set them afire to use as living torches to light his gardens. Hot melted lead was poured hissing down the backs of some. Others had their eyes torn out. Hands and feet were burned while cold water was poured over their bodies.

3. When a person is persecuted because he is willing to die for his faith. It is no accident that the Greek word for martyr is also translated "witness." When one is willing to live his faith even to the point of death, he is persecuted for righteousness' sake. Again the early Christians challenge us at this point. Accounts reveal that some were shut up in sacks of snakes and thrown into the river, some were tied to huge stones and thrown into the river, some were hanged from trees and beaten with rods, others were tied to catapults or wild horses and wrenched limb from limb, still others were tied to the horns of wild beasts or tied up in nets and charged by bulls. They were not only willing to live by their faith, but also to die for their faith.

II. Why persecution is blessed.

A. *Because it tells the Christian who he is.* "Sacrifice to Caesar or die," the Roman judge told Polycarp, the aged bishop of Smyrna. His reply was classic: "Eighty and six years have I served Christ, and he has done me no wrong. How can I blaspheme my King who saved me?" When the Christian suffers persecution, he is assured that the same treatment was given Christians of other ages. Persecution is a painful reminder to the persecuted that he is numbered with the saints of all ages who have suffered because of their righteousness in Christ.

B. *Because it tells the Christian where he is going.* His dwelling place is "in heaven." Such a realization brings joy in persecution and makes it blessed (1 Peter 3:14–17).

C. *Because it tells the Christian what is waiting for him in heaven; his reward will be great.*

Conclusion

During the Depression years, a lonely Christian who had lost his job, his fortune, his wife, and his home was aimlessly walking the streets. He had continued to live the Christian life even in the face of persecution by his friends. He happened upon some masons who were working on a large church. He was particularly interested in one man who was chiseling on a triangular piece of stone that just did not seem to fit anywhere in the building. When asked about it, the workman replied, "See that little opening way up there near the spire? Well, I'm shaping this down here so that it will fit up there." Tears filled his eyes as he walked away, realizing that his persecution on earth was shaping him for heaven.

WEDNESDAY EVENING, MARCH 9

Title: The Command to Love God Supremely

Text: "Jesus said unto him, Thou shalt love the Lord thy God with all thy heart, and with all thy soul, and with all thy mind" (**Matt. 22:37**).

Scripture Reading: Matthew 22:34–40

Introduction

Our Lord defined our first duty toward God in terms of loving him supremely. When the lawyer who was trying to trick Jesus asked him which was the greatest of the commandments, Jesus responded that a person's first responsibility toward God is that of love.

I. People do not naturally love God.

A. *In the natural, people find it impossible to love God, because God has been misrepresented.* From the dawn of human history, Satan has misrepresented the

77

nature and character of God. He has raised questions concerning the goodness of God and doubts concerning the wisdom of God. He has said dark and hard things about God that have caused people to be frightened when contemplating the Creator. Satan has blamed God for all of the tragedy and misfortune that have befallen the human race.

B. *Many do not love God and choose to live in disobedience to his commandments.* They consider his commandments as obstacles to their chosen way of life. They visualize God as some kind of killjoy who would prevent them from doing what they would like to do. Because of sin and because of the moral law that is within the human heart, people know that one day they must face their Creator and give an account of their lives. People identify God with their own sense of shame and guilt, and they do not relish the thought of facing their records.

II. The gospel reveals that God is lovable and should be loved (1 John 4:19).

A. *To hear and believe the gospel makes it possible for a person to consider loving God.* As a person hears the gospel, that person becomes convinced that God is worthy of adoration, devotion, and confidence.

B. *The God and Father of our Lord Jesus Christ is supremely lovable.* He is not only our Creator but also our Redeemer. He wants to guide us and empower us that we might live victorious lives.

C. *God's love is without blemish.*

D. *God's love is all-inclusive and unchangeable.*

E. *God's love is unfailing, and it will never be exhausted.*

III. We must express our love to God.

As the psalmist contemplated the goodness of God, he asked, "What shall I render unto the LORD for all his benefits toward me?" (Ps. 116:12). There are many ways by which we can give expression to our love for God.

A. *We express our love for God by obeying his commands.* Jesus said, "If ye love me, keep my commandments" (John 14:15). Joyful and eager obedience to his gracious commands is perhaps the best way by which we can demonstrate love for him.

B. *We show our love by constant loyalty to God as he reveals his will to us.*

C. *We express our love for him who first loved us by unselfish and devoted service to him and to others.*

IV. The results of obeying the command to love God supremely.

Some people think that living a life of loving obedience to God would be burdensome and boring. An examination of the lives of those who have sought to do so proves the contrary.

A. *To love God supremely is to experience the highest possible manhood or womanhood.* Man at his best is the man who walks and talks with God in a life of fellowship and friendship.

B. *Obedience to the Lord causes one's life to be enriched by the blessings of God.*
C. *To live the life of loving obedience to God causes a person to love his fellow humans more and causes him to spend his life in service to others.*

Conclusion

To love God supremely means that we will be saved from loving something of lesser importance, from becoming idolaters. Only when we love God supremely will other things find their proper place in life. We can show our love for our Lord by obeying his first and greatest commandment, which contains in capsule form all of the commandments that relate to our responsibility to him and to our fellow humans.

SUNDAY MORNING, MARCH 13

Title: The Word of Salvation

Text: "And Jesus said unto him, Verily I say unto thee, Today shalt thou be with me in paradise" **(Luke 23:43)**.

Scripture Reading: Luke 23:39–43

Hymns: "Christ the Lord Is Risen Today," Wesley

"I Saw the Cross of Jesus," Whitfield

"Jesus, Keep Me Near the Cross," Crosby

Offertory Prayer: Heavenly Father, you have given your best to us. Help us to bring our best to you. Help us to offer to you the best of our time, the best of our thoughts, and the best of our talents. Today we bring the fruits of our labors. Bless them to meet the needs of a lost and perishing world, through Jesus Christ our Lord. Amen.

Introduction

The first word that Jesus uttered from the cross was a prayer for his enemies: "Father, forgive them; for they know not what they do." This second word was an answer to prayer. You know the scene. Jesus and two thieves had been condemned to death by crucifixion. They were led from the judgment hall to Calvary, where they were crucified, a thief on either side and Christ in the center. Perhaps Pilate had ordered Christ's crucifixion between two thieves to emphasize the mob's demands. Perhaps the Jewish officials, who followed Jesus to Golgotha, directed it as an additional insult. In any event, it was a fulfillment of Isaiah 53:12, which says, "He was numbered with the transgressors." Christ had been the friend of sinners in his life, and in his death he was crucified with them. Jesus came to identify himself with sinners; their lot was to be his. It was only natural that Christ be in the midst of sinners at his death.

In the midst of his suffering and agony, Christ took time out to deal with the needs of an individual. Jesus always was concerned with individuals. He could

79

preach to multitudes until they forgot day and night, hunger and thirst. He could teach the disciples until their hearts burned within them. But he was at his best when he was face-to-face with an individual. Remember how he spoke with Nicodemus, saying, "You must be born again," or to the rich young ruler as he placed his finger on a covetous heart, or to Martha as he ministered to her sorrow, revealing the concern and compassion of God for the individual.

The two thieves had joined the crowd in their cries. One said sarcastically, "If thou be Christ, save thyself and us." But the other rebuked him: "Dost not thou fear God, seeing thou art in the same condemnation? And we indeed justly; for we receive the due reward of our deeds: but this man hath done nothing amiss.... Lord, remember me when thou comest into thy kingdom." And Jesus said unto him, "Verily I say unto thee, Today shalt thou be with me in paradise" (Luke 23:39–43).

As Jesus dealt with this individual crucified beside him, we find one of the clearest and simplest statements of salvation to be found in all God's Word. Let's view its varied facets and seek its truth. We see:

I. The repentance of a sinner.

Who was the dying thief? We do not know. He was one of the nameless multitude who pass across the pages of history. His life could have started as a picture of promise. But somewhere along the way he took the wrong turn. He fell into evil company, chose an easy life, and decided to take what he could any way he could. Now he was paying for it as the blood dropped from his hands and feet. Only a short time earlier he was mocking the Christ with the mob; now he was yielding to him as Savior.

A. *There was first a conviction of sin.* The other criminal said, "Dost not thou fear God, seeing thou art in the same condemnation?" Conviction started here with a fear of God, for as our Scripture tells us, "The fear of the LORD is the beginning of wisdom" (Ps. 111:10). Then he added, "And we indeed justly; for we receive the due reward of our deeds." Conscience begins to prick and probe and point to Christ. But this man had known of God previously. No doubt his conscience had hurt before. Why the difference? The difference came when he saw the Christ and exclaimed, "This man hath done nothing amiss."

The thief probably had been in the judgment hall and heard the trumped up charges made against Christ. He had heard Pilate say, "I find no fault in this man." He had heard Jesus speak to the women of Jerusalem on the way to the cross. He saw him keep silent as he was nailed to the cross. He had heard him pray, "Father, forgive them; for they know not what they do." Surely this was no ordinary man, and he did not deserve to be on a cross.

"He hath done nothing amiss." The thief was but reemphasizing what others of Christ's day had said. Jesus had stood before his enemies and said, "Which of you convicteth me of sin?" And not one could find one evil

80

deed in his life. Pilate said, "I find no fault in him." Judas cried, "I have shed innocent blood." The Christ was pure and spotless before the world.

The recognition of one's sinfulness is the first step toward salvation. This thief readily admitted his sinfulness. He might have done as so many others have done and compared himself to others. He was no worse than the hypocritical Pharisees who stood by, nor the thief who was crucified with him, nor the mob that jeered and taunted. But in the light of Christ's purity, he was black and sinful in heart.

This is our greatest need today—to see ourselves as sinful in God's sight. The reason we do not is that we have never seen God. When Isaiah saw the Lord, he abhorred himself. When Daniel saw the Lord, he fell at his feet as dead. He saw his sinfulness and confessed to the Christ.

B. *The thief's second step was a confession of faith.* When he saw himself as sinful, he saw the Christ as King and Lord and cried, "Lord, remember me when thou comest into thy kingdom."

1. He confessed Christ as "Lord." "Lord, remember me," he pleaded. Paul tells us that such a confession is salvation: "If thou shalt confess with thy mouth the Lord Jesus ... thou shalt be saved" (Rom. 10:9). If a person does not confess Christ now as Lord, he will someday. One day "every knee should bow ... every tongue should confess that Jesus Christ is Lord" (Phil. 2:10–11).

2. The thief confessed Christ as King. "Remember me when thou comest into thy kingdom." Never did one look less like a king. But faith saw Jesus as the King of Kings.

C. *There came the cry of salvation.* When the thief cried, "Remember me," he was saying in his own limited way, "Save me." He saw Jesus as the Savior in the most unlikely of circumstances. The angel had said, "Thou shalt call his name JESUS: for he shall save his people from their sins" (Matt. 1:21). John the Baptist had called him "the Lamb of God, which taketh away the sin of the world" (John 1:29). Blind Bartimaeus had found him as Savior, as had countless others. But now he was nailed to a tree and, seemingly, helpless to save anyone. Faith, however, cried out, and the Christ responded. Jesus received the thief true to the promise he made during his ministry, saying, "Him that cometh to me I will in no wise cast out" (John 6:37).

II. The revelation of salvation.

A. *This is a perfect picture of salvation by grace.* When this man, in confession of his sins and faith in Christ, yielded himself to Christ, he was saved. It was salvation by grace.

1. There was no goodness in this man to merit salvation. He was a thief, a robber, a murderer. Salvation does not come through good works. Paul emphasized this on every occasion (Eph. 2:8–9).

2. This man could join no church nor be baptized. He had no time or ability to do these things, yet he was saved.

81

3. This man would have done good works, been baptized, and joined the church if he had lived, for he was a Christian and they are acts of obedience. But he struck a death blow to salvation in any other way than by faith and trust in Jesus Christ.

B. *The thief's conversion was immediate.* There may be long periods of training, long periods of conviction, but until one comes to the place of actual faith and trust in Christ, there is no salvation. A choice must be made.

C. *There is hope for the worst of sinners.* There was never a more unlikely man to respond to the Christ, but he did and was saved.

D. *This man will rise up in the day of judgment to condemn us.* He had no Bible, no Christian parents, and no church, yet he believed.

III. The reward of the Savior.

A. *The reward of sin was being realized.* How right he was when he said, "We receive the due reward of our deeds." He was paying for his evil life with his life. The Scripture declares this to be true: "The soul that sinneth, it shall die" (Ezek. 18:4).

B. *Jesus gave the man the reward for faith.* He answered the man's prayer, saying, "Today shalt thou be with me in paradise." In these words Jesus gives assurance for all people.

1. Jesus promised the man a heavenly home. Jesus told this new convert that he was going to heaven with him. He also promises us: "In my Father's house are many mansions: if it were not so, I would have told you. I go to prepare a place for you.... I will receive you unto myself; that where I am, there ye may be also" (John 14:1–3). We do not know much about heaven, but it is a place prepared by Christ, and he is there, and that is enough.

2. Jesus told him that heaven would be immediate. "*Today* shalt thou be with me in paradise." There is no long period of waiting after death, no soul sleep. We go immediately to be with Christ. Paul said that to be absent from the body is to be present with the Lord (2 Cor. 5:8).

IV. The refusal of a sinner.

There were two men crucified with Christ. One turned in faith for salvation; the other continued to curse Christ and reject him. These two men had the same opportunities and received the same offer. One had his heart broken by the scene; the other's heart was hardened. If the first cross is an invitation to all to be saved, this one is a warning not to presume. He was very near the Christ, yet he went out into eternity *lost.*

Grace, in the final analysis, is not irresistible. He who stands knocking at the door of your heart will not force his way. He waits for you to open.

Conclusion

One was lost! One was saved! Jesus died for them both. And so it is today!

Jesus invites all people to come to him for salvation. You will go away as one of these two. William Cowper's poem expresses it:

> *The dying thief rejoiced to see*
> *That fountain in his day;*
> *And there may I, though vile as he,*
> *Wash all my sins away.*

SUNDAY EVENING, MARCH 13

Title: The Christian Is Different

Text: "And he said to them all, If any man will come after me, let him deny himself, and take up his cross daily, and follow me. For whosoever will save his life shall lose it: but whosoever will lose his life for my sake, the same shall save it" **(Luke 9:23–24).**

Scripture Reading: Matthew 5:1–12

Introduction

As we study the Beatitudes, we become increasingly aware that there is a vast difference between Christians and non-Christians.

There are many ideas as to what constitutes being a Christian. Some believe that they are saved if they are baptized, join a church, try to do right, and live by the Golden Rule. Christians often are compared to wheelbarrows (no good unless pushed), kites (always up in the air about something), footballs (can't tell which way they will bounce next), balloons (full of air and ready to blow up), trailers (having to be pulled), and neon lights (on and off). Without a doubt, the world has come into the church and the church has become worldly. Our Lord paints a picture of the difference between Christians and non-Christians in the Beatitudes.

I. The Christian's object of worship is different.

A. *Three beatitudes point out this difference (the poor in spirit, they that mourn, and the meek).*

B. *The non-Christian worships himself.*
  1. Everything revolves around his own selfish desires.
  2. Ultimately, that which keeps him from becoming a Christian is his worship of self. Thus Jesus admonishes his followers to "deny self" (Luke 9:23).
  3. He sees the world only through his own eyes. In New York's Museum of Natural History a room was arranged to look like a room looks through the eyes of a dog. Table legs resembled large pillars, chairs were like thrones, and the ceiling was comparatively high. The object of the experiment was to see just how different the world looks through the

eyes of a dog. One likewise sees the world through different eyes when Christ is his Savior.

C. *The Christian worships God.*

1. He has taken three steps to total commitment. He has realized his spiritual helplessness (poor in spirit). He has expressed sincere sorrow for his sins (they that mourn). He has surrendered every part of his life to Christ (the meek).

2. He strives for self-denial. Where the non-Christian strives for self-expression, self-mastery, self-confidence, self-glory, and self-indulgence, the Christian strives for self-denial.

II. The Christian's goal is different.

A. *One beatitude points out this difference (they who hunger and thirst after righteousness).*

B. *The non-Christian's goal is anything that satisfies him.* He hungers for wealth, status, possessions, and power. Anything that will aid him in the worship of himself becomes a goal in his life. If he prays at all, his prayer is somewhat like the little boy's prayer: "Lord, make me good but not too good—just good enough to keep me from getting a whipping."

C. *The Christian's goal is righteousness.* Above everything else, the Christian wants to be right, live right, and die right with God.

1. The only way to be right with God is through a personal commitment to Christ.

2. The only way to stay right with God is to become more like Christ each day.

III. The Christian's conduct is different.

A. *Three beatitudes point out this difference (the merciful, the pure in heart, and the peacemakers).*

B. *The non-Christian's conduct is determined by self-worship.*

1. One who worships self will do anything to satisfy self.

2. One who worships self will get what self wants at the expense of others.

3. One who worships self has one standard for judging right and wrong: "What will this do for me?"

C. *The Christian's conduct stems from his relationship to God in Christ.*

1. He acts differently because his heart has been cleansed (pure in heart).

2. He takes into consideration the needs and rights of others (the merciful).

3. He is actively concerned about the attitudes of others toward himself and God (the peacemakers).

Conclusion

The Christian is different than the non-Christian. His influence is different (Matt. 5:13–16), as are his actions and the attitudes behind his actions (vv. 17, 48), his motive for service (vv. 1–18), his treasures (6:19–34), and his rule for living (7:12). The Christian and the non-Christian live in two different realms — the realm of selflessness and the realm of selfishness. The Christian lives in the realm of God's kingdom in which the will of God is the supreme good.

WEDNESDAY EVENING, MARCH 16

Title: The Command to Love Your Neighbor as Yourself

Text: "And the second is like unto it, Thou shalt love thy neighbour as thyself" (**Matt. 22:39**).

Scripture Reading: Luke 10:25–37

Introduction

In the two great commandments, our Lord presents in capsule form the total requirements of the law of God as far as our obligations to God and our fellow humans are concerned. We are to love God supremely and steadfastly. We are to love our neighbor as ourselves. In the parable of the good Samaritan Jesus defines the good neighbor as one who ministers in mercy to those who are in need along life's pathway. He uses the example of the Samaritan as a demonstration of the royal law of love.

I. Love is the law of the kingdom of God.

Love is the law of the king; it takes precedence over every other law. To obey the law of love toward God and toward others is to make life royally happy.

A. *We are to love God supremely (Matt. 22:37).*

B. *We are to love our neighbor as ourselves (Matt. 22:39).*

C. *The husband is to love his wife as Christ loved the church and gave himself for it (Eph. 5:25).*

D. *The followers of Christ are to love each other even as Christ loved them (John 13:34).*

E. *The disciples of Christ are to love even their enemies (Matt. 5:43–44).*

F. *John tells us that love for our fellow Christians is one of the proofs that we have a living relationship with God (1 John 3:14). Absence of love in the heart is proof that one does not have eternal life (1 John 3:15).*

II. The royal law of love illustrated (Luke 10:25–37).

Jesus used the example of the good Samaritan to illustrate the love that we should demonstrate for our neighbor. Some of the characteristics of the love that he would commend can be discovered by a study of this incident.

A. *Love reacts to suffering with compassionate concern.*

B. *Love responds to need with action.*

C. *Love is willing to suffer inconvenience for the sake of others.*

D. *Love is generous in its provisions for others.*

E. *Love is courageous in the face of danger and is willing to be exposed to risk.*

F. *Love does not hesitate to cross racial barriers.*

G. *Love ignores religious differences.*

H. *Love is patient and persistent in its expression.*

III. The difficulty of obeying the commandment to love our neighbor.

A. *People are not always lovable.* It is not easy to love some people.

B. *People do not always respond to love.* Sometimes love is rebuffed and rejected.

C. *Christian love is something above and beyond natural love.* Christian love is not superficial and instinctual. It is a persistent, unbreakable spirit of goodwill toward others.

D. *We can be enabled to love the unlovable when we recognize the value of each person in the eyes of God.* God loves people to the extent that he gave his Son to die for them. If God could see something in people that was worth redeeming, then it behooves each of us to follow his example.

Conclusion

Paul describes love as being the supreme gift of the Holy Spirit (1 Cor. 12:31 – 14:1). In writing to the Romans he speaks of the love of God as being poured out in our hearts by the Holy Spirit (Rom. 5:5).

The God who so loved that he gave his Son for us will enable us to live by the royal law of love if we are willing to let his Spirit bestow upon us this capacity, this gift of love for our fellow humans.

SUNDAY MORNING, MARCH 20

Title: The Word of Affection

Text: "When Jesus therefore saw his mother, and the disciple standing by, whom he loved, he saith unto his mother, Woman, behold thy son!" **(John 19:26)**.

Scripture Reading: John 19:25 – 27

Hymns: "Love Divine, All Loves Excelling," Wesley

"Glory to His Name," Hoffman

"I Will Sing of My Redeemer," Bliss

Offertory Prayer: Our Father, this is the day you have made. We accept it as a gift from your loving hand. You are the Giver of every good and perfect gift. We thank you for life, for health, for ability, and for the opportunity to work and earn material benefits for our loved ones. We rejoice in the opportunity to offer on your altar the fruits of our labor as an expression of our grateful worship to the end that the needs of kingdom enterprise might be met. Bless these gifts to the relief of human suffering and to the salvation of souls. In Jesus' name. Amen.

Introduction

Again today we stand at Calvary. We see our Christ on the cross. He has asked for forgiveness for others. He has granted forgiveness to one who repented. Time passes, and the suffering and agony increase. The heat of the day is intense. The pain of the wounds is unbearable. The crowd is still jeering and deriding. The disciples have forsaken him and fled.

There beneath the cross, watching all of this, is Mary, Jesus' mother. She is one of the women of Galilee who came up with him to Jerusalem. She had spent the night of his agony in a sleepless sorrow. She was at the door of Pilate's judgment hall early that morning. She followed Jesus to Calvary. She heard the wailing of the women of Jerusalem and saw the nails driven through his hands and feet. At first she must have stood only on the outskirts of the crowd. As the day wore on, however, the stream of passersby ceased, the soldiers sat down to cast their dice and pass the hours of waiting, the priests and scribes fell back into the shade. It was then that Mary, John, and the women drew near until they stood by the cross to hear with thrilled hearts Jesus' words of recognition and care.

Suspended between earth, which had openly rejected him, and heaven, which had seemingly forsaken him, he remembers his mother, Mary of Nazareth. Hear him as he says, "Woman, behold thy son.... Behold thy Mother." The first word from the cross was addressed to his Father. This third word is addressed to his mother.

In this scene there are three people who stand out. Let us examine them more closely.

I. The mother who sorrowed.

A. *Mary stood by the cross.* As Jesus' mother stood there, her heart must have broken within her. She may have questioned, but surely she never doubted. However, neither did she understand.

Like the brothers of Christ, she had not grasped all that was involved in the incarnation. From the beginning she had had all the wonderful promises connected with her Son. The angel Gabriel had promised, "He shall be great, and shall be called the Son of the Highest" (Luke 1:32). Angels told the shepherds of the birth of "a Saviour which is Christ the Lord" (Luke 2:11), and another angel promised Joseph that Mary's Son would "save his people from their sins" (Matt. 1:21). These divine promises had all foretold something of the wondrous nature of the child that was to be given to her and of the marvelous mission in store for him.

B. *What Mary experienced was a fulfillment of Simeon's prophecy.* After Jesus' birth Mary presented him in the temple as the law required. There she met the elderly Simeon, who predicted that "a sword shall pierce through thy own soul" (Luke 2:35). It was a startling prophecy that the child of whom such great things had been foretold should bring sorrow to her.

Early in Jesus' life, however, Mary began to realize something of the truth of the prophecy. When she was exercising a perfectly natural authority, on the occasion when Christ at the age of twelve remained behind in Jerusalem instead of joining the caravan home, he said to her, "Didn't you know I had to be in my Father's house?" (Luke 2:49 NIV). Later on, when

87

his public ministry had just begun and she asked him to meet a need that had arisen at a wedding feast in Cana, he said to her, "Woman, what have I to do with thee? mine hour is not yet come" (John 2:4). Whatever else there was in these statements of our Lord to his mother, there was a distinct intimation that he knew the work that the Father had given him to do and that the work was to be done by himself, without interference or direction from even his mother. Mary was in a difficult position. While she did not grasp the way in which Jesus' work was to be accomplished, she always believed in him. Therefore, when the hour of trial came and when the agony of the cross arrived, she was there, faithful unto death. "All [the disciples] forsook him, and fled," but his mother "stood by the cross" (Mark 14:50; John 19:25).

This sacrifice of Mary has been sensitively conceived by Holman Hunt in one of his paintings. In it we see the carpenter's shop at Nazareth. Jesus stands at his bench with uplifted arms, and Mary, behind him, sees the shadow of his arms cast on the wall before him—the shadow of a cross. That shadow had now become a reality.

C. *How could such sorrow be borne?* Mary had submitted to God. When God made known to her that she was to conceive and bear a Son of the Holy Spirit, she knew that it meant gossip, misunderstanding, and cruel taunts. But she had said, "Behold the handmaid of the Lord; be it unto me according to thy word" (Luke 1:38). She willingly submitted herself to her God and his will.

II. The Son who suffered.

A. *Now we turn to the central figure.* It is the Christ, not Mary, who is preeminent. In the midst of his agony, Jesus unselfishly looked down from the cross into the face of his mother. Can you imagine the thoughts that must have flooded his mind? He probably saw his home in Nazareth and heard the soothing voice of Mary as she sang him a lullaby and told him the stories of God's Word. He felt the tender care of his mother's arms about him and sensed the pangs of sorrow and misunderstanding that were hers during his ministry.

But now that was over, and he looked to the future. Joseph had died, leaving Mary a widow. With a heart of love and tenderness, Jesus said, "Woman, behold thy son," indicating John, who stood by. "Go with John; he will care for you now. Your future is secure."

B. *The Christ here is setting a wonderful example.* The words God gave to Moses on Mount Sinai have never been repealed: "Honor your father and your mother" (Ex. 20:12 NIV). Paul reemphasized this in Ephesians 6:1: "Children, obey your parents in the Lord: for this is right."

The injunction to honor our parents goes far beyond obedience to their words, although it certainly includes that. It includes love and affection, gratitude and respect.

C. *But Jesus' words to Mary went far deeper than that, for by his words he cut himself off from all earthly ties.* He was saying to his mother, "My human relationship with you is over. I am no longer your Son but your Savior. You, like all others, must come to me as the Lamb of God sacrificed to take away the sins of all the world."

III. The disciple who served.

Jesus looked from Mary to John, who also stood by the cross, and said, "Behold thy mother."

A. *What a privilege this was for John!* Here was an opportunity to render service to his Master when he was needed most. Christ was saying to John, "You are to become my substitute. I am helpless now to care for Mary. You care for her physical needs. You provide the service and love and care I cannot provide." The text says, "From that hour, that disciple took her unto his own home." John obeyed promptly and willingly. But let those of us who would covet John's opportunity remember that Jesus on one occasion called his followers his mother and brothers, giving all believers the opportunity to minister to the needs of others as John did.

Think of what John would have missed had he not been there when Christ spoke. Thomas missed the words of the Master in one of his resurrection appearances. We miss much when we are not present when he meets with his people and speaks to their hearts.

B. *But wait!* What *is* John doing here? Scripture says that the disciples had forsaken Jesus and fled (Mark 14:50). One of the greatest sorrows that Christ suffered was desertion by his disciples. It was bad enough that his own people, the Jews, should despise and reject him; but it was far worse that the Eleven who had been with him so long should desert and forsake him in his hour of trial.

Perhaps you are in that condition now. In a moment of weakness, you have deserted Christ, forsaken his company, denied your relationship to him. Perhaps your heart has become cold and indifferent. Christ has not forsaken you. He loves you still and stands to receive you in repentance.

John, in his experience of rededication, risked his own life, ignoring the mocking of the crowds, and stood by his Master ready to serve. In like manner Christ looks for us to help today.

On the cross our Savior remembered his mother. So today he remembers the single mother who is anxious and worried, the youth who is confused and perplexed, the man who faces trial and temptation, the parents who have sorrow and grief. He remembers them all and is ready to help.

Conclusion

Jesus provided an earthly home for Mary by entrusting her to John. But even while he spoke, while the world jeered, he was providing a heavenly home for her by sacrificing his life. He did not do this for Mary alone, but for all who believe. He said, "In my Father's house are many mansions.... I go to prepare a place for you." This home is ours by faith, and the door is the cross.

SUNDAY EVENING, MARCH 20

Title: Salt of the Earth

Text: "Ye are the salt of the earth: but if the salt have lost his savour, wherewith shall it be salted? it is thenceforth good for nothing, but to be cast out, and to be trodden under foot of men" **(Matt. 5:13)**.

Scripture Reading: Luke 14:25–35

Introduction

Jesus has spent the night in prayer. Coming down from the mountain early in the morning, he chooses the Twelve and takes them back up into the mountain, where he delivers the Sermon on the Mount.

From this vantage point, overlooking the Sea of Galilee, he and the apostles have a ringside observation seat.

The fishermen have spent the night fishing. Now they are docking their boats and crating their catch. Since there is no refrigeration, the fish are packed in layers of salt. On board each ship is a salt barrel. As the disciples glance down at the ships, they see a familiar sight. A husky fisherman plunges his calloused hand into the salt barrel, draws out a heaping handful of salt, and throws it into an empty crate. Then he carefully lays a layer of fish on the salt and continues to alternately layer salt and fish until the crate is full. Perhaps Jesus looks away for an instant to this sight and then turns to his disciples with these words: "Ye are the salt of the earth."

I. The timeless teachings of Christ.

A. *The fact that Jesus spoke of salt is an illustration of his timelessness.* In the average gallon of sea water, there is one-fourth pound of salt. One statistician figured that all of the world's oceans would yield enough salt to build a wall 180 miles high and one mile thick, which would be long enough to reach around the world at the equator.

B. *The world changes; the teachings of Jesus are changeless.* More scientific discoveries have been made in the last fifty years than in the previous five thousand years. But the teachings of Jesus have never changed. They are as timeless as salt.

II. A rotten world.

Just as fish need salt to keep them from rotting, this world needs the salty influence of Christians to keep it from rotting.

A. *Moral rot.*
1. Alcoholism.
2. Drug addiction.
3. Pornography.
B. *Theological rot.*

1. Many so-called Bible scholars view heaven and hell as mythological.
2. Many ministers do not believe in the virgin birth.
3. Many scholars try to explain away events recorded in the Old Testament, such as the flood, the parting of the Red Sea, and Jonah's being swallowed by a large fish.

III. The Christian's place of influence.

A. *Salt is salt because it is different.* When asked, "What does salt taste like?" one can only answer, "It tastes like salt." It is unique. The influence of the Christian must remain a unique force in the world.

B. *Salt is pure.* One of the purest elements known to humankind is salt. It is easily taken from salt pits and salt mines because it is so pure. Likewise, the Christian should be characterized by purity.

C. *There is no substitute for salt.* If it loses its ability to salt, nothing can take its place. No one can take the place of the witnessing Christian whose life always corresponds to his lips.

D. *Salt can be useless.* When dirt got mixed with salt, the precious salt was treated like dirt; it was thrown on the slippery paths around Jerusalem and other ancient cities. The saddest sight on earth is a Christian who has lost his influence for Christ. He is like precious salt being treated like common dirt.

Conclusion

Born Drunk was his name. He was the son of a prostitute who actually was drunk when he was born. His friend Jim had found a new life in Christ. Born Drunk had carefully observed Jim's conversion. "I want to be like Jim," he said.

"Well, don't you want to be like Jesus?" asked a friend.

"I don't know nothin' about Jesus, but whatever happened to Jim, I want it to happen to me," was his reply.

Jim had been the salt of the earth!

WEDNESDAY EVENING, MARCH 23

Title: The Command to Guard against Covetousness

Text: "He said unto them, Take heed, and beware of covetousness: for a man's life consisteth not in the abundance of the things which he possesseth" **(Luke 12:15).**

Scripture Reading: Luke 12:13–21

Introduction

Jesus' words are always interesting. His sayings have commanded the attention of earth's greatest scholars. His words have encouraged the despairing and the despondent pilgrim on life's highway. His words have inspired contemplative youth. His words have comforted grieving hearts. His words have served as pointing fingers to the highway of happiness. His words have served as stoplights on the road to destruction. It is such a word of warning that we find in our text: "Take heed, and beware of covetousness: for a man's life consisteth not in the abundance of the things which he possesseth." Each of us would live a richer and fuller life if the words of this command from the heart of our living Lord could be written on our hearts and minds with the point of a diamond.

No one ever confesses to being guilty of the sin of covetousness. An honored and revered pastor once said, "I have spent forty years in the pastorate. In counseling men concerning their problems, every sin in the catalog has been confessed except the sin of covetousness." We do not recognize our guilt, because we call it by some other name. We do not recognize it as a sin, because our economic system encourages it. Covetousness cooperates with our natural acquisitive instinct. Advertising agencies appeal to and develop our tendency to become covetous.

We need to listen intently and responsively to the warning of our Lord when he commands us to beware of covetousness.

I. The nature of covetousness.

A. *The common definition of covetousness is "to want something that belongs to someone else."*

B. *The dictionary defines covetousness as "marked by inordinate desire for wealth or possessions or for another's possessions."*

C. *Covetousness is not only an act but also an attitude.* If we interpret Christ correctly, covetousness is that attitude that judges success in terms of material things. Covetousness is the belief that the good life is a life of material affluence. By studying the parable of the rich fool, we can discover that covetousness is selfishness in action. The covetous person is primarily concerned about his own comfort and pleasure, is far more interested in time than in eternity, and considers "making a living" as the chief object in life. The covetous person majors on feeding his stomach and clothing his back while starving his spirit and dwelling in spiritual nakedness. The command of Jesus our Lord is that we must beware of covetousness. We must not tolerate it. We must flee from it. We must avoid wrapping our life around that which is material, visible, tangible, and perishable.

II. Covetousness has been and is the curse of God's people.

We have been guilty of desiring that which was either unlawful, improper, forbidden, or unnecessary. The desire for such has often led us astray from the will of God (1 Tim. 6:6–11).

A. *Covetousness for equality with God caused Adam and Eve to fall into sin.*

B. *Covetousness caused Lot to choose the well-watered plain that led to Sodom.*

C. *Covetousness caused the children of Israel to murmur against Moses and to desire to return to Egypt.*

D. *Covetousness for material things caused the society of Israel to decay to the point of utter corruption during the days of Jeremiah (Jer. 6:13).*

E. *Covetousness for material things caused the people of Malachi's day to withhold tithes and offerings from God (Mal. 3:8–10).*

III. How can we avoid covetousness?

A. *We can avoid covetousness if we realize that covetousness defiles a man's spiritual nature and twists his moral vision (Mark 7:20–23).*

B. *Recognizing God's attitude toward covetousness can help us to guard against it (1 Cor. 5:11).*

C. *We can overcome covetousness if we will fully recognize the temporary value of material things in contrast to the doing of God's will (1 John 2:15–17).*

Conclusion

God has commanded us not to be getters and keepers but rather givers and sharers. When God bestows a blessing on us, he does so not that we might indulge ourselves and grow fat but that we might minister to others and help those in need.

In the final analysis, the only way in which we can avoid being overcome by covetousness is to define our objective for living in terms of an opportunity to be a giver of the good news of God's love to a lost and needy world. Our Lord has commanded us to avoid covetousness. We are obligated to do so if we want to prove our love for him.

SUNDAY MORNING, MARCH 27

Title: The Word of Desolation

Text: "And about the ninth hour Jesus cried with a loud voice, saying, Eli, Eli, lama sabachthani? that is to say, My God, my God, why hast thou forsaken me?" **(Matt. 27:46).**

Scripture Reading: Matthew 27:39–49

Hymns: "Crown Him with Many Crowns," Bridges

"The Lily of the Valley," Fry

"There Is a Green Hill Far Away," Alexander

Offertory Prayer: Holy Father, you who are the Creator and Sustainer of life, to you we come with gratitude for the inner disposition that causes us to want to worship you. We thank you for the inward prompting of your Holy Spirit that ever draws us closer to you. As an act of worship we bring our tithes and offerings for your ministry of mercy in your world. Bless both the gifts and the givers for Jesus' sake. Amen.

Introduction

In all of the Bible there is no verse more perplexing than this word of Christ from the cross. When one is faced with it, he begins to look for some excuse to bypass it. Martin Luther even felt this temptation—great scholar that he was. He once began a study of this verse and for a long time continued in prayer, fasting, and meditation. At length he arose and exclaimed in amazement, "God forsaken of God! Who can understand that?"

Let us first try to picture the scene. Jesus was crucified at 9:00 in the morning, at "the third hour," the hour of the morning sacrifice, the hour at which the lamb had been, for generations, offered daily in the temple. After he had hung on the cross for three full hours, at high noon, when the sun, which burns so intensely in Palestine, was at its brightest, darkness suddenly fell on the whole land and continued until the ninth hour, three o'clock in the afternoon. This was the hour of the evening sacrifice, when again a lamb was offered daily in the temple, foreshadowing the sacrifice of the Lamb of God, the Lamb slain from the foundation of the world. During that time of darkness no sound came from Jesus on his cross. Then as the darkness passed, he cried, "Eli, Eli, lama sabachthani?" "My God, my God, why hast thou forsaken me?"

How can we understand this scene? How can we express its meaning? We can grasp some of its wonder by examining three areas.

I. The desolation of the Christ.

Was there ever a cry so filled with desolation as "My God, my God, why hast thou forsaken me?" Many misunderstood the cry. Those who stood by said, "He is calling for Elijah to help him."

A. *This was no new experience for Christ.* From childhood the Christ had been misunderstood. Members of his own household refused to recognize him as the Messiah and even accused him of being insane. When he cast out demons, his contemporaries accused him of being in league with Beelzebub, the prince of demons. Because he associated with publicans and sinners, they charged him with being a gluttonous man and a winebibber. When he said to them, "Destroy this temple, and in three days I will raise it up" (John 2:19), they thought he spoke of the temple in Jerusalem. When he said that he was a king and spoke of a kingdom, they accused him of treason. He said that he was the Son of God, and they charged him with blasphemy. They did not understand.

B. *Now, as he came to the cross, they misunderstood again.* Listen to their words: "He saved others; himself he cannot save. Let [him] descend now from the cross" (Mark 15:31–32). They laughed at him and jeered, but they did not understand.

1. They were right. He had saved others. He had saved the blind from their darkness. He had saved the disabled from their lameness. He had even saved some from death. He had saved sinners from their sin. What a testimony of Christ's power, from the lips of his enemies!

2. They were also right when they said that he could not save himself. Why couldn't he? If he wanted, he could have called legions of angels to his

94

side and destroyed the rabble around the cross. But, in a real sense, he could not save himself, for his heart was set on saving others. He had come to seek and to save the lost, not to save himself. His inability to save himself was of his own volition. He knew that "without shedding of blood [there] is no remission" of sin (Heb. 9:22). He could not save himself, for he had come to save you.

II. The separation from the Father.

More profound than all the mysteries of time and eternity is the mystery of what was happening in the midday darkness. "Why hast thou forsaken me?"

A. *Can you find a word filled with more pathos than this word "forsaken"?* One immediately pictures a city abandoned by its citizens, a child deserted by his parents, a wife forsaken by her husband.

This was no new experience for Christ. All of his life he had been forsaken. His own family turned from him. "He came unto his own, and his own received him not" describes his own nation's rejection of him. His disciples all forsook him and fled. He had known what it meant to be forsaken, yet he was always conscious that he was not alone, for the Father was always with him. He said at the Last Supper, "Behold, the hour cometh, yea, is now come, that ye shall be scattered, every man to his own, and shall leave me alone: and yet I am not alone, because the Father is with me" (John 16:32). But now he cried, "Why hast thou forsaken me?" No one stood by him. There was no opening of the heavens nor voice of God. There was no strengthening angel by his side as in Gethsemane. He was alone, forsaken by God.

But does God ever forsake his own? All history, all human experience, all Scripture indicate that he does not. David could say, "Yea, though I walk through the valley of the shadow of death, I will fear no evil: for thou art with me" (Ps. 23:4). God has promised, "I will never leave thee, nor forsake thee" (Heb. 13:5). He did not forsake Joseph in Potiphar's prison, Israel in Egypt, David when he faced Goliath, nor Daniel in the lions' den. Yet here he forsook the Christ.

B. *What can it mean?* The answer is to be found in the significance of Christ's death.

1. Certainly this was not an actual, eternal separation from God. The divine nature could not be separated from the human; Jesus was eternally God. Nor could the Father be separated from the Son in the Godhead.

2. It could not mean that the Father had forsaken the Son in the sense that he ceased to love him, for God truly was well pleased with Jesus for sacrificing himself in behalf of others and doing God's will even to the point of death.

3. It was because all the sin of humankind was placed on Jesus. "He was made to be sin," said Paul. Therefore God forsook the Son. God abandoned the Christ, for God is holy and cannot bear sin.

95

C. *This explains Gethsemane.* To be forsaken of God was the cup that Christ found difficult to embrace. Yet he was obedient unto death, saying, "Not my will, but thine, be done."

D. *The sin of the world is what separated Christ from the Father.* And let us never forget that it is always so. Sin separates from God. It was so when God drove Adam and Eve from the garden and from his presence. It was so when David lied and murdered. His fellowship with God was broken, and he cried out, "Restore unto me the joy of thy salvation" (Ps. 51:12). It was true with God's people in the past. It is true with us today. Isaiah cried out, "Behold, the LORD's hand is not shortened, that it cannot save; neither his ear heavy, that it cannot hear: But your iniquities have separated between you and your God" (Isa. 59:1–2). Sin always separates from God, but the door of return is always open in Jesus Christ.

III. The substitution for our sin.

In some marvelous and miraculous way, the Christ, in this moment of desolation and separation, was taking our place on that cross.

A. *Paul interprets the scene for us when he says, "[God] hath made [Jesus] to be sin for us, who knew no sin" (2 Cor. 5:21).* Jesus was made to be a sin offering for our sins. All of the sin and iniquity of all the world was placed on him. Think of all the sin of all the world—all the murder, hate, greed, lust, covetousness, etc.—and see it all placed on Christ. As the Passover Lamb was slain to symbolize the redemption of Israel from their bondage to sin, as the high priest symbolically placed the sins of the people on the scapegoat, so Christ bore the sins of all the world. Isaiah 53 foretold it: "He was wounded for our transgressions, he was bruised for our iniquities: the chastisement of our peace was upon him; and by his stripes we are healed" (v. 5).

B. *Consequently, all the wrath of God was poured out on Christ, who became sin for us.* All the punishment that our sins deserved was placed on him. Every nail driven into his body was for our sin. Every stripe upon his back was for our sin. Every thorn that pierced his brow was for our sin. The spear thrust into his side was for our sin. All of this he did for us.

IV. The proclamation of the scene.

As paradoxical as it may seem, these words proclaim a message of faith and victory.

A. *It was a word of trust.* There was the ever-present temptation to doubt, but Christ could still say, "My God, my God." He held firm to his strong faith in God. Though we may be abandoned by the world's favor, the friendship of others, and earthly prosperity—seemingly forsaken by God—yet God himself always stands near to those who can cry, "My God, my God." Christ, like Job, was saying, "Though he slay me, yet will I trust in him" (Job 13:15).

B. *It was a cry of victory.* Here Jesus was finishing what he came to do. He was accomplishing the will of the Father. This was his supreme moment of triumph, and God authenticated it by accepting his sacrifice. The veil of the temple was rent from top to bottom, as if God reached down from heaven and tore it apart, saying to humankind: "Come now through the sacrifice of my Son. You no longer need a priest to intercede for you."

Conclusion

"Salvation is found in no one else, for there is no other name under heaven given to men by which we must be saved" (Acts 4:12 NIV). Christ, who bore your sin, who took your place, will save you today.

SUNDAY EVENING, MARCH 27

Title: Salt and Saints

Text: "Ye are the salt of the earth" (**Matt. 5:13**).

Introduction

The Englishman who invented potato chips sold only a few packages a week until he thought of putting salt on them. At first, inventor Frank Smith fried thin slices of potatoes and peddled them on a very small basis. Then he tucked a little pinch of salt wrapped in blue paper into each package. His business boomed to the point that he had to purchase a huge farm to grow his potatoes. Today the potato chip business has spread all over the world. But without salt it would have died in England generations ago.

Likewise, without the salty influence of Christians, the Christian movement would have died long ago. Perhaps all of the uses of salt both ancient and modern should be applied to the Christian.

I. Some uses of salt related to God.

A. *The sacrifices and offerings were salted (Lev. 2:13; Ezek. 43:24).*

B. *Salt also symbolized the irrevocable character of God's covenant with Israel (Num. 18:19; 2 Chron. 13:5).* The sacred incense (Ex. 30:35) and the shewbread (Lev. 24:7) were seasoned with salt. God never changes. His promises to and his demands on his people are equally just as changeless.

II. Some uses of salt.

A. *Salt preserves.* Perhaps this was the primary use in the mind of Jesus when he used salt as an illustration. Plutarch said that meat is part of a dead body and would, if left to itself, go bad. He concluded, however, that salt preserves it and keeps it fresh and that salt is "like a new soul inserted in a dead body."

B. *Salt prevents further decay.* Salt not only prevents corruption, it also controls corruption that already exists. It is applied to fresh meat to prevent decay. When it is applied to living flesh, it creates an environment unfavorable to disease, thus allowing natural healing powers to work. The Christian does not seek to legislate morals, but he supports legislation that creates the moral environment for reform.

III. Some observations about salt.

A. *Salt is useless unless it is scattered*. In fact, it is distasteful any other way. If left in the saltshaker, it may draw moisture and harden. It is best when spread on watermelon, tomatoes, steak, or corn on the cob.

Henry Ward Beecher said, "If you want your neighbor to see what the Christ spirit will do for him, let him see what it has done for you." This is shared Christianity.

B. *A little salt goes a long way*. The casual witness of life and word has often reaped eternal dividends. It is noteworthy that our Lord often spoke of leaven to indicate the small beginnings of some things that grew into powerful forces. Is it any wonder that a pinch of salt is often sprinkled on dough to aid in the rising process?

C. *Salt never calls attention to itself except when it is in the wrong place*. When sprinkled on food, it brings out the natural flavor; one is hardly aware of its presence. But let the ice cream salt seep into the ice cream, and salt is out of place! Let the Christian compromise with the world's ways and find himself in the wrong places doing the wrong things, and he, too, is out of place.

D. *Salt is composed of two poisons*. Its technical name is sodium chloride. Sodium and chloride are poisonous when taken separately. But God joins these two poisons to make salt, a condiment on every table.

The Christian is poisoned by sin. In Christ, his body becomes the temple of the Holy Spirit. God's transforming work makes the Christian's witness a necessity for the world. In Christ, the image of God that was marred by man's fall is restored by the Holy Spirit.

E. *Salt is composed of many different sizes of grains*. When viewed through a microscope, salt grains are different sizes and shapes. Christians are this way too. Some are more capable than others. Some are better prepared than others. But all Christians of all ages and of all stations in life make up the salt of the earth.

Conclusion

"Did they laugh at you for being a Christian?" a friend asked a young man attending a secular college.

"No, they never did know that I am a Christian," was the reply.

Is it any wonder that the world wonders about some Christians?

"I would be a Christian if I could see one," said a great leader of another country. Another echoed, "I would be a Christian if it were not for Christians."

Christians—for the sake of souls—be what you are: the salt of the earth!

WEDNESDAY EVENING, MARCH 30

Title: The Command to Give

Text: "Give, and it shall be given unto you; good measure, pressed down, and shaken together, and running over, shall men give into your bosom. For with the same measure that ye mete withal it shall be measured to you again" **(Luke 6:38)**.

Scripture Reading: Luke 6:27–38

Introduction

As we contemplate obedience to the commandment of our Lord, it would be wise for us to recognize that there is always a promise involved or implied in every commandment of our Lord. There are many surprises in store for the person who studies the commandments of the Lord with this truth in mind. For some reason we usually think of a commandment as either placing restrictions on us or making undesirable demands on us. Because of this improper understanding of the nature of the commandments of our Lord, we often overlook the precious promises that are contained in them. Particularly is this true with regard to God's commandment to give.

I. The command to concentrate on giving.

There is only one word of command in the text. That command is found in the first word of the text in which Jesus said, "Give."

A. *Giving is the way to maturity.*

B. *Giving is the way to usefulness and fruitfulness.*

C. *Giving is the way to happiness (Acts 20:35).* Our Lord would have each of us focus our attention and efforts on the activity of giving. We should be intelligent and generous givers in every area of life.

II. What can we give?

Almost automatically one thinks in terms of giving money when the subject of giving is introduced. Because of our built-in tendency to be selfish, and because of our pocketbook protection instinct, we usually react negatively to the opportunity and the responsibility of being a giver.

There are many things that a child of God can give and be enriched, instead of impoverished, by giving.

A. *We can give Christian love to those about us.* Christian love has been defined as a persistent, unbreakable spirit of goodwill toward others.

B. *We can give mercy to those who are unfortunate and undeserving (Luke 6:36).*

C. *We can give understanding and toleration to those with whom we disagree (Luke 6:37).*

D. *We can give forgiveness to those who mistreat us (Luke 6:37).*

E. *We can give praise to those who are serving faithfully.*

99

F. *We can give encouragement to those who are struggling.*

G. *We can give inspiration to those whose lives come under our influence.*

H. *We can give gratitude to those who are generous.*

I. *We can give the gospel to those who are lost.*

III. The promise connected with this commandment.

Because of our negative attitude toward giving, we miss the promise of the text. Look again at the words of Jesus. Following the one word of command, the promise is this: "and it shall be given unto you; good measure, pressed down, and shaken together, and running over, shall men give into your bosom."

Jesus declares that the person who lives to be a giver will without fail receive a bounty from his fellow humans as well as the blessings of a generous God.

Conclusion

Apart from the obedience to the command to give, one can never experience the promise that is connected with it. Our Lord said, "If you love me, you will obey what I command" (John 14:15 NIV). We prove our love for our Lord who gave his life for us by imitating his example and giving ourselves and all that we are in unselfish service to others.

APRIL

■ **Sunday Mornings**

Continue with the theme "The Seven Words from the Cross" through Palm Sunday. Follow with an Easter sermon focusing on one of Jesus' postresurrection appearances.

■ **Sunday Evenings**

Continue the series on the Sermon on the Mount.

■ **Wednesday Evenings**

Continue the series "The Commands of Jesus Christ."

SUNDAY MORNING, APRIL 3

Title: The Word of Anguish

Text: "After this, Jesus knowing that all things were now accomplished, that the scripture might be fulfilled, saith, I thirst" **(John 19:28)**.

Scripture Reading: John 19:28–29

Hymns: "Praise Him, Praise Him!" Crosby

"The Old Rugged Cross," Bennard

"When I Survey the Wondrous Cross," Watts

Offertory Prayer: Holy Father, we remind ourselves that nothing is hidden from you. You have placed within our care many blessings over which we are to serve as managers for you. Help us to be your servants in every area of our lives. We present to you a portion of the fruits of our labors as an act of worship. Accept them and bless them to the increase of your kingdom, to the salvation of the lost, and to ministries of mercy through Jesus Christ, our Lord. Amen.

Introduction

Of all the words that Christ spoke from the cross, his cry "I thirst" was the shortest. At the same time, it was the only one relating to his own anguish. He had prayed for others, "Father, forgive them; for they know not what they do." He had answered the prayer of a penitent thief. He had considered the needs of his mother. He had prayed to the Father in the darkness. Now he cried, "I thirst."

Bystanders had heard the most awful cry to fall from human lips, "My God, my God, why hast thou forsaken me?" Now they heard one of the most common phrases spoken by people, "I thirst." They could hear this word any hour, on every hand, in this parched land. Now, though, they heard it from the Son of God. He who had scooped out the oceans with his hand, who had drawn the rivers with his fingers, who brought forth water from the rock to quench the thirst of Israel, now cried, "I thirst."

What does it mean? What are its implications? Let us look at its varied facets and try to catch its significance.

I. It was a cry as man.

A. *Here we are brought face-to-face with the supreme paradox of all time.* The Christ was truly the God-man. He was God incarnate.

1. He was divine — "very God of very God." Before the foundations of the world, he was. He existed from all eternity in the glory of heaven. John says, "In the beginning was the Word, and the Word was with God, and the Word was God. The same was in the beginning with God" (John 1:1–2). The New Testament declares him to be God. Jesus claimed to be God, and the disciples recognized him as God.

2. He was human, and the cry "I thirst" stresses this. Our Lord's words remind us that he was partaker of a true humanity. That the Son of God was truly incarnate is a fundamental doctrine of the Christian faith.

   The evidence of our Lord's incarnation is as clear and convincing as its necessity was obvious and urgent. A real, vital, complete assumption of human nature by the second person of the Trinity is plainly taught in Scripture. He was born of a woman. He grew. He had the natural appetites of a man. He performed all the ordinary actions of a man; he ate, he drank, he walked, he sat, he wept, he slept, and at length he died. If these proofs are not sufficient, he is repeatedly and expressly styled a man. He grew in knowledge; he expressed human emotions; and he is said to have been like his fellow humans in all things. Our Lord's dying exclamation, "I thirst," reminds us of his incarnation and is one evidence of its truth.

   What a contrast this is! Yet his life had been one of contrasts. He was the Son of God, yet he was born in a stable. He knew all things, yet he grew in wisdom. He had equal authority with God, yet he was subject to his mother. He fed hungry multitudes with a few small loaves and fish, yet his own hunger in the wilderness was an occasion of satanic temptation. He said he was meek and lowly in heart, yet he declared himself greater than Solomon. He wept at the grave of Lazarus, yet he raised him from the dead. With such contrasts in the life of Christ, we need not wonder that he who stood in the temple and cried, "If any man thirst, let him come unto me, and drink" (John 7:37), should hang upon the cross, and, in an extremity of suffering, cry out, "I thirst." A. W. Pink, in stressing Christ's humanity, pointed out that God does not thirst, nor do the angels thirst. But we thirst because we are human, and so did Jesus.

B. *"I thirst" stresses not only Jesus' humanity but also his suffering.* To realize the full impact of these words, we must recall what preceded them. He had observed the Paschal meal with his disciples and instituted the Lord's Supper. He had gone from there to Gethsemane, where he sweat, as it were, great drops of blood in his agony. He had been arrested and dragged from trial to trial throughout the night and early morning. He had been mocked and ridiculed, slapped and scourged. Now the nails had been driven through his hands and feet. The crown of thorns had pierced his brow. It had been eighteen or twenty hours since he had had anything to drink. For six hours he had been on the cross. Throughout all of this he never complained nor cried out for pity. But now he cried, "I thirst."

Jesus suffered, and his suffering was real. Gnosticism, an early heresy, denied the reality of his suffering, but the New Testament stresses it over and over. This is what Paul meant when he declared, "Christ had to suffer" (Acts 17:3 NIV). It is what the writer of Hebrews meant when he said, "Because [Christ] himself suffered when he was tempted, he is able to help those who are being tempted" (Heb. 2:18 NIV). It is the emphasis of Peter when he wrote, "Christ suffered in his body" (1 Peter 4:1 NIV).

C. *Jesus suffered though he was the Son of God.* God did not exempt his "only begotten Son." He suffered, and so must we. We are not exempt nor immune. Sorrow and heartaches, grief and pain, belong to all of us.

II. It was a cry on behalf of man.

A. *Jesus cried, "I thirst."* But why? Why was he suffering? Why was he dying? It was on behalf of others that he suffered. Peter described this scene: "For Christ died for sins once for all, the righteous for the unrighteous, to bring you to God" (1 Peter 3:18 NIV). He suffered in life that we might not have to suffer in death. He cried, "I thirst," on the cross that we might not cry, "I thirst," in hell.

B. *Jesus did not have to suffer.* At the beginning of the crucifixion, Jesus had been offered an intoxicating drink to deaden the pain of the cross. He refused this drink, choosing rather to suffer the agony and pain, choosing to taste the full bitterness of this cup that was his. Jesus knows, therefore, all that we endure. This means that "we do not have a high priest who is unable to sympathize with our weaknesses, but we have one who has been tempted in every way, just as we are — yet was without sin" (Heb. 4:15 NIV). He understands our grief and pain, our sorrow and heartache, our suffering and anguish. We can cast all of our cares on him, for he cares for us (1 Peter 5:7). He proved that he cares for us by suffering in our behalf.

C. *Why did Jesus wait until he had been on the cross for six hours before he cried out, "I thirst"?* The Scripture says that it was not until Jesus knew "that all things were now accomplished" that he cried, "I thirst." Not until his murderers had been forgiven, a penitent thief had been saved, his mother had been provided for, and sin had been encountered and conquered did he think of himself. After Jesus had encountered and defeated Satan in the wilderness at the beginning of his ministry, he was hungry. Now he had met Satan again in a battle for the souls of humans. With the battle over and the victory won, "knowing that all things were now accomplished," he said, "I thirst." Why not sooner? He was too busy meeting the needs of the world. The Scripture says, "for the joy set before him [he] endured the cross" (Heb. 12:2 NIV).

III. It was a cry to man.

A. *The cry "I thirst" was not a prayer offered to the Father, as Christ had done earlier.* Had he petitioned the throne of God, the Father could have satisfied his thirst in countless ways. Instead, he cried to those beneath the cross. He cried for their help even as he cries today for our service. In that hour he was utterly dependent on their help. His hands were nailed to the cross and could not lift the drink to his lips. His feet were tied to the tree and could not seek a cooling stream. He was helpless, dependent on those who cared. His feet cannot walk our streets. His hands cannot minister to our world. His voice cannot speak his truth. His arms cannot embrace a world in love. He is dependent on us. He cries to us for help.

B. *Out of the many who stood by, there was only one who gave him drink to quench his thirst.* A soldier ran and offered a sponge of bitter wine. This deed reminds us of Jesus' words, "If anyone gives even a cup of cold water to one of these little ones because he is my disciple,... he will certainly not lose his reward" (Matt. 10:42 NIV).

Don't you envy that soldier? Wouldn't you have liked to have been the man who gave Christ the drink? Well, you can be, for through the lips of thousands today he still speaks this word. We hear it in those who thirst for love and kindness, in those who thirst for concern and compassion, in those who thirst in suffering and sorrow, in those who thirst for forgiveness and assurance. We hear the cry and can satisfy the thirst! And in doing so we are ministering to the thirst of the Christ. It was he who said, "Inasmuch as ye have done it unto one of the least of these my brethren, ye have done it unto me" (Matt. 25:40). Where there is need, where there is sorrow, where there is loneliness, where there is sin, there is the Christ today. Listen and you can hear his cry—"I thirst."

Conclusion

In this hour Jesus thirsts for your service, for your love, for your presence. But, perhaps, like the disciples, you have forsaken him and fled—you have backslidden. He thirsts for your return.

Jesus thirsts for lost souls today. It was for this purpose that he suffered. Once he asked a lost woman for a drink of water to quench his thirst, and in turn he offered her living water that she might never thirst. She opened her heart and received the Christ. In doing so she satisfied the thirst of the Savior.

One day, if you do not accept Jesus as your Savior, you will utter this same cry, "I thirst." Like the rich man in hell, you will thirst for all eternity (Luke 16:19–31). It was to save us from this thirst that he cried, "I thirst."

On the other hand, if Jesus is your Savior, you will never thirst again, for heaven is yours, where you "shall hunger no more, neither thirst" (Rev. 7:16). Jesus' invitation is to you. "If any man thirst, let him come unto me, and drink" (John 7:37).

> *I heard the voice of Jesus say,*
> *"Behold, I freely give*
> *The living water; thirsty one,*
> *Stoop down and drink, and live."*
> *I came to Jesus and I drank*
> *Of that life-giving stream;*
> *My thirst was quenched, my soul revived,*
> *And now I live in him.*

SUNDAY EVENING, APRIL 3

Title: The Light of the World

Text: "You are the light of the world. A city on a hill cannot be hidden. Neither do people light a lamp and put it under a bowl. Instead they put it on its stand, and it gives light to everyone in the house. In the same way, let your light shine before men, that they may see your good deeds and praise your Father in heaven" (**Matt. 5:14–16 NIV**).

Scripture Reading: Luke 11:29–36

Introduction

The glow of a cigarette on a dark night is visible three-fourths of a mile. The glare of a match can be seen for a mile. Light from a good flashlight is visible for one and a half miles. Light from a 100-watt lamp can be seen for twelve and a half miles. The headlights from your automobile are visible for twenty miles on a clear night.

Our Lord taught that Christian influence can light the whole world! Christian influence is described as preservation (salt of the earth) through demonstration (light of the world).

I. The Christian's light can light the world.

A. *When Jesus said, "Ye are the light of the world," he related the mission of the Christian to a familiar Palestinian object.* William Barclay described the light with which those who heard the Sermon on the Mount would be familiar (William Barclay, *The Gospel of Matthew, Chapters 1–10,* Daily Study Bible Series, vol. 10 [Philadelphia: Westminster, 1958], 119). He indicated that the houses in Palestine were very dark and had only one small circular window not more than eighteen inches across. Each home had a lamp that was no more than a gravy boat filled with oil with a floating wick. The lamp stood on a lampstand that was a small, roughly shaped wooden table. For safety's sake, the lamp was removed from its stand and put under an earthen bushel measure so that it might burn without risk when the family was away from the home.

B. *Light exposes darkness.* The primary duty of the lamp's light was to be seen. Thus our Lord indicates that Christians are to love in such a way that others might see Christ in our lives.

C. *As it shone through the small window and as its rays reached the rooms of the house, the lamp served as a guide.* The best guide to the better life is that of a Christian whose influence counts for Christ.

D. *As it shone through the small window, the light warned travelers of dangerous obstacles along the road.* The Christian's influence should serve as a warning sign for all to observe. Our lives should say, "Warning! Walk this way!"

E. *An elderly blind man was seen carrying a lantern on a dark night.* "Since you can't see, why are you carrying a lantern?" asked an interested friend. "I carry a lantern at night," he said, "so that others won't stumble over me."

II. Only Christians can be the light of the world.

"You" is in the emphatic position. No one else can take the place of Christians as the light of this world, which is dark with sin.

A. *While Jesus was on earth, he was the Light of the World (John 8:12; 9:4–5; 12:35–36).*

B. *Since Christ left the earth, Christians have been given the responsibility of demonstrating him to the world (Phil. 2:15).*

C. *The radiance of the Christian's life depends on how close he or she is to Jesus Christ (2 Cor. 4:6–7).*

III. The Christian's light cannot be hidden.

A. *Like "a city set on a hill," the Christian's influence cannot be hidden.* A city with shining lights can be seen from all sides on a dark night.

B. *Not all lights have the same wattage.* Some are only 15 watts and others are 500 or even 1,000. God has use for even a dim bulb on a dark night. Regardless of how dimly it shines, the light of a Christian's influence is being observed by someone.

C. *"Bury my influence with me" was the request of a Christian whose light had not shone very brightly for Christ.* When he came to die, he was filled with regret that he had done so little for Christ. But Jesus taught that one's influence cannot be buried with him.

IV. There is a place for every Christian's light.

A. *The Christian is not fired up to fizzle.* Lights are lit for the purpose of shining. They are never lit for the purpose of being covered.

B. *There is a place for every light.* Just as each light in the Palestinian houses sat on its own particular table so that it would shine through the small window and to the rooms of the house, each Christian has a particular place from which he or she is to shine.

C. *Without the elevation of the lamp, the light is wasted.* A lighthouse at Charleston, South Carolina, boasts of twenty million candlepower and is visible for twenty miles. But the secret to its success is the 140-foot structure on which it sets. Christians must find the will of God for their lives and shine in it to the best of their abilities.

Conclusion

Light makes no noise. Lighthouses sound no drums. They merely shine. Christians' influence causes others to see Christ in them. But for what purpose? Surely not for their own glory! Christians influence the world toward Christ for the glory of God. With Paul, Christians assert, "I have been crucified with Christ and I no longer live, but Christ lives in me" (Gal. 2:20 NIV).

WEDNESDAY EVENING, APRIL 6

Title: The Command to Have Faith

Text: "And Jesus answering saith unto them, Have faith in God" (**Mark 11:22**).

Scripture Reading: Mark 11:15–23

Introduction

The besetting sin of God's people, both in the past and in the present, is the sin of little faith. When faith departs, fear captures the citadel of the soul.

The men and women who have become spiritual giants are those who out-prayed and out-trusted their contemporaries. They responded to God's promises in a positive manner and trusted him to be as dependable in the future as he had been in the past.

Jesus Christ always responded creatively and redemptively to the faith of those who trusted him implicitly. He healed the centurion's servant because of his faith (Matt. 8:5–10). He healed the palsied man because of his faith and the faith of the four who brought him (Mark 2:5). He healed the daughter of the Canaanite woman because of the faith that she indicated by her persistence (Matt. 15:21–28). Many have failed to live the genuine Christian life because they have not yet recognized that it is a life of faith.

I. To have faith is not always easy.

A. *We are people of flesh.*
B. *We want to walk by sight.*
C. *The unfaithfulness of others often discourages our faith.*
D. *The confused, uncertain, and troubled condition of the world makes a simple faith difficult for some.*

II. To have faith is reasonable.

A. *Creation encourages faith.*

B. *The history of those who have trusted God makes faith reasonable.*

C. *Personal experience makes faith reasonable, at least for some.*

III. Faith is absolutely essential ...

A. *If we are to have personal assurance of security with God.*

B. *If we are to make personal ventures involving risks.* That is, we must believe that God is going to help us.

C. *If we are to please God (Heb. 11:6).* To have no faith is to cast doubt upon God's truthfulness.

D. *Without faith we will not worship, pray, or witness.*

IV. How can we have a great faith?

A. *We can pray for a greater faith (Luke 17:5).*

B. *We can believe the testimonies of the Word of God (Rom. 10:17).*

C. *We can believe the testimonies of others who have lived by faith (Heb. 11).*

D. *We can use the faith that we have.*

Conclusion

Clearly our Lord commanded his disciples to exercise faith. If we obey this command, we will discover that our faith is increased. By obedience to this command, we will prove our love and at the same time experience the abundant life that our Lord has planned for us.

SUNDAY MORNING, APRIL 10

Title: The Word of Victory

Text: "When Jesus therefore had received the vinegar, he said, It is finished: and he bowed his head, and gave up the ghost" **(John 19:30)**.

Scripture Reading: John 19:30–37

Hymns: "I Will Sing the Wondrous Story," Rowley

"'Man of Sorrows,' What a Name," Bliss

"Jesus Paid It All," Hall

Offertory Prayer: Gracious God, help us to be ever conscious that we are but stewards of your grace. Help us to be good managers of that which you have entrusted to our care. We bring a tithe and an offering to show the sincerity of our love and concern that all of the world might hear the gospel of your redeeming love through the missionary outreach of the church. In the name of our Lord we pray. Amen.

Introduction

In the early days of our country one great achievement was the laying of tracks for a transcontinental railroad. Progress and union awaited the day when the East and West would be united by a rail running from the Atlantic to the Pacific. Over many years the task was advanced at difficulty and sacrifice. A ceremony was held at Promontory, Utah, on May 10, 1869, at which a golden spike was driven, symbolizing the completion of the railroad, the uniting of East and West. The crowds cheered, and the news was spread. This simple message was sent to the media by telegraph: "It is finished."

Two thousand years ago on the border between heaven and hell, four spikes were driven into the hands and feet of the Son of God. They were not of gold but of crude iron that tore the flesh. When these men had done their evil work, the word was shouted, "It is finished." Heaven and earth were now joined. Man and God were now united. It was finished, for "God was in Christ, reconciling the world unto himself" (2 Cor. 5:19).

This cry was the sixth word that Christ spoke from the cross. To those who stood there that day, the word had many meanings. Perhaps for every person it had a different meaning. To the soldiers it was the end of a day's work. Their job was finished and could be forgotten, as a hundred other crucifixions had been. To Mary it meant sorrow and grief, for her Son was dead. To Pilate it meant that, although his conscience would continue to accuse him, the threat to his authority was over. To Annas and Caiaphas and the other religious leaders, it meant that the threat to the "establishment" was over; the undermining influence of this religious innovator was finished, and they could return to the status quo. To the crowd it meant that the excitement of the day was done, and they could return to their homes and businesses as usual. To Jesus' enemies it meant that this impostor was dead, and they could rejoice. To his friends it meant the end to their hopes that he was the Savior of Israel. It was finished. His disciples could go back to their fishing and hide their shame in Galilee.

But the crucial point is not what Jesus' words meant to people then, but what they meant to him and to his Father and what they mean to us today.

I. They were the words of a Prophet.

    A. *A prophet was one who had been called and commissioned by God to do a work.* Such was the task of our Christ. At the age of twelve, in the temple, he said, "Didn't you know I had to be in my Father's house?" (Luke 2:49 NIV). To his disciples he said, "My food is to do the will of him who sent me" (John 4:34 NIV). In John's gospel alone the Lord is spoken of as being "sent." In Gethsemane Jesus cried, "Not my will, but thine, be done" (Luke 22:42). Now, on the cross, this "Prophet" of God cried out, "It is finished." He had completed the work that the Father had sent him to do.

    B. *Prophets were sent to speak forth for God, to declare his will and purpose, to reveal God's nature and character to sinful people.* This is what our Christ had done through his life. To Philip he declared, "He that hath seen me hath seen the Father" (John 14:9). John wrote concerning him, "No man hath seen God at any time; the only begotten Son ... hath declared him" (John 1:18). No longer do people have to wonder about God, for Christ has shown him to be a God of love—"[God] commendeth his love toward us, in that, while we were yet sinners, Christ died for us" (Rom. 5:8). Now on the cross Christ cried, "It is finished." A complete revelation had been given, and he illustrated it by his death.

II. They were the words of a Priest.

A. *Here on the cross our Savior assumed the role of the High Priest.* But there is a difference. He was not like those of the old dispensation, who offered the blood of sheep and goats. He offered himself on the altar of Calvary.

1. Jesus was qualified, for he was sinless. John the Baptist had cried, "Behold the Lamb of God, which taketh away the sin of the world" (John 1:29). Now Jesus became the Lamb without spot and blemish. We are not redeemed with corruptible things, such as silver and gold, but by the precious blood of Christ himself. As the writer of Hebrews said, "By his own blood he entered in once into the holy place" (Heb. 9:12).

2. This sacrifice was sufficient. "The blood of Jesus Christ his Son cleanseth us from all sin" (1 John 1:7). Now Christ cried from the altar, "It is finished." Nothing more is needed for our forgiveness and redemption. All we can do is open our hearts and receive it by faith.

B. *As our High Priest, he has fulfilled and finished all of the types, the ceremonies, the rituals, and the sacrifices.*

1. The shed blood of every sacrificial lamb came to full fruition here in Christ's sacrifice. The scapegoat, who bore the sins of the people, here found its consummation.

2. The priesthood itself is done away with. "It is finished!" The priest wore robes of scarlet, but Christ's scarlet was in the blood he shed as a priest after the order of Melchizedek. The priest wore the names of Israel on his shoulder (Ex. 28:12), but Christ "hath borne our griefs, and carried our sorrows" (Isa. 53:4). The high priest wore a crown of gold, but our High Priest wore a crown of thorns. The high priest could enter the Holy of Holies only once a year, but our High Priest ever lives to make intercession for us. The priest offered sacrifices repeatedly, but our High Priest offered himself once for the sins of the world. The priest shed the blood of lambs, but our High Priest shed his own precious blood.

3. Now the veil of the temple has been torn in two. God reached down and tore it down the middle. People no longer need a priest to intercede for them. We "come boldly unto the throne of grace" ourselves.

C. *The faith of all those who went before is now vindicated in Jesus' perfect sacrifice.*

All the saints of ages gone by—Abraham, Isaac, Jacob, Moses, Joshua, and others—were in heaven on credit. Their redemption had not been completely paid for, but God had promised it would be. Now as Christ cried out, "It is finished," all of these who looked forward to the coming of the Messiah and offered their sacrifices in faith could rejoice. Christ had redeemed them. The perfect sacrifice had been offered by their Priest— the Christ. When the Savior said, "It is finished," God stamped in red letters, "Paid in full."

III. They were the words of a King.

A. *Never did one look less like a king.* Jesus' crown was a crown of thorns. His scepter was a reed. He had no power because he was nailed to a tree. He had a cross instead of a throne. Yet when he cried, "It is finished," he spoke as a king. This was not a despairing sob nor a word of resignation. This was the tremendous shout of a king who reigned from a cross.

1. Pilate had a sign made that read, "The King of the Jews," and had it placed on the cross above Jesus' head. It was written in three languages for all to behold and read. Hebrew was the language of religion, Greek the language of culture, and Latin the language of law and government; and Christ was declared King in them all. Micah had foretold Jesus' kingship—"But thou, Bethlehem ... out of thee shall he come forth unto me that is to be ruler in Israel" (Mic. 5:2). He refused the crowd who would have made him a political king (John 6), for his was to be a spiritual reign. Pilate asked him, "Art thou the King of the Jews?" Jesus answered, "Thou sayest that I am a king. To this end was I born, and for this cause came I into the world, that I should bear witness unto the truth. Every one that is of the truth heareth my voice" (John 18:37). How then was Jesus to become King? The answer can be seen in Paul's words, "And being found in fashion as a man, he humbled himself, and became obedient unto death, even the death of the cross. Wherefore God also hath highly exalted him, and given him a name which is above every name: That at the name of Jesus every knee should bow, of things in heaven, and things in earth, and things under the earth; and that every tongue should confess that Jesus Christ is Lord, to the glory of God the Father" (Phil. 2:8–11).

   What is this "name which is above every name"? Revelation 19:16 says that it is "KING OF KINGS AND LORD OF LORDS" (NIV). "It is finished." Jesus is now King eternal!

2. The thief on the cross was the first to recognize the Christ as king. He addressed Jesus as Lord and entreated him, "Remember me when thou comest into thy kingdom" (Luke 23:42).

B. *The picture is that of a king who has gone forth into battle.* The enemy has been engaged. Victory has been won. Now he returns home and faces

111

his subjects with the news: "It is finished—accomplished." The King of heaven has met the enemy, Satan, in mortal conflict. Evil has done its worst to defeat the Christ, but Christ is victor. Colossians 2:15 says, "And having spoiled principalities and powers, he made a shew of them openly, triumphing over them." This is the King returning in victory, leading "captivity captive" (Eph. 4:8).

This does not mean that Satan no longer resists. It means the battle has been won and the final outcome has been settled. D-day in World War II meant that the enemy had been defeated. The Nazi forces continued to fight, but the final outcome was not in doubt. That had been decided, and it was only a matter of time. So it is with the cross of Christ and the defeat of Satan.

C. *The cross then means that "It is* finished*."* Love has triumphed over sin. Life has triumphed over death. Christ has triumphed over Satan. Today the King of Kings is on the throne of this universe. His hand is on the helm of this world, and he rules in human affairs.

> *I'm a child of the King,*
> *A child of the King!*
> *With Jesus, my Savior,*
> *I'm a child of the King!*

Conclusion

Jesus is our Prophet, our Priest, and our King. Let us recognize him as such and give him the honor and glory due his name. Let us sing with Edward Perronet:

> *All hail the pow'r of Jesus' name!*
> *Let angels prostrate fall;*
> *Bring forth the royal diadem,*
> *And crown Him Lord of all.*
>
> *Ye chosen seed of Israel's race,*
> *Ye ransomed from the fall,*
> *Hail Him who saves you by His grace,*
> *And crown Him Lord of all.*
>
> *Let ev'ry kindred, ev'ry tribe,*
> *On this terrestrial ball,*
> *To Him all majesty ascribe,*
> *And crown Him Lord of all.*
>
> *O that with yonder sacred throng*
> *We at His feet may fall!*
> *We'll join the everlasting song,*
> *And crown Him Lord of all.*

SUNDAY EVENING, APRIL 10

Title: "Not to Destroy But to Fulfill"

Text: "Think not that I am come to destroy the law, or the prophets: I am not come to destroy, but to fulfil. For verily I say unto you, Till heaven and earth pass, one jot or one tittle shall in no wise pass from the law, till all be fulfilled. Whosoever therefore shall break one of these least commandments, and shall teach men so, he shall be called the least in the kingdom of heaven: but whosoever shall do and teach them, the same shall be called great in the kingdom of heaven" **(Matt. 5:17–19).**

Scripture Reading: John 14:15–26

Introduction

The Sermon on the Mount can be divided into three major divisions: the Christian's character (the Beatitudes), the Christian's influence (salt and light), and the Christian's conduct (Matt. 5:17–7:12).

Our text for this message points to the inner motivation for Christian conduct. It illustrates ways in which our Lord "internalizes" the external demands of the scribes and Pharisees.

I. Jesus fills the law full of meaning.

A. *Many have the wrong impression of the relationship of law to grace. Jesus' disciples had lived under the law of Moses and the Prophets.* Both called for obedience to God's commands. What now? Are Christians released from these commands? Jesus emphatically said that he did not come to destroy the Law and the Prophets but to "fulfill" them.

B. *Jesus fills them full of meaning by emphasizing the inner motivation rather than the overt act.* He gives no by to sin because the Christian lives under grace. Like Paul, Jesus asserted the validity of the Old Testament's ethical code (Rom. 6:15).

C. *God makes no fewer demands under grace than he did under law.* The very coming of Christ binds people closer to the law. "One jot or one tittle [one Greek *iota* or one breathing mark] shall in no wise pass from the law, till all be fulfilled."

How long will the law last? "Till heaven and earth pass." Peter speaks of "a new heaven and a new earth, the home of righteousness" (2 Peter 3:13). H. H. Hobbs said of the law's permanency: "The law will then pass into nonexistence as it gives way to its goal, the righteousness of God. Even then the 'law' will not be repealed. It will simply find its full realization as it passes from word to spirit, from demand to acceptance as the full and glorious will of God" (*The Beam*, September 1961, 28).

II. Jesus demands a righteousness of heart.

A. *The new birth is indicated through the remaining verses in Matthew 5.* As Martin Luther said, "Good pious works do not produce good pious men, but good pious men produce good pious works."

B. *Sin is basically a disease of the heart.* All sin begins in the heart and works out into the life. Jesus fills the law with meaning by treating the "germs" that cause sin rather than the symptoms that indicate sin.

   1. Anger leads to murder (5:21–22).
   2. Lust leads to adultery (5:27–28).
   3. Adultery leads to divorce (5:31–32).
   4. The lying heart leads to profane oaths (5:33–37).
   5. Personal regard leads to retaliation (5:38–40).
   6. Self-love leads to hateful actions (5:43–48).

In *The Taste of New Wine,* Keith Miller presents a gripping account of how he struggled to find new life only to realize the new life comes with new birth. After an interesting account of his conversion experience, he says: "But something came into my life that day which has never left.... God, I realized, doesn't want your time. He wants your *will,* and if you give Him your will, He'll begin to show you life as you've never really seen it before" (Keith Miller, *The Taste of New Wine* [Waco, Tex.: Word, 1966], 39).

III. Jesus properly relates character and conduct.

Character is not the result of conduct, but conduct is the result of character. Jesus dealt with the Christian's character in the Beatitudes before he even mentioned the Christian's conduct.

A. *When one controls anger, he will not murder.*

B. *When one controls lust, he will not commit adultery.*

C. *When one keeps the marriage vow, he will not seek a divorce.*

D. *When one controls the desire to lie, he will not use oaths to cover up falsehood.*

E. *When one controls the selfish desire to get what he feels is coming to him, he will not seek revenge.*

F. *When one crucifies self, he can love even his enemies.*

Conclusion

A beautiful tree that had stood for years at the corner of a house suddenly fell across the street. There was no wind that day. The tree had given every indication of life. Its leaves were green, and its limbs were healthy. A city employee was called to the scene to investigate and make arrangements for the tree to be removed from the street. He found that the tree had been sabotaged by parasites that had eaten out its inside and severed its roots. Outwardly, it was beautiful. Within, it was corrupt. When it comes to Christian conduct, Jesus deals first with the inner person.

WEDNESDAY EVENING, APRIL 13

Title: The Command to Stop Fearing the Future

Text: "Let not your heart be troubled: ye believe in God, believe also in me. In my Father's house are many mansions: if it were not so, I would have told you. I go to prepare a place for you. And if I go and prepare a place for you, I will come again, and receive you unto myself; that where I am, there ye may be also" (**John 14:1–3**).

Introduction

People have always stood in fear of the mystery of death. One motive behind our Savior's coming to the world and dying on the cross was that he might deliver us from the fear of death (Heb. 2:14–15).

The apostle Paul implied that man's fear of death is due to his being a sinner (1 Cor. 15:55–56). It may be idle speculation, but we could assume that if physical death had been a part of God's original plan for the human race, people would have approached this experience in the garden of Eden without any fright at all. It is the reality of sin in the life of each of us that causes us to have anxious thoughts concerning our eternal destiny.

Throughout his ministry our Lord said little in a direct manner about heaven. As he approached the end of his ministry, he sought to comfort and challenge his disciples with the assurance of the reality of an eternal home where they would be rewarded according to their works. During this time of the year when the resurrection is prominent in the minds of many, it can be profitable for us to look at some of the things the Bible has to say about heaven. Even a partial understanding of that which our Lord is preparing for those who love him can help us to be obedient to his command not to worry about the future.

I. Heaven is a prepared place for a prepared people (John 14:3).

II. Heaven is a place where God dwells in love with his people (Rev. 21:1–3).

The joys that God intended for humans in the garden of Eden will be realized in the holy city the Lord is preparing for those who love him.

III. Heaven is a place of perfect holiness (Rev. 21:27).

The evil that has caused so much unhappiness and trouble here on earth will be unknown there.

IV. Heaven is a place of exemption from all suffering and pain (Rev. 21:4).

The things that people have known here on earth that cause weeping and suffering and death will be things of the past.

V. Heaven is a place where rewards will be bestowed and enjoyed (Rev. 22:12).

The privilege of entering heaven is the gift of God's grace to those who receive Jesus Christ as Lord and Savior. We do not work for the privilege of going to heaven. The heavenly Father will reward in heaven those who have labored to carry out his purpose on earth. We serve our Lord out of gratitude because we are going to heaven. Instead of worrying about the future, we should rejoice and anticipate that which our Lord has in store for us beyond this life. Heaven is described as a tabernacle where God dwells with his children (Rev. 21:1–8), as a city (vv. 9–27), and as a garden (22:1–5).

Conclusion

By virtue of our Lord's resurrection from the dead, we can be assured of the certainty of an eternal home where sickness and sorrow, suffering and death will be strangers. Let us trust him. Let us obey him. Let us love him. Let us serve him. By all means, let us urge others to get ready for heaven.

SUNDAY MORNING, APRIL 17

Title: The Word of Committal

Text: "And when Jesus had cried with a loud voice, he said, Father, into thy hands I commend my spirit: and having said thus, he gave up the ghost" **(Luke 23:46)**.

Scripture Reading: Luke 23:46–49

Hymns: "At Calvary," Newell

        "The Way of the Cross Leads Home," Pounds

        "Beneath the Cross of Jesus," Clephane

Offertory Prayer: Holy and loving Father, you have given us the rich treasures of your grace. We thank you for every blessing that has come to us in the past. We praise you for your blessings on us in the present. Today we recognize and express our gratitude for the blessings you have in store for us in the future. In our tithes and offerings we bring the fruit of our labors as proof of our gratitude and love. Accept these tithes and offerings as symbols of our desire to give ourselves completely to you. In Jesus' name. Amen.

Introduction

"Hosanna! Blessed is he who comes in the name of the Lord!" (Mark 11:9 NIV). This was the shout of the crowd on Palm Sunday as Jesus entered Jerusalem. They threw palm branches before him and acclaimed him King. The problem, however, was that they were not receiving Christ as their eternal King but rather as a "king for a day." Only five days later some of these same people were shouting, "Crucify him! Crucify him!"

Now their evil desires had been granted, and Christ was on the cross. For six hours he had hung there, suspended between heaven and hell. He had completed the work the Father sent him to do. Atonement had been made for sin. Humankind and God were now reconciled. Jesus had said in the upper room, "I have glorified thee on the earth: I have finished the work which thou gavest me to do.... I have manifested thy name unto the men which thou gavest me out of the world.... I have given unto them the words which thou gavest me.... And now come I to thee" (John 17:4, 6, 8, 13). Now that "it was finished" he was ready to return to the Father. And so he said, "Father, into thy hands I commend my spirit."

These last words of Christ are filled with significance. Let us look at them carefully and allow them to speak to our hearts.

I. The prayer Jesus offered.

A. *These are the words of prayer.* Praying at all times was characteristic of our Savior. He had begun his ministry in prayer, continued it in prayer, and now finished it in prayer. In every crisis of his life, he turned to prayer for his strength and support.

Jesus had exhorted his disciples to pray. He had taught them that prayer was the antidote to temptation (Mark 14:38), the means of overcoming discouragement (Luke 18:1), the way to receive God's abundance (Mark 11:24), the method of overcoming hate (Matt. 5:44). Now, in the hour of suffering and separation, he was simply practicing what he had taught his disciples to do. He was praying!

B. *These words are a quotation from Scripture.* Jesus turned in his mind to Psalm 31 and drew forth the passage that was then being fulfilled. Again this was like the Christ. When he was in the wilderness being tempted of Satan, he combated each temptation by quoting Scripture, saying, "It is written." When he inaugurated his public ministry in Nazareth, it was by quoting the Scriptures. When his enemies sought to ensnare him, his answer again and again was: "Have you not read?" referring to the Scripture. We would do well to follow his example by becoming so saturated in a knowledge of God's Word that when the exigencies of life come, we are steeled against the assaults of Satan by the power of the Word. "Thy word have I hid in my heart."

C. *These words are a contrast with Jesus' life.* During all of his ministry, Christ had been in the hands of men. He came to his own, and his own did not receive him. In the garden of Gethsemane, as the disciples lay sleeping, Jesus said, "The Son of man is betrayed into the hands of sinners" (Matt. 26:45). Now for the past twelve hours he had been in the hands of men. They had scourged him, slapped him, beaten him, and plucked his beard. They had spat upon him and reviled him. Three hours on the cross he suffered separation from God. Now it was over. "Into *thy hands* I commend my spirit," he said to his Father. What a contrast—from the hands of men to the hands of God, from the hands of Satan to the hands of the Father. Never again would they mock and abuse him, for now he was in the hands of God.

Now Jesus is at the right hand of the Father awaiting the time when he will come again and all the world will be in *his* hands. Men had dared to judge the Christ, but when he comes, he will judge them. Once they cried, "Away with him"; then he will say, "Depart from me." Once he was in their hands; then they will be in his.

D. *These are words of faith and trust.* Every Jewish mother instructed her child to say this nightly prayer: "Into Thy hands I commend my spirit, for Thou hast redeemed me, O Lord, Thou God of truth." How many times Mary, Jesus' mother, must have put his little hands together and taught Jesus to say these words. Now with his hands held wide apart to the world, he prayed, "Into thy hands I commend my spirit."

"Into thy hands I commend my spirit." The word "commend" literally means "to deposit," "to entrust to the care of." Here the Son is entrusting his spirit into the hands of the Father for safekeeping. Paul expressed the idea: "I know whom I have believed, and am persuaded that he is able to keep that which I have committed unto him" (2 Tim. 1:12).

Now Jesus is in the hands of the Father, exactly where Jesus told all believers they were. "And I give unto them eternal life; and they shall never perish, neither shall any man pluck them out of my hand. My Father, which gave them me, is greater than all; and no man is able to pluck them out of my Father's hand" (John 10:28–29).

II. The peace Jesus experienced.

When he had prayed, Jesus bowed his head and serenely "yielded up his spirit." What a picture of peace and tranquility for a dying man! It was a peace based on:

A. *Communion with the Father.* Only a short time before, Jesus had cried out of the darkness, "My God, My God, why hast thou forsaken me?" The Father had turned his back on the Son as he became a sin offering for the world. Now the Son looked into the face of the Father and said, "I'm coming home. The work is finished." Jesus no longer said, "My God"; he said, "Father." He is back in fellowship with his Father.

B. *Certainty of the Father.*

1. "Into thy hands," says Jesus. There is no doubt of the Father's loving care and concern. There is no question of the Father's ability to receive and keep his spirit.

   In the hands of God! In the hands of a loving Father! This means not only security but also providential care. Whatever the experiences of life, God is watching over his own and is active in the affairs of their lives. Paul explains it in Romans 8:28, "We know that all things work together for good [God is at work in all things for good] to them that love God, to them who are the called according to his purpose."

   Can one call this cross "good"? No, not in itself, but God is at work in it and transforms it from the ugly instrument of execution into a glorious instrument of redemption. He can transform our worst into his glorious best.

2. In this cry of certainty we come to understand Christ's attitude toward death. To our Christ the cross was a crisis but not a catastrophe. It was not a horrible ending; it was a glorious beginning. It was not an ignominious defeat; it was a marvelous victory.

Jesus was here experiencing what every one of us must experience. Hebrews 9:27 says, "It is appointed unto men once to die." We have an appointment with death. There is a legend that Philip of Macedon kept a particular slave whose sole duty it was to awaken his master each morning with the solemn warning, "Remember Philip, that thou must die!" This slave is every man's companion.

How then shall we face this hour? How shall we view it? Walter Savage Landor wrote concerning death:

> *I strove with none, for none was worth my strife.*
> *Nature I love, and after nature, art;*
> *I warmed both hands before the fire of life;*
> *It sinks, and I am ready to depart.*

To Landor death was the dying of the fire and the exit into the cold. Contrast this with words of Dwight L. Moody toward the end of his life. "One day you shall read in the newspaper that Dwight L. Moody is dead. Don't you believe it! I shall be more alive than I have ever been."

This was Christ's view of death. He had told his disciples, "In my Father's house are many mansions: If it were not so, I would have told you. I go to prepare a place for you. And if I go and prepare a place for you, I will come again, and receive you unto myself; that where I am, there ye may be also" (John 14:2–3). Jesus was saying that death is simply going into another room of the Father's house, going into the Father's presence alive and complete. He spoke of God as "the God of the living." Abraham, Isaac, and Jacob were not mere handfuls of dust. They were living personages in the hands of the Father.

C. *Completeness for the Father.*

1. Jesus had completed the Father's will for him. It was only after he could cry, "It is finished," that he was ready to go to the Father. His life was not one of tragic incompleteness. He was not struck down by evil men in the prime of life. He deliberately surrendered his life. There was no compulsion but that of love. He said, "No man taketh [my life] from me, but I lay it down of myself. I have power to lay it down" (John 10:18). Augustine said, "[Jesus] died *because* he willed it, *when* he willed it, and *as* he willed it." He had completed the Father's purpose, so now he could "yield his spirit" into his hands.

2. What a peace this indicates! What a contrast with us! So much of our life is characterized by incompleteness. We think of Schubert's

Unfinished Symphony, of Leonardo da Vinci's *Mona Lisa,* of Coleridge's *Kubla Khan,* of Raphael's *Transfiguration.* We hear Joshua saying at his death, "There remaineth yet much land to be possessed." But not our Christ—his work was completed. Oh, to be able to say with Paul, "I am now ready to be offered, and the time of my departure is at hand. I have fought a good fight, I have finished my course, I have kept the faith" (2 Tim. 4:6–7).

III. The pattern he set.

Peter said that Christ was "leaving us an example, that ye should follow his steps" (1 Peter 2:21). All of his life Jesus had been an example for us as Christians. Now in his hour of death he was also an example. He set a pattern for us in his words, "Father, into thy hands I commend my spirit."

A. *It was a pattern for death.* These words are a challenge for us to come to the conclusion of our lives saying, "Into thy hands." Others have! Augustine did! Polycarp did! Jerome did! Luther did! So did John Huss! The priests jeered as Huss was led away to be executed for heresy. They had placed a dunce cap on his head with figures of the Devil on it, and in their hearts they were consigning his soul to Satan. But Huss knew differently and kept repeating, "Father, into Thy hands I commend my spirit."

James Stewart tells of a little girl who looked into the face of her widowed father every night and said, "Good night, Father. I'll see you in the morning." She became ill and gradually grew weaker, to the point of death. Just before her death, she whispered, "Good night, Father. I'll see you in the morning."

When we can say this, there is nothing to fear in death. We can say with David, "Yea, though I walk through the valley of the shadow of death, I will fear no evil: for thou art with me" (Ps. 23:4). As Clement of Alexandria has said, "Christ turns all our sunsets into dawns."

B. *It was a pattern for life.* If Jesus had not lived each moment of his life to do his Father's will, if each day he had not been conscious of being in the Father's hands, he could (or would) not have committed himself into the Father's hands at death. So with us. Our death shall be like our life. If we have rebelled in life, we will rebel in death. If we have denied in life, we will deny in death. If we have submitted in life, we will submit in death. If we have walked with God in life, we will walk with him in death.

There is a word of warning here to the unsaved. The unbeliever who cannot say, "Into thy hands I commend my spirit," will realize that "it is a fearful thing to fall into the hands of the living God" (Heb. 10:31).

C. *There is a pattern of service.* As Christ committed his spirit to God, he was also committing his work to us. He gave his spirit to the Father, but he gave his gospel to us (1 Cor. 9:17). He goes to the Father, but we must go to the world (2 Cor. 5:19).

120

Conclusion

This is the end of the greatest life ever lived here on earth. The crucifixion is drawing to a finish. What was the effect on those who stood by? The answer is seen in verses 47–49.

1. The centurion witnessed Jesus' crucifixion and was deeply moved. He confessed the Christ as the Son of God and as his Savior (v. 47). This is what all people ought to do.
2. The crowd "came together to that sight, beholding the things which were done, smote their breasts, and returned" (v. 48). They were unmoved and unchanged by it all. They continued to see but also continued to sin. They looked but were lost. They returned to their old way of life. This is what all too many do.
3. The disciples had been standing afar off, but now they stood beholding (v. 49). They later understood the meaning and significance of Jesus' crucifixion. Then they went throughout all the world telling the Good News. This is what we must do.

SUNDAY EVENING, APRIL 17

Title: Righteousness That Exceeds

Text: "For I say unto you, That except your righteousness shall exceed the righteousness of the scribes and Pharisees, ye shall in no case enter into the kingdom of heaven" (**Matt. 5:20**).

Scripture Reading: Ephesians 2

Introduction

Have you ever had a dream in which you found yourself placed in an impossible situation? Take this one, for instance: You are attending a track meet. The announcer informs all present that the fastest man in the world is to run in the next race. You listen to the names of the other participants. Then *your* name is called! You are told that you must run in the same race with the champion. Reluctantly, you take your place. But there is more. You must not only keep up with the champion, you must overtake him and win the race. What a dream!

Those who heard the Sermon on the Mount must have felt that way when they heard Jesus say, "Except your righteousness shall exceed the righteousness of the scribes and Pharisees...." The scribes and Pharisees were the religious champions of that day. Herein we have a contrast between pseudo and genuine righteousness.

I. Pseudo righteousness is entirely external.

A. *The scribes had expanded the Old Testament law to hundreds of little rules and regulations.* For instance, they had formulated over twelve hundred rules from one command, "Remember the Sabbath day to keep it holy."

1. They defined work as the carrying of a burden. "But what is a burden?" someone would ask. The scribes decided that a burden was enough food equal to the weight of a dried fig, enough wine for mixing in a goblet, enough milk for one swallow, enough honey to put on a wound, enough water to moisten an eye salve, enough ink to write two letters of the alphabet, and on and on!

2. They argued over whether one could wear his false teeth on the Sabbath, carry a cane, move a lamp, or travel over a "Sabbath day's journey." Someone has aptly said, "They could split a hair in twelve ways and have plenty of hair left."

3. Did the tailor who accidentally left his shop the day before the Sabbath with a needle in his robe and wore the robe to temple services break the Sabbath? Yes, said the scribe.

4. Should one eat eggs laid on the Sabbath? No. Some even taught that a woman should not look at herself in a mirror on the Sabbath for fear that she might see a gray hair and pluck it out.

B. *The Pharisees were dedicated to the task of living by these rules and regulations with no emphasis whatsoever on inner motivation.*

1. Visibly, the Pharisees were righteous people. The well-dressed Pharisee wore many different garments of all colors, which were held to his body by an embroidered belt inlaid with precious stones. The inner garment went to the heels, and a blouse or shirt hung over the belt. The more ruffles there were on the blouse, the more righteous the Pharisee.

2. Our Lord spoke of their practice of enlarging "the borders of their garments" (Matt. 23:5). They wore phylacteries, little boxes of Old Testament Scripture, on the forehead (so that the Word of God would be near the head) and on the left arm (so that the Word of God would be near the heart when the arm was bent). These little boxes gave our Lord the occasion to say, "But all their works they do to be seen of men" (v. 5).

3. They used the Scripture as a teaching aid but not as a guide for their lives (vv. 1–4).

4. They did their good works to be seen and praised by others (v. 5).

5. They went to church to parade their piousness (v. 6).

6. They tried to usurp the place of Christ in their teaching (vv. 7–12).

7. They used public prayer to cover up private sins (v. 14).

8. They made promises without any intention of keeping them (vv. 16–22).

II. Genuine righteousness begins in the heart.

A. *It is possible to perform religious acts without one's heart being right with God (Matt. 15:3).*

B. *It is possible to serve God with the lips but deny him with the heart (Matt. 15:8).*

C. *The heart is the seedbed of sin (Matt. 15:11, 19–20).* No sin ever came into a person's life that was not first manufactured in his or her heart.

It is possible to act righteous without being righteous. A young preacher pulled off his new overcoat (the first he had ever owned) and hung it at the back of the rescue mission in Fort Worth, Texas, where he was leading a service one evening. During the invitation at the close of the sermon, a man staggered to the altar, where he went through all of the "proper motions." He seemed repentant and said the right things, but he was just sizing up the place so that, when the right time occurred, he could make his way to the coat rack at the back, steal the young preacher's overcoat, and get lost on the crowded street outside.

III. Genuine righteousness is attained through the new birth.

A. *Paul taught that "Christ is the end of the law of righteousness to every one that believeth" (Rom. 10:4).* God bestows genuine righteousness upon one through Christ.

B. *When one believes or commits his life to Christ in the new birth experience, he experiences true righteousness.*

C. *Righteousness is external (light of the world and salt of the earth), but it begins as an internal experience of God's grace (Eph. 2:8–9).*

Conclusion

"Except" is the key word in the text for this message. Three other verses in the New Testament are noteworthy at this point:

1. "Except ye repent, ye shall all likewise perish" (Luke 13:3).
2. "Except ye be converted, and become as little children, ye shall not enter into the kingdom of heaven" (Matt. 18:3).
3. "Except a man be born again, he cannot see the kingdom of God" (John 3:3).

WEDNESDAY EVENING, APRIL 20

Title: The Command to Forgive

Text: "Jesus answered, 'I tell you, not seven times, but seventy-seven times' " **(Matt. 18:22 NIV).**

Scripture Reading: Matthew 18:21–35

Introduction

Peter's question about forgiveness probably arose because of ill-treatment by others either toward himself or toward the Lord. His was a logical and responsible question in view of the fact that the pagan world had no place for the word *forgiveness* in its vocabulary. His suggestion that a person might forgive a repeated offender as many as seven times was actually an indication of a rather generous spirit on his part. There was a custom that one should be forgiven as many as three times. To forgive an offender seven times was far above the average.

The disciples were probably as shocked as some modern-day readers are when they heard Christ say that they should forgive "seventy-seven times." Actually Jesus was saying, "You must not place any limitations on the range of your forgiveness."

As surprising as it may seem, these guidelines for forgiveness were given by our Lord for the benefit of the offended. When we fully recognize this, we will see the logic behind his commandment that his disciples maintain a disposition to forgive.

I. The problem of ill-treatment by others.

Many of us live between two expectations as far as others are concerned. Some of us are unrealistic in that we expect perfect treatment from others. Some of us are overly pessimistic because we expect others to act like scoundrels.

A. *People are mistake makers.* Because we make mistakes, ill-treatment of self and others is simply one of the facts of life with which all of us must deal.

B. *Some injury is inevitable.* Some people inflict injury deliberately. Others inflict injury unconsciously. Still others inflict injury indirectly.

C. *Some, with selfish, malicious intent, inflict injury upon others.* The question of how to deal with injury at the hands of others has been a pressing problem through the ages. Our natural impulse is to retaliate in kind and to inflict injury upon those who have injured us. To do so is to break a number of our Lord's commandments. To retaliate with injury for injury contradicts the very nature of our faith.

II. The high cost of placing limits on forgiveness.

It is always difficult to forgive someone who has injured us. It never has been easy for the follower of Christ to forgive those who were guilty of inflicting injury either upon themselves or upon their loved ones. There are at least three reasons why we must determine to forgive others.

A. *To limit or to refuse forgiveness prevents a person from living by the principle of love.* He who carries a grudge lives for the day when he can retaliate. Unconsciously he begins to plan for his revenge, and hate begins to fill his heart and mind. Hate is a powerful force that can have explosive consequences if it is permitted to express itself.

B. *Limiting forgiveness causes a person to be preoccupied with the faults and mistakes of others to the extent that he becomes blind to his own shortcomings.* To major upon the splinter in the eye of a brother is to discover eventually that one has a plank in his own eye (Matt. 7:3–5).

C. *Limiting forgiveness places the present and the future under the tyranny of the past.* To refuse to forgive enables the past, with its errors and mistakes, to sit in on the present as a constant troublemaker. We would be wise if we would take all of the old mistakes of others and place them out of circulation. We need to destroy all of our lists of complaints against others.

III. What is forgiveness?

God wants to deal with each of us on the basis of his forgiveness of all of our sins. God wants each of us to relate to each other in terms of forgiveness.

Forgiveness is something infinitely more than ignoring the offenses and errors of others. Forgiveness is more than simply forgetting a debt or obligation owed us by another.

Forgiveness has been defined as involving at least three responses.

A. *To forgive means to "Hold it against him no longer."* This involves remitting or renouncing the right to retaliate. By the decision of the mind and heart the offended decides that he will refuse to inflict injury upon the offender.

B. *To forgive is to determine to remove resentful feelings.* To do this is often exceedingly difficult. At this point one must depend on the grace of God and decide to follow the example of our Lord. We must also recognize that if we do not purge out of our hearts all malice and hatred, the source of our joy will be poisoned. We must recognize that the only way by which we can be assured of the forgiveness and grace of God is on the condition that we forgive those who have sinned against us (Matt. 6:14–15; Col. 3:13).

C. *To forgive is to put forth an effort to revive friendly relationships.* Forgiving is remembering and yet loving, accepting, and restoring broken relationships. Such is necessary in all areas of life if we want to live a life of joy and victory.

Conclusion

A number of things can help us be more forgiving toward others. We need to remember that God has forgiven us (Eph. 4:31–32).

It might be helpful for us to recognize that many of our injuries are just supposed and imaginary. We must guard against letting our pride and sense of self-importance cause us to magnify small things out of proportion. It will also be helpful if we will distinguish between malicious intent and errors or misjudgments on the part of others.

If we will seek all of the light or information that we can concerning the situation or the person involved, it will help us to be more understanding and tolerant toward those who have injured us. It will be impossible for us to forgive those who mistreat us unless we let the light of the love of God fall on the offender.

While it may be costly to forgive those who have offended us, the cost of not forgiving is much greater.

SUNDAY MORNING, APRIL 24

Title: Appearance by the Sea

Text: "Jesus showed himself again to the disciples at the sea of Tiberias" (**John 21:1**).

Scripture Reading: John 21:1–19

Hymns: "Praise to God, Immortal Praise," Barbauld

"Rejoice, the Lord Is King," Wesley

"Is Your All on the Altar?" Hoffman

Offertory Prayer: By your providence, O Lord, we are placed on a kindly earth. We confess that our actions sometimes spoil the heritage you have given us. Make our hearts tender to care for the needy, and make our minds strong to solve the problems that frustrate us. Consecrate these offerings that your name and way may be known and loved, through Jesus Christ our Lord. Amen.

Introduction

It is difficult for us to feel what Jesus' disciples felt in their sense of utter defeat at Calvary and the joy of triumph in his resurrection appearances. We know the end of the story by the time we know the beginning. But for those who experienced it initially, it was a time of great suspense and surprise, sorrow and joy. Never have human beings felt such a wide range of emotions in so short a space of time as they passed from the depth of despair to a victory that defied comprehension.

Jesus had risen from the dead. The disciples had seen him and heard him speak. Yet as the postresurrection days stacked themselves upon each other, they seemed to have found themselves with time on their hands. Peter made the simple announcement, "I'm going fishing," and six other disciples said in essence, "Me too."

The disciples' night of hard work on the open Sea of Galilee was fruitless. In the early dawn they saw someone standing on the shore whom they took to be a stranger. He called out a greeting and, either from his vantage point or from supernatural knowledge, he gave instructions for the next net casting. Following his advice, they made a great catch of fish. Bringing their catch to the shore, they recognized the risen Christ.

Jesus' postresurrection appearance by the sea and the circumstances of the disciples' great catch are beautiful suggestions that life is not all tragedy, that there is purposeful activity that makes sense. But there is more than symbolism and analogy here. Three accomplishments may have been intended through this appearance by the sea.

I. Reality of the Resurrection.

Many people said that the appearances of the risen Christ were nothing more than visions the disciples had. Jesus' sudden appearance behind locked doors and his disappearance in the same manner added to the mystery. The Gospels go far out of their way to establish the fact of an empty tomb and a risen Christ who had a body that still bore the marks of the nails and the sword thrust in his side.

The appearance by the sea adds to the firmness of the resurrection foundation. Jesus pointed out a place to cast their net. He had kindled a charcoal fire and already had begun to cook fish before the disciples reached shore. Such things as these certainly could not have been the figment of someone's imagination; it was not the appearance of a spirit or ghost.

II. Reminder of the disciples' calling.

The appearance by the sea may well have been a reminder of their calling.

These seven disciples needed to be reminded of the work to which they had been called. We can imagine the ridicule they faced on the village streets and the puzzlement they had within their own minds. They had seen the risen Lord, he had made them promises and had called them to high service for him and the world. Yet nothing happened that could give them a "handle to latch onto." Still they waited, and there were more days when they did not see him than days when he appeared. These delays put strain on tired minds.

Quite suddenly, we may guess, Peter announced, "I'm going fishing," and as the others joined him, they got that accustomed feel of something to do. What were they thinking as they moved away from the shore? Were they getting a feel for the fisherman's life again? Were they going to turn their backs on the great adventure, to settle down, disillusioned if not outright cynical, contemptuous of all idealism? Was Christ's call to them fading out? Notice what the Scripture has to say.

A. *"That night they caught nothing" (v. 3).* This is more than a note of mere human failure. The Bible makes a good case for the sanctity and dignity of common work, but that is not the point here. For people who are called to serve God vocationally, an occupation of their own choosing different from God's call, however useful in human estimation, is destined for disappointment.

B. The Scripture goes on to say, *"Just as day was breaking, Jesus stood on the beach; yet the disciples did not know that it was Jesus" (v. 4 RSV).* Note the contrast between night and day. They went their own way during the night, and their efforts were fruitless. Daylight brought revelation and identity. Note also the contrast between the lake and the shore. On the lake they toiled without success. On the solid ground of the shore, Jesus gave rewarding directions and prepared breakfast. Could their failure to recognize Jesus be traced to their failure to follow him?

C. *Jesus asked them while they were out on the lake, "Children, have you any fish?"* They answered him, "No" (v. 5 RSV). The affectionate form of address used here by Jesus suggests his special sympathy for them, his tender, almost fatherly, care for men who had so quickly forgotten their true calling and had come up against the brick wall of failure.

D. *Jesus was preparing breakfast and soon invited them to gather around and eat.* After breakfast Jesus asked Peter three times, "Do you love me?" After the apostle's affirmative reply each time, Jesus said successively, "Tend my lambs," "Shepherd my sheep," and "Tend [or feed] my sheep" (vv. 15–17). The lesson Jesus was teaching them seems to be this: The ministry to which they were called, the apostolic life, required that they learn to trust him to provide for their daily bread.

The renewal and deepening of their call dates from this appearance by the sea. With this experience to look back upon, there would be no more turning aside from the duties of apostleship. Christ's commands here are set in the complex context of fishing and a meal: fishing because the apostles must draw people to Christ; a meal because they must provide for the new converts as he has provided for them.

George MacDonald has described these experiences of Peter and the disciples in a way that appeals to many of us.

The Boat

I owned a little boat a while ago,
And sailed the morning sea without a fear,
And whither any breeze might fairly blow
I steered my little craft afar or near.

Mine was the boat,
And mine the air,
And mine the sea,
Nor mine a care.

My boat became my place of mighty toil,
I sailed at evening to the fishing ground,
At morn my boat was freighted with the spoil
Which my all-conquering work had found.

Mine was the boat,
And mine the net,
And mine the skill
And power to get.

One day there came along that silent shore,
While I my net was casting in the sea,
A Man who spoke as never man before.
I followed Him; new life began in me,

Mine was the boat,
But His the voice,

And His the call
Yet mine the choice.

Ah! 'twas a fearful night out on the lake,
And all my skill availed not, at the helm,
Till Him asleep I waked, crying,
"Take Thou the helm—lest water overwhelm!"

And His the boat,
And His the sea,
And His the peace
O'er all and me.

Once from the boat He taught the curious throng
Then bade me cast my net into the sea;
I murmured but obeyed, nor was it long
Before the catch amazed and humbled me.

His was the boat,
And His the skill,
And His the catch,
And His my will.

The appearance by the sea aided in the establishment of the reality of the resurrection, and it was for the disciples a reminder of their calling. There was a third accomplishment in this appearance: the restatement of the church's function.

III. Restatement of the church's function.

Jesus' threefold question to Peter about love cannot be confined to the individual disciple. From it, all of us must learn that the essence of discipleship is love and that the response of that love is service. Love does not ask permission to do good things; it has done them already. The church, to the extent that it is truly Christ's people, loses its life in a ministry to the world. The church should have no time to fuss about itself, its image or prestige. The church denies its Lord when it becomes self-centered and pampered, fondling its own achievements, admiring its own righteousness or orthodoxy, caressing its own virtues. The church's function in the world is to be light and salt.

Conclusion

The church is not a reservoir where the Water of Life is stored; it is the spring where the Water of Life arises in the lives of Christ-centered Christians and flows out to others. If you love Christ, you will serve him through a love that reaches out to gather in the sheep and tend the flock of God.

SUNDAY EVENING, APRIL 24

Title: "Thou Shalt Not Kill"

Text: "Thou shalt not kill" (**Ex. 20:13**).

Scripture Reading: Matthew 5:21–26

Introduction

Is there a murderer in the house?

Certainly any congregation would feel uneasy if a known murderer who had never been prosecuted for his crime were sitting in church this Sunday. How would you feel sitting next to a killer who might strike again at any minute?

If the truth were known, perhaps many murderers worship in our churches every Sunday.

I. Jesus prohibits the inward steps that lead to the outward act of murder (vv. 21–22).

The gradual movement from anger to contempt to personal insult is noted by our Lord. Gradual punishment from the judgment (local court) to the council (the Sanhedrin) to hell is also indicated.

A. *Continuous anger is prohibited. Thumos* is the Greek word for anger that blazes up quickly and soon dies out. But *orge* is the word in our text. It speaks of anger that will not forget, wrath kept warm, feelings that refuse to be pacified, and revenge. This kind of anger "worketh not the righteousness of God" (James 1:20). It refuses to forgive. It says, "I just can't stand that person!" It asserts, "Well, I'll forgive but I sure won't forget!"

It is sinful to murder. But what of the one who harbors hate in his heart? "Whosoever hateth his brother is a murderer" (1 John 3:15). This is the inward step that leads to the outward act!

B. *Contempt or scorn is prohibited.* If a person does not control his anger, it will finally control his tongue. The one he hates will become a topic of conversation. When a person refuses to talk to God about someone who "bugs" him, he usually talks to others about him!

Finally, one develops an overestimation of himself. The pride of birth, possessions, position, or knowledge finally causes the angered one to cry out at the one who causes him to be angry, "You empty head [*Raca*]!"

C. *Personal insult and character assassination are prohibited.* At last the angry heart cries out, "Thou fool!" This word is from the root word for immorality. It is used when one wants to murder the character of another with his tongue.

James said that the undisciplined tongue is "set on fire of hell" (James 3:6). The only instance in the New Testament in which the feminine ending is given to the word translated "slanderer" is 1 Timothy 3:11. The Greek word for slanderer is also translated "devil." Paul is teaching that a woman who slanders the character of another is a "she-devil." It follows, therefore, that a male slanderer is a "he-devil."

These are drastic words! But what do they mean? Paul, James, and Jesus are telling us that the people who seem to glory in character assassination are not the kind of people that will be found in heaven. Their future dwelling place is hell!

Gossip, slander, and backbiting are among the most devilish traits possessed by human beings. The writer of Proverbs said, "He that hideth hatred with lying lips, and he that uttereth a slander, is a fool" (Prov. 10:18). One of Shakespeare's characters said, "I will speak daggers to her, but use none" and "Words are razors to my wounded heart."

II. Anger, contempt, and slander hinder the Christian (vv. 23–26).

A. *Worship is hindered (vv. 23–24).*

1. The Christian should take the initiative in reconciliation. If he has wronged another or if another person feels that he has been wronged, the Christian's only alternative is to be reconciled!

2. Revival would sweep many churches if Christians would not say things behind one another's backs that they have not said to their faces.

   A pastor called his church to prayer for revival. "I have done everything I know to do," he told the congregation.

   "There will never be revival in this church until Brother Brown and I speak to each other," cried one of the church's deacons. The deacon made his way to a man to whom he had not spoken for ten years. Then both men asked the church to forgive them for their failure.

   "Pastor, I have been unfair," said another member. "I have said things about you that were not true, and I want you to forgive me." For several minutes men and women stood to apologize to each other and to the church. The pastor reported that the church soon experienced the greatest revival in its history!

B. *Influence is hindered (vv. 25–26).* Our Lord admonishes us to agree with our adversaries "while thou art in the way" between your house and the courthouse. The Christian who will not be reconciled runs the risk of hurting the influence of the whole church by taking his case to court (1 Cor. 6:1).

Conclusion

But what must the Christian do? The psalmist gives us good advice: "Let the words of my mouth, and the meditation of my heart, be acceptable in thy sight, O Lord, my strength, and my redeemer" (Ps. 19:14).

Here are some practical suggestions:

1. Watch your thoughts.
2. Refuse to harbor anger.
3. Catch yourself before you speak angrily.

4. Look at others through the eyes of Jesus.
5. Seek the forgiveness of those you have wronged.
6. Commit your heart and tongue to Christ.

No man can tame the tongue (James 3:8). But God can!

WEDNESDAY EVENING, APRIL 27

Title: The Command to Pray

Text: "And he spake a parable unto them to this end, that men ought always to pray, and not to faint" **(Luke 18:1)**.

Scripture Reading: Luke 18:1–14

Introduction

By means of a parable our Lord lovingly commanded his disciples to pray.

In the Sermon on the Mount we find our Lord assuming that his disciples would pray (Matt. 6:5–7). In these verses there is no specific command that people give themselves to prayer. Our Lord says, "But thou, when thou prayest." It is only normal that a loving parent would assume that a devoted child would hunger for fellowship and communication. People should not need a command to encourage them to give themselves to prayer.

Perhaps our Lord gave this command in the form of a parable because he knew that people would become too busy to pray or because they would sometimes feel unworthy to pray. Or perhaps he gave this parable that teaches persistence in prayer to encourage the faith of those who prayed without receiving a specific answer to prayers offered in the past.

We need to recognize the benevolent motive of our Lord in giving this parable that can be interpreted as a command to pray. Our Lord knew that the lives of his disciples would be greatly enriched if they would develop the habit of prayer and then not break it. He knew that their lives would be greatly impoverished and hindered if they did not give themselves to prayer.

I. Prayer is the divinely appointed channel by which the children of God are to receive the things that they need from God (Luke 11:9–13).

II. Through prayer we draw close to God and permit him to draw close to us in our times of danger from evil (James 4:7–8).

III. Through the prayer of confession and faith we receive the assurance that our sins have been forgiven (1 John 1:9).

IV. Through the prayer of faith and thanksgiving we obtain the peace of God that surpasses all understanding (Phil. 4:6–7).

Conclusion

Many have thought of prayer as being a monologue in which the child of God brings his needs to God's throne of grace. Prayer in its highest form is a dialogue between God and his children. When we listen to what God has to say, we receive assurance of sonship, of forgiveness, of his abiding presence, and of the peace that surpasses all understanding even in the midst of storm.

If we want to prove our love for our Lord, we should do so by being obedient to his command to enter again and again into the presence of the heavenly Father in prayer. To be disobedient at this point is to deprive ourselves of the joy of fellowship with God and to rob our God of the services that we could render if we would but let him communicate with us.

MAY

■ **Sunday Mornings**

Follow up Easter with a post-Easter sermon on the first Sunday of the month. Then on the second Sunday focus on Mother's Day. In the Sundays that follow, use the theme "Living in the Power of the Spirit."

■ **Sunday Evenings**

Continue the series on the Sermon on the Mount. This month's messages deal primarily with moral purity, absolute honesty, and the need for kindness in all human relationships.

■ **Wednesday Evenings**

Conclude the series "The Commands of Jesus Christ."

SUNDAY MORNING, MAY 1

Title: The Disciples' Refresher Course

Text: "These men who have turned the world upside down have come here also" (**Acts 17:6 RSV**).

Scripture Reading: Romans 8:14–16, 26–27; Galatians 5:22–25

Hymns: "All Hail the Power of Jesus' Name," Perronet

"Dear Lord and Father of Mankind," Whittier

"Speak to My Heart," McKinney

Offertory Prayer: O Lord God, who has given us an example of the shared life, send your Spirit on us. May we give out of the money we have so that those who have not may receive what they need. Through Jesus Christ, our Lord. Amen.

Introduction

Many things in the church year point toward Easter. It is the big day, the big occasion, but what do you do after it is all over? What happens as a result of the Easter event is the real question. What keeps happening day after day and year after year in the light of Christ's resurrection?

Now that we have celebrated Christ's resurrection, we must settle down to a more costly task of living it. Because of the resurrection, we live rather than die, we hope rather than despair. That the good outweighs the bad is not always immediately discernible, because physical death, pain, separation, worry, and

134

fear still exist. But the ultimate victory has been won on the cross and in the tomb for the believer.

During the forty days between Jesus' resurrection and ascension, the disciples had a refresher course. And that is what we need. There is a striking contrast between the world in which the disciples lived and the world in which we live. They had no church buildings or hospitals or Christian schools. They had no organizations or written creeds. They did not have the New Testament. They had no semblance of Christian government or nation. They did have a unique Person in the world. His uniqueness was evident in his life, character, crucifixion, and resurrection from the dead. These eleven followers of that unique Person were sometimes fearful and despairing, sometimes mistaken, but they were there. They had a fellowship, a place to meet (the upper room), a memorial feast to keep, and good news to share. After their refresher course, they went into the world and turned communities upside down. "These who have turned the world upside down have come here also," said some people in Thessalonica (Acts 17:6).

I. Back to Galilee.

The refresher course was offered in Galilee. Jesus met the women who were returning from his empty tomb to tell the disciples. After greeting them and receiving their offering of worship, Jesus said to them, "Go and tell my brothers to go to Galilee; there they will see me" (Matt. 28:10 NIV). Why go back to Galilee? Possibly to get away from troubled Jerusalem, but there were probably other reasons too. Their hearts would be more at ease back home in Galilee where they had lived and met the Master.

It can be a notable event in one's pilgrimage when he or she goes back to familiar surroundings and focuses on the essential rather than the accidental. "There they will see me," Jesus promised. We need to seek out the powerful, glorified Christ and become saturated with his personality. In our lesson today, let the power of association help you recall his teaching and see it from the perspective of postresurrection meaning.

II. Intimate contact with Jesus.

The curriculum of the disciples' refresher course was weighted with intimate contacts with Jesus. They had been close to him before, but now, through enlightenment of who he was, a new intimacy developed. Their deepest natures felt a new warmth and friendship. By this intimacy, Jesus quickened the memories of the disciples. For example, he gave special attention to Thomas and Peter, who had doubted and denied him.

By this intimacy Jesus taught his disciples concerning his eternal presence. His physical presence was now intermittent. He appeared behind locked doors, and they were being prepared for postascension days. In this intimacy Jesus promised to be with them always.

Christians today need a refresher course by which they can learn how to live intimately with God. The seventeenth-century monastery cook Brother Lawrence said that God was as close and real to him in the kitchen among his pots and pans as in times of more formal prayer and worship in the chapel.

III. The results of the disciples' refresher course.

Twenty years or so after Jesus' ascension, Paul and Silas in Thessalonica were described in words that the world has never forgotten. Moffatt translates it, "These upsetters of the whole world have come here, too." These people were in the succession of the prophets. Elijah, Nathan, Amos, Jeremiah, John the Baptist, and others were troublers of Israel. They often made those in authority uneasy.

Conclusion

Our approach, generally, is to try not to upset anyone. Too much of what the church does depends on satisfied customers. Our techniques and policies are designed to be more soothing than upsetting. Certainly there is no virtue in being an upsetting force for the sake of disturbance, but it is to our shame that the church is not more of an upsetting force. We have become quite skillful in detouring around and leaping over the real conflicts of our times. H. E. Luccock said, "That charge of being an upsetting force in a settled world is a high tribute and an unconsciously accurate appraisal of the real nature of Christian truth."

SUNDAY EVENING, MAY 1

Title: "Thou Shalt Not Lust"

Text: "Ye have heard that it was said by them of old time, Thou shalt not commit adultery: But I say unto you, That whosoever looketh on a woman to lust after her hath committed adultery with her already in his heart" **(Matt. 5:27–28).**

Scripture Reading: Matthew 5:27–30

Introduction

Martin Luther once said, "You can't prevent the devil from shooting arrows of evil thoughts into your heart; but take care that you do not let such arrows stick and grow there." As our Lord discussed the subject of sexual purity, he indicated that adultery begins with thoughts that are allowed to grow.

I. What is lust?

    A. *An inward attitude.* Throughout this portion of Matthew 5, Jesus emphasizes the inward attitudes that lead to sinful acts. The Pharisees said that the commandment on adultery could be broken only by the overt sexual act. Our Lord indicates that when one uses his eyes to excite lust and passion outside of marriage, he has committed the inward sin that leads to the overt sexual act. That person suffers from the guilt of the act even though he has not committed the act.

B. *An evil thought.* What did Jesus mean? He certainly did not mean that look-ing at a woman is a sin. One may look upon a woman to admire her grace and beauty. One may look at a woman and see gentle motherhood and loving mercy. The sin is not in the looking but in the evil purpose of the look.

Temptation becomes sin when one looks upon another and says, "I would commit the act of adultery if I had the opportunity."

II. What harm can lust do?

A. *Lust transforms good into evil.* The right hand and right eye are considered the best hand and the best eye. Our Lord is teaching that nothing should be kept in our lives that leads to sexual impurity—no matter how good it may be.

There is nothing evil about sex within marriage (Gen. 2:24). Within marriage sex is good and noble; outside of marriage it is reduced to sin. When lust leads to fornication or adultery, it transforms good into evil.

B. *Lust destroys.* Casting away and plucking out speaks of destruction. Lust can destroy a person's body, influence, and character. In the final analysis, lust may destroy a person's soul.

C. *Lust leads to forgetfulness.* What you think, you are! If one thinks lust, he will finally act out adultery (Jer. 7:9; Mark 7:21).

1. Lust causes you to forget that your body is a "living sacrifice" that is to be presented to God (Rom. 12:1–2).
2. Lust causes you to forget that your body is the "temple of the Holy Spirit" and is not to be defiled by fornication or adultery (1 Cor. 6:18–20).

III. How can one overcome lust?

A. *Work at it.* John Ruskin once said, "No one can ask honestly or hopefully to be delivered from temptation unless he has himself honestly and firmly determined to do the best that he can to keep out of it."

B. *Practice God's presence.* What you are afraid to do in man's presence, be afraid to think in God's presence. The destruction of sin begins in the heart (Ps. 24:3–4). Someone has well said, "What you want to become tomorrow, your thought life must be today."

C. *Mortify evil habits and deeds (1 Cor. 9:27; Col. 3:5).* A philosopher once said, "I can't prevent a bird from flying over my head, but I *can* prevent him from building a nest in my hair."

D. *Refuse to feed the flesh.* The apostle Paul admonishes, "Clothe yourselves with the Lord Jesus Christ, and do not think about how to gratify the desires of the sinful nature" (Rom. 13:14 NIV). We are to "abstain from all appearance of evil" (1 Thess. 5:22).

We feed the flesh through the eyes, the ears, and the lips. Christians must avoid magazines that feed the flesh with scandals and pornography.

They must also choose wisely which television shows and movies they view. And they must be discerning in what they hear and cautious in repeating it (Rom. 8:13).

Conclusion

In one of Homer's Greek mythologies, he tells the story of an island that is inhabited by beautiful, seductive maidens whose singing caused several ships to perish on the reefs that surrounded the island.

Ship captains had tried several methods to foil the temptation. They filled the ears of their sailors with wax so that they would be deaf to the seductive songs of the sirens. Ulysses plugged his sailors' ears with wax and tied himself to the mast of the ship. As he heard the seductive singing, he was kept safe by the rope that bound him.

But Jason and his crew found the best method. He took on board his ship Orpheus, the sweetest singer of his day. As they neared the island, Orpheus played his lyre and sang a song that was far grander than the songs of the maidens. The cheap, seductive songs of the sirens were no match for the sweet singing of Orpheus.

A Christian can best overcome lust and bypass adultery by filling his mind and life with things that are noble, just, pure, lovable, gracious, excellent, and admirable (Phil. 4:8).

WEDNESDAY EVENING, MAY 4

Title: The Command concerning Our Children

Text: "Suffer the little children to come unto me, and forbid them not: for of such is the kingdom of God" (**Mark 10:14**).

Scripture Reading: Mark 10:1–16

Introduction

There must have been something attractive about Jesus: his personality, the beauty of his spirit, the charm of his conversation, and the love that he had for all. Without doubt he was tasteful and neat in dress, courteous in manner, gentle, tender, cheerful, social, a delightful companion and friend. All sorts of people were attracted to him.

He was the friend of children. They loved him, and he loved them. On one occasion some parents brought their children to him that he might bless them. Evidently he was busy or occupied in some manner, and his disciples rebuked those who were bringing children to Christ. Imagine their surprise when they were rebuked and the parents were encouraged to bring their children to him.

I. Christ welcomes the children.

A. *The children of today are the leaders of tomorrow.*

138

B. *A child is much more responsive to the message of God's love than is an adult.*

C. *Christ extends a special invitation to children.*

II. Parents are to bring their children to Christ.

Fathers and mothers are indeed wise in bringing their children to Christ and leading them to trust him as Savior at a very early age. Dr. Gaines S. Dobbins has said that three-fourths of those who are won to faith in Christ Jesus are won in childhood.

Parents can bring their children to Christ in the following manner.

A. *By means of a beautiful Christian home life.*

B. *By means of earnest prayer on their behalf.*

C. *By teaching them Christian principles from day to day.*

D. *By regular worship habits both at home and at church.*

Conclusion

The Christ who commands us to bring our children will help us with our children. We can trust him for grace and guidance. We can lean on him for wisdom and insight. We can look to him for the capacity to love should our children conduct themselves in an unlovable manner. Christ will work in their minds and hearts and wills if we cooperate with him in teaching them.

We can prove our love for our Savior by cooperating with him and his purpose of redeeming and using our children for the extension of his kingdom on earth.

SUNDAY MORNING, MAY 8

Title: A Mother's Wages

Text: "Pharaoh's daughter said to her, 'Take this baby and nurse him for me, and I will pay you.' So the woman took the baby and nursed him" (**Ex. 2:9 NIV**).

Scripture Reading: Exodus 2:1 – 10

Hymns: "All Hail the Power of Jesus' Name," Perronet

"O Blessed Day of Motherhood!" McGregor

"Faith of Our Mothers," Patten

"'Tis So Sweet to Trust in Jesus," Stead

Offertory Prayer: Gratefully and humbly, our Father, we bow in your divine presence this morning. We come to this point in our service with hearts that are happy for the opportunity to bring to you a tangible expression of our gratitude for all the blessings that you have poured out on us during the past days. We are ever mindful that "every good gift and every perfect gift is from above, and cometh down from the Father of lights." We give to you our tithes and offerings from hearts of love with the earnest desire that you will take them and multiply them in your kingdom's use. Through Christ our Lord we offer this prayer. Amen.

Introduction

Dark were the days of the Israelite slaves in Egypt, those whose backs felt the sting of the whip as it left its mark, those whose greatest joy—the birth of a son into the home—had now turned into the greatest of life's sorrows through the decree of the pharaoh. The Hebrew people had reached the point where life had become so oppressive that it had almost lost its meaning for them. Yet there was a thread of faith that kept the flame of hope flickering in their lives. One such person of faith was a Hebrew housewife, Jochebed, who looked with joy into the face of her newborn son and then became sad as she remembered the pharaoh's decree that all Hebrew boy babies must be slain. She followed her God-given motherly instinct—to preserve her small son at all costs—at the risk of losing her own life if apprehended for her daring scheme. She prepared a basket from the reeds growing nearby and coated it with "bitumen and pitch" (Ex. 2:3 RSV). Then she placed her little son in it and carried it secretively to the river near the place where the pharaoh's daughter bathed each day. In due time the princess of Egypt came for her daily swim, and when she saw the basket among the reeds she sent her maid to get it. Seeing the baby, "she had compassion on him" (v. 6). Miriam, the baby's sister, approached the princess with the suggestion that she find a nurse from among the Hebrew women to care for the little lad. Receiving an affirmative response, she dashed off to her own house and brought her mother to Pharaoh's daughter, who gave her a command: "Take this baby and nurse him for me" (v. 9 NIV). The remaining part of her command to Jochebed forms the text for our thinking this morning—"and I will pay you" (v. 9 NIV).

What are a mother's wages? Abuse, overwork, heartache? In our modern way of life, all too often this seems to be the type of reward a mother, especially a mother of a teenager, may expect. However, a godly mother can look beneath the surface and see what the real rewards are. We can look at the story of Jochebed, the mother of Moses, and see truths pertinent to the role of motherhood today.

I. A godly mother's characteristics.

Certain characteristics are a part of a Christian mother's way of life. Among these are:

    A. *Faith.* To house a crying baby for three months with guards passing through the area required of this mother a type of faith that called forth courage on her part. To have faith in the future when everything pointed to the ultimate destruction of her race required a faith in the power of Almighty God to control the future. Faith that her "crazy scheme" to preserve her baby's life had been planted in her heart by God and that he would see that scheme through to its fruition was born out of personal experience with God. For a mother in our day to give birth to a son and to believe that he will see a better day ahead or will be able to have the Christian stamina to withstand the evils of his day requires faith in God through Christ Jesus, a faith that may be likened to that of Eunice and

Lois, the mother and grandmother of young Timothy (2 Tim. 1:5). Faith is required of a godly mother. As Thomas à Kempis in *Imitation of Christ* said, "Faith is required of thee, and a sincere life, not loftiness of intellect, nor deepness in the mysteries of God."

B. *Hope.* Against all odds, Jochebed found that hope welled up in her heart, hope that her son Moses would be saved from Pharaoh's sword and saved to a life of useful service. It was a hope born out of faith not in her own scheme but in the power of God to save and to sustain unto the uttermost. Today every godly mother has hope in her heart for each child God gives to her, hope that her child will grow up to take a useful place in life's drama, but more especially, a place of service in Christ's kingdom.

This hope a mother carefully imparts into the heart and soul of a child while he is yet at her knee. I recall quite vividly the surprising revelation my mother made to me on the day of my graduation from seminary. She said, "Son, on the day you were born I dedicated you to God to be a servant in his kingdom." Through the years she had kept this fact from me to prevent undue influence on my decision concerning my life's work. Yet through the years she had been shaping and molding my life as best she could that I might be a fit vessel for service should the Lord accept her gift!

C. *Love.* Every godly mother must have a love that is submissive to the will of God. Jochebed technically carried out the pharaoh's edict, for she did "throw" her son into the river! Actually, however, she was casting him on the love of God, realizing that his power and love were sufficient for her great need. In that heartrending moment on the riverbank, the love of a mother for her babe and the love of God met and performed a miracle of salvation through human instrumentality, a miracle that was to change the course of history for a great race of people, a miracle that was to change the way of life for the great Judeo-Christian segment of the human race! In that moment on the riverbank, Jochebed found that "perfect love drives out fear" (1 John 4:18 NIV).

II. A mother's task.

I would not be so foolish this morning as to attempt to name all of the many functions a mother must perform for her children — wiping noses, scrubbing grimy hands, tying shoelaces, applying a psychology book "to the seat of understanding," serving as social secretary and chauffeur to young teenagers — for these are too numerous to count. There are certain general areas into which I shall delve, however, as I attempt to define the task of a godly mother.

A. *To curb the child's lawlessness.* A mother has only a few short years at best to instill into a young life the ideals and precepts for life's best living. As the author of Proverbs expressed it: "Train up a child in the way he should go: and when he is old, he will not depart from it" (22:6).

B. *To cool the fevered brow.* There is no touch like the touch of a mother's hand when a child is sick. The ministry of a mother's love to the physically sick child leaves a memory indelibly imprinted on the mind and heart of the child. Each time I behold a mother hovering over the bed of a critically ill child, I almost feel that I have glimpsed divine love in action.

C. *To point the way to God.* In Port Gibson, Mississippi, there is (or was) a church building located on the main thoroughfare. The building itself is rather commonplace with but one exception—at the top of its steeple there is fixed, not the usual spire or cross, but a hand, the forefinger of which points heavenward toward God. The greatest task a godly mother has is to point her children to God. During those formative years while Jochebed was acting as nurse to her own son, she was able to implant a knowledge of the God of the Hebrews in the heart of the young lad, a knowledge that seemingly lay dormant for many years until the time was right in the sight of God for that knowledge to awaken into action. Every mother's opportunity, as well as her divine commission, is to teach the way of salvation to her child that he or she may come to know Christ as Savior and Lord at an early age.

III. A mother's wages.

Pharaoh's daughter said to Jochebed, "And I will pay you" (Ex. 2:9 NIV).

A. *Early payment.* At first Jochebed may well have asked herself, "Is the pain of motherhood really worth it?" Did not her son while in a fit of anger go against all her early teachings and commit murder? Was he not forced to flee from Egypt as a common criminal? No doubt the thought of probably never seeing him again was almost more than she could bear. Heartache upon heartache—was this to be the payment of motherhood? Today innumerable mothers of teenagers are asking themselves that same question.

B. *Later payment.* Jochebed may not have lived long enough to see the great role played in history by her three children who were instrumental under God's guidance in leading the children of Israel out of bondage into freedom. However, the lives they lived created, figuratively speaking, a great monument to her memory, erected against the skyline of history with the epitaph, "How great was thy faithfulness!" The greatest reward or wages that can be bestowed on any mother are the following:

1. Children who are obedient.
2. Children who are morally pure.
3. Children who make a contribution to God's kingdom.
4. Children who throughout life's journey stand on the side of right.
5. Children who have been born again.
6. Children who are active soul winners.

Corsages may bring a temporary smile of gratitude to our mothers' faces on

Mother's Day, but that which brings real and abiding joy to a godly mother are the things just mentioned.

Conclusion

Today I would ask you to consider this: Is your life bringing joy to your Christian mother? Are you living so close to the Lord that the wages enumerated a moment ago are being bestowed on your mother? If you are not a Christian, do you realize that your godly mother is praying for you, is longing to see you give her the greatest gift of all—a child who has repented of his sins and has turned to Christ as his Savior? Let Christ come into your heart and life this morning.

SUNDAY EVENING, MAY 8

Title: Except for Fornication

Text: "It has been said, 'Anyone who divorces his wife must give her a certificate of divorce.' But I tell you that anyone who divorces his wife, except for marital unfaithfulness, causes her to become an adulteress, and anyone who marries the divorced woman commits adultery" **(Matt. 5:31–32 NIV)**.

Scripture Reading: Matthew 19:1–9

I. Biblical teachings on marriage and divorce.

A. *Marriage is the one-flesh union of one man and one woman that is to be broken only by death (Matt. 19:4–5).*

B. *God's ideal is that one man and one woman shall remain together in this one-flesh union (Gen. 2:18; Rom. 7:2; 1 Cor. 7:10–11).*

C. *Since two people are joined together by God (Gen. 1:27–28), this union is not to be broken by man (Matt. 19:6).*

D. *Moses did not command divorce, but he gave permission to divorce (Deut. 24:1–4; Matt. 19:1–8) because of Israel's moral inferiority.*

E. *Jesus granted the right of divorce only on the ground of marital infidelity (Matt. 5:32; 19:9).* Our Lord indicated that when a man divorces his wife without this ground, he may cause her to be debauched, thereby causing her and any man whom she marries to share in adultery (Matt. 19:9).

F. *Jesus taught that marriage after divorce, without the ground of marital infidelity, is adultery.*

G. *Jesus implied that the spouse of an adulterer has a right to remarry after divorce (Matt. 5:32; 19:9).*

Our Lord said, "except for marital unfaithfulness" in these two passages. This phrase indicates that the "innocent party" in the divorce has grounds to remarry.

H. *Jesus taught that divorce was never in God's original plan for marriage (Matt. 19:6).* Jesus never really attempted anywhere to set forth a law concerning divorce, but he intended to emphasize that the marriage union can be broken only by adultery.

II. Some conclusions on divorce and remarriage.

One might draw the following conclusions from a study of the Scriptures on this subject:

A. *Any person who puts away his partner for any other reason than adultery, and marries again, commits adultery.*

B. *The "innocent party" in a divorce case is free to marry again.*

C. *While divorce is permitted by God in case of adultery, it is not commanded.* There is no evidence that one would be living in adultery if he or she continues to live with an adulterous mate.

III. Some suggestions for a happy home.

A. *Before considering marriage, persons should be sure that their love is the everlasting kind.*

B. *Persons should be mature before they marry.* The highest divorce rate is among teenage couples.

C. *Persons should marry with the determination to make the union last.*

D. *One should recognize what really matters in marriage.* Alfred Sutro once wrote a play called *A Maker of Men,* in which a bank clerk returns home after missing a promotion and says, "I see other men getting on; what have I done?"

His wife answers: "You have made a woman love you. You have given me respect for you and admiration and loyalty and devotion—everything a man can give his wife except luxury, and that I don't need. Still you call yourself a failure, who within these four walls are the greatest success!"

E. *Persons contemplating divorce should count the cost to self, spouse, children, parents, relatives, church, and society in general.* They should ask, "Can this divorce be justified from the Christian viewpoint?"

F. *Persons already divorced must ask God for help in finding his will.*

Conclusion

Shortly after a British jet crossed and recrossed the Atlantic in about eight hours, a cartoon was printed in the *New York Times.* It pictured a jet traveling at fantastic speed. The plane was labeled "Man's Scientific Progress." On the ground was a huge turtle moving slowly and ponderously. The turtle was labeled "Man's Moral Progress."

In a vivid way, this cartoon symbolized what could be the tragedy of the modern age and the most compelling reason for greater attention to the biblical principles for the Christian home.

WEDNESDAY EVENING, MAY 11

Title: The Command to Be Ready

Text: "Therefore be ye also ready: for in such an hour as ye think not the Son of man cometh" **(Matt. 24:44)**.

Scripture Reading: Matthew 24:36–51

Introduction

Our text comes from a section of the gospel of Matthew that emphasizes the coming judgment on the nation of Israel and the certainty that one day the Lord Jesus Christ shall come back as King of Kings and Lord of Lords to claim his own. Our Lord was instructing and encouraging his disciples to be ready for both of these events. Repeatedly he emphasized judgment and the certainty of his victorious second coming. He urged them to be ready for whatever the future might hold for them.

A careful reading of the New Testament will reveal that one of the most prominent emphases that was made in the early church was concerning the second coming of Christ. It was in the hope of his return that the early Christians lived and labored and suffered and gave of themselves completely to the cause of Christ.

As the centuries have gone by, some have given up hope that the Lord will return. It is possible that some Jews had given up hope for the coming of the Messiah in the first place. In the fullness of time, he came, and in the fullness of time, he will come a second time. Those who have diligently studied the New Testament at this point declare that the return of Christ is mentioned more than three hundred times. We need to give heed to our Lord's promise to return and his command to be ready.

I. Consider the promises of Jesus' coming.

    A. *His second coming is implied by God in Genesis 3:15.*

    B. *Jesus made many personal promises concerning his return (John 14:1–3).*

    C. *The angels said that he would return (Acts 1:11).*

    D. *All of the New Testament writers believed that Christ would return for his own.*

II. Observe the manner of Jesus' coming.

Some have thought that Jesus fulfilled his promise to return in the coming of the Holy Spirit at Pentecost. Others have thought that he fulfilled his promise by coming into the believer's heart in the conversion experience. And yet others have believed that he fulfilled his promise to return in the destruction of Jerusalem. To believe any of these things is to ignore much that the New Testament teaches concerning his coming.

    A. *His return will be personal (John 14:3).*

    B. *His return will be visible (Acts 1:11; Rev. 1:7).*

    C. *His return will be in great power and glory (1 Thess. 4:16; 2 Thess. 1:7–10).*

III. Recognize the purpose for Jesus' second coming.

 A. *He will come that his lordship might be recognized (Phil. 2:9–11).*

 B. *He will come to raise the dead (1 Thess. 4:16–18).*

 C. *He will come to receive his own (John 14:1–3).*

 D. *He will come to complete our salvation (Heb. 9:28).*

 E. *He will come to reward the faithful (Rev. 22:12).*

 F. *He will come to judge the wicked (Acts 17:30–31).*

 G. *He will come to establish peace (Isa. 2).*

IV. How can we be ready for Jesus' second coming?

 A. *If we want to be ready for the second coming of Jesus Christ, we must be saved.* We must trust Jesus Christ as Lord and Savior from the tyranny of sin. We must experience the new birth. Apart from this experience of trust and commitment to Jesus Christ, one cannot possibly be ready for his coming.

 B. *If we want to be ready, we must be busy about our Master's business until he comes (2 Peter 3:14).* We must not be lax about spreading the message of his death and resurrection to the ends of the earth.

 C. *If we want to be ready, we must be faithful (2 Peter 3:17).* It is not enough that we be faithful for a time. We must be faithful all of the time. Our Lord will come suddenly and unexpectedly.

 D. *If we want to be ready, we need to be looking forward to his coming expectantly (Rev. 22:20).*

Conclusion

John, the beloved apostle, loved the Lord and labored in the hope that the Lord would return during his lifetime. It is interesting that this revelation should come to a close with a prayer and a benediction that the grace of the Lord Jesus might be with all of his followers until his victorious return for his own.

SUNDAY MORNING, MAY 15

Title: Departure without Tears

Text: "Then he led them out as far as Bethany, and lifting up his hands he blessed them. While he blessed them, he parted from them. And they returned to Jerusalem with great joy, and were continually in the temple blessing God" **(Luke 24:50–53 RSV).**

Scripture Reading: Acts 1:1–11

Hymns: "Rejoice, the Lord Is King," Wesley

    "Jesus Shall Reign," Watts

    "Crown Him with Many Crowns," Bridges

Offertory Prayer: O God, we acknowledge your goodness to us beyond measure. We acknowledge, too, our debt to the forefathers of our Christian faith. As a result of what you have put in their hearts and minds, the influence of our offering today will be felt in many parts of the world. May our material resources be made increasingly available to your work so that the Good News can be proclaimed more universally. Through our Savior's name. Amen.

Introduction

No one enjoys saying good-bye to a loved one. Some people will go to much trouble to avoid this unpleasant experience. Joseph Parker, one of the great English preachers of former days, preferred that visitors in his home not say good-bye upon departure. He and his wife, early in marriage, agreed not to say good-bye to each other upon parting, and they lived up to the promise.

We are not likely to go to such extremes in dealing with life's inevitable separations. Yet our unpleasantness is pronounced in varying degrees, depending on how close the departing person is to us and the degree of finality we fear is in the good-bye.

One would expect, therefore, that the disciples would be heavyhearted when Jesus left them. His ascension had all the marks of finality about it, yet they shed no tears over his departure. There can be no question about their love for him. They were heartbroken and puzzled when he told them, prior to his crucifixion, of his departure. We might have expected an account of Jesus' ascension to read as follows: "And it came to pass that he parted from them and was carried up into heaven, and they worshiped him and returned to Jerusalem with hot tears that blinded their eyes and with hearts breaking in the sorrow of farewell. And they said one to another, 'It was beautiful while it lasted, and now we must get on without him in a world that in his absence has turned cold and bleak and gray.'"

As strange as it may seem, there is nothing of this gloom and sadness surrounding the ascension of Jesus. Instead, those early Christians "returned to Jerusalem with great joy, and were continually in the temple blessing God."

I. Consider, first, the scriptural basis for this observation—departure without tears.

Jesus met his disciples in the vicinity of Jerusalem for private instructions. Then "he led them out as far as Bethany, and he lifted up his hands and blessed them." This is an exact reversal of the triumphal entry and symbolizes their following him to the ends of the earth. "And it came to pass, while he blessed them, he was parted from them, and carried up into heaven." How appropriate that the last recollection the disciples have of their Lord is of his blessing them as they stood together on the high ground overlooking Jerusalem!

"And they worshipped him, and returned to Jerusalem with great joy." This verse follows logically from the thought of the previous one. Worship was properly given to the ascended Christ because he was ascended. The disciples returned to

Jerusalem, obedient to the Lord's previous command and in expectation of the fulfillment of the promise.

The account in the book of Acts has much to add. It tells of a cloud receiving Jesus out of the disciples' sight. The "cloud" is to be understood both literally and symbolically. It seems that an actual physical cloud hid Jesus from the disciples' view and that when the cloud lifted he was no longer visible. But there is more involved than the literal. God's relation to his people and the world was often through the use of a cloud. At the time of the exodus, the Lord led and protected his people by a cloud. The cloud covered the mount at the giving of the Law. When the tabernacle was completed, the cloud came upon it to signify the abiding presence of God. On the Mount of Transfiguration the cloud signified the presence of God. In the ascension the cloud was without doubt, for the disciples, a powerful symbol of the return of Jesus to the Father.

The Acts account talks about "two men standing by the disciples in white apparel." The appearance of angels in the narrative suggests that, for the disciples, there was the dawning realization of spiritual truth, which the author, and probably the apostles, could express in no other way. "Ye men of Galilee, why stand ye gazing up into heaven?" (Acts 1:11). This is a contrast between the insignificant and earthly as over against the divine and eternal. It is the realization that the Lord who is tabernacled *here*, really belongs *there*. They sense that this is the last appearance of its kind. But there is to be a future coming, in some sense, for so he promised. How? When? Where? Who can know? In some way his coming will be similar to his departure—mysterious but certain. Greater precision than this is hardly to be expected in speaking of the mystery of the consummation of all things.

II. There was departure without tears because the disciples had no sense of loss.

The ascension was not in any sense a good-bye. It expresses a certain finality as far as its place at the end of a group of narratives is concerned. It marks the end in time of the whole series of events that the Gospels proclaim. The events of the thirty-plus years of Jesus' earthly life can be narrated somewhat, but not exactly, as ordinary earthly events can be narrated. The "event" that started the series of earthly events on its way and the "event" that brought the series to its close cannot be confined to the language of narration. The incarnation and the ascension are the "brackets," so to speak, that enclose the earthly life of the Lord. Or, to change the metaphor from mathematics to music, they are the "bridge passages" that link the earthly events to the eternal world.

What happened at the ascension does not, however, reverse what happened at the incarnation. The world is not the same place after the Lord's ascension as it was before he became man. It is permanently different from what it was because of what he accomplished. Jesus remains eternally man—"the same yesterday and today and forever" (Heb. 13:8 NIV). In him man has been raised to the throne of God. The Godward aspect of this truth is expressed in the epistle to the Hebrews as the eternal intercession of Christ as High Priest on behalf of humankind. The manward aspect is expressed in the Pauline phrase, "Our citizenship is in heaven" (Phil. 3:20 NIV). The unity of heaven and earth for the Christian is guaranteed by the indwelling of the Spirit, through whom Christ is eternally present on earth.

The ascension marks the completion of a ministry, beginning with the resurrection, in which Jesus successfully aimed at carrying the sense of his presence beyond the need of the senses. Without seeing, hearing, or touching him, they knew him to be near. Read the New Testament carefully, remembering that the Epistles were written before the earliest Gospels, and you will recognize that the apostles preached Jesus' risen power and abiding presence more than they preached the glory and splendor of his life.

Jesus went out of the sight of his disciples, and after Pentecostal power had come upon them, they went out to be witnesses of what they had seen and heard. They heralded the Good News, the news commanded attention and produced conviction, and salvation by faith in Jesus followed. As they witnessed to that truth by word of mouth and by their daring, holy living, the old Roman Empire, which was falling to pieces, was captured for the living Christ.

Conclusion

The New Testament leaves no doubt about the believer's reunion with the ascended Christ. It will be in the Father's house, in the completeness of our human nature, and it will never end. So we must not try to stay on the mount of vision. Returning to our Jerusalems, let us continue on our way rejoicing.

SUNDAY EVENING, MAY 15

Title: "Thou Shalt Not Swear"

Text: "Swear not at all" (**Matt. 5:34**).

Scripture Reading: Matthew 5:33–37

Introduction

George Fox once was commanded by the judges at Lancaster to "take an oath in court." His reply was as follows: "Ye have given me a Book here to kiss and to swear on, and this Book which ye have given me to kiss says, 'Kiss the son,' and the Son says in this Book 'Swear not at all.' Now, I say as the Book says, and yet ye imprison me. How chance ye do not imprison the Book for saying so?"

When Jesus said, "Swear not at all," did he mean that we are not to take an oath in court? Does he not go much deeper than merely testifying in court?

I. What is an oath?

An oath is a promise or a covenant.

A. *God made some promises to man that were considered a part of his covenant with man.*

1. Man would have freedom of choice because he was made "in the image of God" (Gen. 1:27; 2:7–9).
2. God would send a Savior to save man from his sins and restore the image that was marred by sin (Gen. 3:14–15). The remainder of the Old Testament tells the story of God's redemptive plan for man.
3. God would not destroy man by water. The rainbow is an eternal reminder of this covenant (Gen. 9:11–13).
4. The Jews would be a covenant people through whom Jesus Christ would be born into the world (Gen. 17:1–5).

B. *God's people have made some covenants between each other.*
1. Abraham and his servant made a covenant to find a wife for Isaac (Gen. 24:8–9).
2. Isaac and Abimelech made a covenant of peace (Gen. 26:27–29).
3. The Old Testament covenants are too numerous to mention. However, we notice that covenants were made between Jacob and his sons, Joseph and his brothers, and Jonathan and his father.
4. As men made covenants and promises with each other and to each other, the name of God became associated with these covenants because he was a witness to them. Paul could say, "I call God for a record upon my soul" (2 Cor. 1:23). On one occasion he said, "Before God, I lie not" (Gal. 1:20).

II. The Pharisees' perversion of oaths.

A. *The Pharisees contended that an oath in which God's name is used is binding.* In other words, if one uses the name of God in an oath, he must be telling the truth. They conceived of God as a partner to transactions in which his name was used.

B. *However, if God's name was not used in an oath, the Pharisees did not have to be truthful.* Again, God was not considered a partner to a transaction in which his name was not used. Eventually the Pharisees used in their oaths things that were related to God, such as heaven, earth, Jerusalem, and the head. However, they felt no obligation whatsoever to be truthful in their speech as long as God's name was not used.

III. Christ's teachings about oaths.

A. *Truth is absolute—not relative.* Our Lord teaches that the Christian should be so truthful in his speech that he would not have to depend on an oath to fortify his lies.

Chaucer said, "Truth is the highest thing that man can keep." Thomas Huxley once said, "Truth is the heart of morality." The late Henry R. Luce, editor in chief of *Time, Life,* and *Fortune* magazines, once said, "The most dangerous fault in American life today is the lack of interest in the truth."

When Jesus said, "Let your communication be yea, yea, and nay, nay," he meant that the Christian's yes should mean yes and his no should mean no. He commands truthfulness (cf. James 5:12).

B. *God cannot be compartmentalized.* There is not one language for church, another for the shipyards, another for the factory, and another for the office. There is not one standard for the church and another standard for the business world. All words are spoken in the presence of God!

C. *Truth begins in the heart.* As one lets Christ cleanse his heart, he learns to be so truthful that he needs no oath.

Conclusion

In Korea a few years ago, army intelligence officers found an interesting fact in the use of the polygraph. The lie detector worked best on those who had had much contact with the Christian faith. Those who knew nothing of Christianity, however, seemed to be able to lie without guilt.

Jesus Christ is the embodiment of all truth. He said, "I am the way, the *truth,* and the life" (John 14:6).

WEDNESDAY EVENING, MAY 18

Title: The Command to Tarry for Spiritual Power

Text: "And, behold, I send the promise of my Father upon you: but tarry ye in the city of Jerusalem, until ye be endued with power from on high" **(Luke 24:49)**.

Scripture Reading: Luke 24:36–53

Introduction

The Lord's disciples were amazingly inadequate for the task that he commanded them to accomplish. A study of the Scriptures will convince you that these men and women were ordinary human beings. Yet despite their weaknesses due to being Adam's heirs, the Lord committed to them the tremendous task of evangelizing the world. They were to begin in Jerusalem, where he had been crucified, and move out to Judea and then to Samaria and on to the uttermost parts of the earth.

How did Jesus' disciples achieve that which has amazed the world? The apostles were a baffled and disappointed group of Jewish peasants. Though unrefined by society, these men launched a movement that established their Leader in the affections of the world in the first three centuries of the Christian era. We must remember that this Leader had been executed by the authorities of the civil government as if he were a common criminal.

These apostles did not enjoy political endorsement or social prestige. They lived in a society that was materialistic and antagonistic to anything spiritual. They went from one world center to another proclaiming Jesus Christ as Lord of Lords and King of Kings. What was the secret of their success?

While many factors may have contributed to their success, none is more important than their obedience to our Lord's command to tarry for the spiritual power that they would need to accomplish their task. Modern-day Christians must recognize their need for this same spiritual power if they are to be effective in today's world. We must recognize and respond to our Lord's command to tarry until we have been endued with the power of the Spirit of God before we can effectively minister to a needy world.

I. The disciples were promised a power from heaven.

A. *We are familiar with many types of power:*
1. Muscle power.
2. Mechanical power.
3. Electrical power.
4. Nuclear power.
5. Financial power.
6. Political power.
7. Military power.

B. *Jesus was talking to his disciples about spiritual power, the very power of God.* He was talking about the power by which God created the world and the power by which he had been raised from the dead.

II. Is this power available today?

A. *Our Lord promised that the Comforter would come to abide with his disciples forever (John 14:16–17).* This promise concerning the abiding presence of the Holy Spirit was made in deliberate contrast to his brief sojourn with them.

B. *The Great Commission speaks of the authority and power of the Savior, who has promised to be with his obedient disciples always (Matt. 28:18–20).*

III. How can we have this power in the present?

A. *We need to recognize that without this power we are defeated before we begin (Zech. 4:6).*

B. *We need to respond to both the presence and the power of the Holy Spirit in genuine faith.* If we do not believe in his presence and power, we will not experience his power.

C. *Jesus taught that the power of the Holy Spirit was given to those who recognized their need and who made requests (Luke 11:13).*

D. *In discussing the task of witnessing to the unsaved, Peter said that God gives the Holy Spirit to those who obey him (Acts 5:32).*

Conclusion

He who departs to win the world to Christ without first seeking the power of the Holy Spirit is as foolish as the soldier who departs for battle without his weapons. He who neglects to let the Holy Spirit fill his heart and life is acting with the foolishness of an airplane pilot who departs for a long journey with only enough gasoline to get his plane off the ground.

It is neither incidental nor accidental that our Lord spoke to his disciples at the beginning and said, "Come unto me," before he commanded them, "Go." One must tarry in the presence of God for spiritual power before he can go out into the world and render effective service for God. The command to tarry for spiritual power is just as relevant and necessary for the present as it was for the apostles long ago. One cannot do God's work without God's power. If we want to do God's work effectively, we must obey Jesus' command to tarry for the endowment with spiritual power.

SUNDAY MORNING, MAY 22

Title: The Spirit of the Lord

Text: "The Spirit of the Lord is upon me, because he hath anointed me to preach the gospel to the poor" (**Luke 4:18**).

Scripture Reading: Luke 4:14–19; John 14:16–18

Hymns: "Break Thou the Bread of Life," Lathbury

"Holy Spirit, Faithful Guide," Wells

"Breathe on Me, Breath of God," Hatch

Offertory Prayer: Holy heavenly Father, open our eyes and help us to see the world's great need for the good news of your love through Jesus Christ. Open our eyes to the suffering of the unfortunate. Help us to see the needs of unfortunate children and needy young people. Help us to see that we are to be sharers of that with which you have blessed us. Help us as we bring our tithes and offerings to do so out of devotion for our Savior and love and concern to meet the needs of those about us. Help us to overcome our selfishness. Help us to rise above the material and to live for the spiritual. In the name of our Savior we pray. Amen.

Introduction

When Jesus returned to Nazareth after the beginning of his ministry, he was given the privilege of reading the Scripture on the Sabbath. He selected a messianic passage from Isaiah that revealed the nature and scope of the ministry that he as the Messiah would fulfill. He began to read where it is declared, "The Spirit of the Lord is upon me." This was more than just a place to begin reading from the scroll; it was a proclamation to the effect that his messianic ministry was being made possible by the presence and power of the Holy Spirit. This affirmation takes on special significance when one recognizes that it was in the power of this same Spirit that our Lord intended for his disciples to serve in the world.

If we can see how it was that our Lord ministered in the power of the Holy Spirit, perhaps we will be encouraged to make a more positive response to the Holy Spirit, who came to dwell in our hearts in our conversion experience. As our

153

Lord said (Luke 4:18), "The Spirit of the Lord is upon me," his followers can say, "The Spirit of the Lord has come to dwell within my heart" (cf. John 14:16–17; 1 Cor. 3:16; 6:19).

I. Jesus and the Holy Spirit.

It is helpful for modern-day followers of Jesus Christ to discover how our Lord labored in the power of the Holy Spirit, for this same Holy Spirit is available and is eager to enable us as we seek to render ministries in the name of Christ today.

A. *The birth of Jesus was by creative act on the part of the Holy Spirit (Matt. 1:20; Luke 1:35).* In addition to recognizing the virgin purity of Mary, we should recognize the work of the Holy Spirit in the miraculous conception of the Word that became flesh.

B. *Jesus was anointed and identified as the Messiah during his baptism by John the Baptist (John 1:32–34).*

C. *Jesus overcame temptation with the assistance of the Holy Spirit (Luke 4:1).* The Holy Spirit led Christ into confrontation with the Evil One, and by means of Christ's pure manhood, his reliance on the Word of God, and the assistance of the Holy Spirit, he overcame Satan's temptations.

D. *In the power of the Holy Spirit, Jesus healed the sick, cast out demons, and led his listeners to a new understanding of the nature and purpose of God (Matt. 12:17–18).*

E. *Through the eternal Spirit Christ offered himself on the cross for the forgiveness of our sins (Heb. 9:14).*

F. *The Holy Spirit was at work in Christ's resurrection.* By his resurrection from the dead, he was declared to be the powerful Son of God (Rom. 1:4).

II. Disciples of Jesus and the Holy Spirit.

There are remarkable parallels between the ministry of the Holy Spirit in Jesus' life and the ministry that he wishes to render in the lives of Jesus' followers.

A. *By a spiritual birth experience, we become the children of God through faith in Christ Jesus (John 3:3, 7; Gal. 3:26; Titus 3:5).*

B. *The Holy Spirit identifies the believer as a child of God and gives him assurance of salvation (Rom. 8:16).*

C. *By the power of the Holy Spirit, believers are to minister in the name of Christ in the world (Acts 1:8).*

D. *The Holy Spirit was sent into the world to dwell in the heart of each believer as a divine Teacher and Guide into the truth about God (John 14:16–18, 26; 16:13).*

E. *The presence of the indwelling Spirit in the heart of the believer is God's guarantee of his final and complete salvation from the presence of sin when Christ Jesus returns for his own (Rom. 8:11; Eph. 1:13–14).*

Conclusion

The Lord Jesus Christ lived, loved, and labored in the power of the Holy

Spirit of God. Modern-day followers of Jesus Christ will utterly fail to be true followers of Christ if they neglect to properly respond to the guidance and power that are available through the Holy Spirit.

We need to make a response of faith to the presence and purpose of the Holy Spirit, who has come to dwell in our hearts. We must make the response of cooperation and obedience as he leads us in our growth and in our ministry to others. We need to respond by depending on him to bless both the efforts of our hands and the testimony of our lips as we share the good news of God's love.

The Holy Spirit is in the world today speaking with a tender voice to those who need to receive Jesus Christ as Lord and Savior. Each person must hear and respond if he wants to have abundant life in Christ Jesus, the way, the truth, and the life (Heb. 3:7–8).

SUNDAY EVENING, MAY 22

Title: Turning the Other Cheek

Text: "Ye have heard that it hath been said, An eye for an eye, and a tooth for a tooth: But I say unto you, That ye resist not evil: but whosoever shall smite thee on thy right cheek, turn to him the other also. And if any man will sue thee at the law, and take away thy coat, let him have thy cloak also" (**Matt. 5:38–40**).

Scripture Reading: Romans 12

Introduction

A communist leader once said, "We communists have many things in common with the teachings of Jesus Christ." He continued, "My sole difference with Christ is that when someone hits me on the right cheek, I hit him on the left so hard that his head falls off."

Someone has said, "It is hard to get ahead of a fellow when you are trying to get even with him." Because retaliation is a universal instinct, Jesus deals with the urge to get even.

I. Some guidelines to interpretation.

Perhaps this verse is the most controversial in the Sermon on the Mount. People have discussed it from many different viewpoints. Some have found it to teach pacifism while others have interpreted it as a prohibition of capital punishment.

A. *This is not a literal command.* When our Lord spoke of the right cheek, he was speaking of being slapped with the back of someone's hand — the greatest symbol of insult that one could inflict upon another in Jesus' day. The Lord was not being literal to the point of saying that the only time this verse can be used is when someone slaps you. He was speaking of any kind of insult. A vindictive spirit is prohibited in *every* case.

B. *This admonition is for born-again people.* Our Lord never intended for this command to be applied to society. A lost world does not know how to use these words. These words are addressed to people who have been born again and have committed their lives to Jesus Christ.

C. *The Christian should apply this verse to personal and social relationships.* Thus the gospel of Jesus Christ has social implications that are to be recognized by the individual Christian, who is the salt of the earth and the light of the world. The gospel of Jesus Christ is not a social gospel. It is a soul-saving gospel with social implications!

II. Old Testament background.

A. *A control of violence.* In the Old Testament the command was "an eye for an eye and a tooth for a tooth" (Ex. 21:23–25; Lev. 24:19–20; Deut. 19:21). The original purpose of this command was to control violence and the desire for revenge. The death of one man might lead to a war and the death of many. It was determined that the judges would allow the one who was wronged to extract equal merchandise from his assailant.

The punishment was limited only to those who had injured others. The right of retaliation was not in the hands of individuals but in the hands of the judges (Ex. 18:19–23).

B. *A time for tempers to cool.* Scholars generally agree that this law was never literally carried out. It slowed people down long enough to think about the situation and to determine that one may be taking a good eye for a bad eye or a good tooth for a bad tooth.

Thus what seems to this enlightened age to be an archaic teaching may have been quite modern in Old Testament times. The law of retaliation in the Old Testament was certainly an improvement over what they had.

III. The Pharisees' perversion of the law of retaliation.

A. *They changed the permission to retaliate to a positive command.* The Pharisees taught that one *must* retaliate when he is wronged.

B. *They made it a personal matter and suggested that people go around the judges and do their own retaliating.*

C. *Their approach was legalistic.* They thought only of one's own rights and not the rights of others. In some cases the Pharisees were even acting as judges themselves.

IV. The teachings of Jesus on retaliation.

A. *We are to resist evil.* Our Lord admonishes us to forget if we have been wronged. It is a good idea not to talk about it, for the rehearsal of wrongs done to us often leads to a bitter spirit.

B. *Anytime a Christian is insulted he should not return insult for insult.* We often are insulted with the tongue, with a look of disgust, or by someone's actions. But we must not retaliate!

C. *Become indifferent to personal criticism.* As the Christian becomes less and less conscious of himself, he becomes more and more indifferent to the criticism of others.

D. *Do more than is expected of you.* The coat was the inner garment. It was lawful for one to take the inner garment permanently; however, the cloak (the outer garment) was both the robe and a blanket. It was not lawful to take it permanently from another person. But our Lord said that the Christian should not insist upon his personal rights. He must do more than what is expected of him. When asked for the coat, give the cloak too!

E. *Enthrone Jesus Christ in your life.* Jesus practiced this precept when he was slapped (John 18:22–23). He gladly gave up the right to defend himself in order to speak in defense of the truth.

Peter, who stood watching that night, later wrote, "When they hurled insults at him, he did not retaliate; when he suffered, he made no threats. Instead, he entrusted himself to him who judges justly" (1 Peter 2:23 NIV).

Conclusion

Christians are to have no part in retaliation. As the proverb says, "Do not say, 'I'll pay you back for this wrong!' Wait for the LORD, and he will deliver you" (20:22 NIV). When we show love to those who wrong us instead of striking back, the world will see that we are followers of Christ.

WEDNESDAY EVENING, MAY 25

Title: The Command to Missionary Activity

Text: "Therefore go and make disciples of all nations, baptizing them in the name of the Father and of the Son and of the Holy Spirit, and teaching them to obey everything I have commanded you. And surely I am with you always, to the very end of the age" **(Matt. 28:19–20 NIV).**

Scripture Reading: Acts 1:1–8

Introduction

Our text contains the Great Commission. These words from the Master provide his church and the individual Christian with a missionary mandate. It is personal in its application and obligation. It is pressing in its urgency as far as world need and our obedience are concerned.

Our world is in desperate need of our making a personal response to this missionary mandate. Our day is a day in which the world is plagued with great physical hunger. Our day is a day of growing world tension. Our day is a day of major social, economic, and political revolution. Our day is a day of incalculable suffering. Our day is a day of possible unlimited destruction. Our day is a day of desperate spiritual need. Our day is a day of glorious opportunity for proclaiming the gospel that provides the only hope for our salvation, personally and collectively.

I. This command to missionary activity reveals God's eternal purpose for the world.

    A. *God's eternal purpose is verbalized in John 3:16.*
    B. *God's purpose has been revealed through the ages.*
       1. It was revealed to Abraham.
       2. It was made plain to Moses.
       3. The psalmist sang about it.
       4. The prophets proclaimed it.
       5. It was announced at the birth of Christ.
       6. It was disclosed in the teachings of our Lord.
       7. It was demonstrated and manifested in Christ's sacrificial death on the cross.
       8. It is plainly declared in Christ's great commission.

II. The Master's missionary mandate reveals God's will for our individual lives.

    A. *God's purpose is that the gospel should be proclaimed to everyone throughout the whole world.* Our purpose for being should be related to God's eternal purpose for the world.
    B. *God's program, that of making disciples, should be our program.*
    C. *Our Lord promised his personal presence to those who would be obedient to his missionary command.*
    D. *God's energy, wisdom, and power are available to those who are obedient to this command.*

III. The Master's missionary mandate is directed to me and to you personally.

    A. *We need to rediscover the world's need for Christ.* While those about us may have great needs for many things, the greatest need that anyone has is the need for a right relationship with God through faith in Christ Jesus.
    B. *We need to recognize our personal responsibility.* Many have applied the imperative of this missionary mandate to those who are in the clergy or to those who have received a call to go to the foreign mission fields. Actually, the emphasis in this command is on "making disciples." This is the only imperative in the command. The word that is translated "go" is a participle that means "in your going about from place to place make disciples." This command was not to be limited to the apostles. It is a command that comes down through the centuries to this hour to each follower of Jesus Christ.
    C. *We need to rejoice in our opportunity.* The greatest opportunity that one ever

faces is the joyful privilege of leading someone to receive the gift of eternal life and to have his sins forgiven through faith in Christ Jesus.

D. *We need to radically commit ourselves to the work of our triumphant Savior.* Our God went to the extreme expense of giving his Son to die on the cross to save us from our sins. We need to make a sacrificial investment of our time, talents, treasure, and testimony in being obedient to the Lord's command to make disciples.

Conclusion

If each disciple of Jesus Christ were to seriously commit himself or herself to being obedient to this missionary mandate, the world could be evangelized in less than ten years. You and I have no control over what others do. As individuals, let us determine that we will be obedient to our Lord's missionary mandate in our own personal world.

SUNDAY MORNING, MAY 29

Title: The Recovery of Sight

Text: "The Spirit of the Lord is upon me, because he hath anointed me to preach the gospel to the poor; he hath sent me to heal the brokenhearted, to preach deliverance to the captives, and recovering of sight to the blind, to set at liberty them that are bruised" **(Luke 4:18).**

Scripture Reading: Luke 4:14–21

Hymns: "Guide Me, O Thou Great Jehovah," Williams

      "Will Jesus Find Us Watching?" Crosby

      "Open My Eyes, That I May See," Scott

Offertory Prayer: Holy Father, open our eyes to help us to see the evidences of your grace and mercy. Help us to see the bounty of your provisions for us. Help us to recognize that every good and perfect gift is from you. Help us, Lord, to recognize that as we have received so we are to give. Help us to believe that the abundant life is to be found in a life of unselfish devoted giving. Accept these tithes and offerings and help us to worship you in spirit and in truth as we dedicate the fruits of our labor for the advancement of your kingdom. Through Jesus Christ, our Lord. Amen.

Introduction

Have you ever wanted to be an ophthalmologist? An ophthalmologist is a physician who specializes in the treatment of the eyes. He seeks to prevent disease that afflicts the eyes and to eliminate diseases that are destroying one's eyesight. He seeks to improve the ability of his patients to see. There are times when by surgery he is the means for the recovery of sight.

To restore sight to a blind person is to open up for him many new worlds: new avenues of instruction, usefulness, and delight.

I. There are three major types of blindness.

A. *Physical blindness.* Erasmus said, "In the country of the blind the one-eyed man is king." The Lion's Club is a service club that has encouraged its members to donate their old glasses and will their eyes for the benefit of the blind. Many people have been able to recover physical eyesight because of the activities of this service club.

B. *Mental blindness.* There are none so blind as those who will not see. Some are mentally blind because of a closed mind or because of prejudice. Some are mentally blind because they have never opened their eyes to see the world about them.

C. *Spiritual blindness.* Jesus dealt repeatedly with the problem of spiritual blindness. He declared that only the pure in heart could really see God (Matt. 5:8) and that a divided loyalty made it impossible for one to see clearly (6:22–23). John declared that hatred causes one to dwell in the darkness of spiritual blindness (1 John 2:11).

II. The nature and results of spiritual blindness.

A. *Unawareness.* He who has never looked through a microscope knows little of that which is very small. He who has never looked through a telescope is unaware of much that is present in the universe. He who has never seen an X-ray film cannot fully understand what is on the inside of a person. He who has never utilized the eye of the soul is blind to the spiritual reality in our world.

B. *Distortion.* We are familiar with the story in which one blind man felt of an elephant's side and described him as being like a wall. Another blind man felt of one of the elephant's legs and described the elephant as being like a tree. The third blind man felt the elephant's tail and described him as being like a rope. They had a distorted image of what an elephant is like. He who is spiritually blind has a distorted concept of God, self, life, and others.

C. *Darkness.* How dark is the world of the blind man? To dwell in perpetual darkness is a fate that none of us covets, but to live in eternal darkness is a far worse fate.

III. Christ wants to open our eyes and help us to see.

A. *He wants to open our eyes and help us to see that God is a God of love, grace, and mercy.*

B. *He wants to open our eyes and help us to see the deadly nature of sin.*

C. *He wants to open our eyes and help us to see that the abundant life is a life of unselfish devoted giving of self for the welfare of others.*

D. *He wants to open our eyes and help us to see the need of an unsaved world for the good news of Jesus Christ.*

E. *He wants to open our eyes and help us to see the spiritual resources that are available to those who walk by faith and who seek to live a life of loving obedience.* Paul declared, "Eye hath not seen, nor ear heard, neither have entered into the heart of man, the things which God hath prepared for them that love him" (1 Cor. 2:9). Some have quoted this as referring to the blessings and the joys that heaven holds for the redeemed. A closer examination will reveal that it describes the present experience of those who are followers of Christ and who are sensitive to the leadership and guidance of the Holy Spirit (1 Cor. 2:10). Christ continues to open the eyes of those who will let him.

IV. Christ wants to remove the blindfolds that keep people in a life of unbelief (2 Cor. 4:4).

Paul was grieved over the fact that many were blind to the glorious gospel of Jesus Christ. Because of their spiritual blindness, they were either neglecting or refusing to put their faith and trust in Jesus Christ as Lord and Savior.

Of the evil work that Satan does, perhaps the most devilish is that in which he blindfolds the minds of people lest the light of the glorious gospel of Christ should shine into them that they might be saved. Satan seeks to blindfold the minds of people to a number of different facts and truths.

A. *People are blind to the lostness of their own souls.*

B. *People are blind to the emptiness of life without God.*

C. *People are blind to the hopelessness of self-effort to redeem themselves.*

D. *People are blind to the brevity of life and to the length of eternity.*

E. *People are blind to their need for new life and the grace to live for God and others.*

F. *People are blind to the wonders of God's love and to the greatness of the salvation that he offers to them through Jesus Christ.*

Conclusion

The worst blindness that one can know is spiritual blindness. Through the preaching of the gospel, God wants to open our eyes to the wonders of his grace. Through those who live the love of God and demonstrate the spirit of Jesus Christ, he wants to open our eyes to the truly good life.

Let us devotionally study God's Holy Word and pray that he will open our eyes to see his wonderful plan for our lives.

If you have been living in spiritual blindness, Christ wants to enable you to recover the sight that will make it possible for you to see God, trust him, and love him. Follow the sight that you have, and trust him with the faith that you have.

SUNDAY EVENING, MAY 29

Title: Go the Second Mile

Text: "And whosoever shall compel thee to go a mile, go with him twain. Give to him that asketh thee, and from him that would borrow of thee turn not thou away" **(Matt. 5:41–42).**

Scripture Reading: Matthew 5:33–48

Introduction

Two Christian men were arguing with each other. A disagreement had begun in their profession that seeped through to their community, family, and church life.

"Look," said the first, "I have bent over backwards to settle this thing; I have gone the second and now the third mile, but you won't come an inch to meet me!"

The other man said he had already gone two miles. Yet they were miles apart. In fact, they were not even within shouting distance of each other. The truth is that neither had gone the first mile, for when one walks the first mile with Christ, he becomes a candidate for the second mile.

I. Background of the second mile.

A. *Roman requirements.* There is an interesting picture in our Lord's command to go "the second mile." The Roman government had authorized all of its civil service workers, postmen, and soldiers to commandeer free labor anywhere on the highway to help carry their baggage. They were limited to requiring one mile of baggage carrying per person.

B. *Jewish rebellion.* Most Jews had driven a stake one mile from their home. In case they were commanded to carry a burden for a mile, they would know exactly when their duty was done. How it must have surprised Jesus' hearers when he told them to go the second mile.

II. Signposts along the second mile.

As one walks the second mile, there are some signposts to Christian living that he will note.

A. *Live above the law.* A man once made a journey to a distant community on an unusual mission. He had been a failure in business nine years before in the very same community. At the time, he had settled all accounts at fifty cents on the dollar and had been declared free of any legal obligations from his creditors. Because of the embarrassment of it all, he finally moved away.

During the nine-year period from the time he left, he worked as hard as possible. He saved everything he could. Then he took his strange journey back to his hometown. For several days he moved from house to house, store to store, and office to office, carrying his notebook of accounts. Dollar per dollar he paid the legally forgiven debts. To each creditor, he declared that he was operating under grace, not just law. There was a written law on the table of his heart more apparent than the law on the statute books at the courthouse. He completed these transactions because of the inner prompting of his soul, not because of fear.

The Christian lives under grace, not law. The requirements of law are "The wages of sin is death" and "The soul that sinneth, it shall die" (Rom. 6:23; Ezek. 18:4). But the grace of God goes beyond law (Eph. 2:8–9) and declares that "the gift of God is eternal life through Jesus Christ our Lord" (Rom. 6:23).

B. *Do more than "your duty."* A man was quite impressed by a bus driver on a city bus. He noted that he was unusually courteous to everyone. Finally, he moved up close to the driver to compliment him on his courtesy.

"Well," explained the driver, "about five years ago I read in the paper about a man who was included in a will just because he was polite. I thought this just might happen to me. So I started treating passengers like people. It made me feel so good that I enjoyed doing it. Now I honestly do not care whether or not I am mentioned in anyone's will."

The bus driver had learned the joy of going beyond his duty. Admittedly he had started wrong, but his motives were purified along the second mile.

C. *Go beyond the minimum requirements.* Many people do just enough on their jobs to keep from getting fired. But the real joy of Christian living comes when one goes beyond the minimum and shoots for the maximum.

When the Jews in Jesus' day went just one mile, they continued to embitter their lives by hating the Romans, but when they went the second mile, they conquered the power of Rome and their own self-centeredness.

Conclusion

Mr. Chen, a member of a Taiwanese Baptist Chapel in Pingtung, Taiwan, was advised by his lawyer to testify in court that his friend had stolen his motorcycle. The truth of the matter, however, was that Mr. Chen's friend had borrowed the motorcycle and had not returned it. In court Mr. Chen testified, "I loaned my motorcycle to my friend, and he hasn't returned it." Later he said, "Being a Christian cost me my motorcycle, but I found peace."

Strangely enough, peace is always found along the road of the second mile.

JUNE

■ **Sunday Mornings**

The theme this month is "Living without Regrets." On the third Sunday of the month, feature a Father's Day message.

■ **Sunday Evenings**

Continue the messages based on the Sermon on the Mount. This month's messages focus on the Christian's motives for service.

■ **Wednesday Evenings**

Begin the series "The Person and Work of the Holy Spirit."

WEDNESDAY EVENING, JUNE 1

Title: The Person of the Holy Spirit

Text: "No one who is speaking by the Spirit of God says, 'Jesus be cursed,' and no one can say, 'Jesus is Lord,' except by the Holy Spirit" **(1 Cor. 12:3 NIV).**

Scripture Reading: 1 Corinthians 12:1–11

Introduction

The Holy Spirit is the third person of the Trinity. He is first mentioned in the Bible in Genesis 1:2: "And the Spirit of God moved upon the face of the waters."

Dr. Herschel H. Hobbs has pointed out that the Holy Spirit is the most neglected member of the Trinity. "There are six reasons for this neglect. (1) The doctrine of the Holy Spirit is difficult to understand: 'But the natural man receiveth not the things of the Spirit of God: ... neither can he know them, because they are spiritually discerned' (1 Cor. 2:14). (2) The Holy Spirit is placed third in the Trinity (Father, first; Son, second; Holy Spirit, third). Thus we unknowingly relegate Him to a place of unimportance. (3) There is also a tendency to refer to the Holy Spirit as 'it.' To speak of a person as 'it' makes of him a nonentity. (4) Emotional excesses of some tend to defame the Holy Spirit. (5) There is a fear of sin against the Holy Spirit. For this reason men avoid Him. (6) The use in the King James Version of Holy Ghost is unfortunate. In A.D. 1611 *ghost* meant spirit; today it means the spirit of a dead person or 'haunt'" (*Fundamentals of Our Faith* [Nashville: Broadman, 1960], 51–52).

Dr. R. A. Torrey said, "Any one who does not know the Holy Spirit as a person has not attained unto a complete and well-rounded Christian experience" (*The Holy Spirit* [London: Revell, 1927], 12).

It is imperative that we understand that the Holy Spirit is a person and that we know him as a person. Let us look at some reasons for believing that the Holy Spirit is a person.

I. Designations proper to personality are given the Holy Spirit.
A. *The Holy Spirit is referred to as "he" and not "it" (John 14:26; 15:26; 16:7–8).*
B. *The use of the word "Comforter" in John 14:16–18 indicates that he is a person.* The word "Comforter" cannot be translated "comfort." It cannot be taken as an abstract influence. The Holy Spirit comforts us because he is our Advocate, Instructor, and Helper.

II. The use of the Holy Spirit's name in connection with other persons implies personality.
A. *The Holy Spirit's name is used with Christ.*
B. *The Holy Spirit's name is used with Christians (Acts 15:28).*
C. *The Holy Spirit's name is used with the Father and the Son.* The Great Commission commands baptism in the name of the Father, Son, and Holy Spirit (Matt. 28:19). Paul clearly distinguishes Father, Son, and Holy Spirit (2 Cor. 13:14). The source of blessings for believers comes from Father, Son, and Holy Spirit (1 Cor. 12:4–6).

III. The Holy Spirit possesses the characteristics of personality.
A. *The Holy Spirit knows as a person (1 Cor. 2:10–11).*
B. *The Holy Spirit wills as a person (Eph. 4:11–14).*
C. *The Holy Spirit feels as a person (Rom. 8:27).*
D. *The Holy Spirit loves as a person (Rom. 15:30).*
E. *The Holy Spirit speaks as a person (John 15:26; Acts 13:2; 16:6–10).*

IV. The Holy Spirit is affected by the acts of others.
A. *One may grieve the Holy Spirit (Eph. 4:30).*
B. *One may quench the Holy Spirit (1 Thess. 5:19).*
C. *One may lie to the Holy Spirit (Acts 5:3–4, 9).*
D. *One may resist the Holy Spirit (Acts 7:51).*
E. *One may insult the Holy Spirit (Heb. 10:29).*
F. *One may blaspheme the Holy Spirit (Matt. 12:31).*
G. *One may receive the Holy Spirit (John 20:22).*

V. The Holy Spirit acts as only a person can act.
The Holy Spirit works to makes us the right kind of person. He guides us (John 16:13), reproves us (John 16:8), strives with us (Gen. 6:3), helps us

(Acts 1:8), comforts us (John 14:16–18, 26; Acts 9:31), and prays for us (Rom. 8:26–27). He searches the deep things of God and reveals them to us (1 Cor. 2:10).

Conclusion

When the Holy Spirit deals with us, it is a personal power, not an impersonal influence or power. God help us to follow the leadership of the Holy Spirit!

SUNDAY MORNING, JUNE 5

Title: Give Them the Flowers Now

Text: "But Jesus said, 'Let her alone; why do you trouble her? She has done a beautiful thing to me'" (**Mark 14:6 RSV**).

Scripture Reading: Mark 14:3–9

Hymns: "God Who Touchest Earth with Beauty," Edgar

            "Joyful, Joyful, We Adore Thee," Van Dyke

            "More Like the Master," Gabriel

Offertory Prayer: O God, who has permitted us to see this new day and to greet its light in your house, we know not what to render to you for all your benefits. We confess that often in the enjoyment of your gifts we forget the Giver. May our hearts never be so carried away by material success that we make idols of wealth, station, or pleasure, and in striving after them become estranged from you. Help us, Lord, to be more fervent in our devotion to your service, more faithful to our duties, and more helpful to our fellow humans. Through Jesus Christ, our Lord. Amen.

Introduction

Often at a funeral service we look upon a display of flowers — potted plants, cut flowers, and artificial floral arrangements sent by loved ones and friends to pay tribute to the memory of the deceased. The thought comes often to some of us: "What joy and gladness these flowers might have brought to our deceased friend who needed encouragement and friendship in his latter years."

Leigh Hodge wrote:

> *What to closed eyes are kind sayings?*
> *What to hushed heart is deep vow?*
> *Naught can avail after parting,*
> *So give them the flowers now.*

And Berton Braley expressed the same thought in words which you probably have heard:

If you think that praise is due him,
Now's the time to slip it to him,
For he cannot read his tombstone
When he's dead.

Proverbs 25:11 says, "A word fitly spoken is like apples of gold in pictures of silver." It is important to know when to speak and how to speak words of encouragement. The ministry of fitly spoken words includes the tone of voice, the expression of the eyes, the lines of the mouth, and other body language.

Sometimes the "Give them the flowers now" spirit can be carried out in deeds better than words. An example of this is found in the woman's anointing of Jesus with expensive perfume (Mark 14:2–9). The woman expressed her love in an extravagant manner in an hour of the Master's greatest need—just before his arrest.

I. Let us examine this bouquet.

Let us take these flowers in hand, as it were, and look at them. Jesus was in Bethany in the house of Simon, a rich Pharisee, for supper. As he was sitting at supper, an unusual thing happened. A woman came with a container of precious ointment. It was equal to a year's wages of a day laborer. It was customary to sprinkle a few drops of perfume on a guest when he arrived at the house or when he sat down to a meal, but this woman broke the container and poured the contents on Jesus' head.

The record gives the impression that Jesus was deeply stirred by the unmeasured generosity of her giving. "It was a glorious maximum of sacrifice which never stopped to calculate what might have been a passable minimum," someone observed. She didn't pour out a few drops and say, "Well, I guess that ought to be enough. That puts me in the 'average' category." Instead, she was lifted clear out of herself, refusing to let her devotion be smothered with caution and prudence. She was lifted clear out of arithmetic into love—one of the greatest leaps a person can ever take.

Some of those present said, "Why this waste? The perfume might have been sold for over 300 denarii, and the money given to the poor" (vv. 4–5 paraphrased). We should not be too harsh on these people. They were of limited means, and through hard experiences they had learned that frugality was a necessity. Their thoughts were conditioned by the issues and values of the marketplace.

Jesus replied, "Let her alone ... she has done a beautiful thing to me." He was deeply moved. The woman had given "her flowers now," and it was a thing of instantaneous beauty and joy.

II. Consider the need in our day for the exercise of this spirit.

There is a hard anonymity about modern life that tends to turn persons into mere cogs of a great machine or mere hands in a vast, impersonal crew. Persons are hungry for feeling wanted and appreciated.

Take, for instance, those whom we refer to as "public servants." Good government officials, school teachers and administrators, editors, radio and television personnel, ministers and denominational employees, and hosts of others often are taken for granted. One man has told of going to see the religion editor of a large newspaper. The editor bristled up in self-defense, and hardly realizing it, she asked, "What's wrong?" Her visitor replied, "Nothing is wrong. I just dropped in to thank you for the many favors you have done for our church and the good service you render to our community, and I wanted to tell you what a fine job you are doing." So accustomed to harsh criticism, the editor could hardly believe what she was hearing. Too many people are long on criticism and fault-finding, short on appreciation and the expression of that appreciation.

> *What to closed eyes are kind sayings?*
> *What to hushed heart is deep vow?*
> *Naught can avail after parting,*
> *So give them the flowers now.*

Conclusion

People are discouraged. They are discouraged with their failures or imagined failures, and they need a bracing word. The woman in the text probably had heard the Master speak a word of forgiveness and hope to some discouraged person, and she felt the same need. Having received it, she used her experience to bring blessings to others.

SUNDAY EVENING, JUNE 5

Title: "What Do Ye More Than Others?"

Text: "Ye have heard that it hath been said, Thou shalt love thy neighbour, and hate thine enemy. But I say unto you, Love your enemies, bless them that curse you, do good to them that hate you, and pray for them which despitefully use you, and persecute you; that ye may be the children of your Father which is in heaven: for he maketh his sun to rise on the evil and on the good, and sendeth rain on the just and on the unjust. For if ye love them which love you, what reward have ye? do not even the publicans the same? And if ye salute your brethren only, what do ye more than others? do not even the publicans so?" **(Matt. 5:43–47).**

Scripture Reading: 1 John 3:13–24

Introduction

Years ago at a base in West Germany, 252 United States soldiers were read the following statement: "We hold these truths to be self-evident, that all men are created equal, that they are endowed by their Creator with certain inalienable rights, that among these are life, liberty, and the pursuit of happiness."

The soldiers were not told that the sentence came from the Declaration of

Independence. They were told merely to sign the statement if they agreed with it and not to sign if they didn't. Seventy-three percent refused to sign.

The Berkshire County High School Student Union once conducted a similar experiment in Pittsfield, Massachusetts. The group circulated the First Amendment, explaining that they intended to submit it to Congress as a petition. The First Amendment, of course, guarantees to all United States citizens freedom of religion, speech, press, peaceable assembly, and the right "to petition the government for a redress of grievances." Of 1,154 persons polled, only 4 percent agreed with the statement; 35 percent disagreed, and 23 percent refused to commit themselves.

Here were some of the comments of adults to the student pollsters: "People like you make me sick." "I'll ask my husband." "I'd punch you in the mouth, but you're a girl." "I never sign anything." "I work for the federal government, so I can't comment." "No, the Constitution is all right the way it is." "Children should be seen, not heard."

We often are ignorant about great documents. Some may believe that the Old Testament actually teaches, "Thou shalt love thy neighbor and hate thine enemy." However, this was merely the Pharisees' interpretation of the Old Testament. Nowhere in the Old or New Testament does one find this admonition. Our Lord used this mistaken interpretation to illustrate true Christian love.

I. The need for Christian love.

A great philosopher who once spoke in New York amazed all who heard when he said, "The root of the matter is a very simple and old-fashioned thing, a thing so simple I am ashamed to mention it for fear of derisive smiles with which cynics will greet my words. The thing we need is love—Christian love. If we could have this, we would have a motive for existence, a guide for action, and a reason for courage."

Why did these words cause such excitement? They were not spoken in a church, and the speaker claimed to be an atheist!

II. Love—the mark of a Christian.

How shall people know that you are a Christian? By the fact that you belong to a certain church? By your orthodoxy? By your stewardship of possessions? Jesus indicated that none of these important traits proves that one is a disciple of Jesus Christ. He said, "By this all men will know that you are my disciples, if you love one another" (John 13:35 NIV).

A. *Four words for love.* The Greeks had four words for love. *Storge* described the love between children and parents. *Eros* described the love between husband and wife. *Philia* described the warm, tender affection that one friend had for another. *Agape*, the Greek word used in the New Testament to describe Christian love, is difficult to translate but is probably best translated "self-giving devotion and dedication to God and man."

The first three words describe a love that comes naturally. Parents and children automatically love each other. A man and a woman are said to "fall in love" as if they have no control over this natural impulse. Close friends are naturally affectionate toward each other. But Christian love is a love that we have to work at. It is a love that turns the other cheek and goes the second mile, that forgets about one's own feelings and rights, and that concentrates so much on giving that it forgets about getting.

B. *Loving the unlovely.* Our Lord admonished us to bless those who curse us. This means that we are to reply to bitter words with kind words and return good deeds for cruel deeds.

We are to pray for those who despitefully use us and persecute us. In prayer we analyze one's actions and say, "Why does this person act this way? What is it in his background that makes him this way?"

In prayer we take our burdens to the Lord and leave them there. A well-known doctor has indicated that the verbal expression of animosity toward others causes a certain biological reaction within our bodies that can ultimately cause disease. He believes that many diseases develop when we "fatten grudges by rehearsing them in the presence of others."

Christian love loves the unlovely. A Christian's love for others never depends on what they are. It never depends on what others do *to* the Christian nor what they do *for* him.

We are never any more like God than when we are loving (1 John 4:7–11).

III. How to live by Christian love.

How does one live the love life?

A. *By dying to self.* In the new birth, one dies to self. The more selfless one becomes, the more he learns to love other people.

A society lady went to a psychotherapist, who said, "Tell me all about yourself." For several weeks she made her weekly visit and told him everything. The psychotherapist finally told her, "Madam, I can do no more for you now. I advise you to take the first train to Niagara Falls and take a long, lingering look at something bigger than yourself."

B. *By forgiving and forgetting.* The key to the apostle Paul's life was that he was able to "forget those things which are behind" (Phil. 3:13).

After the death of Abraham Lincoln, Mrs. Lincoln asked John F. Parker, the deceased president's bodyguard, "Why were you not at the door to keep the assassin out?"

Parker bowed his head and said, "I have bitterly repented it. I did not believe anyone would try to kill so good a man. The belief made me careless. I became so interested in the play, I failed to see the assassin enter the presidential box."

"You should have seen him. You had no right to be careless," said Mrs. Lincoln, covering her face with her hands and weeping uncontrollably.

Recovering her composure, she said to Parker, "Go now. It's not you I can't forgive. It's the assassin."

Tad Lincoln, who had overheard his mother, said, "If Pa had lived, he would have forgiven the man who shot him. Pa forgave everybody."

Conclusion

Jesus Christ makes the difference in every life. Through him one can do more than others. Without Christ, one is bound to the code of the Pharisees and scribes: "Love those who love you and hate those who hate you."

WEDNESDAY EVENING, JUNE 8

Title: The Work of the Holy Spirit

Text: "When he is come, he will reprove the world of sin, and of righteousness, and of judgment: of sin, because they believe not on me; of righteousness, because I go to my Father, and ye see me no more; of judgment, because the prince of this world is judged" **(John 16:8–11)**.

Scripture Reading: John 16:1–15

Introduction

The great English preacher Charles Haddon Spurgeon "once preached what in his judgment was one of his poorest sermons. He stammered and floundered, and when he got through he felt that it had been a complete failure. He was greatly humiliated, and when he got home he fell on his knees and said, 'Lord, God, Thou canst do something with nothing. Bless that poor sermon.' And all through the week he uttered that prayer. He woke up in the night and prayed about it. He determined that the next Sunday he would redeem himself by preaching a great sermon. Sure enough, the next Sunday the sermon went off beautifully. At the close the people crowded about him and covered him with praise. Spurgeon went home pleased with himself, and that night he slept like a baby. But he said to himself, 'I'll watch the results of those two sermons.' What were they? From the one that seemed a failure he was able to trace forty-one conversions. And from that magnificent sermon he was unable to discover that a single soul was saved. Spurgeon's explanation was that the Spirit of God used the one and did not use the other" (Walter B. Knight, *Knight's Master Book of New Illustrations* [Grand Rapids: Eerdmans, 1956], 288).

God pity the Christian who tries to do the Lord's work without the ministry of the Holy Spirit. We can do nothing without him. Yet there are those who depend on other things rather than the work of the Holy Spirit. Some depend on logic, eloquent salesmanship, organization, psychology, impressive ritual, or emotionalism.

It is dubious that anyone should try to separate the work of God the Father, God the Son, and God the Holy Spirit. Yet it seems that the work of the Holy Spirit is clearly indicated in the New Testament.

I. The work of the Holy Spirit in relation to the Word of God.

A. *The Holy Spirit inspired people to write the Word of God (2 Tim. 3:16; 2 Peter 1:21).*

B. *The Holy Spirit instructs in the Word of God (1 Cor. 2:10–12).*

C. *The Holy Spirit imparts power in communicating the truth of the Word of God to others (1 Cor. 2:4–5; 1 Thess. 1:5).*

II. The work of the Holy Spirit in relation to the sinner.

A. *The Holy Spirit convicts of sin (John 16:8–11).*

B. *The Holy Spirit makes sinners new (Titus 3:5–6).*

C. *The Holy Spirit works through Christians to bring the gospel to the sinner (Acts 8:29–38).*

III. The work of the Holy Spirit in relation to the Christian.

The work of the Holy Spirit with the child of God is manifold: he assures (Rom. 8:16; Gal. 4:5–6), he seals (Eph. 1:13–14; 4:30), he imparts joy and comfort (John 14:16, 18), he strengthens (Eph. 3:16), he guides (John 16:13), he makes people Christlike (Gal. 5:22–23), he fills the heart with the love of God (Rom. 5:5), he teaches believers to pray aright (Rom. 8:26–27), he leads in acceptable worship (Eph. 5:18–20), he gives liberty (2 Cor. 3:17), and he imparts power to witness (Acts 1:8).

IV. The work of the Holy Spirit in relation to the church.

A. *He adds members to the church (Acts 2:47).*

B. *He instructs what to teach and preach (1 Cor. 2:12–13).*

C. *He maintains harmony (Acts 2:46–47).*

D. *He imparts different gifts for the Lord's work (1 Cor. 12:8–11).*

E. *He appoints and sends out ministers (Matt. 9:38; Acts 13:2–3; 15:27–28; 20:28).*

Conclusion

The work of the Holy Spirit is all-important. Let us be attentive to the workings of the Holy Spirit and follow his leadership in all things.

SUNDAY MORNING, JUNE 12

Title: A Stern Schoolmaster

Text: "It is good for me that I have been afflicted; that I might learn thy statutes" (**Ps. 119:71**).

Scripture Reading: Ps. 119:65–72

Hymns: "Have Faith in God," McKinney

"In the Hour of Trial," Montgomery

"Jesus, Saviour, Pilot Me," Hopper

"Jesus, I My Cross Have Taken," Lyte

Offertory Prayer: Heavenly Father, into your loving hands we again dedicate our time, talents, and energies. At the same time we lay at your feet our symbols of honesty to you — our tithes — and the symbols of our love — our offerings. Accept these symbols as representative of our renewed dedication to your kingdom's great outreach. In the name of Jesus Christ, our Savior, we make this prayer. Amen.

Introduction

Life is not always a bed of roses; in fact, it seldom is. But life has a way of molding us into creatures who are either spiritually mellow and golden or else hardened and bitter. I like to think that life is a schoolmaster that brings out the best in people, especially Christians. The adversities in the pathway of a Christian's life are the chastisements that discipline and ultimately mold him into a vessel of adequate service. We cannot help but think of Helen Keller, unable as a small child to communicate either by sight or sound, as a marvel of the century, as a person who transformed her tragic handicap into a blessing for the rest of the world. Edgar Helms, founder of Goodwill Industries, found defeat in his chosen field of politics, but he found his real life by losing it in service to the handicapped people of the world. The apostle Paul, as a young student of Gamaliel, dreamed of the day when he might become the head of the Sanhedrin, but due to the "adversity" of a dramatic personal experience with the Lord Jesus on the road to Damascus, he gave his life to the very Person whose followers he had formerly persecuted. As a result of this "adversity," Paul led in spreading the gospel through the then-known world. The psalmist is speaking in this text of something that he had learned from the hindsight of a mellowed life of faith.

I. The psalmist's former life (v. 67).

He reminisces over his early life, shaking his head sadly over the way he had conducted himself and over his attitude toward his personal and spiritual life. He says, "I went astray."

A. *The psalmist's early fleshly life.* He was carefree and headstrong. Physically speaking, his life was typical of the teenage days when one feels that life is just begging to be lived and when anything that may present barriers must be rebelled against. He had probably gone astray from the wishes of parents, the mores of society, and the will of God in order to have his pleasure for a moment.

B. *The psalmist's early spiritual life.* Spiritually speaking, his feeling represents for us that stage of rebellion against God so characteristic of unregenerate man. Thus the psalmist was saying that in his former life he had been carefree of any responsibility to God. He had followed the will of pleasure rather than the will of God. In his early life he had gone astray in that he was so busy with the seeking of pleasure, with the "keeping up with the Joneses," and with good — but not best — activities, that he had ruled God out of his thinking.

II. Affliction made a change in the psalmist's life (v. 71).

It is truly a wise man who can look back over his life and realize that the seeming catastrophes along life's journey have actually been stepping-stones to the richer and fuller life that he now enjoys. The psalmist is grateful to God for the afflictions that have beset his journey through life, for they have been the cause of his turning back from going astray, and they have been the elements of teaching whereby he has learned the great lessons of physical and spiritual life.

A. *Through affliction the psalmist recognized a higher power.* Affliction taught him that there is power greater than himself. Strong-willed humans are too often of the opinion that they are self-sufficient. The psalmist indicates in verses 67 and 71 that such may have been his case. Affliction brought him to his knees before his God.

B. *God spoke to the psalmist through the voice of affliction.* He realized that God sometimes speaks to humans in harsh ways in order to draw them back into *the way.* Disasters such as tornadoes, floods, or hurricanes may well be allowed to happen by God's permissive will to cause people to think seriously of their own spiritual condition and to come to that point of surrendering their stubborn wills to the loving, cleansing power of the Lord. Affliction is God's shepherd dog to drive us back to the fold.

C. *Affliction caused spiritual growth.* An untempered blade may easily break when first tried. An unpolished stone lacks beauty and may actually be used as a dangerous instrument. The afflictions of life have a way of giving a Christian spiritual insight into life. Robert Leighton has well said, "Adversity is the diamond dust Heaven polished its jewels with."

III. Fruits of affliction.

In the golden years of life old schoolteachers like to reminisce over bygone days and see in their mind's eye the parade of pupils who have passed in and out of their classrooms. They delight to hear from time to time of the accomplishments of their former pupils. These accomplishments are in part due to the fruits of their labor over the years. The psalmist discussed in this great spiritual poem the fruits of affliction in his life, fruits that may well coincide with those in our own lives.

A. *Afflictions made a believer out of the psalmist.* He said, "I have believed thy commandments" (v. 66). Some years ago I stood beside the hospital bed of one of the men of our city. He had been steadily growing worse in spite of all the knowledge and skill of medical science. He looked up at me and said, "It's a shame that it took this to draw me to the Lord, but I have certainly come to accept him." Life's great afflictions may be necessary to make believers out of sinful people.

B. *The lesson from affliction caused the psalmist now to be able to keep God's Word (v. 67).* This stern schoolmaster, affliction, caused the psalmist to realize the necessity of a life centered in the Word of God and the necessity of keeping God's commandments. I once knew a sensuous young man who lived for the pleasures of each day. One day while in a drunken stupor he was instrumental in causing the driver of the automobile in which he was riding to wreck the vehicle and be killed. This proved to be such a sobering experience that he changed completely from that way of life to a new way of life in Christ Jesus. So thorough was his conversion that now he is a faithful Christian who is highly respected in his church and community. Today, remembering the past, he lives by the commandments of God.

C. *Now the psalmist had a desire to know more about God's Word.* "Teach me thy statutes," cried this poet of God (v. 68). In gratitude to God for the salvation of his soul, the new Christian instinctively cries out:

> *More about Jesus would I know,*
> *More of His grace to others show,*
> *More of His saving fullness see,*
> *More of His love who died for me.*

D. *Affliction caused the psalmist to take great delight in God's law (v. 70).* He found great delight in the study of God's law and in fellowship with God. Obviously his prayer life increased in quality after affliction had mellowed his spiritual life to the extent that he came to find such deep and abiding pleasure in the knowledge of God's law. Nels F. S. Ferré tells of an experience in a chapel service at his seminary. " 'I have come to the seminary to learn to pray,' said 'Mother Alice' Kahokuoluna of the Kalaupapa Leper Colony speaking in chapel. 'That is my biggest need as I face my situation.... Before the missionaries came to Hawaii,... my people used to sit outside their temples for a long time meditating and preparing themselves before entering. Then they would virtually creep to the altar to offer their petition and afterward would again sit a long time outside, this time to "breathe life" into their prayers. The Christians, when they came, just got up, uttered a few sentences, said, "Amen," and were done. For that reason my people called them *haolis*, "without breath," or those who fail to breathe life into their prayers' " (*Strengthening the Spiritual Life* [New York: Harper & Row, 1951], 13). The psalmist had learned through affliction to find pleasure in waiting on the Lord; he did not rush through his spiritual exercises.

E. *Affliction gave the psalmist a new sense of values.* "The law of thy mouth is better unto me than thousands of gold and silver" (v. 72). How beautiful are the smiles that twinkle from the wrinkled faces of our elder saints! As one gazes on these smiling faces, one sees the afflictions of long years of life, afflictions that have done more than put wrinkles in their faces, afflictions that have caused them to be able to smile because of a faith mellowed through life's trials.

Some years ago there was an older couple in our church who had not had an easy life, but they had always had their love for each other and their faith in the Lord, which had brought them through. One day the husband was told by the doctor that he had a malignancy; as a result, all of his nose had to be removed. This necessitated much painful and tedious plastic surgery to restore a semblance of normal features. Shortly thereafter the wife had a stroke and was confined to the bed for many months. The husband was the main "nurse" to care for her during that long period prior to her death. Through all of this time he was able to smile and reassure us that his faith was still bright and that the Lord was the one who was giving him strength for each hour. His sense of eternal spiritual values kept him on an even keel during all that time. Affliction, when understood from God's viewpoint, teaches us that spiritual values are far more to be desired than material values.

Conclusion

The psalmist learned much from the afflictions of life and became a much better person because of them. This morning are you examining your heart concerning your afflictions? Do you see them as blessings instead of curses? Do you realize that God is endeavoring to speak to you through them and to draw you back into *the way* and to cause you to be of more value in kingdom service than ever before? Some here who are not yet Christ followers need to realize that that disturbing feeling in your hearts may be the convicting power of God's Holy Spirit afflicting you, urging you to turn from your sins to salvation. If you feel such a sensation in your heart this morning, won't you let Christ come into your heart and life as Savior and Lord?

SUNDAY EVENING, JUNE 12

Title: "Be Ye Therefore Perfect"

Text: "Be ye therefore perfect, even as your Father which is in heaven is perfect" (Matt. 5:48).

Scripture Reading: Ephesians 4:1–13

Introduction

Many have read and reread today's text and asked, "Did Jesus really say that?" Others read it, understand it, and ask, "Did Jesus really mean what he said?" Through the years there have been many reactions to this verse. It has been glorified, denied, explained away, and ignored. But let us meet it head-on and be quick to assert that Jesus Christ expects perfection!

I. An impossible possibility.

In the same breath, however, let us also declare that perfection is impossible. It is one of the "impossible possibilities" of the Christian life.

A. *Trying the impossible.* One of the secrets of the Christian life is that we continue trying to do that which we know we can never fully accomplish.
B. *What perfection is not.* Just what does it mean to be perfect? It means more than merely cleaning up the outward symptoms of sin in one's life. It means more than going without a cigarette for thirty days, knocking the drinking habit, or abstaining from the use of profanity. Although these would be worthy goals for any life (and would be victories for many), they do not communicate the full meaning of our Lord's words when he said, "Be ye therefore perfect."
C. *Perfection in love.* To be sure, our Lord was discussing perfection in love. He was indicating that our love should be like God's love. However, he was implying that Christians should maintain a holy dissatisfaction between what they are and what they ought to be.

II. A desire to be perfect.

Oliver Cromwell once said, "He who stops being better stops being good."

A. *When a man is saved, he tastes of perfection and is thereby given the desire for perfection.* One of the secrets of the Christian life is that we "hunger and thirst after righteousness." One never hungers or thirsts for something he has never tasted.

The cheetah is one of the fastest animals alive. It has been clocked at a speed of seventy miles an hour. One of the interesting features of the cheetah is his determination. When mealtime comes, he spots an animal that he plans to kill and eat. He starts running toward that one animal. Of course, it runs from him. He may chase it for hours, but he never takes his eyes off that one animal until he catches it. Several other animals might be easier to catch, but he never turns aside from the one he is chasing.

B. *The Christian should be just as determined as he moves toward perfection in the Christian life.* The English statesman Joseph Chamberlain once said that his favorite verse was Genesis 12:5, "They went forth to go into the land of Canaan; and into the land of Canaan they came." From this verse Chamberlain claimed two qualifications for success: (1) Have a goal for which you start, and (2) keep on going after you have started.
C. *Salvation makes us uncomfortable in sin.* One of the marks of a Christian is that he cannot sin and enjoy it. Once he has been saved, he hungers for perfection.

III. An effort to accomplish your purpose for being.

The Greek word translated "perfect" in our text is *teleios.* It means to realize the purpose for which something is planned.

One is perfect who fully realizes his purpose for being created and sent into this world. In the Greek language, an animal without spots that was suited for sacrifice was called *teleos*. A student who had mastered a subject was called *teleos* as over against a learner who was just beginning to master his subject.

IV. Total surrender to Jesus Christ.

Jesus told the rich young ruler, "If you want to be perfect, go, sell your possessions and give to the poor" (Matt. 19:21 NIV). Our Lord was not teaching that the surrender of possessions would make one perfect. He was teaching that one must be willing to give up everything for his Christian faith.

Our Lord admonishes us to get rid of past sins and to commit the future to him. Total surrender is one of the first steps to perfection.

Conclusion

Our text is not looking to the present or the past. Our Lord says, "Be ye." He is not saying, "From here on out, try to be perfect." He is calling for a perfection that no one can really attain. He is speaking of the glory of a faith that we cannot live up to. A great symphony conductor once said, "We try only music that is so great it really can't be played."

Jesus calls us from the sins, failures, difficulties, and disappointments of the past and the present to a life of service in the future.

He challenges us to ask three questions.

1. Do I have the desire to be perfect?
2. Have I found my purpose in life?
3. Have I totally surrendered my life to Jesus Christ?

Then, he declares, "Be ye perfect."

WEDNESDAY EVENING, JUNE 15

Title: The Fruit of the Holy Spirit

Text: "But the fruit of the Spirit is love, joy, peace, longsuffering, gentleness, goodness, faith, meekness, temperance: against such there is no law" **(Gal. 5:22–23).**

Scripture Reading: Galatians 5:16–26

Introduction

People out from under the control of the Holy Spirit produce works of the flesh. When people are not controlled by the Holy Spirit, their degenerate nature produces horrible evils: adultery, fornication, uncleanness, lasciviousness, idolatry, witchcraft, hatred, variance, emulations, wrath, strife, seditions, heresies, envyings, murders, drunkenness, and revelings. This catalog of evils is not exhaustive but only representative of the works of the flesh, of people out from under the control of the Holy Spirit.

On the other hand, when people's lives are controlled by the Holy Spirit, their lives are indeed beautiful. When they live in the Spirit, they walk in the Spirit. The fruit of their lives is love, joy, peace, longsuffering, gentleness, goodness, faith, meekness, and temperance.

The fruit of the Holy Spirit is not to be confused with the gifts of the Holy Spirit in 1 Corinthians 12:8–10—word of wisdom, word of knowledge, faith, healing, miracles, prophecy, discerning of spirits, tongues, and interpretation of tongues. Dr. W. A. Criswell has pointed out that "the ninefold gifts of the Spirit are for power, service, and ministry" (*The Holy Spirit in Today's World* [Grand Rapids: Zondervan, 1966], 191).

The fruit of the Spirit results when the child of God is under the control of the Holy Spirit. Dr. W. T. Conner said that the "fruit of the Spirit" is the natural result of the working of the Spirit in us and that "these ripened qualities of Christian character do not come so much by man's striving and energizing as they do by yielding oneself to the Lord" (*The Work of the Holy Spirit* [Nashville: Broadman, 1949], 117–18).

Let us take a brief look at the fruit of the Spirit:

I. The fruit of the Spirit is love.

Love heads the list of the nine graces that make up the fruit of the Spirit. Paul wrote, "And now these three remain: faith, hope and love. But the greatest of these is love" (1 Cor. 13:13 NIV). Jesus said, "By this all men will know that you are my disciples, if you love one another" (John 13:35 NIV). Again Paul said, "Hope does not disappoint us, because God has poured out his love into our hearts by the Holy Spirit, whom he has given us" (Rom. 5:5 NIV). Christians are living demonstrations of the love of God. They walk in love, and they manifest their love for God and for people in numerous ways.

Jesus tells us the greatest of all commandments are: "Thou shalt love the Lord thy God with all thy heart, and with all thy soul, and with all thy mind.... Thou shalt love thy neighbour as thyself" (Matt. 22:37, 39).

II. The fruit of the Spirit is joy.

Joy dwells in the Spirit-filled life. There can be no true Christian joy without the indwelling of the Holy Spirit. Happiness depends on happenings, but joy is the result of the indwelling of the Holy Spirit in our lives.

A. *There is joy in the salvation provided by Jesus (1 Thess. 1:6).*
B. *There is joy in serving Jesus (Acts 16:23–32).*
C. *There is joy in suffering for Jesus (James 1:2).*

III. The fruit of the Spirit is peace.

Paul said, "For the kingdom of God is not a matter of eating and drinking, but of righteousness, peace and joy in the Holy Spirit" (Rom. 14:17 NIV). When the Holy Spirit comes into a life, he gives peace to the soul in the midst of all external agitations. When the Holy Spirit takes control, calm comes into one's life instead of chaos.

IV. The fruit of the Spirit is patience.

The Holy Spirit will supply God's children with everything needed to make them effective servants. He will give them patience in the face of persecution, affliction, and distress. He will give them patience in their dealings with others and in their efforts to help those who are spiritually weak or are perishing in their sins. God help us to be patient toward those who need his help!

V. The fruit of the Spirit is gentleness.

Paul expressed the meaning of "gentleness" when he wrote: "Be ye kind one to another, tenderhearted, forgiving one another, even as God for Christ's sake hath forgiven you" (Eph. 4:32).

A. *The Holy Spirit would have us be gentle with our words.* Sharp and unkind words should not flow from our lips. The art of saying appropriate words in a gentle way is an art that never goes out of fashion. An unknown author has written:

> *Thoughts unexpressed,*
> *Fall to the earth dead.*
> *But Heaven itself can't recall them*
> *When once they're said.*

B. *The Holy Spirit would have us be gentle in the Lord's work.*
C. *The Holy Spirit would have us be gentle in witnessing.*

VI. The fruit of the Holy Spirit is goodness.

Barnabas is a good illustration of a good man. Luke wrote, "He was a good man, full of the Holy Spirit and faith" (Acts 11:24 NIV). The Holy Spirit makes us upright in heart and life. Every true Christian finds delight in goodness!

VII. The fruit of the Spirit is faith.

Faith is one of the gifts of the Holy Spirit (1 Cor. 12:9) and one of the graces of the Holy Spirit. Faith is given to us to do the work of God and is exhibited in our lives by the Holy Spirit. Christians are those who trust in God and are faithful to him.

VIII. The fruit of the Spirit is meekness.

Jesus said: "Blessed are the meek: for they shall inherit the earth" (Matt. 5:5). Meekness is not weakness. Meekness pictures a wild horse that has been tamed and is obedient to the one who holds the reins. Moses is a classic example of meekness (Num. 12:3).

IX. The fruit of the Holy Spirit is temperance.

Temperance means "one holding control" or "holding in." The word *temperance* covers the entire range of moral discipline. The fruit of the Spirit is a controlled life.

Conclusion

The fruit of the Spirit as described by Paul in Galatians 5:22–23 portrays Christ and the Christian. Are you a Spirit-filled person?

SUNDAY MORNING, JUNE 19

Title: A Father of God's Own Choosing

Text: "And God said, Sarah thy wife shall bear thee a son indeed; and thou shalt call his name Isaac: and I will establish my covenant with him for an everlasting covenant, and with his seed after him.... And he said, Take now thy son, thine only son Isaac, whom thou lovest, and get thee into the land of Moriah; and offer him there for a burnt offering upon one of the mountains which I will tell thee of" **(Gen. 17:19; 22:2).**

Scripture Reading: Genesis 17:15–19; 22:1–2

Hymns: "God, Our Father, We Adore Thee," Frazer

"Faith of Our Fathers," Faber

"I Am Coming to the Cross," McDonald

Offertory Prayer: Our gracious Master, in you we place our confidence daily, realizing that from you will come all of life's needs. In the past you have blessed us far more than we have deserved. In the present moments you are blessing us with refreshment of soul, and thus in the future we are confident that your blessings will be forthcoming. We offer to you a thank offering as a visible expression of our love and gratitude to you. Accept it, we pray, in the spirit in which we offer it. Amen.

Introduction

Abraham was a father of God's own choosing. He lived up to his role of father in a way uniquely illustrated in an episode with his young son as told in Genesis 22. Here we see all the emotions of a loving father who has his faith in the Lord tried and tested. On this Father's Day it would be good for us to study the life of this great father and see what there was in his life that would cause him to be a father of God's own choosing, a father who was to be the progenitor of God's covenant nation.

I. Abraham was a meek and humble man.

When we think of the words *meek* and *humble,* too often we think of the connotations "wimpy" or "easily walked on," but these are not the meanings the Bible gives. Moses is referred to as "very meek" (Num. 12:3). Humility or meekness denotes that Abraham was:

A. *Subservient to God.* He was a big man in that he was able to stoop low before his God. I like to think of every good father as being one who is humble before his God and subservient to him. He is one who is not ashamed to let the world know that he recognizes himself as being on a lower plane than the Divine Being, that he has surrendered to the lordship of almighty God in his heart and life.

B. *Concerned about the welfare of his fellow man.* In pointing up this characteristic in the life of Abraham, we have but to turn to two episodes:

1. When his cattle and the cattle of his nephew Lot became so numerous that it was difficult for both to subsist in the same area, it was decided that it would be best for the two to part company. Abraham gave Lot the first choice as to the area where he preferred to take his flock; he willingly took second choice.

2. When God announced to Abraham the impending doom of Sodom and Gomorrah, Abraham cried out for the safety of the righteous people who resided in the wicked twin cities. He continued to plead that these cities might be spared for the sake of the righteous in them, finally asking, even at the risk of angering God, if God would turn aside his wrath if only ten righteous people could be found there. Some would suggest that Abraham's only concern was for his nephew Lot, but the Scripture indicates that it was for all the righteous people found in those two wicked cities.

II. Abraham was a loving father.

Little is told in the sacred Scriptures of the early relationship between Abraham and his son Isaac. Reading between the lines, we are able to discern that Abraham wisely and deeply loved his child.

A. *Abraham loved his son wisely.* It is obvious from the text that it was not unusual for the father and his son to be together on trips away from the home tent, for the lad indicated no surprise or concern about this particular trip to a mountain in the land of Moriah (22:2) where they were to go to worship. If Isaac's father said that they should make the trip, there was no question in Isaac's mind concerning the rightness of the trip. Discipline by the father had created obedience on the part of Isaac. In this modern age, some children scarcely know what their father looks like, for he is seldom at home and almost never takes time out to be with them. In too many other cases, fathers of our generation are "absentee fathers," leaving child rearing to the mothers from whom they are divorced. A father must be on hand to teach obedience and to guide in proper principles of living. I once was told by the director of the Peninsula Boys' Club that the problem boys among the hundreds who attend his club are those from homes where no father is present. This is truly a tragedy of our age. It is a small wonder that juvenile delinquency is so prevalent in our day. Fathers who do not care enough about their children to be involved in their lives daily do not create trust in themselves.

B. *Abraham loved his son deeply.* A verbal picture containing great pathos is the scene of Abraham and Isaac trudging forlornly up the mountainside, Abraham's face revealing his heartbreak. Orders from God to sacrifice Isaac were ringing in his ears, mingled with the incessant chatter of the boy following behind. Abraham's love for the boy was pictured in his intense but silent grief. How could he slay his son whom he loved more than life itself? Was not this the son of promise? The son of his old age? His only "legitimate" son? The child who had brought such sunshine into the sunset years of his life? How he wished that the Lord had commanded him to offer up himself as a sacrifice instead of offering up Isaac! It was obvious to Abraham in these moments that God wanted him to offer up something dearer to him than his own life—his son Isaac.

III. Abraham was a father who gave preeminence to the Lord.

In our day too much of the religious training in the home is left up to mothers. As a result, Christianity sometimes, in its outward observance at least, gives the appearance of being only for women and children. A father is failing to live up to his God-given responsibility to his children if he does not take the lead in family worship, in promoting church attendance, and in teaching the Christian disciplines of life. Abraham was a devout follower of God, and he took the lead in family worship experiences. Abraham was a man of great faith.

A. *The test of Abraham's faith.* Before Abraham could meet the requirements of God concerning his being the father of the covenant nation, he had to pass a great test to determine if the Lord God was really on the throne of his heart and life. God said to Abraham, "Take now thy son, thine only son Isaac, whom thou lovest, and get thee into the land of Moriah; and offer him there for a burnt offering upon one of the mountains which I will tell thee of" (Gen. 22:2). What could come nearer turning a man's very soul inside out than this? Was God really on the throne in his heart? Or was his beloved son, Isaac, first in his heart's affections? Fathers in the congregation this morning, do you love the Lord God more than your sons and daughters? How great is your faith in and love for God?

B. *The results: God first, son second.* The greatness of Abraham's faith was revealed to God and to all humankind in that crucial hour on Mount Moriah. Abraham passed his great test with flying colors. Once and for all time it was settled for all posterity to know. Only when God saw that Abraham was actually obedient to his great command and that he, the Lord Jehovah, was actually preeminent in the heart and soul of Abraham, only then did he stay the downward swing of Abraham's arm and tell him to substitute a ram caught in the nearby bushes as his offering. How many of you fathers could pass that test this morning?

The fitness test for fatherhood at its best has not really changed from the day of Abraham; a man must love the Lord God first before he is fit to be the undershepherd of God to the children in his home. Otherwise he can never expect to guide them in the right way for and to the Lord.

Conclusion

This great man of God would leave in his wake many lessons for fathers of our day. Among these are the following: Every father should be humble in the sense that he would love the Lord God with all his heart, soul, and mind. Every father should unashamedly let his love be obvious to his children, allowing them to see his love for them in action as well as frequently telling them of his love for them. Every father should place God first before love of family or possessions. This heritage left by a good father will always be cherished in the hearts of his children.

SUNDAY EVENING, JUNE 19

Title: Theatrical Religion

Text: "Be careful not to do your 'acts of righteousness' before men, to be seen by them" (**Matt. 6:1 NIV**).

Scripture Reading: Matthew 6:1–18

Introduction

The Pharisees did all of their good works to be seen of men. The Greek word for to be "seen of men" is *theathanai*. It is the word from which we get our word *theater*. It means "to gaze upon." In the theater one gazes upon the actors on the stage. The actors are not really themselves; they are acting their parts. They are doing something to be seen by others. Thus the Pharisees' religion was "theatrical religion."

Certainly, our Lord commands his disciples to let their light shine before men, but the motive makes all the difference!

I. The actors—the Pharisees and the hypocrites.

T. S. Eliot wrote in *The Cocktail Party* that "half of the harm done in the world is due to people who want to feel important. They do not mean to do harm—the harm does not interest them because they are absorbed in the endless struggle to think well of themselves."

    A. *In Greek plays the actors wore false faces.* The word *hypocrite* comes from the Greek word for "mask." In the Greek plays, actors were at a minimum, so one actor would have to play several parts. He did this by changing his voice and putting on another mask. One actor might act the part of a woman, a man, a boy, and a girl in the course of one play. From the word that meant "the mask that the actors wore" comes the word *hypocrite*. It denotes "play-acting." The person is not actually the one whom he portrays; he is merely "playing like."

    B. *The hypocrite is a play actor in life.* His actions reflect not the motive of Christian love but the motive of self-glorification.

184

II. The audience—"Before men."

A. *Our Lord forbids us to perform our good deeds merely to gain attention and applause from others.*

B. *The Pharisees used religion as a means toward an end—their own glory.* The Christian is commanded to seek first the glory that God gives (John 5:44). We are to let our light shine before others but for a purpose other than self-glory—"that they may see your good works, and glorify your Father which is in heaven" (Matt. 5:16).

III. The performance.

A. *The Pharisees wore the mask of alms to be exalted.* They did the most good where the most eyes could see them. Would more be done for Christ in our church if we did not care who received the credit?

B. *The Pharisees wore the mask of prayer to be praised by others.* They prayed public prayers to be heard. When our Lord said that the Pharisees "love to pray," he was indicating that they were enjoying their masquerade.

When Bill Moyers was press secretary to President Lyndon B. Johnson, he was called upon many times to return thanks before meals. Upon one occasion he was praying in a quiet tone of voice. "Speak up, Bill," cried the president, "I can't hear you." Moyers paused, looked up, and said, "Mr. President, I was not speaking to you."

C. *The Pharisees wore the mask of fasting so that they might be complimented.* Our Lord is referring here to the voluntary individual fasts. He alludes to the outward signs of humiliation that often accompanied fasting, such as being unshaven or unkempt. The Pharisees possessed "a holier than thou" attitude that dripped with piousness.

IV. The curtain call.

A. *There comes a time when all actors take off the masks and take a bow just as they are.* If one is acting for his own glory, he has already received his reward. Popularity with humans is temporal. True greatness comes with humility. The curtain call will reveal how we have acted on the stage of life.

B. *"They have their reward" is the recurring judgment on these religious play actors throughout this passage (Matt. 6:1, 2, 5, 16).* The Greek word *apecho* occurs frequently in the papyri to denote a receipt such as a tax collector might use. It was translated, "I have received." Jesus is saying that those who are pious for praise have already signed the receipt for their own reward. They bargained for the applause of men, they received their wages, and the account is closed.

Conclusion

Throughout this passage there is the recurrence of the plea for the Christian to become less conscious of self and more conscious of God's presence. He is admonished not to let his left hand know what his right hand is doing (Matt. 6:3). This admonition calls for his mind to be taken off of himself. The Christian is to give alms, pray, and fast as though he were in the presence of God and no one else.

WEDNESDAY EVENING, JUNE 22

Title: How to Be Filled with the Holy Spirit

Text: "And be not drunk with wine, wherein is excess; but be filled with the Spirit" **(Eph. 5:18).**

Scripture Reading: Ephesians 5:15–20

Introduction

The filling of the Holy Spirit is mentioned four times in Luke's gospel. John the Baptist was filled with the Holy Spirit from his birth (1:15). Elizabeth was filled with the Holy Spirit for the singing of a sacred song (vv. 41–42). Zechariah was filled with the Holy Spirit for the uttering of prophecy (v. 67). Jesus was filled with the Holy Spirit for his work (4:1). All of these references appear before Pentecost.

Eight times in Acts and once in Ephesians the filling of the Holy Spirit is mentioned (Acts 2:3–4; 4:7–8, 31; 6:3–5; 7:55; 9:17; 11:24; 13:9–10; Eph. 5:18). A study of these usages of the term will lead to certain conclusions: to be filled with the Holy Spirit is the normal condition of the Christian's life; one is filled with the Holy Spirit for special work; and one is filled with the Holy Spirit for life and service.

Paul says, "Be filled with the Spirit" (Eph. 5:18). The word *plerousthe*, "be filled," is a command. We are commanded to be filled with the Holy Spirit because it is impossible to live the Christian life on any other basis. The Christian's life is to be lived in the power of God and not self. It cannot be lived in our own weak strength but must be lived by reliance upon the Lord and his power and resources. Merrill F. Unger says, "God's dynamic to live the Christian life is the indwelling Holy Spirit, whom every regenerated soul possesses. The Christian life can only be lived by relying upon the Holy Spirit. The normal Christian life is the Spirit-filled life" (*The God-Filled Life* [Grand Rapids: Zondervan, 1959], 68).

I. What is meant by being filled with the Holy Spirit?

The answer to this question can be found by understanding the teachings of the New Testament about being filled with the Holy Spirit.

   A. *Being filled with the Holy Spirit is an experience that is commanded.* The injunction "be filled with the Spirit" is a command. It is not optional, and it lays responsibility on the believer. The Christian is to live out his life under the power of the Spirit of God. He is not to grieve the Spirit by lukewarmness, indifference, frivolity, or worldliness. Let it be clearly understood that the child of God is commanded to be filled with the Spirit.

B. *Being filled with the Holy Spirit is an experience that can be repeated.* Greek verbs express action. *Plerousthe* is in the present tense and denotes continuous action. The experience of being filled with the Spirit is an experience repeated again and again—one baptism, many fillings.

C. *Being filled with the Spirit is an experience that brings about a changed person.* The word *plerousthe* is in the passive voice. The passive voice denotes the subject as acted upon. The blessed third person of the Trinity, the Holy Spirit, desires to control the Christian's life. He desires to control the thoughts, words, and deeds of the child of God.

II. How can a child of God be filled with the Holy Spirit?

A. *One may be filled with the Holy Spirit as he accepts the Holy Spirit's indwelling presence.* The Holy Spirit enables a person to become a child of God (1 Cor. 12:3). He takes up his abode in the believer the moment he puts his trust in Jesus as Lord and Savior (Acts 10:44; Rom. 8:9; 1 Cor. 6:19). Let the believer accept and acknowledge the Holy Spirit's indwelling!

B. *One may be filled with the Holy Spirit when he abandons his life to the Lord.* Wherever wholehearted, absolute, unquestioning, positive, final, and complete abandonment of the life to God takes place, that life becomes filled with the Holy Spirit (Rom. 6:13; 12:1; Eph. 4:30–32). The difference between the Spirit-filled life and the life that is not filled with the Spirit is the difference between a life abandoned wholly to the will of God and a life that wants to have its own way. People will do almost anything except go to the cross and die to self. The Spirit's activity cannot take place in one's life until that life is abandoned to God.

C. *One may be filled with the Holy Spirit as he abides in Christ.* To abide in Christ is to love him and obey him. The Holy Spirit is given to them who obey him (Acts 5:32). The Holy Spirit fills the surrendered vessel. He never fills a disobedient believer. If the believer is to be filled with the Holy Spirit, let him abide in God's Word and will!

III. What can a child of God expect when he is filled with the Holy Spirit?

A. *Victory over sin (Rom. 8:2–4).*

B. *Fellowship with Jesus (Eph. 3:16–17).*

C. *A Christlike life (Rom. 8:9; Gal. 5:16, 22–26).*

D. *Power in the Lord's work (Acts 1:8; 4:31).*

Conclusion

The filling of the Holy Spirit is an experience every child of God should enjoy. Turn your life over to him today and let him fill you with his Spirit!

SUNDAY MORNING, JUNE 26

Title: Climb the Highest Mountain

Text: "I have written unto you, young men, because ye are strong, and the word of God abideth in you, and ye have overcome the wicked one" (**1 John 2:14**).

Scripture Reading: 1 John 2:12–14

Hymns: "All Glory, Laud, and Honor," Theodulph of Orleans

        "Arise, O Youth of God," Merrill

        "Onward, Christian Soldiers," Baring-Gould

        "Give of Your Best to the Master," Grose

Offertory Prayer: Our Father, this morning we assemble ourselves before you to pour out our hearts' adoration and love. We feel that in these moments of presentation of our tithes and offerings we are best able to show forth that love and adoration. Accept, we pray, these manifestations of our sense of stewardship and love in the spirit in which we present them. Bless them and multiply them in your kingdom's service, for we pray in our Savior's name. Amen.

Introduction

In the lives of our young people we have the hope of our tomorrows. Youth is that which spells out hope, strength, and zeal for the future. In John's first letter he expresses so beautifully the faith that he has in youth: "I have written unto you, young men, because ye are strong, and the word of God abideth in you, and ye have overcome the wicked one" (1 John 2:14).

John wrote to the young men of his day because:

I. "Ye are strong."

The strength about which John was speaking was no doubt the strength of:

A. *Enthusiasm and unquenchable zeal.* At times this enthusiasm and zeal may be extremely difficult to live with, causing us to declare that young people have foolish ideas. Robert Louis Stevenson cried out, "Give me the young man who has brains enough to be a fool." By this he no doubt meant a young man who got hold of an idea and had brains enough to pursue that idea through to fruition. Did not the people of Christopher Columbus's day call him a fool for pursuing the idea that the world was round? Did not the citizens of Edison's day refer to him as a "tinkering fool" and to Henry Ford as an "impractical mechanic"? The unquenchable zeal and enthusiasm of youth, with proper direction, will build up; without that proper direction it may well blow up!

B. *One blessed with a vision.*

1. While yet young, Paul literally had a vision in the night concerning his approach to the task of missions: "Come over into Macedonia, and help us" (Acts 16:9). This vision sped up the Christianizing of

the then-known world, for Paul was faithful to the command found in that vision.

2. Martin Luther read God's Word and interpreted it for himself; he had as it were a vision of a purer religion—salvation through faith and not by man's works. Because he was faithful to pursue the teaching of that "vision," a great spiritual reformation caught fire and has warmed the hearts of people through the centuries.

3. In England a shoe cobbler named William Carey labored away at his cobbler's bench with a vision of the great spiritual needs in India. At a meeting of his association, he was asked to propose a subject for discussion. Welling up in his heart was his vision and burden, and he proposed the subject of "whether the command given to the apostles to teach all nations was not obligatory on all ministers to the end of the world." The venerable moderator of the association, John Ryland Sr., reprimanded him: "Sit down, young man. You are a miserable enthusiast to ask such a question. When God wants to convert the world, he can do it without your help; and at least nothing can be done until a second Pentecost shall bring a return of the miraculous gifts." Undaunted, young Carey pressed forward until his vision became a reality and the Word of the Lord was being preached in faraway places. The church of the living God has a solemn duty—giving direction to youth that their hopes, visions, aspirations, and ambitions may lead them to reach high and lofty goals for the future.

C. *Dauntless spirit.* Paul said with determination, "Forgetting what lies behind and straining forward to what lies ahead, I press on toward the goal for the prize of the upward call of God in Christ Jesus" (Phil. 3:13–14 RSV). I know a young man who rose above many misfortunes. His mother died when he was but a few weeks old; his aunt, who was endeavoring to rear him, died when he was scarcely ten years old. His father, never very adept at proper guidance of youth in the home, left him to his own devices. Somehow, through it all he grew up, and as he grew a vision was constantly before him—that of becoming a medical doctor. Against all odds he pulled himself up by his own bootstraps, working his way through college and medical school. Almost every day along life's way he could have "thrown in the towel" and have quit his struggle to climb his great mountain, but he never wavered from his dream. Today he is an outstanding radiologist. Dauntless spirit!

D. *Potentiality.* Many of the "greats" of history had already accomplished some of their greatest achievements during their youth. At thirty-three, Alexander the Great mourned because there were no other worlds to conquer. At twenty-two George Washington was a colonel in the English army. Joan of Arc had lived and died—and gained lasting fame—at the age of nineteen years. Wolfgang Amadeus Mozart captured the great heart of Europe with his symphonies as a youth. John Calvin had achieved great standing in theological circles when twenty-one. Roger Williams had made his mark as a Baptist heretic at age thirty. Yes, youth is full of potentiality; it can be the greatest strength or the major weakness of our nation.

II. "The word of God abideth in you."

The strength of the youth to whom John was writing lay in the fact that they had a knowledge of and love for the Word of God. If our young people today are obedient to the teachings of God's Word, they will be able to avoid the following dangers so prevalent in our society:

A. *Religious regimentation without spiritual regeneration.* All too often in religious circles young people are herded into church membership by right-meaning adults through special classes on doctrine, catechism, or simply because they are at the proper age. Thus many of these young people have become church members before they have become born-again believers. For the strength of youth that John was speaking of, there must first of all be a personal confrontation with Christ Jesus and a surrender to him.

B. *The danger of being laughed into atheism by pseudointellectualism.* In many of the colleges of our day there are some pseudointellectual professors who desire more than anything else to catch the attention and imagination of their young scholars by questioning everything once held sacred by them. The very existence of God and his power and love are often ripped to shreds in the minds of the young students by the ridiculing of the sacred by these so-called intellectual professors. Because of this pressure, the old tried and tested truths learned back home may give way to religious skepticism or agnosticism.

C. *The danger of being overcome by sensual indulgence.* America is not in so much danger of onslaught from without today as from spiritual and moral decay from within. Likewise, youth are not in nearly so much danger from physical harm from without as they are from moral and spiritual decay from within. On every hand there is being flung at youth temptations to drink, use drugs, and have sex. With these pressures on them, youth must have the righteousness of the Lord to help them in their fight against these evils. Euripides said, "Youth is a curse to mortals, when with youth a man hath not implanted righteousness."

III. "Ye have overcome the wicked one."

John no doubt looked with great pride on the young men of the kingdom to whom he was addressing himself in this text. They had already acquitted themselves in the eyes of John, for they had come through the troubled waters of repentance and reached the farther bank of faith in Christ. They had now begun to live the life befitting the Christian faith. Overcoming the Wicked One involves:

A. *Realizing one's need for the Lord.* Too many young people try to be proudly independent, expressing no need for anyone. The young people of this day as in every other age must recognize themselves as sinners before God and be truly repentant of that sinful condition and turn away from it. We are told that Lord Byron always was afflicted with a foolish self-pity, that he had a sentimentality about the sins which he never ceased to love. He was pleased to think of himself as the unfortunate prey of fleshly lusts, while he gloried in his shame. Today young people must be aware of their sinfulness, be sorry about their condition, and turn away from that way of life and thought..

B. *Turning to the source of salvation.* Today in our enlightened age the recipe for salvation is the same as it has been from that day when Jesus died and rose again for man's atonement and justification—faith in Jesus Christ as Savior and Lord. Jesus has the same message to inquiring youth today that he had to Nicodemus when he sought him out one night to ask the way to life. Jesus told him, "Except a man be born again, he cannot see the kingdom of God" (John 3:3). Today youth must experience the birth pangs of repentance and faith and surrender to Christ if they are to experience salvation.

C. *Offering up a surrendered life to Christ.* Youth can know no limits to what can be done in life spiritually and physically if they are in Christ and Christ is in them. When youth surrender to Christ to serve him, they can sing with the songwriter, "I'll go where You want me to go, dear Lord, o'er mountain or plain or sea. I'll say what You want me to say, dear Lord; I'll be what You want me to be."

Conclusion

Let youth dream dreams, see visions, swing into action! Let not even the highest mountain of obstacles along life's journey daunt them! Let youth know their Master and serve him each day. As a young person, will you surrender today to the Master of life, trusting him completely for your soul's salvation and your life's plan? Let him have his way with you.

SUNDAY EVENING, JUNE 26

Title: Payola Piety, Part 1

Text: "Be careful not to do your 'acts of righteousness' before men, to be seen by them" (**Matt. 6:1 NIV**).

Scripture Reading: Matthew 6:1–18

Introduction

Payola is a slang expression for an undercover payoff. For example, a disc jockey might be paid off by a record company to promote a particular record.

If Jesus were to preach from our text to a congregation of today's Americans, he might well title the sermon "Payola Piety."

Payola piety is characterized by doing the right things with the wrong motives.

I. Doing good deeds to be seen of men (vv. 1–2).

A. *Theater-type religion.* The key to the whole passage is in the first verse. Jesus says that the Christian is not to do his good deeds to be "seen of men."

Jesus, in Matthew 6:2, adds more emphasis to this when he says that the "hypocrites" do their good deeds in such a way that others can see their generosity.

B. *The importance of alms.* The Jews attached much weight to the giving of alms. In Jesus' day, almsgiving meant giving money and gifts to those in need—usually beggars on the streets. Today we might well equate almsgiving with the doing of good deeds for others.

In one of the books written in Old Testament times but not contained in our Bible, there are the words: "It is better to give alms than to lay up gold. For almsgiving saves from death and purges away every sin" (Tobit 12:8). In another noncanonical book we find these words: "Almsgiving to a father shall not be blotted out, and as a substitute for sins it shall stand firmly planted. In the day of affliction it shall be remembered to thy credit. It shall obliterate thine iniquities as the heat, the hoar-frost" (Sir. 3:14–15). It is quite certain, then, that almsgiving stood at the top of a Jew's list of good works.

C. *A look at motives.* There is no doubt about it—the Pharisees thought that it was good to give alms. We would all agree today that it is good to give to charity, to help the poor, to tithe, and to give offerings in the church. But God looks first at the inner motive rather than the outward act of charity. When people do their good deeds to have the glory and praise of others, they are guilty of payola piety. Someone has well said that much more work for the Lord would be done in our churches if we didn't care who got the credit for doing it. This is doing the right things with the wrong motives. This is payola piety.

II. Praying to be heard by men (vv. 5, 7).

Jesus mentions a second area in which some are doing the right things with the wrong motive—prayer. Jesus presented two negative arguments against this sin. Again, he turned to the hypocrites and Pharisees of his day for an illustration.

A. *Many prayers—mini religion.* The Jews prayed about eighteen times a day at set times. A Pharisee would be sure to be in a public place when it came time to pray in order that others might see him as he prayed in his arrogant manner. He loved to be in the synagogue, where he would stand (never humble enough to kneel) with his arms stretched to heaven while he "prayed." Another favorite place is mentioned in Matthew 6:5: "in the corners of the streets." This means the crossings of the main thoroughfares of each city. In other words, when a Pharisee prayed on the corner of a street, he was standing in the middle of a crossroad so that people could see him from four sides. It was not an uncommon thing in Jesus' day for traffic to be stalled while a Pharisee said one of his eighteen memorized prayers. It is plain to see that the hypocritical Pharisee prayed only to be seen by others. He was doing the right thing with the wrong motive.

B. *Vain repetitions.* In Matthew 6:7 Jesus says that the Christian's prayer is not to be filled with "vain repetitions." Actually the Greek uses a verb that means "to babble repetitions" (cf. NIV). This is saying words with one's lips without ever thinking about their content or meaning. This is the type of prayer that the prophets of Baal made to their god on Mount Carmel when they danced around an altar for several hours crying out, "Baal, help us!" This is a picture of a person who thinks that God owes him an ear because he prays the loudest or the longest. He thinks that he can wear God out and finally get him to grant a request. Or perhaps he "informs" God of some event or person as though the all-knowing God needs such information. Such a prayer was once delivered by a radio preacher at the close of his broadcast: "Lord, you know that our address is Box 333, Del Rio, Texas. Now please lay it on someone's heart to write down this address and send us some money." One has the wrong motive when he prays to be heard of men. This is payola piety. The payment is the praise of men.

III. Fasting to appear religious (v. 16).

In Jesus' day there was one day in each year (the Day of Atonement) on which every Jew was required to fast (Lev. 16:31). From morning till evening the Jews would go without food and water, bathing, grooming, and shoes. William Barclay indicates three reasons for the Jewish fast.

A. *It was a deliberate attempt to draw the attention of God to the person who fasted.*
B. *It was thus meant to be a proof for repentance.* But the Pharisees made it a substitute for repentance.
C. *It was for the sake of others.* It was not for the purpose of saving one's own soul but to liberate the nation from its distresses.

Conclusion

The Pharisee and hypocrite of Jesus' day chose Monday and Thursday to do his fasting, since those were market days and more people would be in town than any other time during the week. They would walk through the streets on these days unshaven and unkempt, for they wanted everyone to know that they were religious. They were doing the right thing with the wrong motive.

How about you? What are the motives behind your good works?

WEDNESDAY EVENING, JUNE 29

Title: The Sin against the Holy Spirit

Text: " 'Every sin and blasphemy will be forgiven men, but the blasphemy against the Spirit will not be forgiven. Anyone who speaks a word against the Son of Man will be forgiven, but anyone who speaks against the Holy Spirit will not be forgiven, either in this age or in the age to come' " **(Matt. 12:31–32 NIV)**.

Scripture Reading: Matthew 12:22–37

Introduction

The most solemn, severe, and sober warning ever uttered by Jesus has to do with the person of the Holy Spirit. All of the Synoptic Gospels record this warning (Matt. 12:31–32; Mark 3:28–29; Luke 12:10). Many other Scriptures fortify Jesus' teaching of the sin against the Holy Spirit (Gen. 6:3; Prov. 1:24–31; Jer. 7:16; 11:14; 14:11; Heb. 10:26; 1 John 5:16–17).

Jesus said his own words may be rejected, his own person may be spoken against, and these things forgiven. However, those who blaspheme the Holy Spirit will not be forgiven in this world or in the world to come.

I. What is the sin against the Holy Spirit?

Blasphemy against the Holy Spirit is called the sin against the Holy Spirit or the unpardonable sin. The word *blaspheme* means to speak reproachfully, to rail at, to revile.

Dr. A. T. Robertson, in describing the sin against the Holy Spirit, said, "What is the blasphemy against the Holy Spirit? These Pharisees had already committed it. They had attributed the works of the Holy Spirit by whose power Jesus wrought miracles (Matt. 12:28) to the devil. That sin was without excuse and would not be forgiven in their age or in the coming one. People often ask if they can commit the unpardonable sin. Probably some do who ridicule the manifest work of God's Spirit in men's lives and attribute the Spirit's work to the devil" (*Word Pictures in the New Testament* [New York: Harper and Brothers, 1930], 96–97).

The sin against the Holy Spirit is seeing the work of God's Son, knowing it to be the work of God's Son, failing to believe in it as the work of God's Son, and ascribing it to a diabolic source.

II. What are some of the characteristics of the sin against the Holy Spirit?

A. *It is a sin against the light of the gospel.* To commit this sin one must have felt the power of the Holy Spirit. God reveals himself through his Son Jesus Christ, and people must accept him or reject him. Some blaspheme him!

B. *It is a sin of crystallized character.* It is no impulsive, hasty act. It is committed by one whose moral vision is perverted and who serves evil habits. It is committed by one who is insensible to the Holy Spirit's leadership.

194

C. *It is a sin of hate.* Some people hate the gospel of our Lord and Savior Jesus Christ. The gospel exposes sins, reveals chains and fetters, and advertises bondage, pride, lust, and greediness. The Holy Spirit strives, but people resist. Some hate the Lord and his work and ascribe it to the Devil.

D. *It is a willful sin (Heb. 10:26–29).*

E. *It is a sin that draws false conclusions.* The Pharisees said, "This fellow doth not cast out devils, but by Beelzebub the prince of the devils" (Matt. 12:24). How wrong can one be?

III. Why can't the sin against the Holy Spirit be forgiven?

A. *The sin against the Holy Spirit cannot be forgiven, because it brings eternal damnation (Mark 3:29).*

B. *The sin against the Holy Spirit cannot be forgiven, because the individual is indifferent to his own condition.*

C. *The sin against the Holy Spirit cannot be forgiven, because the person who commits it loses the power of moral discrimination.*

D. *The sin against the Holy Spirit cannot be forgiven, because the person is bitterly hostile to the Lord.* When a person hates God, spiritual deterioration and ruin set in. When a person becomes hostile toward God, he cannot perceive the truth.

Conclusion

Let us never ascribe the work of the Lord Jesus to the Devil. Let us seek, ask for, and follow the Holy Spirit's leading in our lives. Let us respond to the gospel as it is revealed to us by the Holy Spirit.

> *Spirit of the living God, fall fresh on me,*
> *Spirit of the living God, fall fresh on me,*
> *Break me, melt me, mold me, fill me—*
> *Spirit of the living God, fall fresh on me.*

JULY

■ **Sunday Mornings**

An appropriate Independence Day sermon is suggested for July 3. On the following Sundays, continue with the theme "Living without Regrets."

■ **Sunday Evenings**

Continue the series on the Sermon on the Mount. The messages this month deal with the Christian's motives and the Lord's Prayer.

■ **Wednesday Evenings**

"Some Prayers of the Psalmist" is the theme for Wednesday evenings. A few of the many petitions to be found in the Psalms have been selected for examination and repetition by those who would like to worship more meaningfully.

SUNDAY MORNING, JULY 3

Title: Christianity and American Freedom

Text: "Stand fast therefore in the liberty wherewith Christ hath made us free, and be not entangled again with the yoke of bondage" (**Gal. 5:1**).

Scripture Reading: Psalm 33:12–19

Hymns: "God of Our Fathers," Roberts

"America the Beautiful," Bates

"Mine Eyes Have Seen the Glory," Howe

Offertory Prayer: Our God and our Father, who has been our help in ages past, we lift our voices in adoration of you today. Our gifts are but a small token of the gratitude that swells within our hearts. For the truth that has made us free and for the Christ who came to proclaim it, we thank you. As we celebrate the independence of our great nation, we acknowledge anew our abiding dependence on God in whom we trust. In Christ's name we pray. Amen.

Introduction

Charles Rann Kennedy, in his drama of the last days of Jesus, *The Terrible Meek*, confines the action at the foot of the cross to conversations between the Roman captain; Mary, the mother of Jesus; and others. The scene takes place during the night following Christ's death, and darkness covers the stage. As the play ends, Mary, in the depth of despair, is bewailing the death of her Son. The captain comforts her by saying that her Son is not dead.

> *"I tell you, my good woman, this dead son of yours,*
> *Disfigured, shamed, spat upon,*
> *Has built a kingdom this day that shall never die.*
> *The living glory of him will forever rule it.*
> *The earth is his and he made it.*
>
> *He and his brothers have been moulding and making it*
> *Through all the long ages.*
> *They are the only ones*
> *Who ever really can possess it*
> *Not the proud, not the idle, not the wealthy,*
> *Not the vaunting empires of this world. . . . No!*
>
> *Something has happened up here on this hill today,*
> *To shake all our kingdoms of the blood and fear to the dust.*
> *The earth is his, the earth is theirs, and they made it.*
> *The meek, the terrible meek,*
> *The fierce, the agonizing meek*
> *Are about to enter into their inheritance!"*

([New York: Harper and Brothers, 1912], 39)

This truth still stands! Across the centuries Christianity has made its influence known, and today it is of great significance to American freedom.

Historian Clinton Rossiter contends that any study of early American history that ignores religion is essentially unsound. Charles Beard, in his book *A Basic History of the United States,* asserts that in the founding and development of every colony, religious considerations played an important role.

If this be true, what are some of Christianity's contributions to American freedom?

I. An optimistic yet realistic philosophy of history.

A. *The cyclical philosophy of history that is basically pessimistic began with the Babylonians.* It asserts that life and history are really going nowhere. People can do nothing to change the hopeless boredom of history. There may be different actors in different costumes and on different stages, but the drama of history is always the same and the plot and ending never change.

Plato believed that every 36,000 years God withdraws from the world, allows fate to wipe out life, and then the drama of life and history begin all over again. Seneca, a Greek Stoic, believed the cycle took only 10,800 years. The Hindu faith asserts that everything begins all over again every 4,300,000 years.

In more recent times, Oswald Spengler, in his book *The Decline of the West,* restated this old philosophy as he asserted that all civilizations in history move through four unavoidable stages—birth, growth, maturity, and decay.

B. *Christian philosophy would diagram history, not as an endless circle, but as a straight line.* At one end we would write the words, "In the beginning God ...," and at the other end of this line we would write, "I come quickly and my reward is with me.... I am ... the beginning and the end." This line moves forward and upward, ending only with the return of Christ and the ultimate triumph of righteousness.

II. A practical demonstration of democracy.

A. *In the early church, we see pure democracy in action at the baptism of the family of Cornelius and when the seven deacons are elected by the church.*

B. *Roger Williams, in his Rhode Island experiment, transplanted the concept of democracy to America.* Former Chief Justice Charles Evans Hughes said that the charter of Rhode Island was the ancestor of the Federal Constitution adopted 124 years later. Evidence that Thomas Jefferson was influenced by Williams is seen in a striking similarity of ideas in the Declaration of Independence and an earlier declaration written by Williams.

A well-used book in Jefferson's library that expounds complete religious liberty and church-state separation was *A True Picture of the Anabaptists.* Further indications that Jefferson was influenced by New Testament democracy were sermons in his library by preachers such as Robert Hall of London, Thomas Baldwin of Boston, and Richard Furman of Charleston, South Carolina.

III. A needed emphasis on the worth of the individual.

Communism preaches, "The individual is nothing—the party is everything!"

A. *Christ seems to take quite a contrary position on this matter.* By his own life he stressed the worth of the individual. He sought out the man born blind who was cast out of the synagogue for expressing his belief that Christ was of God.

Christ's belief in the worth of the individual sprang from his ability to see people, not for what they are, but for what they can be. And so he called unlikely men such as Matthew, Zacchaeus, Peter, and Simon the Zealot to be his followers.

B. *The Christian faith brought to America the doctrine of the worth of the individual.* The Great Awakening brought this same renewed emphasis. As a result of this spiritual revival, scores of social reforms were seen.

George Whitefield's orphanage in Georgia was the first benevolent institution of its kind in America. Humanitarian interest in slaves, prison reform, and care for the insane all were born out of the revival of the Christian faith in America.

This basic Christian emphasis could be stated no better than it is in the Declaration of Independence: "We hold these truths to be self-evident: That all men are created equal; that they are endowed by their Creator with certain unalienable rights; that among these are life, liberty, and the pursuit of happiness."

IV. Encouragement and preservation of education.

From the days of Paul until now the Christian faith has encouraged the attainment of knowledge. "Study to shew thyself approved unto God, a workman that needeth not to be ashamed" (2 Tim. 2:15) reflects the Christian attitude toward the matter of knowledge and education.

During the Dark Ages, what little scholarship remained was kept alive in religious circles. The Reformation, a revival of religion, followed the Renaissance, a revival of learning. Great men such as Martin Luther, John Calvin, Huldrych Zwingli, and John Knox were brilliant, well-educated men who advocated the education and enlightenment of the masses. One who contends that Christianity has held back education lacks a proper knowledge of history.

Most of England's great universities were founded by religious groups. In America almost all of the first universities were established by Protestant faiths. Some of these are Brown, Columbia, Rochester, Princeton, Colgate, Rutgers, and the University of Chicago.

An outgrowth of the Great Awakening's emphasis on the worth of the individual was mass education through a system of public schools.

V. A proper incentive for a strong capitalistic economy.

An oft-repeated verse of some of the early Christian colonists was, "If any would not work, neither should he eat" (2 Thess. 3:10). This verse expresses the pioneering spirit of the founding fathers of America. Upon this principle our nation was built and must continue to stand.

Why does the United States have the highest standard of living in the world and yet is the youngest of the leading nations? The answer is found in the Christian faith. Christianity so changes a person that it makes him want to live above the level of mediocrity. It gives him a fresh incentive and a new and wholesome pride.

VI. Separation of church and state.

Jesus enunciates this principle in his words, "Render therefore unto Caesar the things which are Caesar's; and unto God the things that are God's" (Matt. 22:21).

Many believe that Roger Williams became the real founder of the new republic and that his policy of separation of church and state at Providence accounts for this practice in America today. In the Rhode Island Charter of 1644, written 132 years before the Declaration of Independence, Williams guaranteed that "no person within said colony, at any time hereafter shall be in any wise molested, punished, disquieted, or called in question for any differences in opinion in matters of religion."

Sir Winston Churchill contended that Williams, a preacher, was the first to put into practice the complete separation of church and lay government.

VII. Religious liberty.

Up to the time of the Revolutionary War, nine of the colonies supported an established church. Rhode Island alone guaranteed full religious liberty.

John Leland, a minister concerned about religious liberty, was encouraged by scores of people to run against James Madison for the office of delegate to the Constitutional Convention to be held in 1789. Madison, advised by friends that Leland would defeat him, went to Leland. Leland withdrew upon Madison's promise that he would support a bill specifically defining complete religious liberty. Madison kept his promise.

Conclusion

> *My country, 'tis of thee,*
> *Sweet land of liberty,*
> *Of thee I sing:*
> *Land where my fathers died,*
> *Land of the pilgrims' pride,*
> *From every mountainside*
> *Let freedom ring!*

SUNDAY EVENING, JULY 3

Title: Payola Piety, Part 2

Text: "Do not sound a trumpet before thee, as the hypocrites do ... that they may have glory of men" (**Matt. 6:2**).

Scripture Reading: Matthew 6:1–18

Introduction

The philosophy behind payola is "If it'll pay, I'll play-like." This philosophy was behind much of what was termed "religion" in Jesus' day. The scribes and Pharisees did many of their pious deeds to be seen by others. They were "playing-like" as far as religion was concerned. They were playing for a price—the glory of men. They gave their money to the church in such a way that everyone would see and know that they were good stewards. They prayed in places and in such a manner as to bring the praise of men for their piety. Their kind of religion might well be called payola piety.

I. Payola piety is rewarded in time instead of eternity.

A. *Paid in full.* The sad thing about payola piety is that it has no reward in heaven. It is possible for a person to be very religious in the eyes of humans but to be lost in the eyes of God.

After each instance of doing the right thing with the wrong motive, Jesus added, "Verily I say unto you, They have their reward." The verb for "they have their reward" is in the present tense. The idea is that they are having their reward right now. In other words, as people do their good works to be seen by others, pray to be heard by others, and fast to appear religious, they are receiving their reward when others applaud them. The meaning is that they have their reward; they will get no more than the praise of humans.

B. *The applause of humans.* Good deeds done to be seen by others are rewarded by the admiration of others. Prayer to be heard by others is rewarded by the reputation of being a devout person. Fasting to appear religious is rewarded by acclaim in religious circles.

Two young men had the idea that they would like to fast. So they told their pastor that they planned to stay after church on a particular Sunday afternoon and fast. The pastor was delighted. He told others about it and even announced it from the pulpit. The boys may have received a blessing from the session with the Lord, but it is plain to see that their only reward was the praise of others that lasted for a short time.

II. Payola piety can be defeated by a consciousness of the presence of God.

Jesus gave the admonition to give alms, pray, and fast in secret. This means that a Christian is to do good deeds, pray, and fast with a consciousness of the presence of God. Jesus says, "Thy father which seeth in secret himself shall reward thee."

A. *Such consciousness causes a person to do good deeds without being conscious of himself (v. 3).* This is the meaning of "Let not thy left hand know what they right hand doeth." This verse carries also the idea of natural giving. The Christian whose heart and billfold are dedicated to the Lord never has to argue with himself on Sunday morning to decide how much he is going to give. He never puts the right hand into his pocket and asks, "Should I give the twenty-dollar bill, which would be my tithe, or should I give five dollars?" He knows beforehand what he is going to do. He merely reaches down into his pocket and draws out God's money. It does not matter to him how much it is or how much it leaves him. He merely believes that this is the will of God for Christians in the financing of a local New Testament church.

B. *Such consciousness causes a person to realize that God meets personal needs (vv. 9–13).* Although this is not the full meaning of the Lord's Prayer, the idea of a consciousness of God's presence motivates the prayer. One who realizes that God is near will not hesitate to follow the model prayer in asking for provisions.

Petition for personal needs is not a major part of the model prayer. However, the whole prayer leads up to a request for personal need. The prayer begins by identifying the source of personal provision. "Our Father" indicates that this is the prayer of a Christian. "Hallowed be thy name" is a petition that the Christian may acknowledge as holy the things that belong to God. It is through God that there can be unity in the world. The prayer says, "Thy kingdom come; thy will be done." This is two ways of saying the same thing—the kingdom comes in the hearts of individuals and the world when the will of God is done in those hearts and those groups.

Then there are the three petitions for personal needs—both physical and spiritual. "Daily bread" denotes a basic necessity; Jesus did not say, "daily cake," because he knew that cake is not a necessity. Then there is the plea for personal forgiveness and the indication that one must forgive others their sins before God will forgive his sins. The prayer closes with the request "Lead us not into temptation."

Thus the prayer is the outcome of a consciousness of the presence of God in the world. One would not pray for bread, forgiveness, and delivery from temptations in this world if he did not believe that God was already in the world.

Conclusion

It goes without saying that payola piety as such cannot be a part of a true Christian's life. However, it should be noted that every real Christian should be on the lookout for the attitudes and philosophy behind such piety. The best method of doing this is to live every minute of life with a consciousness of the presence of God.

WEDNESDAY EVENING, JULY 6

Title: "Lord, Who Shall Abide in Thy Tabernacle?"

Text: "Lord, who shall abide in thy tabernacle? who shall dwell in thy holy hill?" (Ps. 15:1).

Scripture Reading: Psalm 15

Introduction

The psalmist questioned God concerning the qualifications of character and conduct that make it possible for one to dwell in the house of God. His was a personal question that has significance for the sincere worshiper. What kind of person must I be if I want to enjoy fellowship with God? What kind of conduct is pleasing to God? What attitudes or actions would cause me to be deprived of the privilege of enjoying fellowship with God?

I. The value of abiding in God's house.

The psalmist assumed that everyone would want to dwell in the house of

God. "For a day in thy courts is better than a thousand. I had rather be a door-keeper in the house of my God, than to dwell in the tents of wickedness" (Ps. 84:10).

    A. *To dwell in God's presence brings safety.* "He that dwelleth in the secret place of the most High shall abide under the shadow of the Almighty" (Ps. 91:1).

    B. *Dwelling in God's presence brings satisfaction.* "Thou wilt shew me the path of life: in thy presence is fulness of joy; at thy right hand there are pleasures for evermore" (Ps. 16:11).

    C. *Dwelling in God's presence brings stability to life.* "He that doeth these things shall never be moved" (Ps. 15:5; 1:3).

II. The psalmist's question concerning dwelling in God's house.

    A. *His question was of personal concern.* He wanted to be among those who would dwell with God and with God's people.

    B. *His question is of personal significance for us.* The God of the psalmist is the God and Father of our Lord Jesus Christ. That which was required then continues to be required of those who would dwell with God. "One thing have I desired of the LORD, that will I seek after; that I may dwell in the house of the LORD all the days of my life, to behold the beauty of the LORD, and to inquire in his temple" (Ps. 27:4).

III. Guests whom God welcomes.

In reply to the psalmist's question, God speaks in both the positive and negative to describe the characteristics that are pleasing to him.

    A. *The positive.*

        1. The guest of God walks uprightly. He does not harbor sin in his life.

        2. The guest of God loves righteousness. His life is dedicated to deeds of positive goodness.

        3. The guest of God speaks words of perfect truthfulness (15:2, 4).

    B. *The negative.*

        1. The guest of God refuses to use his tongue destructively (15:3). He is not a slanderer or talebearer who spreads false reports.

        2. The guest of God is never guilty of doing evil to his neighbor (15:3).

        3. The guest of God refuses to whitewash iniquity (15:4).

        4. The guest of God refuses to profit from the pain of the unfortunate (15:5).

Conclusion

Only by the grace of God can we experience the new life that causes us to hunger and thirst after righteousness (Ps. 42:1–2). The divine Spirit that came to us at the time of conversion will lead us and empower us to become the kind of persons who can enjoy the fellowship of God's presence if we will but cooperate with him from day to day (Phil. 2:12–13).

SUNDAY MORNING, JULY 10

Title: The Judgment of God

Text: "Therefore thou art inexcusable, O man, whosoever thou art that judgest: for wherein thou judgest another, thou condemnest thyself; for thou that judgest doest the same things. But we are sure that the judgment of God is according to truth against them which commit such things. And thinkest thou this, O man, that judgest them which do such things, and doest the same, that thou shalt escape the judgment of God?" (**Rom. 2:1 – 3**).

Scripture Reading: Romans 2:1 – 6

Hymns: "Awake, My Soul, Stretch Every Nerve," Doddridge

          "We're Marching to Zion," Watts

          "The Lord Will Come," Milton

          "Will Jesus Find Us Watching?" Crosby

Offertory Prayer: Heavenly Father, we come to you again this morning with gratitude in our hearts because of your many blessings to us. We can truly say that "morning by morning new mercies we see." Because we are grateful for your blessings, we come to you with our gifts of love and devotion. Bless our gifts this morning, Father, and use them to your service and glory. And may we love you more because of this privilege of giving. In Jesus' name. Amen.

Introduction

In our Scripture passage under consideration this morning, Paul is not overlooking the great doctrine of salvation by grace as found in Ephesians. He is, however, stressing that believers ought to act like believers—that every person, believer and unbeliever, Jew and Gentile, is going to have to give an account of himself or herself before God. God's judgment is a subject that certainly is not exhausted in our text, for obviously only certain facets of the whole truth are brought to light here. Among these facets are the following:

I. Judgment is of God, not man (v. 1).

Too often along life's highway we encounter people who seem to feel that they have been divinely appointed judges or critics of their fellow humans. Paul speaks pointedly on this subject in verse 1.

    A. *Man who judges others is inexcusable.* Man is trying to play the role of God if he attempts to pass judgment on his fellow man, for God is the only Judge. Those who play the role of critic or judge in the community are behaving as a deranged person once did. Such a person once slipped into the judge's chambers, put on the judge's robe, and entering the courtroom, sat in the judge's seat behind the bench, trying to pass himself off as a judge. Just as absurd is the person who attempts to sit in judgment on his neighbor. Paul said emphatically concerning the critic, "Thou art inexcusable, O man, whosoever thou art that judgest" (v. 1).

B. *One who passes judgment on his neighbor passes judgment on himself.* Paul said, "For wherein thou judgest another, thou condemnest thyself" (v. 1). Does not the town gossip soon have the wrath of the local citizens on her neck? Do they not shun her? Can she ever expect to have close friends who will confide in her? I once knew a person in the community where I lived who arose early to get her household chores cared for so that she might begin making the rounds of the neighbors' homes to glean all the latest bits of news and choice tidbits of gossip. People dreaded her arrival at their homes and found many excuses not to let her in. Unfortunately, she never understood why people seemed not to prefer her company.

C. *The one who condemns is usually guilty of the same fault.* The person who sits in judgment on other people, condemning them for character imperfections, all too often is guilty of the same things — or worse. Jesus pointed out that man can see the slightest imperfection in his neighbor's character or personality but has not the slightest idea that his own character is far from lily white and that his own personality reeks with undesirable traits. "Judge not, that ye be not judged," said Jesus (Matt. 7:1). In a certain church there were some prominent businessmen who were successful by the world's standards. They presumed to sit in judgment on their pastor and deacons for the way they administered the affairs of the church. They would have been horrified, however, if their pastor had criticized them concerning the way they operated their respective places of business.

II. God's judgment is true.

Paul expresses the deep and abiding conviction that he and all real Christians have concerning the judgment of God — it "is according to truth against them which commit such things" (Rom. 2:2).

A. *God's judgments are true to divine standards.*

1. God judges not by inadequate human standards, by manmade laws with all of their frailties and absurdities. Some of the most entertaining reading a person can do is to read old law books that contain laws that have no present-day significance or that never did make sense. I am told that in a certain state there used to be a law that said that when two trains approached an intersection at the same time, each was to wait until the other had passed — a more than somewhat difficult task!

2. God's judgments are equitable. There are laws in our land that seem to protect the guilty and to penalize the innocent. For instance, a brave citizen heard a noise in an adjoining apartment and, knowing that the occupant of that apartment was out of town, went into that apartment to investigate. He apprehended two men in the process of robbing the apartment of its valuables, and he held at bay the two culprits until the police could arrive. The result of this heroic action was that the robbers

were sent to jail for four months. The brave neighbor was sentenced to prison for two years for illegal possession of a gun—manmade justice! God's judgment is equitable.

B. *God makes no mistakes in his judgment.*

1. God's judgments are accurate. God looks down into the heart of the one being judged, and his system of judgment is more accurate than a lie detector. His judgments are just. As Joseph Addison once said, "To be perfectly just is an attribute of the divine nature."

2. God cannot be misled by circumstantial evidence. Many years ago a man was sentenced to death on the gallows because a jury had declared him guilty of murder. The condemned man firmly declared his innocence, but circumstantial evidence was against him. On that fatal day, he was led to the gallows, the noose was put in place, and finally the trap door was sprung. In the hush of those moments following, there arose a murmur of excitement. Unexplainedly, the noose broke and the condemned man simply fell a few feet to the ground. It was decided that he would not have to undergo the trip to the gallows again but that he would be sent to prison to remain for the rest of his life. Some twenty years later in a distant town a man lay dying. He called the minister close to his bedside and whispered into his ear his confession of the murder for which the other man had been convicted. God, the righteous Judge, cannot be misled.

C. *God's judgment is tempered by love.* The person standing before God's judgment throne who is joined to Christ in faith is not looked upon as a stranger but as a beloved heir. The love of God reaches across his bar of justice to reassure the trembling person that divine justice is tempered by divine love. As we stand before the throne of God to answer to him for the deeds done in the flesh, he will see us not in our own goodness—or lack of it—but as followers of and believers in his only begotten Son.

III. Man cannot escape his judgment (vv. 3, 6).

Some people live as though they expected to live on this earth forever, as though there will never be a day of accounting to almighty God. Paul speaks emphatically against such an idea, for he says that:

A. *Those judging others cannot escape God's judgment.* Humans receive some elements of judgment while yet on this earth. Paul is saying that in due time God is going to sit in judgment on *every* person; no one can hope to escape that judgment.

B. God *"will render to every man according to his deeds" (v. 6).* There will appear before God's judgment seat a variety of "cases." Paul describes some here:

1. Those who despise the riches of God's goodness, forbearance, and longsuffering (v. 4). Humankind living in this age will have much to answer to God for on this score, for never has there been such a time of indifference to the goodness of God. People today are busily engaged

in vaulting up the ladder of self-esteem, quite forgetful that it is God who gives them the very breath of life.

2. Those who are hard-hearted (v. 5). The hardness of heart that causes people to continue to say no to the call of God's Holy Spirit is the cause of this great and unpardonable sin. Hardness of heart creates rebellion toward God and enmity with God. This sin of unbelief will cause many to hear the fatal words of the righteous Judge: "Depart from me, ye cursed, into everlasting fire, prepared for the devil and his angels" (Matt. 25:41).

3. Those who continue to refuse to repent of their sins (v. 5). How tragic it is that many people see no need of turning away from their sins. Also tragic is that many plan to wait until the last minute of their earthly lives to seek forgiveness.

4. Those who patiently continue in faith and well-doing shall receive eternal life (v. 7). Faith that lasts until death is a saving faith, indeed! Faith that puts words into practice in day-to-day living is faith that counts. Some standing before the great judgment throne are going to hear the Master say, "Well done, thou good and faithful servant: thou hast been faithful over a few things, I will make thee ruler over many things: enter thou into the joy of thy lord" (Matt. 25:21).

Conclusion

Paul speaks to us in a very pointed way, cautioning us not to sit in judgment on our fellow humans. We as Christians ought to take into our hearts Paul's admonition to us and resolve not to speak harshly of others or to gossip about others in the future. More to the point, Paul reminds us that there is going to be a judgment of each one of us by God, the righteous Judge, and that we must be prepared for that great day. This morning will you examine your hearts and see if you find therein the assurance that you are ready to meet the Master face-to-face? If you find that you are not prepared, will you open your heart and let your faith flow out to God through Christ Jesus and in return allow his saving power to reach into your soul?

SUNDAY EVENING, JULY 10

Title: The Lord's Prayer — What It Is Not

Text: "But when ye pray, use not vain repetitions, as the heathen do: for they think that they shall be heard for their much speaking" **(Matt. 6:7)**.

Scripture Reading: Matthew 6:7–15

Introduction

A great scholar could not sleep one evening. He arose to study the Lord's Prayer. He studied it all night. At daybreak he was convinced that in a lifetime he could not fathom its depth.

I. Some impressions.

A. *It is profound.* We are immediately impressed by its brevity. There are sixty-six words in the Lord's Prayer just as there are sixty-six books in the Bible. One can say this prayer in less than a minute.

We are impressed by its profound nature. It is quoted in many languages around the world by just about every race and creed of people.

B. *Our ignorance of it.* Many years ago when prayer was allowed in public schools, a schoolteacher in Maine asked each of her pupils in the first through twelfth grades to recite the Lord's Prayer every day. One day she gave the high school students a test and asked them to write what they remembered of the Lord's Prayer. Here are some of their answers.

A senior girl, age eighteen, wrote, "Our Father who art in heaven, Halloween our name."

A sophomore, age sixteen, wrote, "Give us our daily bread and forgive our dinners."

A freshman, age fifteen, wrote, "Our Father who art in heaven, thou'll be our name. Thou Kingdoms come thou will be done on earth as it is in heaven. And give us this day our daily trespassest."

A sophomore, age fifteen, wrote, "Forgive us our tresmasses as we forgive our trespasses."

In Shakespeare's *Hamlet*, the king who miserably fails in prayer says, "My words fly up, my thoughts remain below; / Words without thoughts never to heaven go."

To many people the Lord's Prayer has become words without thought.

II. It is not a definition of prayer.

Nowhere in these verses does one find a definition of prayer. They exemplify different qualities and aspects of prayer, but they do not explain that prayer is praise or adoration or thanksgiving. These verses do not define prayer as confession or petition or intercession. Nor do they explain prayer as initial meditation or experienced reflection or deep contemplation. They teach by example, as the poet James Montgomery put it:

> *O Thou, by whom we come to God,*
> *The life, the truth, the way,*
> *The path of prayer Thyself hast trod:*
> *Lord, teach us how to pray!*

III. It is not a ritual to be repeated.

In verse 7 of the chapter in which the Lord's Prayer appears, our Lord warns against "vain repetitions." It may be that the Lord's Prayer has become nothing but a vain repetition to many.

IV. It is not necessarily for use in church services.

A. *Early traditions.* Cyril indicated in his writings that during the time of Lent and Easter, as early as AD 50, the Lord's Prayer was used in church services. In Jerusalem the Lord's Prayer was "prayed" just before the Lord's Supper was observed.

In an old document, *The Teaching of the Twelve Apostles*, which has been dated as early as AD 50, the Lord's Prayer seems to have been reserved for those who had been baptized in the name of Christ.

Tradition may be on the side of those who use the Lord's Prayer as a part of ritualistic worship services. However, our Lord does not indicate that the Lord's Prayer is to be repeated as any part of a ritual.

B. *Lost meaning.* The Lord's Prayer often loses its meaning when it is repeated as part of ritualistic worship. One man testified, "The Lord's Prayer doesn't mean much to me." He went on to say that, while he was in the army, he heard the Lord's Prayer recited so many times without any feeling and meaning in chapel services that it had lost all of its meaning for him.

It may well be that one of the things furthest from the mind of our Lord when he gave the Lord's Prayer in the Sermon on the Mount was the primary manner in which it is used today.

V. It is not a magic formula.

The Jews repeated certain prayers for the events of life. At the sight of fruits, vegetables, wine, or any produce of the earth, they said, "Blessed art thou that created the fruit of the tree, fruit of the vine, and the fruit of the earth."

At the sight of shooting stars, earthquakes, lightning, thunder, or storms, they said, "Blessed is he whose might and power fill the earth."

When they saw mountains, hills, rivers, or deserts, good Jews would say, "Blessed is the author of creation."

When they heard bad tidings, they said, "Blessed is he, the true Judge."

When they acquired something new, they said, "Blessed is he who hath given us life."

A good Jew thought one should pray every time he entered or left a city.

Certainly, the Lord's Prayer is not such a magic formula. When our Lord said, "Pray ye," he used the Greek present, active imperative. This verb tense indicates continuous action. In other words, Christians should make prayer the habitual practice of their lives.

Conclusion

The daughter of an atheist said to a friend, "I was brought up without any religion. I do not believe in God." Then she said wistfully, "But the other day in an old German book I came across a German prayer, and if the God of that prayer exists, I think I could believe in him."

"What was the prayer?" asked the friend. In German, she slowly repeated the Lord's Prayer.

WEDNESDAY EVENING, JULY 13

Title: "Open Thou Mine Eyes"

Text: "Open thou mine eyes, that I may behold wondrous things out of thy law" **(Ps. 119:18)**.

Scripture Reading: Psalm 119:1–24

Introduction

The psalmist prayed that God would open the eyes of his soul that he might be able to understand the truth in the divine Word of God. Perhaps he had read the Word of God with a seeing eye and an understanding heart and hungered for a return of this blessed privilege.

If we would properly understand and respond to the revelation of God that is contained in the Bible, we must pray that our eyes be opened by the Holy Spirit.

Paul wrote to the Corinthians concerning the work of the Holy Spirit in opening our eyes and revealing to us the deep things of God (1 Cor. 2:9–12). One can read the Word of God and become familiar with the narrative and acquainted with the facts of which the Bible speaks. Only when the eye of the mind is opened by the Spirit of God can the divine truth contained in God's Word become real to the reader (Luke 24:25–32). Our Lord opened both the minds of his apostles and the Scriptures that they might really understand the wondrous things written in the Word of God (Luke 24:44–47). The psalmist was praying for an open eye, a capacity to see spiritual reality.

I. Open thou mine eyes—that I might behold the nearness of the Lord.

God is Spirit. No man hath ever seen the eternal God except as he made himself visible in Jesus Christ (John 14:9). The psalmist sang of the abiding presence of the eternal God. He rejoiced that God is always as near as the breath that we breathe (Ps. 139:7–13).

II. Open thou mine eyes—that I may see the spiritual resources that are available for service.

The great men and women of God have been those who were able to perceive that inexhaustible spiritual resources were available through faith and obedience. Most of us are blind to the resources of God, as was the servant of Elisha when the king of Syria made war against Israel (2 Kings 6:16–17). Paul was aware of these spiritual resources and moved forward in faith, believing that God would meet his needs as they arose (Eph. 1:18; Phil. 4:13). These resources can be found in the promise of the Lord to be with his obedient disciples at all times (Matt. 28:20). They are available through the Holy Spirit, who came to dwell within the heart of each believer at the time of conversion (1 Cor. 3:16).

III. Open thou mine eyes—that I may see the multitudes through the eyes of Christ (Matt. 9:36).

Our Lord viewed the needy multitudes in his day with compassion. We need to look upon our world today with the same compassion. We need open eyes that can see beneath the mask of affluence and success and see the heart hunger and the spiritual destitution of those who do not know God.

We need to see people as the objects of supreme concern to our God, who so loved this world that he gave his Son for its redemption.

IV. Open thou mine eyes—that I may be convinced of the power of the gospel (Rom. 1:16).

Paul believed that the divine energy by which lives could be redeemed and transformed from failure into spiritual success was to be found in the preaching of the gospel, the good news of what God had done and was continuing to do in and through Jesus Christ.

Only when our eyes are opened to see the continuing power of the gospel to save the people of our world will we be filled with enthusiasm and truly be the servants of Jesus Christ.

Conclusion

There are none so blind as those who will not see. Let each of us take a position by the roadside that leads from Jericho to Jerusalem, and as Jesus passes by, let us pray the prayer that the blind men prayed: "Lord, that our eyes may be opened" (Matt. 20:33). As our Lord had compassion on them and opened their eyes, so will he give to us the capacity to see spiritual reality.

SUNDAY MORNING, JULY 17

Title: Count the Cost

Text: "Then said Jesus unto his disciples, If any man will come after me, let him deny himself, and take up his cross, and follow me" (**Matt. 16:24**).

Scripture Reading: Matthew 16:24–28

Hymns: "Praise, My Soul, the King of Heaven," Lyte

"Alas, and Did My Saviour Bleed?" Watts

"The Old Rugged Cross," Bennard

"Wherever He Leads I'll Go," McKinney

Offertory Prayer: Into your storehouse, O Father, we bring our tithes and offerings. We make our offerings to you because we love you and desire your kingdom to come in the fullness of glory. We present to you these tangible expressions of our love and devotion to you. We pray that you will accept them in the spirit with which we bring them. Amen.

Introduction

The chief reason that the Jewish nation failed as a nation and failed to continue as God's chosen people was that it failed to be committed to the task assigned to it. Jesus came to select a new covenant people, a spiritual Israel, an Israel that originated through the birth process—the "second birth"—a spiritual birth through repentance and faith. Jesus was careful, however, to warn his followers that they must stop and count the cost: "If any man will be a follower of mine, let him get totally committed to the task by first of all denying himself his own personal desires and whim and, taking up his load of responsibility in kingdom service, following me faithfully" (Matt. 16:24, my paraphrase). Jesus never promised that the Christian life would be easy. In fact, he promised hardship and persecution. He desires of his followers total commitment of life in order that the world might be won to him. Is this too much to ask? All Christians must realize that they are commissioned by Christ to be builders in his kingdom. Let every Christian, therefore, sit down and count the cost of such a building program.

I. It will cost him a deep personal faith in Christ.

We are living in a day in which many people pronounce themselves "Christians" simply because they have been privileged to be born into a Christian home and into a Christian community. To merit the label "Christian," one must first have met the requirements of Jesus for entry into his kingdom.

A. *"Except a man be born again" (John 3:3).* This is a strange saying for mortal ears, yet Jesus has stated this as the mode of entry into his kingdom. Using figurative language to express a great spiritual truth, Jesus was saying that a person must come into a personal relationship with him through the birth pangs of a deep spiritual experience. Natural man must suddenly see himself as he is in the sight of righteous God—unclean in thought and action, rebellious toward the divine will for his life, selfish to the core of his being. After seeing himself in that light, he must have great remorse for his unholy condition and turn away from that way of life. He must then turn to the Creator of both mortal life and the Way of immortal life, Christ Jesus, trusting him implicitly for his soul's salvation and surrendering to him as the Lord of his life. Through such birth pangs must a man emerge into the kingdom of Christ.

B. *"That I may know him" (Phil. 3:10).* To some philosophical minds, God is just an illusion. Ludwig Feuerbach, the most significant and influential representative of illusionism in the modern world, said that God is "nothing else than a product and reflex of the supernatural human mind" and that theology is but "a web of contradiction and delusions" (quoted in Albert C. Knudson, *The Doctrine of God* [New York: Abingdon-Cokesbury, 1930], 22–23). Other thinkers of the day have followed after Freud, who claimed to have found the roots of religion in perverted sexuality (ibid., 23). Not so with the apostle Paul, whose faith was in Christ Jesus as Savior and Lord. He was eager to know his Master better each day. He expressed this feeling beautifully to young Timothy when he told him, "Study to shew thyself approved unto God, a workman that needeth not to be ashamed, rightly dividing the word of truth" (2 Tim. 2:15). A true Christian is one who is hungry to learn more each day about Christ and the things of his kingdom. He will pay the price for that knowledge by diligently studying God's Word, by spending much time in prayer, and by taking careful notice of God's dealings in the lives of Christians. How often have I mourned over disasters that came into the lives of some of my Christian friends, only later to find that those "disasters" had been turned by the Master into "blessings." God's dealings with his followers, when studied in the light of his Word, cause us to come to know him better.

C. *"Let your light so shine before men" (Matt. 5:16).* Each Christian is a translator of God's Word to the people of the world. On one occasion a group of biblical scholars was discussing the merits of the various modern translations of the New Testament. Each scholar differed from the other in his preference of these translations, and each one loudly upheld his preference with rather heated arguments to substantiate his views. One of the scholars present remained silent all during this lengthy, animated discussion. Finally, the others noticed that he had voiced no opinion concerning the merits of any of the translations, so they turned and inquired which one he preferred. He replied, "Well, if you must know, I like my old grandfather's translation best; he translated for seventy-five years God's Word into life, and it was the most effective translation I have ever known."

II. It will cost him service to the body of Christ, the local church.

A stalk of corn is a stalk of corn even though it may be growing in a weed patch. Under such conditions, however, it will not be much of a stalk of corn, and it certainly will not bear any harvest of grain. Conceivably a Christian can be a Christian and not have fellowship with others in the church of Christ, but he will not be much of a Christian, certainly not a fruit-bearing Christian. Every Christian who is truly born again will desire to be an active part of a body of believers, the "called-out ones" of God.

A. *Use your talents in service to the church.* In a church where I was privileged to be pastor, there was a man who literally would have fainted if he had been told he must teach a Sunday school class; to lead in public prayer he could not; to serve in the choir he would not. This man, however, was considered one of the most valuable members of the church, for he used his skills as an electrician in such a great way for his church that the other members felt his contribution was invaluable.

B. *Shoulder the teaching, training, and missionary load of the church.* Every member of the local church should realize that the Lord expects him to be actively engaged in promoting the teaching and training programs of the church. If he cannot lead, he can be the best follower in the church.

How encouraging it is to a church leader to have faithful and enthusiastic followers in his organization. America is fast slipping backward spiritually. We are told that a great percentage of college students—our leaders of tomorrow—make no pretense of having any sort of Christian faith. If we in our local churches do not shoulder the responsibility for teaching and training the young people while they are yet with us, they are apt to go out into life to be advocates of materialistic atheism.

C. *Be faithful in attendance in your church.* If we are thoroughly Christian, we are going to desire to congregate regularly for worship and fellowship. One dear saint of a church member once remarked to me, "I can be a great deal of help by always being in my place at the proper time. I want the pastor to realize that he doesn't need to take his time to see me, but he can spend his time working with those not so faithful and with unchurched people." Most Christians are not as faithful in their attendance as they ought to be. Recently I bemused myself by making a "guesstimate" as to how the average American spends his time. As based on a life span of seventy years, the results were as follows: six years spent in eating, eleven years in working, eight years in amusement, twenty-four years sleeping, five years dressing, three years talking, and only six months in church.

III. It will cost him money.

A dirty word among many Christians is the word *stewardship*, especially when that word has particular reference to the stewardship of money. Yet it is one of the most vital words in the Christian faith. It is a chief determining factor as to whether a Christian has really made Jesus the Lord of his life. Stewardship involves our time, talents, and money. At this time I will speak only of the financial phase of stewardship.

A. *It is the duty of every Christian to tithe.* How can a Christian whine, "I would love to tithe, but, Pastor, I just can't afford to"? Where would the Christian be today if nearly two thousand years ago Jesus had said, "I would love to die for you people, but I just can't afford to give up my sinless life for you sinners"? Old Testament believers while under the law assumed that every believer in and follower of Jehovah God would give at least a tenth of his income. How can a Christian who is under grace—the unmerited favor of almighty God—afford to do less than an Old Testament Jew?

B. *It is the duty of every Christian to promote stewardship in his church.* A church member once said to a friend who was a great man of God in whom he had a lot of confidence, "Our church is always asking for money for such causes as building fund, missions, etc. Some of us members are getting the impression that our pastor and church leaders are more interested in money than in the spiritual needs of our community." The wise man of God replied, "If your church is making too much ado over finances, it is probably because its members have failed to give God his share—that is, they have failed to tithe their incomes. I have never heard a tither complain about requests from the pulpit for money or complain about a sermon on tithing. It is usually the member who owes much in back tithes and offerings to the Lord who complains about stewardship being stressed."

IV. It will cost him spiritual energy.

One of the greatest weaknesses of most Christians is their unwillingness to witness to others of Christ. Jesus has commissioned every Christian to be a soul winner. This is the greatest cost to every Christian in his role of a disciple, but it is the most rewarding of all his endeavors.

A. *It will cost him time.* In our busy lives, we feel that there are never enough "energy hours" left in our schedules to go up the street, down the street, or across town to witness to a lost soul. We are under the same Great Commission to witness as were the first-century Christians. We must, therefore, take time to tell others about Christ.

B. *It will cost him love.* Dietrich Bonhoeffer well said, "It is hardly surprising that so few are granted to see things with the pitying eyes of Jesus, for only those who share the love of his heart have been given eyes to see. And only they can enter the harvest field" (*The Cost of Discipleship* [New York: Macmillan, 1959], 225).

C. *It will cost him effort.* It will cost him effort in self-inventory, in soul-searching prayer, and in spiritual concentration on and consecration to the task of winning that certain soul to Christ. He must have God's power in his efforts or they will be of no avail. Samuel M. Shoemaker has said, "One reason why so much of our Christian effort never gets to the level of awakening is that it is self-effort.... our willfulness and self-effort stand in [God's] way as much as any of our sins" (*By the Power of God* [New York: Harper & Brothers, 1954], 136–37).

D. *It will cost him a righteous life.* Once an entire college football team was sidelined for most of the season because an infection crept into their midst, felling the players, managers, and coaches. When it was discovered that the rest of the student body did not seem to be affected, the origin of the hepatitis was discovered to be in a leaky water pipe that piped the water to the drinking fountain on the practice field. The imperfection in the water pipe had allowed germs to creep into the pipe and thence into the drinking water. A Christian's life must be a righteous channel if God's blessings are to flow through. All the persuasive oratory in the world on the part of the Christian who is attempting to win someone to Christ will be of no avail if that Christian's life does not back up what he is trying to say.

Conclusion

Today will you who are Christians ask yourselves, "Am I totally committed to the cause of Christ? Have I stopped to count the cost of discipleship? Am I sincerely trying to help to bring in Christ's kingdom?" These are the questions every Christian must put to his own heart. And every lost person this morning must ask, "Do I love the Lord more than my sinful way of life? Am I now ready to turn my back on sin and turn to Christ?" Sinner friend, surrender to the Master and let him cleanse your soul and save you for useful service. The cost of discipleship is small in comparison with the blessings you will receive.

SUNDAY EVENING, JULY 17

Title: The Lord's Prayer—What It Is

Text: "But thou, when thou prayest, enter into thy closet, and ... pray to thy Father" **(Matt. 6:6)**.

Scripture Reading: Matthew 6:7–15

Introduction

Do you remember the first letter you ever wrote? Pencil in hand, you stared at a blank sheet of paper. Perhaps you asked an older person, "What should I say?"

Do you remember the first time you stood before people and tried to make a speech? Perhaps your first question was, "What should I say?"

There are two ways your elders may have helped you in these early years of writing and speaking: (1) By giving you a copy of a letter or speech and asking you to copy it down or to recite it from memory or (2) by giving you an outline or a pattern to serve as a guide for what you should say.

The Lord's Prayer is a pattern for prayer. It contains the principles to guide the Christian's prayer life. Our Lord spent whole nights in prayer. Certainly he did not merely repeat these words again and again. Undoubtedly, he used them as his pattern to pray.

I. An outline of the pattern.

The Lord's Prayer falls into a logical outline.

A. *Prelude or invocation*— *"Our Father which art in heaven."* These words teach us that our prayers must not be self-centered. All of God's people can pray because God is *"Our* Father," not *"My* Father."

B. *Three petitions concerning God.*

1. "Hallowed be thy name." God's name is hallowed and holy. We pray that God's name, which is already hallowed, may be regarded for what it is. We begin our prayer by acknowledging his holiness and righteousness.

2. "Thy kingdom come. Thy will be done." The kingdom of God comes into our lives as we let the will of God be done. We ask that God become the sovereign Ruler of our lives.

3. "On earth, as it is in heaven." We acknowledge that there are angels in

heaven and that there is activity in heaven. We ask that God's will in our lives be done on earth as perfectly as it is being done in heaven.

C. *Three petitions concerning people.*

1. "Give us this day our daily bread." We do not pray for our daily "cake"; we ask only for the basic necessities of life.

2. "Forgive us our trespasses." If we harbor in our hearts hatred for a brother or sister, we cannot pray aright. We must have a forgiving spirit as we ask God for his forgiveness.

3. "Lead us not into temptation." When trying times come, we pray that God will lead us around them. We do not pray that God will remove temptations from us. Our prayer is merely that God will deliver us from the clutches of the Wicked One.

D. *Some believe that our Lord's disciples added the appropriate doxology to the Lord's Prayer.* Even if this is so, it is certainly a fitting conclusion to the model prayer.

II. A pattern for living.

A. *Like the Ten Commandments, the Lord's Prayer has two poles — the vertical and the horizontal.* Three petitions are related to God (vertical). Three petitions are related to humans (horizontal). The same religious and social relationships are noted in the Beatitudes — five of them deal with our relationship to God and three deal with our relationships with others.

B. *The Lord's Prayer says, "Give God first place in your life."* Three petitions precede the prayer concerning human needs. The words *I, me, my,* and *mine* do not appear in the Lord's Prayer. Only when God has been given his proper place in a person's life do all things fall into their proper perspective.

C. *The Lord's Prayer teaches us that all of our needs are met in Christ.*

1. The present — daily bread.

2. The past — forgiveness of sin.

3. The future — protection from temptation and deliverance from evil.

Conclusion

This prayer reminds us that God is able to meet all of our needs. God is not limited by the past, present, or future.

When we pray for our present needs, we are reminded of the Creator, God the Father. As we pray for forgiveness of past sins, we are reminded that God revealed himself to us in Jesus Christ and that Christ died on the cross for our sins. When we pray about the future, we are reminded that the Holy Spirit is our Guide, Comforter, and Helper. In the Lord's Prayer, Jesus is telling us to bring all of our lives to an all-sufficient God who can help us in all circumstances — God the Father, Son, and Holy Spirit.

WEDNESDAY EVENING, JULY 20

Title: Blot Out My Transgressions

Text: "Have mercy upon me, O God, according to thy lovingkindness: according unto the multitude of thy tender mercies blot out my transgressions" **(Ps. 51:1)**.

Scripture Reading: Psalm 51

Introduction

Psalm 51 contains the heart cry of a grief-stricken sinner because of the sin that had polluted his heart and deprived him of the joy of fellowship with God. Let us earnestly pray that we might be kept from the sin into which David fell. We would be exceedingly wise to always flee from temptation and to avoid the appearance of evil, for no one is immune to temptation.

A study of the experience of David with Bathsheba is beneficial in this day when moral standards are being abandoned.

Because of his sin, David suffered greatly. Sin always results in suffering. David no longer enjoyed peace of heart and mind (Ps. 32:3–4). He was crushed by the burden of guilt (Ps. 51:3, 9, 11–12). Behind these confessions and petitions one can see the barren destitution of his heart and life before sin was confessed and forgiven.

While few of us have sinned in the manner in which David sinned, we must recognize that all of us are sinners and in need of forgiveness (1 John 1:8–10). David's dealing with his guilt can provide us with insight concerning how we should deal with our transgressions against God.

I. David made a plea for pardon.

A. *The king made an appeal to God's mercy (Ps. 51:1).* The last thing that he wanted at this time was justice. He needed mercy, so he appealed to the merciful God for mercy and received mercy.

B. *David acknowledged his guilt of sin (Ps. 51:3).* David provides us with a pattern for dealing properly with guilt.

   1. He accepted responsibility for his guilt.
   2. He did not blame his companions.
   3. He did not hold Bathsheba responsible for his sin.
   4. He did not rationalize and try to justify his action.

II. David made a plea for purity.

A. *"Wash me thoroughly from mine iniquity."* The word *iniquity* means crookedness or twistedness. David perceived that his life was out of tune and out of touch with God.

B. *"Cleanse me from my sin."* The word "sin" means to miss the mark, to fall short of the aim, to fail to pass inspection. David recognized that sin causes one to be rejected, and he earnestly desired to be cleansed from his sin.

218

C. *"Purge me with hyssop, and I shall be clean: wash me, and I shall be whiter than snow" (Ps. 51:7).* The heart of the king hungered for a divine purification that would cleanse him completely. He eagerly desired that God would deal drastically with his sin and guilt in order that he might again be clean on the inside. David earnestly prayed that God would hide his face from his sins and blot out all of his iniquities. He feared that he would be utterly cast off and that the Spirit of God would depart from him unless God did deal with his sin in mercy. He prayed that God would not only forgive and blot out his transgressions but that he also would renew a right spirit within him. He pledged that, if God would forgive his sin, he would dedicate himself afresh to the service of God. He said, "Then will I teach transgressors thy ways; and sinners shall be converted unto thee.... my tongue shall sing aloud of thy righteousness" (vv. 13–14). He would show forth the praises of God to everyone.

Conclusion

May God not only help each of us to confess our sins, but also grant us to receive his forgiveness and move forward with joy as his redeemed children and servants.

SUNDAY MORNING, JULY 24

Title: God's Great Risk

Text: "And God said, Let us make man in our image, after our likeness" **(Gen. 1:26)**.

Scripture Reading: Genesis 1:24–31

Hymns: "The Spacious Firmament on High," Addison

          "Jesus Shall Reign," Watts

          "Majestic Sweetness Sits Enthroned," Stennett

          "Just as I Am," Elliott

Offertory Prayer: Into your sacred hands we cast our offerings of love and faithfulness. Receive them as you did the loaves and fish beside the Sea of Galilee, multiplying them in order to feed the spiritually hungry of the world. We present anew our love and devotion to you along with our tithes and offerings. Bless us as we wait before you in this hour of worship and adoration, for we offer this prayer in the name of Christ our Savior. Amen.

Introduction

The title of this sermon, "God's Great Risk," is based on an attempt to look at this subject from a human viewpoint. It is by no means an attempt to humanize God.

When we read this account in Genesis, we have a tendency to swell with pride because God has made us with such rich endowments. Our pride begins to melt away and become shadowed with misgivings when we realize the full portent of this truth. What a risk God has taken to create such a creature as man and to place him here on the earth with authority over the rest of God's creation and with the right to make his own decisions morally and spiritually! Some of the reasons why it was such a great risk for God to create man as a free moral agent are these:

I. Man may rebel against God's sovereignty.

While yet in the garden of Eden, Adam set the pattern for such rebellion. The same old story continues today.

A. *Man may seek to remake God's wonderful creation.* Has not man always seemed to think that he could improve on God's work? Scripture says, "And God saw everything that he had made, and, behold, it was very good" (Gen. 1:31). Bertrand Russell presumed to say in a spirit of overconfidence closely akin to rebellion, "It may be that God made the world, but there is no reason why we should not make it over" (*Scientific Outlook* [New York: W. W. Norton, 1931], 151). Man indeed has made great scientific strides forward during these past few years. So many and so great are human-kind's achievements that we must agree with Eustace Haydon: "The world today knows nothing more familiar than man's success in imposing his will on the flow of events.... He changes the face of the earth and alters the habits of men" (*Quest of the Ages* [New York: Harper and Brothers, 1929], 210). Such people imagine that humans by their own resources can decide the direction of all historical development. These are nice, neat, unnoticed forms of rebellion against the sovereignty of God, yet they are destructive.

B. *The creature may turn against the Creator.* "The fool hath said in his heart, There is no God" (Pss. 14:1; 53:1). Atheists, the modern version of the person described in this verse, seek in their proud and stubborn hearts to war with God by spending their time denying that he exists. They seek to destroy the goodness brought about in this world through his providential love and his mercy through his Son Jesus Christ. Some do not speak openly against God but rebuff all who seek to enlist them for Christ.

II. Man may mar and destroy the image of God.

In himself man runs the great risk of:

A. *Marring the image of God's holiness and righteousness.* Isaiah's vision of the holiness of the Lord in Isaiah 6 caused him to cry out, "Woe is me! for I am undone; because I am a man of unclean lips, and I dwell in the midst of a people of unclean lips: for mine eyes have seen the King, the Lord of hosts" (v. 5). Paul said, "Know ye not that ye are the temple of God, and that the Spirit of God dwelleth in you? If any man defile the temple of God, him shall God destroy; for the temple of God is holy, which temple ye are" (1 Cor. 3:16–17). As images of God we are guilty of abusing the picture of holiness and righteousness. We are creating a society full of crime. Some of the outward manifestations of this are:

1. Juvenile delinquency. J. Edgar Hoover once expressed the opinion that in almost every case parents are to blame for the development of young criminals through neglect, unhappiness, insecurity, and parental conflict. Juvenile delinquency is but the reflection of adult modes, morals, and methods. There is no form of juvenile vice, violence, or viciousness that does not have its counterpart on the adult level.

2. Alcoholism and drug addiction. B. C. Holtzclaw, in an address at the Pastor's School of the University of Richmond, said, "Man's purpose in the world, if he is an image of God, is to create good, so far as that is possible, and not to be the source or cause of evil.... He ought to ... aim at producing good" (quoted in the *Religious Herald*, 132, no. 28 [July 9, 1959]). Alcoholism and drug addiction prevent an individual from producing good in this world. More lives have been maimed or ruined and more homes upset by drug abuse than by any of the diseases common to man, and the latter are more easily cured. God must be ashamed of his image wallowing in the gutter of life, selfishly and foolishly trying to enjoy life to the fullest but going about it in the most unrewarding way.

3. Wrong use of freedom of thought and action. For many people freedom means being oneself. This is obviously impossible to accomplish unless a person is at liberty to go contrary to the will of the very God who makes him free. When God placed man on this earth and gave him the privilege of choosing or rejecting him and his laws, he ran a great risk. The very being of man cries out for freedom, and unregenerate man sees freedom as having his own selfish way. Every person longs for freedom.

III. Man may reject God's loving call to salvation.

God has always desired to have fellowship with his created image. As on that cool evening in the garden of Eden when he called to Adam and Eve, so today he calls to each of us to come to him and have fellowship with him. God's great risk in this matter is that he allows us to choose to come to him for fellowship through salvation and submission to his lordship or to reject him completely. Adam and Eve and many of their descendants have stubbornly rejected God, but God has a way of wooing stubborn man, not through force, but through the strongest of all cords—the cords of love.

    A. *He has given a way whereby people may come to him.*

        1. God's part in this way of salvation: he gave his only begotten Son to atone for our sins on Calvary.

        2. Our part:

            a. Repentance—a great sorrow over our sinfulness and a turning away from our sinful way of life.

            b. Faith in Jesus Christ as Savior and Lord.

B. *Some people reject the way of salvation completely and deliberately.* Some are so hard-hearted that they steadfastly refuse to humble themselves and yield to the cleansing power of Christ and to his sovereignty over their lives. They deliberately choose to reject Christ and turn their backs on his loving call to salvation.

C. *Some people unintentionally reject the plan of salvation by procrastinating.* "Tomorrow, next Sunday, next year I shall accept Christ as my Savior and Lord. There are things I must do before accepting him. I must clean up my speech; I must learn to control my temper; I must give up my alcoholic drinks," some say. This is a negative approach and is in a sense an effort to earn salvation by works. That is not God's plan at all, but rather, as Charlotte Elliott wrote, we must come to him as we are and allow him to do the cleansing:

> *Just as I am, without one plea*
> *But that Thy blood was shed for me,*
> *And that Thou bidd'st me come to Thee,*
> *O Lamb of God, I come! I come!*

Conclusion

Did God take a risk in creating you in his image? Over the Greek temple at Delphi are these words: "Know thyself." This morning, I say to you, "Know thyself." Have you used your God-given freedom as a lustful license to serve yourself and your pleasure, or have you given yourself to Christ to serve him? Stop marring the image of God through your rebellion toward him and surrender to his love for you. Accept him today. Come just as you are that he may cleanse your soul and set you free.

SUNDAY EVENING, JULY 24

Title: "Our Father"

Text: "After this manner therefore pray ye: Our Father which art in heaven" **(Matt. 6:9).**

Scripture Reading: John 1:1 – 13

Introduction

God is not the Father of all humans!

Does that statement surprise you? The doctrine of "the fatherhood of God and the brotherhood of man" on which the social gospel movement was founded sounds good, but it is not in the Bible.

Certainly God is the *Creator* of all people; however, he cannot be called the *Father* of all people. It seems wise, therefore, to approach this section of the Lord's Prayer with a discussion of God the Creator before discussing God the Father.

I. God the Creator.

    A. *The Bible plainly declares that all races of people had a common origin with God (Acts 17:24–26).* Since God is the God of all races by creation, one race cannot be superior to another.

    B. *The Bible teaches that man was created "in the image of God" (Gen. 1:26–27).* No one knows exactly what this means, because no one knows God perfectly. Yet we do know that man reflects certain important elements of God's being.

        1. Man is more than an animal. Like an animal, he eats, drinks, and needs sleep, but he was created in God's image.

        2. Rationally, this means that man is a thinker. Morally, it means that man has the ability to know right from wrong. Spiritually, it means that man is a living soul and can commune with the Creator and the created.

    C. *As we seek to understand God the Creator, we are reminded of the following:*

        1. All men are created equal, and God is no respecter of persons (Rom. 2:11; Eph. 6:9; 1 Peter 1:17).

        2. All men are sinners (Rom. 3:23), and the wages of sin is death for all people of all races (6:23).

        3. Christ died for all people (John 3:16).

        4. Christians of all races, therefore, are brothers and sisters in Christ (Luke 13:29).

        5. In Christ there is a common brotherhood (Gal. 3:28; Col. 3:11).

        6. Sin marred the image of God in man, but it is restored for people of all races when they are born again.

        7. When one has this personal relationship to God through Christ, he is able to address God as "Our Father." We address God as "Our Father," not because we have been born into a world created by God, but because we have been born again through the new creation by Christ Jesus (John 1:12). Those who have rejected Jesus Christ have another father—the Devil (John 8:44).

II. God the Father.

    A. *Revealed in Christ.* The greatest privilege afforded mortals is the privilege of calling God the Creator "Father." In Christ, the fatherhood of God is revealed, because "God was in Christ reconciling the world unto himself" (2 Cor. 5:19).

        As a young man, Jesus said to those who were anxious concerning his whereabouts, "Did you not know that I would be about my *father's* business?" In the garden of Gethsemane he prayed, "O my *Father,* if it be possible, let this cup pass from me." On the cross he prayed, "*Father,* into thy hands I commend my spirit."

        It is interesting to note that Jesus did not pray to his Creator, Judge, or Ruler. He prayed to his heavenly *Father.* God is Creator of all, but he is Father only to those who become his children in Christ (1 John 3:1–2).

In Christ we become true children of God, heirs of God and joint-heirs with Christ (Rom. 8:16–17).

B. *What does the fatherhood of God reveal about God's nature?*
1. God loves us supremely. As earthly parents care for their children, so God cares for and loves his children. God is not isolated, detached, or insulated against emotion. God cares for us. Because we have been adopted into his family, we cry, "Abba, Father" (Rom. 8:15).
2. God dearly protects us. In Jesus' day two sparrows were sold for a penny (Matt. 10:29). Bargain hunters could get five sparrows for two pennies. One was thrown in as though he was forgotten. But God's infinite knowledge reaches out to even that forgotten sparrow (Luke 12:6).
3. God will discipline us. The Scriptures teach us, "God dealeth with [us] as sons; for what son is he whom the father chasteneth not?" (Heb. 12:7).
4. God comforts us. We are encouraged to cast all our cares on him because he cares for us (1 Peter 5:7).
5. At death we shall inherit heaven, our "inheritance that fadeth not away" (1 Peter 1:4).

Conclusion

"Like father like son" applies to our relationship to our heavenly Father as well as to our earthly father.

Like Father like son! As the Father speaks the truth in love, his children bridle their tongues and refrain from pride and prejudice.

Like Father like son! God's children possess an unusual compassion for those in need. Their greatest desire, of course, is to see unsaved people brought to Jesus Christ. The Scriptures teach that "the Son of man is come to seek and to save that which was lost" (Luke 19:10).

Like Father like son! As the Father is holy and pure, his children seek to purge themselves from those things that are unholy and impure. In thought, motive, and deed, holiness is the watchword for God's sons and daughters!

Like Father like son! God's children seek not the approval or the applause of the crowd. God's children refuse to live a life of slavery to sin.

WEDNESDAY EVENING, JULY 27

Title: "Teach Us to Number Our Days"

Text: "So teach us to number our days, that we may apply our hearts unto wisdom" **(Ps. 90:12)**.

Scripture Reading: Psalm 90

Introduction

In some respects the ancient Egyptians were wiser than we are. We are told that at every feast there was always an extraordinary guest that sat at the head of the table. He was heavily veiled, and he did not eat, drink, or speak. This guest was a skeleton that they had placed there to warn them, even in the time of their feasting, that there would be an end to earthly life as we now know it.

Several beneficial results could come to us if we would seriously face the fact of death and make a positive response to it. The psalmist recognized the need of taking an inventory of the number of his days that he might spend the balance of his life in a profitable manner. Adjusting life to the fact of death would probably produce at least three results.

First, it could cure us of the cancer of covetousness that causes us to live and labor merely to accumulate and to have things of earthly value.

Second, it could cause us to switch our affections to the things of God and to the things of eternal significance.

Third, if we were to look at sin by the light of death's lantern, we would see the hollowness, shallowness, and futility of living for the pleasures of sin.

It has been said, "A frequent meditation upon death is a healthful antidote to guard against all sin." Another has said, "He who remembers death cannot fall into sin."

I. Let us consider death.

Perhaps there is no subject that we think of tonight to which so little thought is given. The thought uppermost in our minds is the proverb: "We must live." We would be wiser to alter it and say, "We must die."

A. *Consider the origin of death.* We die because of sin (Rom. 5:12).

B. *Consider the certainty of death (Heb. 9:27).* While some things are uncertain, we can be absolutely certain that death will come to each of us if the Lord delays his coming. Greatness will not prevent death as is evident from the lives and deaths of such personalities as Julius Caesar, Napoleon Bonaparte, Winston Churchill, and Barak Obama. Strength of body will not prevent death — Samson, Goliath, and Gideon. Wisdom will not prevent death — Solomon, Paul, Augustine, Webster, and Gladstone. Wealth will not prevent death — Bill Gates and Warren Buffett. Holiness will not prevent death — patriarchs, prophets, apostles, and martyrs. The noble, the strong, the famous, the good, the weak, and the feeble must die.

C. *The time of our death is uncertain.*

D. *The result of death for the saved is blessedness and happiness (Rev. 14:13).* For the unsaved it is to be exiled from God forever (Luke 16:19–31).

II. Let us consider death's warnings.

A. *Are there any empty chairs in your family circle?*

B. *Do you pay any attention to the fact that death walks abroad through the world?* We hear about it on television and read about it in the newspapers.

C. *The advance of age and the decrease in vitality of life should warn each of us of death's approach.*

III. Let us consider preparation for death.

A. *The philosopher, the scientist, and the sociologist can assist us in life, but they have no comforting answer to the question, "If a man die, shall he live again?"*

B. *Christ and Christ alone can help us to be prepared for death (John 5:24–29; 11:25–26; 14:19).*

C. *To walk with God as he is revealed in Jesus Christ through life is to experience a loss of fear as we approach the experience that we call death (2 Cor. 5:1–8).*

Conclusion

Death for the Christian is but the close of an earthly pilgrimage on his journey to be with God, where he will be delivered from the limitations associated with earthly life and where he will be able to worship and enjoy God forever.

SUNDAY MORNING, JULY 31

Title: Walking before the Lord

Text: "I will walk before the LORD in the land of the living" **(Ps. 116:9)**.

Scripture Reading: Ephesians 5:1–10

Hymns: "Trust and Obey," Sammis

"Walk in the Light," Barton

"Footsteps of Jesus," Slade

Offertory Prayer: Heavenly Father, help us not to forget that you are the source of every good and perfect gift. Help us to count our blessings one by one that love might well up within our hearts and that generosity might characterize our spirits. We bring our tithes and offerings as symbols of our love and as indications of our desire to be involved with you in proclaiming the gospel and in ministering to the needy in today's world. Through Jesus Christ, our Lord, we pray. Amen.

Introduction

The psalmist opened his eyes to behold the beauty of God's goodness to him. His heart responded by loving God more completely than he had previously. He rejoiced in the abundance of God's goodness to him in both the spiritual realm and the physical realm.

His grateful heart sought methods by which he could respond to God's love and grace. Among the decisions that he made was that of choosing to "walk before the LORD in the land of the living." His choice would be a wise choice for each of us.

We find many encouragements to walk and talk with God as we study the Bible. It is recorded, "Noah walked with God" (Gen. 6:9). Abraham was instructed by God to "walk before me, and be thou perfect" (17:1). God promised

226

to walk among his people: "I will walk among you, and will be your God, and ye shall be my people" (Lev. 26:12).

Paul challenged the Christians in Rome to "walk in newness of life" (Rom. 6:4). To the Christians in Colosse, he said, "Walk worthy of the Lord unto all pleasing, being fruitful in every good work, and increasing in the knowledge of God" (Col. 1:10). In writing to the Ephesians, Paul detailed the Christian's walk in a manner that commands both our imagination and our enthusiasm.

I. We are encouraged to walk worthy of our Christian vocation (Eph. 4:1).

We are to remember that we wear the name of our Lord. We are to conduct ourselves as the children of God. We have a noble heritage to live up to. We must not bring disgrace upon our Lord and his church by means of character or conduct that would cause others to be repelled.

II. We are encouraged to walk in love (Eph. 5:2).
   A. *God so loved that he gave his Son for us.*
   B. *Christ so loved that he gave his life for us (John 15:13).*
   C. *Our Lord commanded his disciples to relate to each other in terms of love (John 13:34–35).*
   D. *Because of God's great love for us, we are obligated to relate to each other in terms of Christian love (1 John 4:10–11).*
   E. *Without love it is impossible for us to prove that we have a vital, living relationship with Jesus Christ (1 John 3:14–16).*

III. We are encouraged to walk as the children of light (Eph. 5:8).

As the children of light, we are to separate ourselves from the moral evil associated with living in the darkness of spiritual death. We must put away and sever the relationships with those attitudes and habits that are characteristic of the life of faithlessness and rebellion against God.
   A. *We are to remember our command to function as the light of the world, which makes possible life, love, and hope for the world (Matt. 5:14–16).*
   B. *Christians are to shine as lights in a dark world so that people might see the way to God (Phil. 2:14–16).*

IV. We are encouraged to walk in wisdom (Eph. 5:15).

True wisdom is a gift of God (James 1:5). It is that divinely given insight that makes it possible for one to see through to the end of a course of action. This kind of wisdom comes to those who reverently and responsibly study God's Word and communicate with him in prayer. It comes after we listen to and heed the wisdom of the wise and the counsel of the heavenly Father as he speaks with a still small voice while we tarry in the closet of prayer.

Wisdom is the need of everyone. Wisdom from God is an absolute essential if we are to live humbly and creatively in the home, in the school, in the office, and in any of life's relationships.

Conclusion

The Christian's walk — his daily conduct — is more important than the Christian's talk. It is the Christian's walk that authenticates his talk. The world desperately needs to hear the testimony of those who know God. But before we can talk to the world effectively, we must "walk before the Lord" in such a manner as will cause the world to become attracted to the secret that makes our life different.

To walk with God is to walk on a happy road of life, a way that becomes more wonderful as the years go by. "Enoch walked with God: and he was not; for God took him" (Gen. 5:24).

SUNDAY EVENING, JULY 31

Title: "Which Art in Heaven"

Text: "Our Father which art in heaven" (**Matt. 6:9**).

Scripture Reading: Ephesians 4:1 – 10

Introduction

An ocean liner loaded with vacationers was caught in a furious storm. The passengers were donning their life jackets and checking their cabins. In one cabin they found a little girl, all alone, playing on the bed with her dolls. When they told her about the storm, it did not seem to disturb her at all. She remained as quiet as before, playing with her dolls.

Someone asked, "Aren't you frightened?"

Calmly, the little girl replied, "No, the captain is my father."

The Lord's Prayer begins with the realization that, for disciples of Jesus Christ, the captain of this world is our Father!

I. God's address or God's nature?

God, who is in heaven, is also on earth. We live in his presence. The phrase "which art in heaven" is not necessarily God's address.

"Our rocket has bypassed the moon. It is nearing the sun, and we have not discovered God. We have turned lights out in heaven that no man will be able to put on again. We are breaking the yoke of the gospel. Let us go forth and Christ shall be relegated to mythology." These words were spoken to the world on Christmas Day, 1960, from a radio station in Moscow.

When a Russian cosmonaut returned to earth, he was quite proud of the fact that he had seen neither God nor angels in space. But when Colonel John Glenn returned from orbiting the earth, he said, "The God I pray to is not so small that I expected to see him in space."

H. G. Wells was never more correct than when he said, "Until a man has found God, he begins at no beginning and works to no end." So it is in prayer.

Until we realize that we live in the presence of our heavenly Father, we have no beginning and no goal in life or in prayer.

II. Human concepts of God.

A. *The Lone Ranger concept.* To many people God is like the Lone Ranger, who is standing around somewhere ready to hop into our lives when we need him.

B. *The granddad concept.* Others view God as a simple old man who lives in the upstairs apartment and whose legs will not permit him to come down very often.

C. *The philosophical concept.* Some people view God as a problem that finite man must solve.

A doctor said, "When I see God, I'm going to hold a cancerous bone before his eyes and ask, 'Why?'"

Voltaire declared that life is no more than "a bad joke." The questions of those to whom God is a problem are legion: If God is so good, why does he allow evil to exist in the world? If God is so powerful, why does he allow war to exist? If God is so loving, why does he allow hell to exist?

III. The biblical concept of God.

Augustine said, "God is within all things, but is shut up in nothing; outside all things, but excluded from nothing; beneath all things, but not depressed under anything; above all things, but not lifted up out of the reach of anything."

The apostle Paul declared that we live in the presence of "One God and Father of all, who is above all, and through all, and in you all" (Eph. 4:6).

A. *God is present in heaven and on earth at the same time.* When we address God who is in heaven, we are also declaring his presence on earth.

1. God is called "the possessor of heaven and earth" (Gen. 14:19–22).
2. God "made heaven, and earth, the sea, and all that therein is" (Ps. 146:6).
3. God "hath stretched forth the heavens, and laid the foundations of the earth" (Isa. 51:13).
4. God is called "the high and lofty One that inhabiteth eternity, whose name is Holy" (Isa. 57:15).
5. Jesus prayed, "I thank thee, O Father, Lord of heaven and earth" (Matt. 11:25).

B. *Man can never get out of God's presence (Ps. 139).*

1. Nothing on earth is high enough or deep enough to hide us from God's presence (v. 8).
2. One cannot run fast enough to escape the presence of God (v. 9). The wings of the morning are rays of sunlight. If one could run as fast as the speed of light, he would not be able to escape God's presence.
3. Even darkness cannot hide us from the presence of God (vv. 11–12).

Darkness has saved many from their enemies. Darkness has covered many sins that would have been known in the daylight. But the darkness cannot hide us from God's all-seeing eye.

4. We live in the presence of a God who cares for us and who loves us (v. 5). His love and care encircle us.

Conclusion

Before leaving each morning, a fisherman prayed this prayer: "Keep me, O my God. My boat is so small and thy ocean is so great."

William Law advised every Christian to begin his prayers by using "such expressions of the attributes of God as will make you sensible of his greatness and power."

> *They who seek the throne of grace*
> *Find that throne in every place;*
> *If we live a life of prayer,*
> *God is present everywhere.*
>
> *In our sickness and our health,*
> *In our want or in our wealth,*
> *If we look to God in prayer,*
> *God is present everywhere.*

AUGUST

■ **Sunday Mornings**

The theme for the messages is "God's Wondrous Grace." The grace of God is magnified, and a positive response is encouraged.

■ **Sunday Evenings**

Continue the series on the Sermon on the Mount. The messages this month feature some of the petitions found in the Lord's Prayer.

■ **Wednesday Evenings**

The theme for Wednesday evenings this month is "Living Significantly for Christ."

WEDNESDAY EVENING, AUGUST 3

Title: On a Mountaintop with Jesus

Text: "And after six days Jesus taketh Peter, James, and John his brother, and bringeth them up into a high mountain apart" **(Matt. 17:1)**.

Scripture Reading: Matthew 17:1–9

Introduction

It is interesting to note that God has always worked through minorities instead of majorities. Through the ages there have been individuals or small groups who stood in the inner council with God and were given a vision of his plan and purpose. Because of this unique experience, they were then equipped to render a significant ministry to others.

Among the apostles there appeared to be an inner circle composed of Peter, James, and John. These three were invited to go apart with Christ for prayer and communion with God. The time of this experience is significant. Six days earlier Peter had given expression to his personal faith that Jesus Christ was "the Christ, the Son of the living God" (Matt. 16:16). Following this great confession, Jesus had spoken about founding and building his church, and he had revealed to his disciples that he was on a mission for God that would eventually lead to death and resurrection (v. 21). Peter, to whom this wonderful revelation had come, did not understand at all how death by crucifixion could figure in their dreams and hopes in connection with the Messiah. He sought to dissuade Christ from thinking in these terms, only to be rebuked as being the servant of Satan at that time (vv. 22–23). Six days after this—days of loneliness, frustration, and perplexity—Jesus led these three up a high mountain to pray. Eight times Mark states in his gospel that Jesus led his apostles away to a place of privacy for prayer, for instruction, for fellowship, and for communion with God. Our lives would be greatly enriched if today we would put forth the effort to go apart into a private place for communion and prayer.

I. The transfiguration of Christ (Matt. 17:2).

Words are inadequate to describe this revelation of the glory of Jesus Christ, the divine Son of God.

A. *This was not a light from above.*

B. *This was not a reflected light.*

C. *The transfiguration was the shining forth of a divine light from within Christ.* Deity was shining through the veil of human flesh like the light that shines through a lightbulb to illuminate a room. No doubt it was this experience that John referred to in saying, "And the Word was made flesh, and dwelt among us, (and we beheld his glory, the glory as of the only begotten of the Father,) full of grace and truth" (John 1:14).

II. The heavenly visitors.

Moses and Elijah appeared on the mountain. It is significant that these two Old Testament characters would come to the Christ.

Moses was the lawgiver. The law said, "The soul that sinneth, it shall die," and "The wages of sin is death." Elijah, the prophetic revealer, called the people of his day back to the law of God.

Moses was buried by the Lord himself (Deut. 34:5–6), while Elijah was carried up into heaven by a chariot of fire (2 Kings 2:11).

Moses was the lawgiver who revealed that people are guilty of sin and considered unrighteous before God. Elijah represented the great prophets who foretold the death of Christ for the forgiveness of sins and cleansing of people.

Those who wonder concerning the possibility of our knowing each other when we get to heaven could profitably study this passage. Even James and John recognized these spiritual giants of the past.

III. These heavenly visitors discussed Christ's exodus with him (Luke 9:30–31).

The word that is translated "decease" in our English version literally means "exodus." The Greek word is *exodon*, and it refers to Jesus' departure from earth to heaven.

A. *Moses had led the children of Israel from under the tyranny of Egyptian bondage.*

B. *Elijah had called the people back to loyalty to the living God.*

C. *The Christ, to whom these angelic visitors talked, is to deliver humankind both from the slavery of sin and into a life of holy living.* Through his death he is to lead God's people into life.

IV. Thoughts for today.

A. *We can learn from this experience on the mountaintop with Jesus that even the Son of God needed divine encouragement as he faced the task that was before him.* Every person needs encouragement, and the best encouragement comes from an experience with God.

B. *Prayer transfigures one's soul and life.* Each of us needs to discover the immeasurable resources available to us through the avenue that prayer can open up for us. Many of us are laboring in the energy of the flesh, and consequently we achieve only that which human ingenuity or ability can produce. If you want to find the secret of the success of Jesus, you must go apart to a private place and tarry and listen while you pray.

C. *Only those who have served Christ faithfully in the valley of daily duty and have lived close to him can climb the mountain of transfiguration with him.* The revelation of God's glory and grace comes to each of us according to our capacity, and our capacity is developed as we give ourselves in loving loyalty to him. Faithful service in the valley makes possible the mountaintop experience, even as the mountaintop experience makes possible more effective service in the valley.

D. *There is a glory in the Bible and in the living Christ that is beyond our ordinary perception.* This glory is often veiled, but it is always there for those who have eyes to see.

E. *Heavenly experiences are occasionally given to Christians as a foretaste of the glory to come.* Such an experience always creates responsibility. An experience like this is never given merely as a reward but rather as a preparation for a needed ministry to others.

Conclusion

The mountaintop is not a permanent dwelling place for the disciple of the Lord. Following this indescribable experience and contrary to the wishes of Peter, who suggested that he be permitted to build three tabernacles so that they could stay there, Jesus led the disciples back down into the valley, where suffering and human need were present and where a ministry of mercy was needed desperately (Matt. 17:14–18).

If God has given you some rich experience, you should not only praise him, you must be alert to the proper time and place to render a needed ministry. May God help you to see your opportunity and seize it.

SUNDAY MORNING, AUGUST 7

Title: Grace to Save

Text: "For by grace are ye saved through faith; and that not of yourselves: it is the gift of God: Not of works, lest any man should boast" **(Eph. 2:8–9)**.

Scripture Reading: Ephesians 2:1–10

Hymns: "Amazing Grace," Newton

           "Grace Greater Than Our Sin," Johnston

           "Saved, Saved!" Scholfield

Offertory Prayer: Heavenly Father, words are inadequate to express our gratitude for your wondrous saving grace that has brought us into your family and made us fellow workers and joint-heirs with our Lord Jesus Christ. With hearts of love, we now present to you a portion of that which you have enabled us to earn. We earnestly beseech you to accept our tithes and offerings and to bless their use in advancing the cause of Christ. In the blessed name of our wonderful Savior and Lord we pray. Amen.

Introduction

Charis, the Greek word translated "grace," appears in the New Testament 155 times. Grace is one of the greatest words in the Christian vocabulary but is known only where the Bible has gone. Perhaps it holds in its content as much as or more than any other word. This word is so woven through the New Testament that any effort to remove it from its context would cause the whole fabric to fall to pieces. Grace pervades the New Testament as the salt permeates the sea, and yet it is one of the least understood of all the wonderful words recorded in it.

I. What this grace is.

What a far-reaching ministry this word *grace* has exercised through the centuries! Who can tell all that is wrapped up in the word? We talk and sing about grace, but what does it mean?

Some words preclude concise definitions, and *grace* is one of them. The grace of God is the most profound subject of divine revelation. The wealth of the entire revelation of God in Jesus Christ is enshrined in the word. That is why it defies adequate definition. Freighted with deity, grace is as gentle as the morning breeze and as mighty as the ocean's tide. It is the basis of Christian experience.

People of learning have made numerous attempts to define grace. Some of these attempts have been helpful. Grace has been defined as the unmerited favor of God toward sinners, but it is much more than that. Another has defined grace as the favor of God toward the undeserving. This definition is better, but it is not strong enough.

Grace is the spontaneous love and boundless mercy of God freely expressed toward those who are entirely undeserving. In grace all of the qualities of deity are combined and all of the resources of deity are exerted in our behalf. Standing for all that God is, grace represents his abiding and overflowing love and abounding and outflowing power in Christ meeting the needs of lost sinners. As Dr. J. H. Jowett said, "Grace is the energy of the divine affection rolling in plenteousness toward the shores of human need."

The principle of grace distinguishes Christianity from all other religious systems. Other religions make demands, but Christianity offers a gift. Other religions insist on doing, but Christianity speaks of receiving. Other religions outline the works that people say one must do to be saved, but Christianity reveals a work that God has already done to make salvation available to all.

II. Where this grace comes from.

The mystery of grace is that it began in the heart of God before he made this world (Eph. 1:4–6). God the Father is the fountain of all grace, Christ the Son is the channel, and the Holy Spirit is the administrator. The supply of grace is inexhaustible. Grace, which is the infinite expression of God's love for sinners, cannot be increased or diminished. All of the dealings of the Trinity with people are on the basis of grace. Every action of God through the centuries has been for the purpose of setting forth, for the benefit of sinful human beings, the riches of his marvelous, matchless, and infinite grace, which is far greater than our sins.

III. What this grace does.

Grace, which dwelt in the heart of God from the beginning, was hidden from the world until it appeared in the incarnation of Christ (John 1:14; Gal. 4:4–5). God's grace devised the astounding plan of salvation, provided salvation for sinners, and made it available to all classes in every generation—rich and poor, educated and uneducated, moral and immoral, noble and ignoble. His grace was manifested most effectively in Christ's coming into this world to seek and to save the lost.

All people are sinners by nature, choice, and practice, and therefore they need salvation (Eccl. 7:20; Rom. 3:23). By salvation is meant deliverance from slavery to sin. Salvation is neither merited nor solicited by humans. The scriptural teaching of salvation by grace glorifies God, and that is one reason proud and egotistical people do not like to hear it.

Many attempt to achieve salvation through personal efforts and meritorious works in spite of the fact that God's Word repeatedly states that it is an utter impossibility. Salvation cannot be purchased by acts of obedience or service, because it is "not of yourselves." What could be plainer than this statement about salvation: "not of works, lest any man should boast"? According to the Scriptures, man's only hope of salvation is in the grace of God (Gal. 2:16; 2 Tim. 1:9; Titus 2:11; 3:5). No one will ever be able to present the record of his efforts and works to God and receive eternal life in exchange, because salvation is entirely God's gift (Rom. 6:23; Eph. 2:8–9).

Conclusion

Any person who would like to be saved must be willing to allow the grace of God in Christ to lift him out of his sinfulness and self into the glorious liberty that belongs to the children of God. If anyone who hears the gospel of Christ is not saved, it is because he refuses to receive the gift that grace offers (John 3:36; 1 John 5:11–12). One receives salvation upon repentance toward God and exercise of faith in Christ. The grace of God that brings salvation is effectual in the sense that it gets the job done.

Has God's grace, which provides the only hope of salvation, saved you? If not, receive Christ by grace through faith now, and he will most assuredly save you. Then praise God for his wondrous grace throughout the remainder of your life on earth.

SUNDAY EVENING, AUGUST 7

Title: "Hallowed Be Thy Name"

Text: "Hallowed be thy name" **(Matt. 6:9)**.

Scripture Reading: Isaiah 57:13–21

Introduction

A businessman was detained by a blizzard in a small Vermont village. He phoned the nearest telegraph office and asked, "Can I send a telegram to Boston?"

"Yep, you can," slowly came the answer. Then, after a pause, "But it won't git there. The wires is down."

Many people who try to pray often feel that the "wires are down." Most people do not find it easy to pray, and days and weeks pass with no words spoken to God. The Christian knows he *should* pray, and often he really wants to pray, but little or nothing comes forth. The privilege of prayer often becomes commonplace to many Christians.

Perhaps we would pray more if we more adequately reverenced the name of God in our speech and our lives.

I. What does it mean to hallow a name?

A. *Meaning of "name."* The emphasis of this verse is on "name," not "hallowed." In Old and New Testament times, "name" meant much more than it means today. When Andrew brought his brother to Christ, our Lord addressed the new convert, "Simon, son of Jonas." This name meant "shifting sand" and proved to be a good description of Simon Peter. Later, however, Jesus said, "Thou shalt be called Cephas, which is by interpretation, A stone" (John 1:42). The apostle Peter also lived up to this name.

In biblical times a person's name revealed his nature, character, and personality. Mr. Miller was a miller. Mr. Taylor was a tailor. Mr. Smith was

236

a smith. Mr. Johnson was John's son. It could well be that the original Mr. Longfellow was a long fellow.

The psalmist said, "They that know thy name will put their trust in thee" (Ps. 9:10). In other words, those who know what God is like will trust him. Remembering the name of the Lord our God means that we will trust him rather than human securities (Ps. 20:7).

Jesus said, "I have manifested thy name unto the men which thou gavest me out of the world" (John 17:6). In other words, Jesus revealed to man what God is really like.

When we speak of God's name, we speak of God's nature, character, and personality. To hallow his name must, therefore, mean to recognize him for who he is.

B. *Meaning of "hallowed."* The root of the Greek word *hagiazein* is the word *hagios*, which means "holy." That which is holy belongs to a different sphere of quality and being. God is considered "the high and lofty One that inhabiteth eternity, whose name is Holy" (Isa. 57:15). To hallow God's name means that our attitude toward God must be unique.

Moses was reprimanded because he did not "sanctify" God in the eyes of Israel when he struck the rock instead of speaking to it. The word translated "sanctify" is from the root *hagios*. Moses was reprimanded for his lack of reverence for the name of God; he disobeyed and distrusted God by taking the law into his own hands.

When we hallow the name of God, we give God that unique reverence that his character, nature, and personality (as revealed in Christ) truly demand.

II. Some prerequisites to hallowing God's name.

A. *Before we can reverence God, we must believe that he exists.* Kant said, "The moral law within and the starry heavens above drive us to God." The Bible never tries to prove the existence of God. His existence is taken for granted.

B. *Before we can reverence God, we must know what he is like.* Perhaps the outstanding attribute of God is his holiness. When we hear the angels sing, "Holy, holy, holy," we cry, "Woe is me ... because I am a man of unclean lips.... Here am I; send me" (Isa. 6:3–8). The closer we get to God the more sinful we feel. The reason? God is holy!

C. *Before we can reverence God, we must practice his presence.* Whether or not we realize it, we are living in his presence.

III. How to hallow God's name.

A. *By total commitment of life to Christ (Matt. 28:20; John 5:23; Col. 2:9; Heb. 1:3).*

B. *By showing reverence for God's name.* If we would hallow the name of God, we must not use his name falsely, lightly, or profanely.

C. *By showing reverence for his day*. We do not reverence the name of God when we use Sunday as a holiday or as half holy day and half holiday. We reverence his name, however, when we set it aside as a day of rest, worship, and spiritual pursuit.

D. *By showing reverence for his Book*. We cannot claim to reverence the name of God when we do not read his love letter to us.

E. *By showing reverence for his church*. The church is the "bride of Christ." A person cannot claim loyalty to another if he will not respect his bride!

Conclusion

Someone has said that reverence is the anteroom that leads into the audience chamber of the King.

The ancient Jews so reverenced the name of Jehovah God that they would not even write it with a quill or ink that had been used to write something else. They always used a new, fresh quill to write God's name. They even refused to pronounce it. Extreme? Yes. Commonplace? No.

WEDNESDAY EVENING, AUGUST 10

Title: Living on Bread Alone

Text: "But he answered and said, It is written, Man shall not live by bread alone, but by every word that proceedeth out of the mouth of God" (**Matt. 4:4**).

Scripture Reading: Matthew 4:1–11

Introduction

A question that multitudes of people are asking constantly concerns the matter of how they are going to live. How shall we live? What are we going to live on? How will we make a living? If one could give a satisfactory practical answer to these questions, he would be regarded as one of the greatest of all public benefactors.

The Bible is the last place most people go for advice and instruction concerning either the major or minor problems of life. Many assume that the Bible has little or nothing to do with their everyday affairs. When the Bible is consulted, many astonishing answers are found that are at variance with the principles by which most people live their lives. They quickly shut the Book and say, "Fanciful! Idealistic! Impractical!"

Our text offers a suggestion concerning a proper answer to the question "How shall we live?" To understand the advice of Jesus on how we should live, we must examine the story of his temptation from which the text comes.

I. Satan's suggestion and our Lord's reply.

A. *Christ's concern for spiritual interests caused him to completely overlook his physical needs.*

238

B. *Satan, wearing the cloak of benevolence and kindness, made a suggestion that on the surface seemed perfectly natural, simple, and harmless.*

C. *Satan urged Jesus to use his divine power to meet a personal need.*

D. *Christ refused to use his divine power selfishly.* If he had yielded, he would have been saying, "Bread is indispensable to the support of life. I can live only as I have bread. I will perish if I do not have bread." Satan's suggestions are never good.

E. *Christ responded to this suggestion by Satan with the Word of God (Deut. 8:3).* Jesus declared that man cannot live on bread alone.

II. There are two ways of life opened to man.

A. *Satan, as the prince of this world, announced his philosophy of life and sought to win Christ's assent to it.*
1. Satan says that man lives by bread alone.
2. "Bread" here is an all-inclusive term that refers to the basic physical needs of life.
3. Satan would imply that the main object in life is to make a good living.
4. Lot, the nephew of Abraham, accepted the bread theory of life and pitched his tent toward the wicked city of Sodom because there was prosperity and plenty in that direction (Gen. 13:10–14).
5. The rich fool lived by the bread theory of life and was interested only in building bigger barns to preserve the products of the field (Luke 12:16–21).

B. *Christ, as the Teacher who came from God, seeks to set us on the right road.*
1. Man shall not, cannot, really live by bread alone. While bread is good, proper, and necessary, it is but a means to life and must not become the end for which one lives.
2. Bread is not to be the main thing in one's thoughts and activities (Matt. 6:25–34).

III. Men are constantly tempted to accept the bread theory of life.

A. *Man has some legitimate physical needs.* By the sweat of our brow we are instructed to secure and to acquire the basic essentials for life.

B. *Each of us must beware lest we let material things become the main objective for which we labor.*
1. The bread theory of life leads downward.
2. The bread theory of life dwarfs the soul.
3. The bread theory of life robs one of the real purpose of life.

IV. The real purpose of life.

Christ instructs us and encourages us to live by the Word of God.

A. *Christ directs our attention to the Giver of the bread that is essential for physical life.*

B. *Living by the Word of God is a life of trust in the goodness of God.*

C. *Living by the Word of God is a life of loving obedience to the God who so loved that he gave his Son for us.*

D. *Living by the Word of God is a life that brings inward satisfaction and refreshment (John 4:31 – 34; 6:48 – 51).*

Conclusion

A person who lives by bread alone has nothing when the bread is gone. Bread alone does not satisfy the deepest hunger of the human heart. To live by bread alone will always bring disappointment and frustration. Christ is the Bread of Life, who brings nourishment, refreshment, and strength to the person who will trust him and follow him in a life of loving obedience (John 6:35; Acts 5:32).

SUNDAY MORNING, AUGUST 14

Title: Grace to Sustain

Text: "And he said unto me, My grace is sufficient for thee: for my strength is made perfect in weakness. Most gladly therefore will I rather glory in my infirmities, that the power of Christ may rest upon me" **(2 Cor. 12:9)**.

Scripture Reading: 2 Corinthians 12:1 – 9

Hymns: "Once for All," Bliss

"I Will Not Forget Thee," Gabriel

"God Will Take Care of You," Martin

Offertory Prayer: Holy Father, we sincerely thank you for your presence with us and for the wonderful privilege of worshiping you. You have been gracious and merciful in saving us and sustaining us, and we thank you for doing so. We pray that you will receive, sanctify, and use our tithes and offerings, which we now lovingly present to you for the furtherance of the glorious gospel of the Christ whom we delight to honor and serve. In his name we pray. Amen.

Introduction

God's grace is sufficient to save and to sustain the believer. Grace carries forward his salvation (Rom. 6:14). When one is made a child of God, he does not receive a stock of grace with which to go on for the rest of his life. He has grace for that day, but he must receive additional grace on each succeeding day. One receives salvation upon believing on Christ, but day by day he needs to draw upon the mighty reservoirs of blessing from God's grace. No matter what the circumstances are, by his grace God infuses into the Christian a sufficiency of divine strength. The storehouse of his grace, with all its vastness and fullness of supply, is open for our use.

God's wondrous grace is adequate to sustain his children.

240

I. In life's temptations.

By temptation we mean enticement to sin. Temptation is something within or without a person to get him to cease to be what he ought to be or to fail to do what he knows is right. All temptations come directly or indirectly from Satan.

Frequently Christians yield to temptation, but their indulgence in sin never makes them happy. A real Christian can never be happy as long as sin stands between God and him.

Maybe your sin is that of a cold heart toward God. Maybe you have been living a prayerless life. Maybe you have neglected the study of God's Word. Maybe you have been withholding God's money and using it for yourself. Whatever your sin, confess it to God and ask him for forgiveness and restoration to his favor and fellowship (1 John 1:9). Let God flood your soul again with the joy you lost when you yielded to temptation. Through grace God will enable you to overcome temptation and be victorious in the Christian life.

II. In life's troubles.

The prospect of trials and troubles looms before all (Job 5:7; John 16:33). Problems and perplexities are always confronting us and causing us concern. Blows fall on us when we least expect them. Expect trouble to come your way sooner or later, for it is a part of both human and Christian experience.

There are all kinds of trouble — those of the body, the mind, and the soul. There are troubles we bring on ourselves and those that others bring on us. Expect and be prepared for that which is the common lot of humans.

Many try to manage their lives without God's help and thereby deprive themselves of much strength and many blessings. God knows all about our troubles and wants to help us through them. To us he says, "Call upon me in the day of trouble: I will deliver thee, and thou shalt glorify me" (Ps. 50:15). Even though you may not know the reason for your trouble, God has a loving purpose in permitting it, such as keeping you from sinning, helping you to discover his will, and causing you to love him more and to obey him better. In answer to prayer, God delivers from trouble at the time, in the way, and by the means he sees best. When we call upon him, God delivers us from our troubles, either by granting what we ask or by doing something else for us that is more for our good and his glory.

God's wondrous grace is sufficient to sustain us in all our troubles. When we are called upon to endure unusual suffering, he gives us patience. When extraordinary sorrows come, he gives adequate strength and comfort.

Many Christians have been comforted by Christ's statement, "My grace is sufficient for thee." His grace is sufficient for all believers in all circumstances and in all generations. The supply of sustaining grace has exact correspondence with the need — never too much and never too little, never too soon and never too late.

Conclusion

Imprisoned in Rome and awaiting the hour of his execution, Paul candidly expressed his attitude about dying (2 Tim. 4:6–8). God's grace was sufficient to

241

sustain him in his final hour. When we who are God's children come to the end of the way, we, too, shall discover that the marvelous grace of God will sustain us as we enter the valley of the shadow of death.

SUNDAY EVENING, AUGUST 14

Title: "Thy Kingdom Come"

Text: "Thy kingdom come" (**Matt. 6:10**).

Scripture Reading: Matthew 13:33–52

Introduction

As a young boy, Jesus became separated from his parents, and when they finally found him in the temple talking with the scholars, he said, "Did you not know that I would be about my Father's business?"

About fifteen years later, Jesus defined his "Father's business." One evening he walked away from the carpenter's shop for the last time. Shortly thereafter he preached his first sermon. It was a short sermon: "Repent: for *the kingdom of heaven* is at hand" (Matt. 4:17, emphasis added).

The kingdom of God was the central message of our Lord while on earth. He interpreted his preaching ministry as the preaching of the *kingdom*. At Capernaum he healed the sick all night. Toward daybreak he went out into the desert to pray. People found him and asked him not to leave them. His reply was, "I must *preach the kingdom of God* to other cities also: for therefore am I sent" (Luke 4:43, emphasis added). Since the kingdom was so important to Jesus, it behooves us to understand his interpretation of it.

I. What is the kingdom?

A. *The kingdom of heaven/God:* Many have speculated on the fact that Matthew uses "kingdom of heaven" thirty-two times, while he uses "kingdom of God" only four times. The "kingdom of heaven" was used by Jewish writers to avoid verbal references to God for fear of breaking the third commandment. This phrase was also used in the papyri to denote basically the same thing as "kingdom of God." Since Matthew was the "most Jewish" of the Gospels, Matthew adhered to the Jewish practice of substituting "heaven" for the name of God. Therefore the kingdom of God and the kingdom of heaven are one and the same throughout the New Testament.

B. *The Greek word for kingdom* (basileia) *signifies kingship, kingly rule, reign, and sovereignty.* It implies dominion and the royal power of God. Thus, when speaking of the kingdom of God, the primary reference is not to the territory that belongs to God but to his lordship over individuals who occupy that territory. In short, God's kingdom has reference to God's way with people. The kingdom of God is primarily a personal relation between God as King and the individual as subject.

II. When is the kingdom?

Jesus viewed the kingdom as present, past, and future. He indicated that it is a gift from God that comes to people only when they are willing to accept it. The kingdom is primarily the inward reign of God that manifests itself externally in the Christian's life.

A. *Present.* Jesus speaks of the kingdom as having already come upon the lives of individuals (Matt. 12:28; Luke 11:20; 12:32). It is "preached" (Matt. 4:23; 9:35; 24:14; Luke 9:2) and "proclaimed" (Luke 8:1; 9:60 NIV). The kingdom may be "received" (Mark 10:15; Luke 18:17) and "entered" (Matt. 5:20; 18:3; 19:23; Mark 10:23–25; Luke 18:24–25). One may not be "far from the kingdom" (Mark 12:34). Some scholars say some verses (Luke 7:28; 16:16) teach that the kingdom "is something which by its emergence has put everything that went before it out of date." These references leave no place for the concept of a wholly apocalyptic kingdom.

B. *Past.* Even though the kingdom is a present reality that is within or among individuals (Luke 17:21), it was also a reality of the past. Abraham, Isaac, Jacob, and the Old Testament prophets were a part of the kingdom of God (Matt. 8:11; Luke 13:28). The kingdom will also be a future reality in the lives of some. Joseph of Arimathea waited for the kingdom (Mark 15:43; Luke 23:51). The kingdom would come within the lifetime of some who listened to Jesus (Matt. 16:28; Mark 9:1; Luke 9:27). Jesus himself looked forward to the kingdom (Matt. 26:29; Mark 14:25) and taught his disciples to pray for its coming (Matt. 6:10; Luke 11:2).

C. *Future.* Even though the kingdom is the gift of God, people are challenged to "seek" it (Matt. 6:33; Luke 12:31) and to "press into" it (Luke 16:16). One's entry into the kingdom of God is worth any sacrifice (Matt. 5:29–30; Mark 9:43–48). The kingdom involves a present and future separation among people (Matt. 13:24–30, 37–43, 47–50). The invitation to enter the kingdom can be lost (Matt. 25:1–13), and the privilege can be taken away (Matt. 8:11–12; 21:43; Luke 13:28). To receive the kingdom, one must repent and believe in the gospel (Mark 1:15), be born again (John 3:3–5), become as a little child (Matt. 18:3–4), and be willing to follow Jesus in the continual task of dying to self (Matt. 19:29; Mark 9:47; Luke 9:61–62).

Conclusion

The following conclusions about the kingdom of God are vital to an understanding of the Lord's Prayer:

1. The kingdom of God is the reign of God in the lives of individuals that is begun when they commit their lives to Christ in repentance and faith.
2. Even though God deserves dominion over their lives, he allows them to choose or refuse his reign.
3. However, their acceptance does not constitute their achievement of the kingdom; the kingdom is a gift from God to humans.

4. The kingdom is destined to grow through the individual's life, by which it transforms society.
5. Though the kingdom is a present reality, it will be consummated at the second coming of Christ, when those under God's rule will be caught out of this world to live in perfect fellowship with God.

WEDNESDAY EVENING, AUGUST 17

Title: God's Attitude toward Do-Nothingism

Text: "Curse ye Meroz, said the angel of the LORD, curse ye bitterly the inhabitants thereof; because they came not to the help of the LORD, to the help of the LORD against the mighty" (**Judg. 5:23**).

Scripture Reading: Judges 5:1–23

Introduction

When the Israelites sinned against the Lord, he withdrew his presence, his power, his protection, and his guidance. Because of this divine withdrawal, the Israelites were delivered into the hands of the Canaanites and were sorely oppressed for twenty years (Judg. 4:2–3). Finally, the people awoke to the fact that the root of their problem was their sin of forsaking the true God. When they repented and called upon God for help, a deliverer was raised up to lead them in overthrowing the power of their oppressor.

After the victorious battle, Deborah, the judge and prophetess, who had accompanied Barak and the army, gave voice to an inspired hymn of praise to God for his blessings. Certain persons who had given themselves unreservedly for victory were recognized and praised. Other tribes were cited for failure to participate in the battle that involved the welfare of all of the tribes. The tribe of Reuben was indicted for remaining among the sheepfolds (Judg. 5:15–16). Gilead remained aloof beyond the Jordan, while Dan and Asher were concerned with their ships and the sea (vv. 16–17).

The city of Meroz is marked off for special criticism and for judgment "because they came not to the help of the LORD, to the help of the LORD against the mighty" (Judg. 5:23). It is declared that the judgment of God would fall upon this city that failed to help of the Lord in time of need. There is a principle involved in this pronouncement of judgment on the city of Meroz, for God continues to need the help of those who can provide needed assistance in his redemptive program of delivering people from the awful tyranny of sin.

I. The Lord still has some battles where help is needed.

A. *God abhors evil in all forms and stands in opposition to its destructive effects.*
B. *God is in battle with the spiritual and moral foes of humankind.*
C. *God is seeking to deliver people from the tyranny and folly of sin.*

244

II. The Lord requires the help of people in his warfare of deliverance and liberation.

A. *God could win every battle without the aid of humans.*

B. *By a magnificent display of divine power, God could overwhelm people.*

C. *By the efforts of angelic beings, he could do the work for us.*

D. *God needs and invites human help with his battles.*

III. The help that the Lord requires does not always come forth.

A. *There are occasions when not to act for God is to act against God.* By withholding help, one is helping the enemy. Meroz, the city on which the wrath of God fell, was located in the thick of the battle when the honor of God, the freedom of God's people, and the cause of truth against heathen error were at stake. The kingdom of God was in need of the assistance of the strength and energy of the men of Meroz.

For some reason Meroz had no zeal for the glory of God and no sympathy for their brethren who were in great trouble. Meroz was to discover that to be neutral, to be indifferent, to be undecided and inactive were sins that brought the judgment of God upon them. To be innocent of wicked deeds alone is not enough to preserve one from judgment.

B. *Excuses were offered by some for not coming to the struggle.*

1. Reuben was busy caring for the sheep.

2. Dan needed to stay by his ships.

3. Gilead was far away, on the other side of the Jordan.

4. Was it laziness, was it the love of ease and comfort, or was it the fear of danger that kept some tribes from coming to the help of the Lord? Perhaps they were self-centered and did not care for those about them (Matt. 25:44).

IV. A bitter curse fell on those who refused to come to the help of the Lord.

A. *What became of Meroz?* Has it not disappeared?

B. *A dreadful sense of shame for failure.*

C. *The frown of the Lord.* God is not pleased when people are indifferent and dedicate themselves to do-nothingism.

D. *They lost the joy of participation and the privilege of sharing in the victory.*

E. *They became victims of self-robbery because they did not come to the help of the Lord.*

Conclusion

While there are many who do not come to the help of the Lord, there are always some who do. It has been truthfully said that it is not so much one's ability that counts as it is one's availability. The people who came and willingly offered themselves to the Lord were used to accomplish victory during the days of Deborah. The same can be true in the present. We must stop making excuses, and we must make ourselves available to our Lord for the work that he has for each of us to do, lest the curse that fell upon Meroz fall on us.

SUNDAY MORNING, AUGUST 21

Title: Grace to School

Text: "For the grace of God that bringeth salvation hath appeared to all men, teaching us that, denying ungodliness and worldly lusts, we should live soberly, righteously, and godly, in this present world; looking for that blessed hope, and the glorious appearing of the great God and our Saviour Jesus Christ; who gave himself for us, that he might redeem us from all iniquity, and purify unto himself a peculiar people, zealous of good works" **(Titus 2:11–14)**.

Scripture Reading: Titus 2:1–15

Hymns: "Come, Thou Fount," Robinson

"Yield Not to Temptation," Palmer

"I Need Thee Every Hour," Hawks

Offertory Prayer: We thank you, heavenly Father, for your marvelous grace which has worked the miracle of regeneration within us and enabled us to live victoriously as your children. We thank you for leading us to your house to worship you and praise you. We rejoice in the privilege of bringing our gifts to you as an expression of our love for you, and we pray that you will accept them and use them in promoting your work. In Jesus' name. Amen.

Introduction

Through the coming of Christ into the world and the preaching of his glorious gospel the grace of God brought salvation to all who would believe on him and receive it. His coming was chiefly to reveal God's wondrous grace. This grace has brought salvation, sustenance, and schooling, or instruction in the things of God.

Our text puts the Christian life in its proper setting—between a great fact of the past and a great event in the future. The fact of the past is the appearing of grace; the event in the future is the appearing of the Lord. When a Christian focuses his attention on the past, he thinks of the grace of which he has become a beneficiary. When he focuses his attention on the future, he thinks of sharing the glory that is to be revealed. Titus 2:12 indicates how a Christian should live. His learning must be translated into living.

Grace does not just give us a theory and enable us to grasp lessons; it disciplines us in order that our lives may be transformed. "Teaching" as used in our text means instructing, educating, admonishing, disciplining, molding, and forming character. It means to school and train. Grace does not involve anything that we can earn, but it does include much that we can learn. To us it says, "Do this" and "Don't do that." Grace encourages us to do what we should, and it chastises us when we fail to do so as well as when we do what we should not. In the school of grace, Christians are taught that living for Christ is serious business. The lessons learned in this school should contribute to our happiness and usefulness in this life.

God's grace teaches us two very important lessons.

I. To deny certain things.

According to Titus 2:12, there are two things that are to be laid aside, and they are the epitome of all that is sinful.

A. *Ungodliness.* Ungodliness is whatever is without or against God. Anything that crowds God out of the life and belittles his claims upon us falls in the category of ungodliness. The ungodly life is one in which God does not live.

God's grace has appeared to school us in avoiding the error of living without God in our thoughts, words, and deeds. It teaches us to deny or lay aside the manner of life wherein God is not consulted.

When one is saved, sustained, and schooled by grace, he will think much about God. God's presence will be his joy, God's strength will be the basis of his confidence, and God's glory will be the chief end of his being.

B. *Worldly lusts.* Worldly lusts include selfishness, pride, sensuality, and the desires or longings that attach themselves to the fleeting things of this earthly life. Worldly lusts are those things that attract and pull us in the direction that God does not want us to go. In the school of grace, we learn to say no to the things that drag us down and tie us up with this world in its rebellion against God. If we never learn anything else in the school of grace, it is exceedingly worthwhile to enter it and there be taught how to say no and mean it.

Since Satan is the prince of this world, why should Christians crave its fashions, fads, and fancies? The grace of God calls for a complete break with the cravings of the flesh: "Come out from among them, and be ye separate, saith the Lord, and touch not the unclean thing" (2 Cor. 6:17). In this verse is a call to be heeded and a command to be obeyed. This command to live the separated and dedicated life comes from God and should be obeyed by every one of us. We must lay aside or deny worldly lusts.

II. To do certain things.

Having schooled us to deny certain things, God's grace instructs us to do certain things.

A. *With regard to self.* "We should live soberly." God's grace teaches us that we are to be governed by the Holy Spirit. Each Christian is expected to exercise self-control in eating, drinking, thinking, speaking, and acting. In all our pursuits, we should endeavor to control our desires and to do our best to resist the temptations of Satan.

B. *With regard to others.* "We should live righteously." As living soberly has to do with rightness on the inside, living righteously has reference to rightness in relationship to others. One must be correct in his character before he can be correct in his conduct. Living righteously is simply the outliving of the indwelling Christ. We should be just in our dealings, charitable in our judgments, blameless in our conduct, and active for the spiritual welfare of others.

247

C. *With regard to God.* "We should live godly." Godliness has an internal and an external phase. The internal phase consists of a right knowledge of God, a complete trust in him, a cheerful subjection of will to him, a fervent love for him, and a genuine longing for the full enjoyment of him. The external phase consists of the adoration and worship of God and faithful service for him. Godliness is the nature of God implanted at regeneration and outworking in the daily conduct of believers. Whatever we do should be done for the glory of God.

Conclusion

God's grace schools us to live soberly, righteously, and godly here and now, amid the troublesome brood of rebellious instincts, mutinous appetites, and tempestuous cravings.

SUNDAY EVENING, AUGUST 21

Title: "Thy Will Be Done"

Text: "Thy will be done in earth, as it is in heaven" **(Matt. 6:10)**.

Scripture Reading: Luke 22:39–46

Introduction

John Ruskin once said, "If you do not wish for [God's] kingdom, don't pray for it. But if you do, do more than pray for it. You must work for it."

Can the kingdom of God come to this earth? If you mean *Can a social gospel dedicated to the salvation of society bring in the kingdom?* the answer is no. But if you mean *Can the kingdom of God come to earth through the lordship of Christ in individual lives?* the answer is yes.

I. The kingdom and the will of God.

When communications were carried on almost entirely by the spoken word, it was a common practice to restate a truth in two different ways so that the hearers could better comprehend it. This custom is evident throughout the Old Testament, especially in the Psalms. For example, "The LORD of hosts is with us; the God of Jacob is our refuge" (46:7), and "The LORD is thy keeper: the LORD is thy shade upon thy right hand" (121:5).

Our Lord used this method of teaching many times. When he said, "Thy kingdom come, thy will be done," he was saying the same thing in two different ways. In other words, the kingdom of God comes in one's life when he allows the will of God to be done.

II. The will of God is for now.

Is the kingdom always future, or is it a present reality? To answer this question, one must have a knowledge of ancient Hebrew and classical Greek usage of similar words.

A. *Hebrew use.* The Hebrew equivalent of *basileia* was *malekuth.* The initial meaning of this Hebrew word was kingship or royal sovereignty. It was used extensively in the Old Testament in the secular sense, meaning a political kingdom (1 Sam. 20:31; 1 Kings 2:12). God's sovereignty over all people is also described as his kingdom (Ps. 103:19).

The sharp distinction between the present and future apocalyptic kingdom is first found in the book of Daniel (2:44; 4:22). Daniel's use of the word refers almost exclusively to the succession of human kingdoms. It does not have reference to the earthly, physical kingdom of God that will come in the future.

B. *Greek use.* Classical Greek writers used *basileia* to describe a kingdom, dominion, or hereditary monarchy. It was the kingdom that rightfully belonged to its king as over against a kingdom that was usurped by tyrants. The Greek word for the latter (*turannis*) was never used in the New Testament. It originally described an absolute sovereign unlimited by law or constitution. It was used earlier by Aeschines, Sophocles, and Aristophanes to describe the gods. It was later used to refer to dictators or tyrants who usurped power over a territory. Thus it came to describe the way in which the power was gained rather than the way in which it was exercised.

Basileia, on the other hand, retained the idea of a kingdom that rightfully belonged to its king. The king is not a usurper or tyrant. He has a rightful dominion over his *basileia* and its subjects. However, whether or not the subjects yield to his dominion determines his rule over their individual lives. Some of them may even attempt to gain the throne from their king instead of recognizing his lordship.

It may be concluded, therefore, that the New Testament word for kingdom refers primarily to the lordship of God in the lives of individuals. The kingdom of God comes when God's will is being done through people.

III. How to get into the kingdom.

A. *Realize its value.* Nothing in this life is as valuable as the kingdom of God. It is like a treasure hid in a field. When one finds it, he sells all so that he may possess it. The kingdom of God is like a pearl of great price. Nothing is too valuable to sacrifice for the kingdom (cf. Matt. 13).

B. *Repent.* There is only one way to enter the kingdom—by repentance (Luke 13:3). John proclaimed repentance at the baptism of Jesus (Matt. 3:1–2). In our Lord's first message, he called for repentance (4:17). In the Beatitudes, our Lord declared that the "poor in spirit" are the possessors of the kingdom (5:3).

C. *Commit.* Those who have repented of sin possess a righteousness that exceeds that of the scribes and Pharisees (Matt. 5:48). To pray, "Thy kingdom come," is to pray, "Lord, let your will be done in my life."

Conclusion

When asked, "Are you a Christian?" some say, "I hope I am," or "I think I am." If we lived in England and someone asked, "Is the queen of England your queen?" would we say, "I hope so"? or "I think so"? No, we would say, "Yes, I know she is my queen, because I live under her reign." Kingdom citizens know their King!

WEDNESDAY EVENING, AUGUST 24

Title: I Am Ready

Text: "So, as much as in me is, I am ready to preach the gospel to you that are at Rome also" **(Rom. 1:15)**.

Scripture Reading: Romans 1:1–16

Introduction

In the words of our text, the apostle Paul gives voice to his eagerness to visit the imperial city of Rome that he might preach the gospel of Jesus Christ there. Paul was possessed by eagerness and the readiness to go because of a number of reasons. The factors that motivated him should also lead us to respond to God's command and God's invitation for us to participate with him in redeeming the world from sin.

Can you say sincerely, "I am ready"? A. C. Palmer wrote a beautiful poem that has been set to music and that indicates a readiness of heart to do God's will.

> *Ready to suffer grief or pain,*
> *Ready to stand the test;*
> *Ready to stay at home and send*
> *Others if He sees best.*
>
> *Ready to go, ready to bear,*
> *Ready to watch and pray;*
> *Ready to stand aside and give*
> *Till He shall clear the way.*
>
> *Ready to speak, ready to think,*
> *Ready with heart and mind;*
> *Ready to stand where He sees fit,*
> *Ready His will to find.*
>
> *Ready to speak, ready to warn,*
> *Ready o'er souls to yearn;*
> *Ready in life or ready in death,*
> *Ready for His return.*

There are a number of reasons why each of us should be ready to do the will of our loving Lord.

I. We should be ready because of our spiritual indebtedness.

A. *Each of us is deeply in debt to God. He is our Creator, Sustainer, and Redeemer.*
B. *Each of us is deeply in debt to past generations.* We are the heirs of a noble heritage of those who have suffered and sacrificed to pass on to us the rich blessings that we enjoy.
C. *Each of us is deeply in debt to a needy world.*

II. We should be ready because of our gratitude for God's love.

All of us are guilty of the sin of ingratitude to some degree. We owe much to our parents and teachers. Various friends have rendered services for which we will always be obligated. But we owe our greatest debt of gratitude to God because of his great love for us (John 3:16). Paul stood in amazement before the riches of God's generosity to us in Christ Jesus and declared that it is impossible to describe the greatness of God's love gift to us (2 Cor. 9:15).

III. We should be ready because of God's love for a lost world.

Parents will often treasure highly a rag doll because it is an object of great value to a child. Some belongings are priceless because they are of value to those we love. Such should be the attitude of each child of God as he contemplates the sinful world in which he lives. The world made up of sinful, rebellious, wayward humans is the object of God's supreme concern. God so loved the world that he gave heaven's best to redeem people from sin. Because the world is of such great concern to the heart of our God, each of us should become personally involved in trying to bring this world to God.

IV. We should be ready because of humanity's desperate need for salvation.

When we see people crippled by ignorance, it is natural that we want to be a teacher who can lead them to truth and to new areas of knowledge. When we come into contact with those who suffer, it is natural that we covet the skills and techniques of a physician that we might be the means of relieving their suffering.

Several years ago the world was very anxious for the welfare of some coal miners who were trapped by a mine cave-in. The account of the various activities leading to their rescue became front page news across the country. Mining companies and the oil companies rushed expensive equipment to the site in order that passageways might be drilled deep into the earth to provide them with oxygen and finally with a way of escape. The entire country appreciated the generous expenditure of funds and the exhaustive effort that was put forth by the men involved to rescue the helpless miners. They were in need of escape from a pit of darkness and death.

Newspapers carried the account of a highway patrolman who drove his police car at a speed of one hundred miles per hour at times to get a child who was desperately sick to a hospital for emergency treatment.

Many illustrations of desperate need could be mentioned, but humanity's greatest need is not for an education or health or escape from a mine or delivery at a hospital. Their greatest need is for the knowledge of God through faith in Jesus Christ. We need to let compassion move us to minister redemptively to those about us.

V. We should be ready because of the brevity of time (John 9:4).

Yesterday is gone forever. Tomorrow is but a dream, a mirage, that may never become reality. The only time of which we can be absolutely certain is the present. We need to use today for the glory of God and for the welfare of others.

VI. We should be ready because of the command of the Christ on the cross.

With a love that is beyond our ability to comprehend or to describe, our Savior came, lived, and died for us. In words clear, definite, and specific, he commanded his followers to evangelize the whole world. They were to begin right where they were. Through the centuries the command from the Man on the cross continues to ring. Love and gratitude tell us to obey. World need demands that we obey.

Conclusion

A. C. Palmer declared a spirit of readiness that we could well pray for and seek to develop.

> *Ready to go, ready to stay,*
> *Ready my place to fill;*
> *Ready for service lowly or great,*
> *Ready to do his will.*

This attitude will bring honor and glory to God. This spirit will make life meaningful and significant for each of us. This response on our part will mean salvation for the hearts and lives of many of those about us. Let us pray that God will move in our hearts and cause us to be ready to do his will.

SUNDAY MORNING, AUGUST 28

Title: Grace to Serve

Text: "I can do everything through him who gives me strength" (**Phil. 4:13 NIV**).

Scripture Reading: Philippians 4:1–13

Hymns: "I Surrender All," Van de Venter

"I'll Go Where You Want Me to Go," Brown

"Take My Life and Let It Be," Havergal

Offertory Prayer: Almighty God, our Father, fountain of wisdom and inspirer of people, we thank you for making available to us a sufficiency of grace to save, sustain, school, and serve. We also thank you that through the presentation of our gifts and your blessing on them, we can participate in proclaiming the gospel, introducing people to Christ, and rendering ministries of mercy to those in need. Help us to know the blessedness of giving generously and cheerfully through Christ, in whose name we pray. Amen.

Introduction

God's grace is the most profound subject of divine revelation and that which is beyond the ability of the natural person to comprehend. The "God of all grace" makes full and free provision of salvation, sustenance, and schooling for those who will receive.

I. The purpose of this grace.

Grace is intended to make us disciples of and workers for Christ. We have been saved that we might serve the Lord Jesus. Are you exerting an aggressive influence toward the overthrow of Satan's kingdom, doing something to limit the reign of sin and to increase the number of Christ's followers? If so, one great purpose of this grace is being accomplished. If not, the grace of God has been bestowed on you in vain. When Paul urged his readers not to receive the grace of God in vain, he intimated that grace is intended to effect some worthy ends closely related to the Lord, ourselves, and others.

The one great purpose of this grace, which includes all others, is "that [we] may with one mind and one mouth glorify God, even the Father of our Lord Jesus Christ" (Rom. 15:6). The supreme purpose for which grace is given is that by it we may glorify God (Matt. 5:16; 2 Thess. 1:11–12). By the tone of our tempers and the tenor of our lives, we are to honor God's grace and make manifest his glory: "Whether therefore ye eat, or drink, or whatsoever ye do, do all to the glory of God" (1 Cor. 10:31). God proposes to show the world through you what his grace can do, in order that others may see the workmanship and honor the Workman.

Christians are saved so that they may work for the Lord. Never yet was a soul bought with the blood of Christ and regenerated by the Spirit of God to whom there was not given a work to do. Many church members are not disposed to do any work for the Lord. They think that there is not any work in the church in which they can use their God-given talents, time, money, or influence. Nevertheless, some spiritual work is required of every Christian. By prayer, Bible study, and watching for opportunities, we are to do more than attend worship services occasionally. We are to give time and labor for Christ and others, thereby leaving on our generation some mark for good, something that will enable Christ to say at the Judgment, "Well done, good and faithful servant."

II. The power of this grace.

The grace of God transformed Paul from a lost sinner into a child of God, from a servant of Satan into a saint of God, from a persecutor of Christians into an apostle of Christ, and from a busy person into a fruitful Christian. God's grace created within Paul the desire to serve the Lord and made his efforts fruitful.

Only the grace of God can make an effective worker out of an individual. Paul said, "I thank Jesus Christ our Lord, who hath enabled me, for that he counted me faithful, putting me into the ministry" (1 Tim. 1:12). Paul had been empowered by divine grace for a great life of Christian service. Standing at the height of his glorious career as a servant of Christ, Paul cried out, "By the grace of God I am what I am" (1 Cor. 15:10). It was the grace of God that had enabled him to do the work that he had done for the Lord.

By grace people are selected to serve God in special ways. Concerning the selection of the disciples and calling them to service, Christ said, "Ye have not chosen me, but I have chosen you, and ordained you, that ye should go and bring forth fruit" (John 15:16). Paul had this consciousness of having been selected by grace when he was called to be an apostle (1 Cor. 15:10). It was by grace that he had been saved, selected, sustained, and schooled; and it was also by grace that he had been made effectual in service. We may wonder at the abundance of his labors and their fruitfulness, but the secret of these things was the enabling grace of God.

To meet our Lord's expectation of walking habitually in good works, we need to be made "strong in the grace that is in Christ Jesus." Let us ask God to make us what we ought to be and to give us sufficient grace to do what needs to be done in Christian service.

In the sunset hour of his life, during his imprisonment in Rome, and while awaiting a violent death, Paul wrote, "I can do all things through Christ who keeps on pouring his power into me" (Phil. 4:13, my translation). He had found his way to the source of inexhaustible power. Paul had tried Christ under all conditions and circumstances of life and had found him equal to every emergency. He jubilantly testified to the measureless resources within the realm of absolute reliance on Christ. Paul did not hesitate to acknowledge that the ability to live contentedly, victoriously, and usefully came from the Lord. As long as Christ kept on pouring his power into Paul, the apostle had adequate strength for every need. Christ is the source of all power for victorious living and acceptable service. With peace in his soul and valor in his spirit, Paul was able to do all things that the Lord commanded him, because Christ continued to pour his strength into him just when and as he needed it. To us also Christ administers his undiminished strength in proportion to our needs.

Conclusion

A lesson of paramount importance for us is that we cannot do anything of ourselves but that through God's wondrous grace we can obtain sufficient strength to render the service the Lord requires of us. God's grace is sufficient to enable us to do the will of our Lord, performing to his glory the assignments with which he has entrusted us.

> *Grace is flowing from Calvary,*
> *Grace as fathomless as the sea,*
> *Grace for time and eternity,*
> *Grace enough for me.*

SUNDAY EVENING, AUGUST 28

Title: "On Earth, as It Is in Heaven"

Text: " . . . as it is in heaven" (**Matt. 6:10**).

Scripture Reading: Psalm 40

Introduction

A very moving story to come out of World War II was the sinking of the troop ship *Dorchester* off the coast of Greenland. Four chaplains—two Protestants, a Roman Catholic, and a Jew—gave their life belts to others. Holding hands on the deck, they went down with the ship.

One of these four was Clark Poling. His father described the turning point in the life of this young man. While attending prep school, the boy called his father long distance and told him that he had to meet him. The father was worried, wondering what sort of trouble his son had gotten into. The meeting at the train station was strained. In silence, they drove to the father's office. They walked in, and Dr. Poling locked the door. Clark slumped in a chair near the desk. The father waited anxiously for the boy to begin.

Suddenly Clark lifted his eyes and asked, "Dad, what do you know about God?"

His father was caught off guard. He had not expected this question. Then he began to speak. "Son, I don't know much about God; but what I know, I really know. I have tested Him in joy and in sorrow, in victory and in defeat. . . . I don't know much about God; but what I know, I really know."

That was the day Clark Poling set out on the path that led him into the ministry and eventually to the deck of the sinking *Dorchester*.

When we pray this section of the Lord's Prayer, "Thy will be done in earth as it is in heaven," we admit both our ignorance and our knowledge of God. We pray for the will of God to be done on earth as it is in heaven, yet we do not know just what is being done in heaven.

I. Heaven is where the action is.

A. *Angels abide there.* To say that something is being done in heaven indicates that there are angels there. These heavenly creatures are busy. Heaven is not a place where one merely sits around on clouds and strums a few notes

255

on a heavenly harp. How could one endure the monotony? In heaven God's will is done without reservation—no questions asked.

The will of God should be done in our lives on earth exactly this way. It is always easier, however, to pray, "Thy kingdom go" than it is to pray, "Thy kingdom come."

B. *Doing God's will now.* A Christian planted himself on a busy street of a town and proceeded to stop all who passed by and asked them, "Do you want to go to heaven?"

As one might expect, everyone answered his question in the affirmative. Late in the afternoon a young tenant farmer in overalls came along. He was confronted with the question and startled the Christian witness by saying, "No!"

"Do you mean to tell me that you do not want to go to heaven?" asked the Christian.

The young tenant farmer thought a moment and replied, "Oh, yes, I want to go to heaven when I die. But I thought you were getting up a truckload this afternoon."

When our Lord admonishes us to pray that the kingdom of God be done in our lives on earth as it is being done in heaven, he adds the dimension of "this afternoon" to our lives.

II. Taking the selfishness out of prayer.

A. *Before we pray for ourselves, we must pray for the kingdom of God to come to our lives and the lives of others.* This takes the selfishness out of prayer. There is not a first-person singular pronoun in the whole prayer. All of the pronouns are in the plural.

B. *Scholars have noted that there are four possessives and four objective cases and one nominative case in the Lord's Prayer.* The nominative is always the popular case because one likes to be the subject of the sentence. But the only "we" in this prayer is in "as we forgive our debtors." Our right to be the subject of the sentence is in forgiving those who have wronged us.

C. *When we pray, "in earth as it is in heaven," we ask God to remove our own selfish desire and replace it with his will in the here and now.*

Conclusion

Unexpectedly, a fellow was asked to give his testimony at a Sunday school class luncheon. Not knowing exactly what to say, he turned the meeting into a personal confession service, admitting that he cheated and lied in his business. But he dismissed this with, "But you fellows are in business, and you know how you just have to do this to get ahead."

The man continued, "As you fellows may know, I do a little gambling." But he was quick to remind them that he merely gambled as a diversion. "After all," he explained, "all of us know that we have to relax to get on in this world."

The man also admitted that he liked to party. He was quick to remind his friends that he did not drink in excess and tried never to get drunk any more than "once or twice a year."

"As many of you fellows know, I can curse a little too," he confessed. Again he tried to dismiss this sin by saying, "A fellow gets upset in this competitive world, and he has to talk tough to get action!"

He ended his testimony by saying, "I am very thankful that, even though I am not an angel, I have never lost my religion."

Could it be that only the true Christian can pray, "Thy kingdom come, thy will be done in earth as it is in heaven"? Could it be that those who never allow Christ to control their lives have never entered the kingdom and have never really found any religion to lose?

WEDNESDAY EVENING, AUGUST 31

Title: Religion Made Easy

Text: "Whereupon the king took counsel, and made two calves of gold, and said unto them, It is too much for you to go up to Jerusalem: behold thy gods, O Israel, which brought thee up out of the land of Egypt" **(1 Kings 12:28)**.

Scripture Reading: 1 Kings 12:25–33

Introduction

The Old Testament tells the story of Jeroboam's rebellion against Rehoboam followed by Israel's separation from Judah. Religion remained as a strong link binding the people of Israel to the people of the southern kingdom. The former still looked to Jerusalem and its temple. They still felt that they must observe the feast days. Jeroboam recognized that he must lead the people of the northern kingdom away from the temple if he was to firmly establish himself as the king of the northern kingdom.

Jeroboam built a new secular capitol in Israel. He then erected religious centers at Bethel and Dan. In these he placed golden calves that were symbols of the Baal god with which the people had been familiar in Egypt. The Canaanites had worshiped the Baal gods. To these places of worship he appointed priests who were "not of the Levites," and he ordained religious feast days different from those in the southern kingdom.

Jeroboam then turned to the people with a proposal that was popularly received. He said, "It is too much for you to go up to Jerusalem." He was a clever man who suggested that their fathers had done too much, and he presented an easier way for them to worship. He appealed to their desire for convenience and for the least possible expenditure of effort.

Centuries later when Jesus showed his disciples that he must go to Jerusalem and suffer and be killed, they were greatly bewildered. They inquired as to why he would leave the safety and popularity that he enjoyed in Galilee and return to the perils of Jerusalem. Peter tried to prevent him from returning to Jerusalem and to the task of dying for our sins for which he had come into the world (Matt. 16:22). Jesus responded to this rebuke from Peter by saying, "Get behind me, Satan! You are a stumbling block to me; you do not have in mind the things of God, but the things of men" (v. 23 NIV). Our Lord's reply to Peter reveals the source of Peter's suggestion: it was the Devil's idea. The Devil was using Peter to repeat the temptation that he had presented to our Lord previously.

Satan would have all of us search for the easiest possible way by which to do the work and will of God. He who focuses his mind on convenience and ease will be strongly tempted to depart from the discipline without which success is impossible.

Our Lord came to earth that the kingdoms of this world might become the kingdom of God. Satan tempted him in the wilderness with the promise of the kingdoms of the earth: "All these things will I give thee, if thou wilt fall down and worship me" (Matt. 4:9). Satan was saying that there was a possible detour around the cross. He was trying to make religion as easy as possible for our Lord.

The Evil One is constantly trying to get us to take just one step away from what we know to be God's will. If we take the first step, he will probably lead us completely away without our ever knowing it. Lot, the nephew of Abraham, chose the way of prosperity and success, and this led to his downfall and the ruin of his family (Gen. 13).

I. Jeroboam's statement is heard on all sides.

A. *"It is too much" for one to attempt to apply the teachings of Christ in all of life's relationships.* Consequently, Christianity is thought of as a ritual and a ceremony rather than as a way of life in fellowship with the living Christ.
   1. It is too much to be Christian in business.
   2. It is too much to be Christian in politics.
   3. It is too much to be Christian in home life.
   4. It is too much to be Christian when one is mistreated.
   5. It is too much to be Christian in the giving of oneself in unselfish service.
B. *"It is too much" for one to tithe his income for the work of the Lord.* Consequently, one's giving is left to spasmodic impulses or to the mood of the moment, and the financial support for the work of God's kingdom suffers.
C. *"It is too much" for God to expect us to give up certain common habits that we acquired before we were converted.*
   Satan knows, and we should recognize, that unless the professing Christian puts aside the sins of the flesh and the degrading habits acquired before conversion, there is no possibility of having a wholesome influence over those who need Jesus Christ as their Savior.
D. *"It is too much" for you to take a position of responsibility in the church.* Because some have accepted this philosophy, they have become spectators instead

of participators in the work of the church. For a follower of Christ to refuse to fill his position of responsibility is to miss the joy of fellowship with Christ. It is to miss the thrill of being a servant of Christ. It is to rob oneself of helping someone else find the way to heaven. Those who remain idle and inactive will deprive themselves of eternal rewards.

E. *"It is too much" for one to be truly faithful to the church.* He who neglects to be faithful to his church will discover that he is giving first-rate loyalty to second-rate causes. One must not permit recreation, work, relatives, or laziness to keep him from being faithful to the church, which our Lord commissioned with the task of evangelizing the world.

II. Has some modern Jeroboam approached you with the suggestion, "It is too much for you to go up to Jerusalem"?

Those who accept Jeroboam's philosophy are guilty of robbing God, robbing themselves, and robbing others.

A. *Choosing the easy way is often an act of outright rebellion against God.* God is our sovereign Ruler and Lord. We are not to think of him as the satisfier of our whimsical wishes. He has the right to command us, for we are his servants as well as his children. His commandments to us are all good and benevolent in their purpose.

B. *Choosing the easy way is often an act of base ingratitude.* Most of us are ingrates when it comes to the blessings of God. Instead of counting our many blessings and being grateful, we often look about us and grieve because someone is seemingly more fortunate than we. When we deliberately seek the way of ease, comfort, and luxury and neglect to do the difficult things that must be done, we are showing a lack of gratitude to God for the abundance of his blessings on us.

C. *Choosing the easy way is often an act of degrading compromise.* Such was the case during the days of Jeroboam when he led his people into idolatry by leading them away from the worship of the true God in the temple in Jerusalem. If we neglect to do the difficult things that life requires and that God requires, we are liable to find ourselves on the way to ruin.

Conclusion

God's will for us is revealed in his commandments. His commandments will bring the greatest possible good into our lives. It is always a serious mistake to disobey God, and it is never right to do wrong. Substitutes are never as good as the genuine thing. When religion was made easy and comfortable, it degenerated, and the nation of Israel went to pieces. Instead of asking for the easy, cheap, convenient way that leads to spiritual success and significant achievement, we need to search for the right way and then pray to God for the grace and strength that are necessary to be faithful to the finish.

SEPTEMBER

■ **Sunday Mornings**

This month's Sunday morning services are evangelistic in nature.

■ **Sunday Evenings**

Continue the series on the Lord's Prayer from Jesus' Sermon on the Mount. Then continue with a message on fasting from the Sermon on the Mount.

■ **Wednesday Evenings**

This month's messages consist of a study of "The Good and Perfect Will of God." Two Scripture verses are suggested as a basis for this series of studies. The first expresses the desire of Epaphras for the servants of Christ at Colosse: "that ye may stand perfect and complete in all the will of God" (Col. 4:12). The second is the prayer of the psalmist as recorded in Psalm 143:10: "Teach me to do thy will; for thou art my God: thy spirit is good; lead me into the land of uprightness."

SUNDAY MORNING, SEPTEMBER 4

Title: "While We Were Yet Sinners"

Text: "But God commendeth his love toward us, in that, while we were yet sinners, Christ died for us" (**Rom. 5:8**).

Scripture Reading: Romans 5:1–8

Hymns: "Holy, Holy, Holy," Heber

           "He Lifted Me," Gabriel

           "Jesus Saves," Owens

Offertory Prayer: Our Father in heaven, we rejoice over the fact that our Savior came into this world to rescue us from the waste and the disappointment of sin. Today we give of ourselves that others might come to know him as a personal Savior and as a wonderful Friend. Accept and bless these tithes and offerings that others might hear the gospel and respond by faith. Through Jesus Christ, our Lord. Amen.

Introduction

Every hour hundreds of people die, having left little impact for good on the world. But there is one whose death was not wasted. He died when he was only thirty-three, but what a life he had lived! And through his death the whole world has been lifted up. Look at the text: "While we were yet sinners, Christ died for us." This text compels us to look at ourselves and look at the way out of sin.

I. Look at ourselves.

Too often our vision is poor when we focus on ourselves. Our vision is marred by our own bias. We look at ourselves and see only part of us. We try to convince ourselves that what we see is all right. We live respectable lives, our morals are good, our physical looks will pass, and we let it go at that. But the Bible compels us to take another look—a look at ourselves through the eyes of God. When we look at ourselves this way we will have to admit that:

A. *We are sinners.* "All have sinned, and come short of the glory of God" (Rom. 3:23). "All we like sheep have gone astray" (Isa. 53:6). "There is none that doeth good, and sinneth not" (Eccl. 7:20). "While we were yet sinners" (Rom. 5:8) points back to the time when sin was ruling.

B. *Sin must be punished.* This means that, because we are sinners, we are in line for a terrible beating. "The wages of sin is death" (Rom. 6:23). "The soul that sinneth, it shall die" (Ezek. 18:4). "The way of transgressors is hard" (Prov. 13:15). Yes, sin must be suffered for, and it often brings its own retribution. People would have to admit that this is true even if they did not believe the Bible. The moral conscience of the world would be shocked by the teaching that sin was not to be punished. Civilization itself would be imperiled if we withheld from sin the punishment it calls for.

II. Look at the way out of sin.

A. *Thank God that man does not have to remain in his sin.* He does have one who quiets the accusing cry of conscience. There is a balm in Gilead. "Christ died for us."

B. *This is the central fact of Christianity.* Christianity is the gospel of redemption. One delights to look at Jesus as an example; but if we look at him merely as an example, that will only harass us and add to our burdens, for his example is perfect and ours is defiled and sinful. We love to think of Jesus as Teacher. But we love him most when we think of him as our Redeemer, the one who died for our sins.

C. *The Bible speaks of Jesus as the vicarious sufferer; he died in our place.* Christ's death for sin is the factor that broke Paul's heart and the hearts of his fellow apostles and sent them as flaming evangels for the conquest of the world. The fact that Christ died, not for himself, but for us, the just for the unjust, that we might be brought by him into right relationship with God is the central fact of his gospel.

III. God might have dealt with sinning humanity in one of three ways.

A. *He might have dealt out to the world only stern justice.* If the Lord were to mete out justice, who would stand? We would all be destroyed. "If thou, LORD, shouldest mark iniquities, O LORD, who shall stand?" (Ps. 130:3).

B. *The Lord could mete out mercy without regard to justice or righteousness or law or order.* But to do this would put an end to all moral government. What does he do?

C. *He metes out both justice and mercy at the same time, in the same person, Christ, who suffered in our stead, himself the Just, for us, the unjust, that he might bring us to God.*

Conclusion

Why is Christ the only one who can make atonement for our sins—the only one who can save us and bring us back to the Father?

1. He is divinely appointed for the mission (John 3:16).
2. He is without fault or blemish or sin. If while here in the flesh he had sinned for one moment in deed or thought, he could not have saved us. God's laws require perfection, and if we are to be saved, the high demands of that holy office must be met. At once we see our hopeless situation if left to ourselves. He is the only one who can make atonement for us.
3. He is capable. And why is he capable? He is both God and man in one personality.

SUNDAY EVENING, SEPTEMBER 4

Title: "Our Daily Bread"

Text: "Give us this day our daily bread" (**Matt. 6:11**).

Scripture Reading: Philippians 4

Introduction

Years ago, a nine-year-old boy, whose mother died in November, arrived at the George B. Taylor Orphanage in Rome, Italy, shortly after Christmas. One of his first assignments in school was a composition on "My Favorite Toy."

When asked what he wrote, the boy replied, "I didn't know what to write. I've never had a toy!"

Then to the question, "What did you get for Christmas?" he replied, "A piece of bread."

This Roman orphanage is a long way from prosperous America. Perhaps affluent people may never fully understand the meaning of the petition, "Give us this day our daily bread."

The only place in which the Greek word *daily* appears is in this verse of Scripture. It is not found in Greek writings outside of Christian literature and is used only in this text in the New Testament. This particular word has been translated "spiritual," "necessary," "steadfast," "daily," and "for tomorrow." Many scholars agree that our text is best translated, "Give us bread for the coming day." Even though this does not forbid the accumulation of wealth, it calls for absolute dependence on God from day to day. In these seven words are some eternal truths.

I. God is concerned about human needs.

A. *Bread is the staff of life, the basic need of all.* Our Lord did not teach us to pray, "Give us this day our daily *cake.*" We ask only for the necessities of life, not the luxuries.

B. *One need only follow the footsteps of Christ to observe God's concern for human need.* Christ was grieved when he saw a widow on the outskirts of Nain who had lost her son. The shortest verse in the Bible is "Jesus wept," and this was over the death of Lazarus. He noticed that his followers were hungry, and he fed them. When the woman with the issue of blood touched him, he realized it. He healed the blind, the lame, and the sick. He conversed with lepers, Samaritans, and the demon-possessed. He fixed breakfast for some fishermen early one morning.

C. *Many people are living defeated lives because they think that no one really cares.* God cares that we have groceries to buy, mortgages to pay, school expenses to meet, and other bills to pay.

Henry Ford encountered a young man trying to fix his Model T Ford alongside a road one day.

When he asked if he could help, the young man answered him in such a way as to say, "You don't know enough to help me."

Finally, this great builder of automobiles said, "I am Henry Ford. I made your car, and I know all about its workings."

We are reminded in this section of the Lord's Prayer that God knows all about the working of this universe and that he can help us through any ordeal.

II. We are totally dependent on God for spiritual and physical needs.

A. *In this prayer we pray, "Give us."* We are hereby indicating that we do not have what we need and must ask God to supply our needs.

B. *Ask for bread?* Yes, the production of bread calls for work on our part. God gives us the grain that we plant and causes it to germinate, but we must harvest it. God gives the water that nurtures its growth, but we must separate the chaff from the grain and grind the grain into flour.

C. *God does the saving, but we must do the letting.* A little boy was running home on a dark, cold night. It always frightened him to run past the cemetery. As he heard the rustling of a nearby tree, he ran even faster as he prayed, "Dear Lord, if you will just pick up my feet, I'll lay them down."

Of course, there are some things we can do. However, we must depend on God for the total supply of all our physical and spiritual needs.

III. We find happiness when we learn to live a day at a time.

Today is the tomorrow you worried about yesterday.

A. *We are to pray today only for the bread of tomorrow.* We must depend daily on God and refuse to worry about the future. As the poet said:

> *Keep Thou my feet; I do not ask to see*
> *The distant scene; one step is enough for me.*
>
> —*John Henry Newman*

B. *The psalmist said, "Thy word is a lamp unto my feet, and a light unto my path"* *(Ps. 119:105).* God is not a searchlight, but he is a footlight. He gives us enough light to take the next few steps, and we follow.

Conclusion

A famous prayer from a fourteenth-century prayer manual says, "O God, give us serenity to accept the things we cannot change; courage to change the things that should be changed; and the wisdom to know the difference."

WEDNESDAY EVENING, SEPTEMBER 7

Title: The Perfect Will of God

Text: "And be not conformed to this world: but be ye transformed by the renewing of your mind, that ye may prove what is that good, and acceptable, and perfect, will of God" **(Rom. 12:2)**.

Scripture Reading: Romans 12

Introduction

The will of God is the function, expression, and manifestation of his nature and character.

Jesus thought of the will of God as the sovereign wisdom, justice, and goodness by which all things are governed.

The natural man thinks of the will of God as that which a cruel fate imposes on life. He thinks of it as something to which one must resign himself because of his helplessness. Consequently, the natural man wants to flee from the will of God. He seeks at times to fight God's will.

Our understanding of the will of God will be determined by our understanding of the nature and character of God. Just what kind of God do we worship? How does God express himself?

I. The will of God and the being of God.

We can learn about the nature of God by an examination of the record of his self-revelation in the Scriptures. The supreme revelation of the nature and character of God is to be found in Jesus Christ.

A. *God is eternal (Ps. 92).*

B. *God is personal.* He thinks, feels, and wills.

C. *God is spiritual.* He is not material, tangible, or visible.

D. *God is perfect.*

II. The will of God and the character of God.

God's will is determined by his being and his character.

A. *God is holy.* He is perfect in moral purity. There is no trace of evil in him (1 John 1:5).

B. *God is omniscient (Rom. 11:33).*

C. *God is perfectly just.* He deals with all his creatures impartially. He will vindicate the righteous and punish the wicked.

D. *God is good.* This is an all-inclusive term. His love, mercy, grace, and forgiveness are wrapped up in that word "good."

Conclusion

The will of God is that which is good, acceptable, and perfect in his sight. God's will is good for us and should be acceptable to each of us. God's will will lead us to a full, complete, abundant life if we accept it by faith and respond to it in love.

SUNDAY MORNING, SEPTEMBER 11

Title: Who Is Being Deceived?

Text: "Be not deceived; God is not mocked: for whatsoever a man soweth, that shall he also reap. For he that soweth to his flesh shall of the flesh reap corruption; but he that soweth to the Spirit shall of the Spirit reap life everlasting" (**Gal. 6:7–8**).

Scripture Reading: Galatians 6:1–8

Hymns: "Joyful, Joyful, We Adore Thee," Van Dyke

"Blessed Redeemer," Christiansen

"The Old Rugged Cross," Bennard

Offertory Prayer: Heavenly Father, you gave your Son to die on the cross for us. You have given us the Holy Spirit to dwell in our hearts. You have given us eternal life, which causes us to hunger after you and to love you. Today we give ourselves completely to you. Accept our tithes and offerings as tokens of our desire to belong completely to you, through Jesus Christ our Lord. Amen.

Introduction

I read the obituary of a man's life the other day that was very interesting. It stated:

He brushed his teeth twice a day with a nationally advertised toothpaste. The doctor examined him twice a year. He wore his rubbers when it rained. He slept with his windows open. He stuck to a diet with plenty of fresh vegetables. He relinquished his tonsils and traded in several worn-out glands. He golfed, but never more than 18 holes at a time. He never smoked, drank, or lost his temper. He got at least 8 hours of sleep each night. He was all set to live to be 100.

The funeral was held Wednesday. He is survived by 18 specialists, 4 health institutes, 6 gymnasiums, and numerous health foods and antiseptics.

This man forgot God, lived as if this world was all there was, and now he is with those who say, "The harvest is past, the summer is ended, and we are not saved" (Jer. 8:20).

There are many such people today—people who think that life consists in the things of this world. Today I want to tell you about some people who are being deceived. (*Read the text.*)

I. The person who thinks that he can make light of the things of God is being deceived.

There are several ways that people attempt to mock God.

A. *First, by thinking that sin can be covered, that no one will ever know.* I heard a fellow pastor say that he was an undertaker's pastor and was shown the body of a teenage girl who had taken her own life. She had written a letter addressed to her brothers, who lived in another place. It was an appeal to them to see to it that her younger sister did not travel the path she had traveled. This girl wrote, "The first time I went down into sin my conscience bothered me, but later on I sinned again and again, and my conscience didn't hurt me."

What does that mean? It means that you may trifle with your conscience, it means that you may sin against God's voice in your heart until finally your heart is so cold and so hard that you cannot hear the voice of conscience. You can live in the midst of sin so long that your conscience will be blurred and blighted until it can no longer speak to you.

When this poor girl first started in sin, she had the same devilish philosophy in vogue today—"No one will ever know." But listen to what she wrote: "I'm not fit to live, and I'm not fit to die." She had come to know that she could not look at herself with confidence or self-respect.

B. *Another way people try to mock God is by thinking that the main thing in life is to have a good time.* And far too many think in terms of sin when they describe a good time.

People sometimes think they want sin at any cost. They want sin even though they know it will cause sorrow, shame, heartache, and eternal suffering. They want sin even though they know that the wages of sin is death, hell, and eternal damnation.

Satan's work is to deceive people, and he is very successful. Some people would rather believe him than Christ. Satan would have you think that you can sin and get away with it, that you can break God's holy laws and not get caught, that you can transgress and not have to pay the price of your folly.

C. *You cannot mock God with a false profession.* You cannot mock him with masses and religious service to cover an ungodly life and get away with it.

D. *Satan baits his hook well with the love of money, enticing the sinner to look to riches in his quest for satisfaction.* But those who have reached the summit of the mountain of wealth are almost unanimous in their confessions that that alone fails to satisfy. George Eastman, who headed Eastman Kodak Film Company, stepped into a Rochester, New York, hotel room and put a bullet through his heart. Mr. Fleischmann, of yeast cake fame, ended his life in Los Angeles by plunging into the cold, dark waters of the Pacific. Jesse Livermore, one of Wall Street's greatest "bears" committed suicide; so did Ivar Krueger, who was the head of one of the world's greatest monopolies. These all say, "There is no peace, no lasting satisfaction in wealth."

II. The person is being deceived who thinks that he can reap good where he has sown evil.

A. *You are going to reap exactly what you sow.* You must have a fig tree to gather figs. Never, never, never, can you expect to gather good when you sow evil. Job 4:8 says, "Even as I have seen, they that plow iniquity, and sow wickedness, reap the same."

B. *Good sowing will bring good harvests.* "He that soweth to the Spirit shall of the Spirit reap life everlasting" (Gal. 6:8). Ecclesiastes 11:1 reads, "Cast thy bread upon the waters: for thou shalt find it after many days."

C. *The harvest is always more than the planting.* The farmer can take one ear of corn and sow and reap a sack full, sow that and reap a wagonload, sow that and reap more than a barn full. It is the same with sin. Hosea cried out about idolatrous Samaria, "They have sown the wind, and they shall reap the whirlwind" (Hos. 8:7). Sinners who sow the wind must expect to reap a whirlwind in the judgment.

III. The third group of people who are being deceived are those who keep putting off getting right with God.

This is exactly what Satan wants you to do. You play right into his hands when you wait. He calls your shots for you.

Conclusion

At a Billy Graham crusade in Miami Beach, Florida, I heard Mrs. Bill Brown, formerly British actress Jean Winmill, share her testimony of conversion. Life had become meaningless, and she thought of taking her life. When she heard of God's grace through Christ's death, she was deceived no longer by the Devil and said, "Instead of taking my life, I gave my life to Jesus, and he has made all the difference in the world."

SUNDAY EVENING, SEPTEMBER 11

Title: "Forgive Us Our Trespasses"

Text: "And forgive us our debts, as we forgive our debtors" **(Matt. 6:12)**.

Scripture Reading: Matthew 18:21–35

Introduction

A little boy was asked to define forgiveness. He said, "It is the odor that flowers breathe when they are trampled on." All of us need the forgiving breath of God in our lives.

There is more to this part of the Lord's Prayer than the forgiveness of our own sins, for we are praying, "Forgive us as we forgive others." We actually are asking God to forgive us of our sins only insofar as we forgive others the wrongs that they have done us.

I. The picture of forgiveness.

"Madam," said a spiritual leader to an elderly saint, "I have come to grant you absolution."

"And what is that?" she inquired.

"I have come to forgive your sins," was the reply.

"May I look into your hands?" she asked. Gazing into them for a moment, she turned and looked him squarely in the eye and said, "Sir! The Man who forgives my sins has nail prints in his palms."

A. *The prime illustration of forgiveness is the death of Jesus Christ on the cross.* This one picture is worth a thousand words. On the outskirts of Jerusalem more than nineteen hundred years ago, there was cursing, pain, hunger, and thirst at Golgotha, the place reserved for the death of Roman prisoners.

No one expected to hear a prayer that day. As they nailed him to the cross, lifted the cross into the air, deposited the cross into the earth, and spit on him, Jesus prayed, "Father, forgive them; for they know not what they do."

There, amid pain, darkness, blood, thunder, lightning, cursing, and death, the prayer of forgiveness hovered over the circumstances of the day.

B. *No headlines.* Years ago a Roman Catholic council at the Vatican made headlines across the world when it voted to forgive the Jews of the sole blame for the crucifixion of Christ. The Vatican Council was over nineteen hundred years late. A far more newsworthy event had passed with scant notice, even without the decision of a church council. It was not performed by the cadence of a pounding gavel but by the beat of a hammer as nails were driven into a cross. It was not a prayer to forgive one race of people for a particular sin; it was a prayer of forgiveness for all people of all time.

II. How do we forgive others?

A. *We forgive others when we seek to understand them.* True forgiveness looks behind what one does. It concludes, "They know not what they do."

B. *We forgive others when we forget what others have done to us.* There is never any record where Jesus recalls the harm that was done to him—not even after his resurrection. We have no record of his sitting around the campfire discussing his ill-treatment at the hands of the Romans. Instead of talking about his troubles, he came to his disciples with, "Peace I give unto you."

Two little boys returned to their separate homes after a fight. One declared to his mother, "I will never speak to him again as long as I live."

The next day the mother caught both boys playing together as usual as though nothing had happened the day before. When she questioned her son about his vow to never again speak to his friend, he answered, "Me and Johnny are good forgetters."

C. *We forgive others when we have learned to love the unlovely.* Christian love does not depend on what one is, what one does to us, or what one does for us. How unlovely was the crowd around the cross! They were the blood lovers of the day. Some of them actually got a thrill out of seeing condemned criminals die on the cross.

III. Why can we forgive?

A. *The only way to become forgiving is to experience God's forgiveness.* When one is saved, he dies to self. When one is saved, he realizes how unworthy he is of God's forgiveness. Then he cannot refuse to forgive others. He cries out with the psalmist, "If thou, LORD, shouldest mark iniquities, O Lord, who shall stand?" (Ps. 130:3).

B. *One who comes to know Christ knows that salvation is by grace through faith (Eph. 2:8–9).* How then can he be less gracious toward his fellow man than God has been toward him?

Conclusion

A shepherd and his daughter lived in a highland village. They were together constantly as they tended the sheep, and she loved to hear her father's call to the sheep as it echoed across the lush, green mountains.

When she grew up, she moved to the city and secured a good job. The old shepherd noticed that her letters became shorter and shorter. The day finally came when he no longer heard from his daughter. Someone from the city came by one day and informed the shepherd that he had seen his daughter, but she acted as though she did not know him.

With his smock and shawl wrapped around his shoulders, the old shepherd took his staff in hand and set out for the city to find his daughter. Passersby stared at the crudely dressed shepherd. Day after day he looked for his daughter along the streets, and he even stopped on the busy streets now and then to give his familiar call.

One day in a degraded section of the city, his daughter, sitting in a room with her friends, looked up with astonishment. There was no doubt about it! It was her father's voice. She threw open the door and rushed out into the street. There her forgiving father took her in his arms and carried her back to the highland home where he loved her back to decency and to God.

WEDNESDAY EVENING, SEPTEMBER 14

Title: John's Understanding of the Will of God

Text: "Jesus saith unto them, My meat is to do the will of him that sent me, and to finish his work" **(John 4:34).**

Scripture Reading: John 4:31–42

Introduction

John's gospel makes reference to the will of God in many different situations. Let us learn about the will of God by studying how it is discussed in John's gospel.

I. Spiritual birth is a part of God's will.

"But as many as received him, to them gave he power to become the sons of God, even to them that believe on his name" (John 1:12). Our relationship to God is not on the basis of our merit, our national origin, or our adherence to a legal code. We enter a relationship with God by means of a spiritual birth. We receive the divine nature in this birth experience, and a continuing fellowship with God is then possible.

II. Doing the will of God brings inward satisfaction.

"My meat is to do the will of him that sent me" (John 4:34). Christ found nourishment for the deepest part of his being in doing the will of God. We can find this same inward satisfaction that quenches the thirst of the soul by following him in doing the will of God (John 7:17).

III. The will of God provides for everlasting life.

"And this is the will of him that sent me, that every one which seeth the Son, and believeth on him, may have everlasting life" (John 6:40). Eternal life is something more than everlasting existence. It is the very life of God. It is qualitative in nature. It is something infinitely above the natural.

IV. The will of God includes our resurrection.

"And I will raise him up at the last day" (John 6:40). John did not believe, neither did Jesus teach, the natural immortality of the soul, which is a Greek concept. Jesus taught and John records our Lord's plan to raise from the tyranny of death those who trust him as Lord (John 5:21, 25–26; 14:1–3).

V. The will of God includes heaven.

"Father, I want those you have given me to be with me where I am, and to see my glory, the glory you have given me because you loved me before the creation of the world" (John 17:24 NIV). In his great intercessory prayer, our Lord expressed his desire that those who had trusted him might share his eternal glory in heaven. We can be certain that this prayer of the Son to the Father will become a reality.

VI. The will of God includes service for the present (John 21:21–22).

Our Lord instructed Peter to concentrate on his personal responsibility for service during the present rather than concerning himself with the activities of others. Much of God's will concerns our past. Much of God's will concerns the future. Very definitely his will for us now is that we be busy in a ministry of mercy to those about us.

Conclusion

Instead of fearing the will of God and fleeing from it, let us determine to find it and then, with all of our strength, give ourselves to doing it.

SUNDAY MORNING, SEPTEMBER 18

Title: Is Something Happening to You?

Text: "Being confident of this very thing, that he which hath begun a good work in you will perform it until the day of Jesus Christ" **(Phil. 1:6)**.

Scripture Reading: Philippians 1:3–11

Hymns: "Praise to God, Immortal Praise," Barbauld

"Christ Receiveth Sinful Men," Neumeister

"He Included Me," Oatman

Offertory Prayer: Heavenly Father, you have given your best to us and for us. We praise you for the privilege of receiving the gifts of forgiveness and eternal life. Today we bring tithes and offerings that represent a portion of our lives. We offer them to you, praying that you would help us give ourselves completely to you. Through Jesus Christ, our Lord. Amen.

Introduction

The worst thing that could happen to a Christian is nothing. On a bleak day in February 1809 a rural Kentucky mail carrier is reported to have inquired of a group of men whether they had any news worth telling. One of the men answered, "Nothing ever happens 'round here." A second man added, "Nope, nothing new 'cept a boy young'un born to Tom and Nancy Hanks Lincoln last night." Nothing "new" had happened? How wrong that farmer was! How blind we mortals are!

I. Let us begin at the beginning—God was the initiator.

A. *Our salvation happens because God takes the initiative.* God purposed his work of redeeming humans while they were still sinners (Rom. 5:8). God fashioned his offensive to win control of people's lives because he loves them and covets for his children that which would allow them to share his own life.

B. *Indeed, God's answer to humankind's need is not a plan but a person, his own Son.* Repeatedly the Bible portrays God as actor, worker, lover, initiator—always confronting people with himself in Jesus Christ (Luke 19:10).

C. *Do you remember when you were born again?* It was the greatest day of your life. God may have used your parents, pastor, teacher, friend, or someone else to get his message to you, but thank God you got the message and you were created anew. If you have not yet experienced this, you cannot understand what I am talking about.

II. Look at the basic ingredients of the experience.

A. *A dim view of self and an awareness of incompleteness and a burden of guilt—a sinner (Isa. 53:6; Rom. 3:23).*

B. *A new view of God.* A neighbor commented to the father of a wayward son, "If he were *my* son, I would turn him out of the house." The father replied, "Yes, if he were *your* son, I'd probably turn him out, too, but you see he is not *your* son, he is my son."

 The cross is a double drama depicting how far people will go to say no to God and how far God will go to say yes to people.

C. *The crisis of decision.* We are sobered by the life-or-death message of the gospel as it speaks of unbelievers as "condemned already" (John 3:18). This points up the tremendous importance of one's decision to give himself or herself to Jesus Christ.

D. *The experience called conversion.* Recall your conversion. Did it happen in a flash? Gradually? Was it calm or emotional? Did it occur during revival? Different people are born again under different circumstances, yet all have similar results.

E. *Beginning, not the end.* Salvation is first of all an experience, second a process, and third a consummation. The New Testament deals with the converted person as saved, being saved, and going to be saved.

III. Something should be continuing to happen to you.

Your new life in Christ should be resulting in growth and change because Christ is now living in you. These may seem like strange words and still stranger truth. It sounds almost like blasphemy, and it would be blasphemy had not Jesus himself promised that he would do nothing less than live his life in and through our lives.

Conclusion

To say that our salvation is *in* Christ is to say that our salvation comes *from* him. But it is also to say that we are saved by being brought into a vital relationship with him. Our love for him should be growing. Our witness for him should be expanding. Our compassion for the lost should be deepening. Our selfishness should be lessening.

SUNDAY EVENING, SEPTEMBER 18

Title: "Lead Us Not into Temptation"

Text: "And lead us not into temptation, but deliver us from evil" **(Matt. 6:13)**.

Scripture Reading: James 1:1 – 16

Introduction

A pastor asked a little boy, "Do you pray every day?"

"No, not every day," answered the little boy. "Some days I don't want anything."

For many of us, prayer often becomes "the heavenly 911" to be used in case of emergency. Some have testified that the only time they have prayed is when they were in a foxhole. Others have prayed only when the doctor finally said, "There is no hope for your loved one." When disaster strikes, divorce proceedings have started, or parents are having trouble with their children, people often resort to prayer even though they have spent very few minutes in prayer before these times of tragedy.

This section of the Lord's Prayer teaches that prayer is not just an escape hatch. Our Lord teaches us to pray for God's help even before we actually feel a need for his help. We pray that God will lead us around temptation.

I. Trials are good for us.

Our Lord encourages us to pray for his leadership through our trials. Trials are good for us (James 1:2 – 12).

A. *We often learn to pray through trials and temptations (James 1:5).* Many have learned to pray through some tragedy in their life.

B. *Our faith is often strengthened by trials (James 1:6).* Through one trial in his life, a Christian said, "For the first time, I realize what it means to trust in God. Before, I didn't think I had a need to trust in him, but now I realize that I am nothing without God."

C. *Trials often teach us what is really important in this life (James 1:12).* When we endure our trials, we receive "the crown of life." This means that we learn what life is really all about. Our Lord came to give us abundant life. Some never find that abundant life until some sort of trial or tragedy besets them (1 Cor. 10:13).

II. Trials are universal.

Our Lord said, "Watch and pray, that ye enter not *into temptation*" (Matt. 26:41, emphasis added). "Into" is the key word in this section of the Lord's Prayer.

273

When we yield to temptation, we have fallen "into" it. Our Lord was tempted yet did not sin (Matt. 4:1–11).

A. *Jesus was tempted by the trial of self-preservation.* The Devil tempted him to turn the stones into bread. In this dog-eat-dog world in which we live, we are often tempted to do wrong for the sake of self-preservation. We hear our Lord say, "Man shall not live by bread alone, but by every word that proceedeth out of the mouth of God" (Matt. 4:4).

Moses had explained to the children of Israel that they were not nourished by the manna that fell from heaven but by the words of God that caused the manna to fall (Deut. 8:3). When we are tempted to trust more in ourselves than we trust in God, we too need to be reminded that God will provide.

B. *Jesus was tempted to doubt God.* Satan tempted him to jump from the top of the temple and receive the applause of men by this sensational act. Our Lord's reply was, "Thou shalt not tempt the Lord thy God" (Matt. 4:7).

Jesus refused to put God on trial to test his word. Moses also had refused to tempt God. In the wilderness, the children of Israel complained because they did not have enough water to drink. Moses said, "Why do you quarrel with me? Why do you put the LORD to the test?" (Ex. 17:2 NIV). To tempt God and to doubt God are one and the same (Ex. 17:2; Deut. 6:16). Some people test God by saying, "I will do this if you will do that."

C. *Our Lord was tempted by security.* Satan told Jesus that if he would just bow down before him, he would receive the kingdoms of the world. Jesus quickly informed Satan that man must worship God only.

Like the children of Israel as they entered the Promised Land, our promised land of affluence often tempts us to trust in material security rather than in Jehovah God.

III. Satan turns our trials into temptations.

A. *The very word "Satan" carries the connotation of an "adversary" who pleads the case against us (Job 1:6).* Satan is always pleading to God against each of us.

B. *He is also called "the devil."* He slanders us and makes up cases against us.

C. *The Greek word translated "evil" is better translated "the evil one."* This, of course, refers to Satan himself. Someone has said, "Satan trembles when he sees the weakest saint on his knees." Our adversary, the slanderous Devil, must be resisted daily.

Conclusion

The following suggestions will help carry out the spirit of this section of the Lord's Prayer:

1. Stay on guard. "Get thee behind me, Satan" is a good line for every Christian to remember. Adam and Eve were forbidden to touch the fruit of the Tree of Knowledge of Good and Evil. After they touched it, they also ate it.

2. Pray every day. Consistency in prayer brings consistent strength for living.
3. Follow God's leadership every day. Ask him to lead you around temptation as you follow his leadership.
4. As you ask to be delivered from Satan, also ask to be delivered closer to God.
5. Realize that yielding to temptation not only affects you but others as well. A man was sitting on the front steps of his home talking about a shady business deal with an associate. His wife came out and gave him the baby to hold for a few moments. He looked down into the eyes of his baby and realized that his sin might hurt this defenseless child. He looked up into the eyes of the dishonest business associate and said, "Leave, and don't come back here again."
6. Practice the presence of God. "Would you want Christ to return and catch you at what you are doing?" may be an effective rhetorical question in a sermon, but we already live in the presence of God who sees and knows everything we do. We do not have to wait for the second coming of Christ. The all-seeing eye of God detects our actions here and now. We must watch for, pray for, and look forward to the second coming of Christ, but why wait until then to live for Christ?

WEDNESDAY EVENING, SEPTEMBER 21

Title: The Will of God Provides and Offers Salvation

Text: "For this is good and acceptable in the sight of God our Saviour; who will have all men to be saved, and to come unto the knowledge of the truth" (**1 Tim. 2:3–4**).

Scripture Reading: 1 Timothy 2

Introduction

God's will has provided salvation for every man, woman, boy, and girl who is willing to receive Jesus Christ as Lord and Savior. It is God's will that each one be saved, forgiven, redeemed, restored, delivered, and liberated.

I. God's eternal redemptive program.

From the call of Abraham to the Great Commission voiced by our Lord, the redemptive program of God is revealed to be the same. Humans are the objects of God's eternal quest. God has sought to deliver humans through the ministry of the patriarchs, the Lawgiver, the prophets, the psalmists, and ultimately through the Christ and his church.

II. By the gift of his Son, God reveals his will.

John 3:16 is said to be the little Bible. It contains the gospel, God's eternal redemptive program, in a nutshell. It tells us that God has given his Son, Jesus Christ, in order to make available to humans the gift of eternal life.

275

（Sunday Morning, September 25）

III. By the gift of his Spirit, God has revealed his will.

Our Lord spoke concerning the necessity of the coming of the Holy Spirit that people might be convicted of their need of a Savior from sin (John 16:7–14). The Holy Spirit is in the world today, not only to empower believers for the ministry they are to render, but to convict the unbelieving world of its need for a Savior. Through the continuing ministry of the Holy Spirit, one can detect God's provision and offer of salvation.

IV. The commission of Christ to the church reveals the will of God (Matt. 28:18–20).

Our Lord's parting mandate was to the effect that his disciples busy themselves at the task of evangelizing the world. His disciples were commanded to conduct themselves in such a manner as they went about from place to place that they might effectively lead others to become disciples of Jesus Christ.

V. God's final invitation reveals his will that all people be saved (Rev. 22:17).

Even if the Bible contained only one invitation to salvation from God to humans, it would still be the world's most wonderful Book. The truth is that God offers his gracious invitation to lost humanity repeatedly throughout the length and breadth of the Word of God.

By divine inspiration the last book of the Bible comes to a conclusion with a broad compelling invitation that people come to the fountain of living waters that they might quench the thirst of their souls. As the followers of Christ, we need to recognize that it is God's will that all of those about us hear the gospel and have an opportunity to personally respond to Jesus Christ. It is our obligation and privilege to try to persuade them to trust him as Lord.

Those who have not yet trusted Christ as Savior should be greatly encouraged by the many evidences that it is God's will that they experience the forgiveness of sin and the gift of eternal life. God is ready to receive, to forgive, to bestow the gift of eternal life at this moment.

SUNDAY MORNING, SEPTEMBER 25

Title: Principles of Protestantism

Text: "For Christ is the end of the law, that every one who has faith may be justified" (**Rom. 10:4 RSV**).

Scripture Reading: Romans 10:1–4; Galatians 5:1, 6, 19–26

Hymns: "When Morning Gilds the Skies," Caswell

"A Mighty Fortress Is Our God," Luther

"Word of God, across the Ages," Blanchard

Offertory Prayer: O Lord, we have feasted often on the riches of your grace. Now, in this offering, we give some tangible acknowledgment that we have been with you—and it has been good. In Jesus' name. Amen.

Introduction

Nearly five hundred years ago Martin Luther nailed his Ninety-five Theses to the church door in Wittenberg, Germany. This was a customary procedure in the academic atmosphere of the university where the church was located when one wanted to debate an issue of public interest. The Roman Catholic monk did not foresee the consequences, and years later he exclaimed, "Had I known all in advance, God would have been put to great trouble to bring me to it." Luther, nevertheless, opened the door to a whole new world, a world of the Protestant Reformation.

Protestantism needs to be understood as a movement of God in history. Admittedly, the word has liabilities because it has been misunderstood and misused. "Protestant" to Elizabethan Englishmen did not signify a mere objector or protestor, although there was the idea of dissent in it. It meant one who bore a witness or one who stood for something, proclaimed something in a statement of flaming conviction. The word broken down to its Latin base makes this clear. *Pro* means "on behalf of," "forth," or "openly," and *testor* means "witness to" or "being a witness."

Protestantism is not *a* church, and certainly it is not *the* church. It is a complexity of movements within the one church talked about in Ephesians. Protestantism has no structural unity, no centralized administration, and certainly no creedal finality. It is an effort to hold fast to the Christian faith in an atmosphere of Christian freedom. In the understanding and application of that faith and in the exercise of that freedom, different parts of it have traveled along different roads at varying speeds. Those who want a religion complete, final, unchangeable in behavior as well as creed are not Protestant in spirit. Protestantism is not a closed system. It welcomes new discovery of truth, and it confesses past errors.

Protestants agree to differ on many points. Uniformity of opinion has never been an alluring ideal to Protestants. But Protestants do have beliefs and convictions shared in common. Certain cardinal principles are embedded in the movement. An apt summary has been given as follows: An open mind, an open Book, and an open road. This is an oversimplification, but it can give guidance to our thoughts.

I. An open mind.

Protestants believe in the right to possess and the Christian duty to exercise an open mind. An open mind is a God-given privilege, and consequently we have not only the right but the duty of private judgment. Open-mindedness is not to be confused with empty-mindedness. Ralph Sockman once said, "In opening the mind to the light of truth one does not need to open the windows and let out the warmth of conviction." Persons can be loyal to their understanding of truth without denying the rights of others who differ.

Every Christian has the right to follow the dictates of his conscience, the moral sense that helps him to determine the difference between right and wrong in matters of faith and practice. The Protestant revolt against a system that viewed religion primarily as dogma, duties, and restrictions was an assertion of human rights and freedom.

Granted, freedom is a dangerous thing; it is more dangerous than anything else in the world except one thing—lack of freedom. Protestantism at its best chooses the road between blind traditionalism and nearsighted individualism. Protestants oppose regimented thinking, even when it is upheld by a venerable institution. The authority they respect is that of truth. And truth is found supremely in Jesus Christ. The mind that approaches mystery without prejudice can more nearly be the recipient of God's revelation.

II. An open Book.

It is sometimes said that the Great Reformation simply substituted an infallible Bible for an infallible pope, a formula that is incorrect on both counts. The popes were not generally regarded as infallible before the Reformation. The Vatican Council decreed in 1870 that the pope, when he speaks *ex cathedra*, is incapable of error touching questions of faith and morals. The Reformers did not acknowledge an infallible Bible; they simply asserted the traditional Christian conception that the word of God in the Bible must be the last court of resort in the church. No question was raised about the inerrancy of the Bible. The two questions that were raised were: first, its sufficiency; and second, the right to interpret it.

We believe the message of the Scriptures speaks to the mind and heart of the believer without flesh and blood intermediary. In this regard, we stand with Martin Luther. In 1521 Luther was summoned before the imperial Diet at Worms, Germany, by Charles V, emperor of the Holy Roman Empire, king of Spain, and ruler of Germany. Ordered to recant his heretical doctrines, Luther refused to do so in a speech delivered first in Latin and then in German. Unable to understand either language, Charles V demanded what he called "a plain answer." "Your majesty requires of me a plain answer," responded Luther. "I cannot recant unless I am proved in the wrong by Holy Scripture or plain reason. I cannot act in opposition to the dictates of conscience and the Word of God. Here I stand. So help me, God, I can do no other."

It is to our shame that we call ourselves a people of the open Book yet do not know what the Book says. Or, if we do, we do not do what the Book says. It is much easier and less disturbing to deny the authority of the papacy to interpret the Scriptures than it is to incarnate the biblical messages and spirit in our lives.

The Scriptures are interpreted from the shared experiences of the believing community, the Holy Spirit witnessing in each, and in each to each, of the truth that God would impart to us. We need to know our great Textbook. We should be able to point people to the joyous and hopeful words of Paul: "If you confess with your lips that Jesus is Lord and believe in your heart that God raised him from the dead, you will be saved" (Rom. 10:9 RSV). We should be able to point people to Jesus' clear teaching to soul-hungry Nicodemus: "I say to you, unless one is born anew, he cannot see the kingdom of God" (John 3:3 RSV).

The Bible at its best is the most forward-looking Book in the world. The eternal purpose that God purposed in Christ—is that only behind us or ahead of us too? The Sermon on the Mount—is that a past achievement or a future goal? Think of the great prophets and their vision of a world where men beat their swords into plowshares and their spears into pruning hooks and learn war no more! Think of our Lord with his commission: "Go therefore and make disciples of all nations" (Matt. 28:19 RSV).

The Bible is both a witness and an invitation, a witness to the great things God has done in the past, an invitation to share the greater experience he will make possible today and tomorrow—a redemption that will not only include all people but also all parts of the lives of people.

III. An open road.

Every person has direct access to God through our Mediator, Jesus Christ. Forgiveness and reconciliation are a direct relationship between people and God and do not require the intervention of another human being.

Paul stated the doctrine of justification by faith in Romans and Galatians to explain his own discovery of the redemptive power of God in Jesus Christ. As a Jew, he had believed that God would declare a person "just" at the Last Judgment by virtue of his fulfillment of the regulations of the Jewish law, with what the apostle called "works." But Paul's own experience had convinced him that he could not possibly make himself righteous in God's sight. He might have willed what was good, but the power of sin was such that he found himself doing the evil that he did not want to do. Christianity opened up a new way of redemption apart from the law. By faith, by the glad, ready response of the whole person to God's gracious gift of salvation in Christ, Paul found himself accepted by God in spite of his sin and remade as a new creature by the power of the Holy Spirit.

The principle of "the open road" frees us from clericalism, from an authoritarian priesthood, but it places a responsibility on the shoulders of every Christian in a way that should shake us out of our lethargy (cf. 1 Peter 2:9). Every person is his own priest insofar as he belongs to the "mutual ministry of believers." Every believer is an agent of God in the proclamation and commendation of the gospel, responsible to the head of the church, Jesus Christ.

Conclusion

In the high New Testament sense, we are to "put on Jesus Christ." We must make him our Master. An open mind, an open Book, and an open way lead us to open ourselves to Christ in life-changing ways. Harold Bosley once said, "Christ limited is Christ betrayed." So let us open our lives to his full influence.

SUNDAY EVENING, SEPTEMBER 25

Title: Fasting

Text: "Moreover when ye fast, be not, as the hypocrites, of a sad countenance: for they disfigure their faces, that they may appear unto men to fast. Verily I say unto you, they have their reward. But thou, when thou fastest, anoint thine head, and wash thy face; that thou appear not unto men to fast, but unto thy Father which is in secret: and thy Father, which seeth in secret, shall reward thee openly" (**Matt. 6:16 – 18**).

Scripture Reading: Isaiah 58

Introduction

In Matthew 6:1 – 18 Jesus discusses (1) the Christian's contact with others—doing good deeds; (2) the Christian's contact with God—prayer; (3) the Christian's contact with himself—fasting.

We say a lot about good deeds and prayer, but most of us say very little about fasting. In the average church we do a lot of feasting but not much fasting.

I. What is fasting?

A. *Negative.* When our Lord mentioned fasting, he was not speaking of merely doing without food for physical reasons. Fasting is physically and psychologically good for many people.

B. *Positive.*

1. Fasting is a part of Christian discipline. A disciple of Christ is one who lives the disciplined life. Paul spoke of bringing the body into subjection (1 Cor. 9:27).

2. To fast for spiritual enrichment means to do without food for a period of time because of a deep concern.

   Some fast to pray about specific matters. Others fast merely to adore God in worship. Others fast to meditate on some important problem or decision. Some fast during times of disappointment or tragedy. While some fast in times of need, others fast to give thanks to God for his blessings. When some Christians face great decisions in their lives, they "pray through" decisions without any thought whatsoever of time or food.

3. Fasting entails forgetting ourselves and letting the Holy Spirit fill us.

II. How not to fast.

It is interesting to note that our Lord spoke more of wrong ways to fast than of right ways to fast. We should not fast to call attention to ourselves.

The good Jew fasted only once a year—during the Day of Atonement. The Pharisees fasted twice a week. Most scholars agree that they probably did their fasting on Monday and Thursday, the market days, so that the most people could

280

observe them and hear them. No doubt they were fond of going down on the streets after fasting all day. Their wrinkled clothing, unshaved faces, and generally unkempt appearance testified to the world that they had been fasting.

A humble person does not really know that he is humble. Likewise, one who truly fasts will probably not talk about it.

Conclusion

Jesus did not say, "*If* you fast." He said, "*When* you fast." Our Lord expected us to fast.

What a difference it would make in our lives and in our churches if we really fasted. Instead of seeking sympathy from others, we would take our burdens to the Lord and leave them there! Instead of bungling our lives by going ahead and doing what looks right, we would find the true will of God by waiting on him in prayer. Instead of saying no when offered a position in the church, we might well, having fasted, say, "Yes, in the name of Christ, I will do this job."

WEDNESDAY EVENING, SEPTEMBER 28

Title: Cooperating with the Will of God

Text: "Thy kingdom come. Thy will be done in earth, as it is in heaven" (**Matt. 6:10**).

Scripture Reading: John 6:32–40

Introduction

When Jesus taught his disciples to pray, "Thy will be done in earth, as it is in heaven," he was giving them the divine blueprint by which they were to build a significant life of real achievement. He was leading them to pledge their cooperation with the will of God in a manner that would bring complete satisfaction to their hearts and lives. He was encouraging them to cooperate joyfully with his good and perfect will.

I. God's will is done in heaven.

A. *The universe itself is constantly obedient to the will of the Creator.* Clouds float through the sky in peaceful obedience to his sovereign will. Stars burn in the night according to his will. Planets rotate in their courses according to his will.

B. *The angelic hosts of heaven obey his will perfectly.*
1. There is no interruption in their obedience because of sin.
2. There is no resistance to his will because of temptation.
3. There is no flaw in their doing of his will because of ignorance.
4. There is no pause in the doing of his will because of weariness.
5. There is no pain or guilt in their actions because of a rebellious will.

The obedience of the angelic hosts is free, constant, spontaneous, and happy.

II. The heavenly pattern of cooperation with the will of God is to be our pattern here on earth.

To the degree that we follow the heavenly pattern of submission to the will of God, we cooperate with God in bringing in his kingdom here on the earth. God would have us experience the holy happiness and harmony of a heavenly life here on earth.

When God's will, way, and work have their proper place in our attitudes, ambitions, and actions, the deepest needs of our lives will have been properly met. The priorities of our lives will have been determined.

A. *By cooperating with the will of God on earth, we can be delivered from those forces and powers that are destructive and deadening.*

B. *By cooperating with the will of God, we will be giving ourselves to those things that are right and proper and that bless the hearts and lives of others.* By cooperating with the will of God, we avoid the peril of majoring on minors and minoring on majors.

III. The logic behind this petition.

Our chief business in life should be that of finding and following God's will.

A. *This petition is a plea for help in making the divine will a regulator of our attitudes and ambitions.*

B. *This petition is a plea for help in letting the divine will become the standard and rule for all of our ambitions.*

C. *To sincerely pray this prayer is to accept the will of God as the road map for all of our future activities.*

Conclusion

Joyfully we should pledge ourselves to seek and to follow God's will. With humility and gratitude we should accept his will. In the center of God's will, we will find our highest happiness and our greatest usefulness.

OCTOBER

- **Sunday Mornings**

   The Sunday morning messages are based on passages from Paul's epistle to the Philippians. The theme is "The Life of Christian Joy."

- **Sunday Evenings**

   Continue the series on the Sermon on the Mount.

- **Wednesday Evenings**

   Continue the series "The Good and Perfect Will of God."

SUNDAY MORNING, OCTOBER 2

Title: The Source of Christian Joy

Text: "I thank my God every time I remember you. In all my prayers for all of you, I always pray with joy because of your partnership in the gospel from the first day until now" (**Phil. 1:3–5 NIV**).

Scripture Reading: Philippians 1:1–11

Hymns: "Joyful, Joyful, We Adore Thee," Van Dyke

   "He Included Me," Oatman

   "Blest Be the Tie," Fawcett

Offertory Prayer: Lord of all being, whose glory floods our souls, we bring you our parched souls that they may be restored through fellowship with you and your saints. The goals for which people grasp—the moment of fame, the glitter of gold, and the bread of pleasure—are but vanity and vexation of spirit. And so we look to you for the highest goal in life, eternal fellowship with you and the saints. Draw us close to you and grant us the full joy of our salvation that ours may be lives of Christian joy wherever we go. In our Redeemer's name we pray. Amen.

Introduction

If Christianity does not make a man happy, it does not make him anything at all! Philippians has been called "The Epistle of Joy." Again and again woven throughout the fiber of this letter are the words "joy" and "rejoice." They recur as a brilliant thread that weaves its way through a lovely piece of cloth.

We do well to remember that ours is meant to be a life of Christian joy—full of radiance.

But from what does a Christian derive joy? What was Paul's cause for Christian joy, and what is ours? It is the fellowship of believers. For Paul said, "I thank my God upon every remembrance of you.... For your *fellowship* in the gospel" (Phil. 1:3, 5).

That which brings real joy to the Christian today is not the building in which he worships, the program in which he participates, or the good that he does; if there be any real joy in his life, it comes from fellowship with other believers. The absence of this fellowship well explains the absence of joy in the lives of countless Christians today.

If ours is to be a life of "Christian joy," it must be a life lived in the fellowship of believers.

I. The greeting this fellowship sends.

In Philippians 1:1–2 Paul sends greetings to the saints "which are at Philippi," the first church established in Europe, whose birth is described in Acts 16. What lay behind this church? What are the principles upon which any work of Christ depends and is built?

A. *The obedience of a servant.* In Philippians 1:1 the apostle speaks of "the servants of Jesus Christ." Paul wanted to go to Bithynia, but God closed the door—"the Spirit suffered them not." Then God called him to Macedonia, and he went. Is there not something to learn from this? I think so.

We have almost come to the position where we think it does not matter whether we obey God, because, after all, we can simply turn to 1 John 1 and claim the promise, "If we confess our sins...." We are in serious danger of taking up the attitude that says, "It doesn't matter if I sin."

The lesson that stands out vividly in this passage is that the work of God depends on the obedience of his servants. It matters profoundly if you and I are disobedient to the will of God. Here we find that the existence of a church depends on the obedience of one man who was prepared to accept God's forbidding and prepared to obey God's calling. The whole situation at Philippi turned on the obedience of a servant.

B. *The operation of the Spirit.* "To all the *saints* in Christ Jesus ..." (Phil. 1:1). At the heart of the founding of this church lay the miracle of salvation, the work and operation of the Holy Spirit.

1. The operation of the Holy Spirit reaches all kinds of people in all kinds of ways. Acts 16, which tells us of the origin of this church, shows the universal appeal of the Holy Spirit as it tells of the salvation of three people—Lydia, the slave girl, and the Roman jailer. Lydia was an Asiatic, the slave girl a Greek, and the jailer a Roman. Lydia was of Paul's culture, the slave girl legally was considered not a person but a tool, and the jailer was middle class. Lydia was converted quietly ("whose heart the Lord opened," v. 14), the jailer was converted dramatically, and the slave girl was converted wonderfully.

2. The Holy Spirit sets Christians apart. Those touched by the operation of the Holy Spirit are called "saints" (1:1). This word "saint" means to

284

be set apart for special service to God. It is used in the Old Testament of the priesthood, the tithe, the central part of the temple, and Israel. We are made different by being set apart by the Holy Spirit for the service of Christ.

C. *The opposition of society.* The apostle addressed the Christians "which are at Philippi" (Phil. 1:1). Christianity is seldom popular when God is really working. At Philippi opposition was aroused immediately. Paul and Silas were beaten and thrown into prison. There are always birth pangs when a church is born or God's work is flourishing. One of the sad commentaries on our day is that we expect the Spirit of God to work without cost or pain to us.

II. The gratitude this fellowship shows is expressed in Philippians 1:3–8.

It is a lovely thing when remembrance and gratitude are bound up together. In our personal Christian relationships, it is great to have nothing but happy memories, and that is how Paul thought of the Christians at Philippi. But what are the strands that bind one Christian to another Christian? There are three:

A. *A life common to the fellowship.* Verse 7 is better translated, "Ye are all partakers with me of grace." They had a life common to the fellowship.

1. Christian fellowship is shared by all. The wealthy businesswoman Lydia, the demon-possessed slave girl, and the middle-class jailer all shared the same sweet Christian fellowship.
2. Christian fellowship is gracious toward all. Snobbery has no place in the church. For me to look down on you is impertinence and blasphemy when we both are indwelt by the same Christ.

B. *A constraining love in the fellowship (vv. 7–8).*

1. Such love is "the affection of Jesus Christ" (v. 8 NIV). The apostle is saying, "I yearn for you with the very compassion of Jesus Christ himself." Christ's love flows through us to others.
2. Such love is a dependable love. Theirs was a fellowship "from the first day until now" (1:5). That love had covered a span of ten years. Do people find your love and fellowship dependable?

C. *A Lord central in the fellowship.* "Being confident of this very thing, that *he* which hath begun a good work in you will perform it until the day of Jesus Christ" (1:6). Our fellowship is built around and upon Christ. Verse 6 says that Christ both imparts confidence and makes certain our perseverance.

III. The growth this fellowship seeks (1:9–11).

Although everything may be ever so wonderful, God is never fully satisfied. Our fellowship seeks a growth yet to be realized. It seeks:

A. *That profusion which is the measure of love.* "That your love may abound yet more and more" (1:9). The picture is that of a bucket standing under a stream of water with the water pouring over on every side and overflowing into others. This is the extravagance in love that is unrestrained. Love never asks, "How little can I give?"

B. *That perception that guides the ministry of love (1:9–10).* This is no sentimental love. It is a love guided by true knowledge and wise judgment. Love is always the way to knowledge. If we love any subject, we want to learn more and more about it. If we love any person, we want to learn more and more about him or her. And if we love Jesus, we will want to learn more and more about him and gain that perception that guides the ministry of love. Here Paul is thinking of a love that does not need to be told because it *knows*. Are you then that kind of Christian? You do not need to be told by your Lord or by your pastor because you *know*. You have gained that perception that guides the ministry of love.

C. *That perfection that is the "must" of love.* "That ye may be sincere and without offence till the day of Christ; being filled with the fruits of righteousness, which are by Jesus Christ, unto the glory and praise of God" (1:10–11).

   Here is the standard established by love — *perfection*, "without offence." Often we are frightened by this word, but God isn't. Although we shall never fully attain it in this life, we can at least aspire to it. And our fellowship prods us on to attain it.

   1. The quest for this "perfection" develops purity of character. "That ye may be sincere" means "that ye may be pure." This word comes from two Greek words meaning "sunshine" and "to judge." Thus it describes that which is able to stand the test of the sun without a single flaw appearing. This is the purity to which your Christian character should aspire.

   2. This perfection is winsome to others, "and without offence" (1:10). Some people seem to be faultless but are so harsh and austere that they drive people away from Christ. Their "spirituality" repels others. This was not so with Christ. The Christian is himself pure, but his love and gentleness are such that he attracts others to the Christian way and never repels them from Christ.

   3. The growth this fellowship seeks is a perfection that ultimately achieves the "Christian aim." But what is this aim? To live a life that brings glory and praise to God. Christian goodness is not meant to bring praise and credit and honor to the Christian himself but to God alone.

Conclusion

The cause for Christian joy is the fellowship of believers. And your responsibility and mine is to see that this fellowship is paramount in our church.

My Church

I want my church to be a place
Where men can meet God face-to-face,
And meditate upon His grace.
That I can think each time we meet
A presence comes and takes its seat.

I want here doors to stand so wide
No hungry soul who waits outside,
Will think that he has been denied.
I want my church to be much more
Than stone and timber, pews, and door,
Or carpet laid upon a floor.
But, oh, I know that it can be
No more than is found in me,
A fellowship with man and Thee.

—Jessie Marle Franklin

SUNDAY EVENING, OCTOBER 2

Title: The Mania of Materialism

Text: "Ye cannot serve God and mammon" **(Matt. 6:24)**.

Scripture Reading: Matthew 6:19–24

Introduction

When a young person spends all of his extra money for records or tapes and all of his leisure time listening to them, we say, "He has a mania for music." When a father buys a set of golf clubs and spends every possible minute on the golf course, we observe, "He has a mania for golf." When a woman joins a local bowling team, purchases a bowling ball, and spends every free night at the bowling alley, we say, "She has a mania for bowling." We have come to define "mania" as a fad or a craze. But actually the word describes a type of insanity, a derangement of the intellectual powers.

There is a type of mania to which even the mentally fit are subject—the mania of materialism. When Jesus warns us against laying up "treasures on earth," he is referring to the habit of hoarding wealth to the point that a person's major objective in life becomes the amassing of material things. Such a mania can master one's life.

I. Materialism can master a person's affections (Matt. 6:19–21).

A. *In the context of this passage, "heart" has reference to one's affections.* If man's mind dwells on coveting things and his time is spent hoarding things, his affections are finally controlled by those things for which he seeks. He wants to do only those things that will bring him a profit. Nothing is quite so helpless as a man who is controlled by the desire to get rich. When his affections are controlled by the mania of materialism, he is blinded to the perishable nature of material things.

B. *Our main problem with material things is our failure to realize just how transient they are.* We fail to see the comparison of sixty-five years with eternity. When our perspective is straightened out, we will realize the perishable

287

nature of material things. But if our affections are set on getting and keeping material things, we forget about the hereafter and concentrate only on the here. Thus we become blinded to the nature of the material world.

C. *When man's affections are mastered by materialism, he cannot lay up treasures in heaven.* In this passage Jesus is drawing a contrast between earthly treasures and heavenly treasures. If man's will is controlled by the desire to hoard material things, he will lose all interest in heavenly things — "treasures in heaven."

D. *A Christian may lay up treasures in heaven by deeds of kindness done on earth.* The Jews of Jesus' day also connected a man's character with his treasure in heaven. A person can do many things that resemble Christian service, but if he is not a Christian, he has no basis for a heavenly reward. A man is rewarded primarily for what he is, not for what he has.

Another way of laying up treasures in heaven is the right use of material possessions. A Texas oilman expressed it well when he said, "The best way to lay up treasures in heaven is to invest your money in people who are going there."

II. Materialism can master a person's spiritual insight (Matt. 6:22–23).

A. *Jesus says that if the "light that is in thee" is darkness, your whole life is in darkness.* This refers to a person's ability to tell right from wrong. It implies that if a person is afflicted with the mania for material things, then his spiritual insight — ability to tell right from wrong — will be afflicted also. Such devotion to material things is deceptive; what one thinks is light is really darkness!

B. *Jesus says that the light or lamp of the body is the eye.* If the eye sees a single vision, the body is full of light. But if the eye sees double, the body is full of darkness. What does all of this mean? Jesus is still talking about material things. He says that if one's life is controlled by the mania for material things — the double-visioned eye — his life will be full of darkness, and his ability to see right and wrong will be darkened. And if this is darkened, then his whole life is in darkness.

III. Materialism can master a person's will (Matt. 6:24).

A. *Slavery was a part of Jesus' society.* He knew that those who heard would know what he meant when he said, "No man can serve two masters." The slave was the living tool of his master. He could be beaten, sold, expelled, or even killed by his master. His time was not his own, for he was at his master's disposal every moment. Jesus referred to the customs of his day when he said that a Christian cannot serve God and mammon at the same time.

B. Mammon *is an interesting word.* It comes from the root word that means "to entrust." Mammon was that which described money entrusted to a banker for safekeeping. As one would build up a large bank account, he came to trust in it. So this word came to denote that in which one places his trust. It was spelled with a capital *M* because, when man puts his trust in money, it becomes his god. God cannot be the master of a man's life whose will is already controlled by material things.

Conclusion

Former astronaut and U.S. senator John Glenn, the first American to orbit the earth, once asked: "Is the ultimate objective of America nothing more than the physical improvement of our situation? Less and less work and more and more better living. If so, what do we do with all this extra time when we are not working? What is our purpose in the world? It seems to me that in the past we always seemed to have a national purpose, something we were driving toward. All at once, in our day and time, we no longer see where we are going." Then he added: "It seems to me there has to be something better than just bigger automobiles and bigger houses...."

Let us lay up treasures in heaven.

WEDNESDAY EVENING, OCTOBER 5

Title: Prayer and the Will of God

Text: "Pray without ceasing ... for this is the will of God in Christ Jesus concerning you" (**1 Thess. 5:17–18**).

Scripture Reading: 1 Thessalonians 5

Introduction

It is the will of God that each of his children has the habit of praying. This truth takes on added significance if we recognize prayer as a dialogue between the heavenly Father and each of his children instead of it being a monologue in which the child of God does all the speaking. It is much more important that we hear what God has to say than that God hear what we have to say.

It has been suggested that while we offer our prayers to God, he directs his prayers to us. We are eager to receive answers to our prayers. The heavenly Father is even more eager that we respond to his prayers.

I. Prayer is a part of the will of God for each of us.

   A. *The Bible teaches from beginning to end that God is a prayer-hearing God.*
   B. *The Bible teaches that the heavenly Father is eager to bestow his gifts of love and wisdom on us.*
   C. *The Bible teaches that God gives only the gifts that are good for us as a result of our prayers.*

II. Our prayers are to be in harmony with God's will.

Our Lord teaches that we can expect blessings from God through prayer if we pray in harmony with God's will. "If you remain in me and my words remain in you, ask whatever you wish, and it will be given you" (John 15:7 NIV).

In his first epistle, John discussed praying in harmony with the will of God. "And whatsoever we ask, we receive of him, because we keep his commandments, and do those things that are pleasing in his sight" (1 John 3:22). "And this is the confidence that we have in him, that, if we ask any thing according to his will, he heareth us: And if we know that he hear us, whatsoever we ask, we know that we have the petitions that we desired of him" (1 John 5:14–15).

Prayer is not intended to be a means whereby people can secure that which they wish for in selfish indulgence. Prayer is the means whereby we requisition divine resources that are necessary for the doing of God's will.

III. Praying in the will of God.

We discover God's will as we examine his commands and his promises as recorded in the Bible. We gain insight into his will as we increase our knowledge of the mind of Christ and as we follow the leadership of the Holy Spirit.

A. *The prayer for salvation is always within the will of God (Rom. 10:13).* God never turns a deaf ear to the plea of a sincere penitent who comes in faith and surrender asking for forgiveness and sonship.

B. *The needy child can expect that his prayer will be heard by the loving heavenly Father (Luke 11:9–13).*

C. *The prayer for victory over evil is within the will of God (James 4:7–8b).*

Conclusion

Praying according to the will of God calls for larger blessings rather than for smaller requests. If we are to fully respond to prayer as a part of God's will for us, we need to do what the owner of a two-way radio set does—keep the "receiver set" turned on so that God can communicate with us as we communicate with him.

SUNDAY MORNING, OCTOBER 9

Title: Joy and the Place I'm In

Text: "What then? notwithstanding, every way, whether in pretence, or in truth, Christ is preached; and I therein do rejoice, yea, and will rejoice" **(Phil. 1:18)**.

Scripture Reading: Philippians 1:12–26

Hymns: "Have Faith in God," McKinney

        "Must Jesus Bear the Cross Alone?" Shepherd

        "Faith Is the Victory," Yates

Offertory Prayer: Our Father, we thank you for the refreshment of sleep and for the beckoning glory of a new day and a new week. Lead us in the paths of righteousness for your name's sake. Enable us to fill swift hours with mighty

deeds, to bear the weight of care, the sting of criticism, the drudgery of unap-
plauded toil. Grant that we may think clearly, act kindly, forgive graciously, and
follow faithfully. In our Redeemer's name we pray. Amen.

Introduction

You preach about a life of Christian joy, and that's fine for you, but you don't
work where I work. You don't have the difficulties I have. You don't have to face
the people I have to face every day. You don't have the financial struggle I have.
You don't have the kind of neighbors who live next to me. You don't face the kind
of family life I face at the close of a difficult day. It's all right for you to talk about
a life of Christian joy, but you wouldn't be so joyful if you were in the place I'm in!

That is our attitude toward life. We think that just because we are in a hard
place, we are justified in ceasing to rejoice.

Let's see how Paul managed. He already had been in prison back home for
two years. And there was the dangerous voyage at sea. Now he faced still two
more years in prison at Rome.

This was not an easy situation; this was not life on a downhill drag. Nevertheless, right in the middle of it all, Paul says, "I therein do rejoice, yea, and will
rejoice!" Surely we learn from this that Christian joy is not dependent on the
place we are in.

At least three things can grow out of a difficult situation.

I. A bitterness that can spoil (Phil. 1:13, 15–16).

When you are in a difficult place, it is easy to become bitter, and I have never
yet met a bitter person who was happy. Happiness and bitterness do not blend. If
you are bitter, you are a miserable kind of person. Is there a root of bitterness in
some part of your life that is spoiling the whole?

What had entered into Paul's potential bitterness? He had wonderfully overcome it; he had risen above it and was rejoicing. But potentially the bitterness was
there. What was involved that could have made Paul an extremely bitter man?
There are three things, and if allowed to enter your heart, they can make you
bitter too.

A. *The injustice of your bonds.* In verse 13 Paul mentions "my bonds in Christ."
Already the apostle had heard the opinion of authority three times. "This
man had done nothing worthy of death or bonds," said the captain of
the temple guard when Paul was arrested. Festus asserted, "This man has
done nothing worthy of death." And after consulting together, Agrippa
and Festus concluded, "This man doeth nothing worthy of death or of
bonds." Paul's bonds were branded with injustice.

It is not easy to be happy when you have been treated unjustly, is it?
You were due a raise and it did not come. You should be further on in life;
friends with not nearly so much ability as you have passed you by, and you
are in the same old position. The injustice of your bonds can bring a bitterness that can spoil.

Are you cursed with such bitterness? Are you resentful? If so, you certainly are not living the life of Christian joy. The venom of bitterness is in your home, your work, and your church. It is wherever you are, and you are a bitter person because of the injustice of your bonds!

B. *The hostility of your colleagues (1:15–16).* "Some indeed preach Christ even of envy and strife." Paul's colleagues were fellow Christians preaching Christ and not heresy. But they were making the most of Paul's bad situation by worming their way into places of influence and power. In doing so, they were elbowing Paul out of the way, "supposing to add affliction to [his] bonds" (1:16).

Has anything like this ever happened to you? Have you been elbowed right out of your place? How did you take it? Did destructive bitterness creep into your life? Well, there is no use in talking about living the life of Christian joy, is there? Not so long as others are adding affliction to your bonds. That is a pretty hard place in which to rejoice, isn't it?

C. *The forgetfulness of your Lord.* This must have been in Paul's mind even though it is not specifically spelled out here. Paul was human enough to have had a second thought or two about his Lord's faithfulness during these trying times. Where was God's purpose in such hardships? Paul had been called as an apostle to preach, and he could not preach, he could not be with the churches he founded, he could not move. Had his Lord forgotten that he was in prison?

Thus, when this apostle writes, "I therein do rejoice, yea, and will rejoice," he is no impractical soul. He is in a place far more difficult than yours, yet he steadfastly refuses to become the victim of destructive bitterness.

II. A blessedness that can surprise (1:12–14, 19).

The blessings that are born out of a difficult situation are often a real surprise. The word "furtherance" in verse 12 pictures the cutting away of undergrowth and the removing of obstacles in the path of an army. So Paul's being in prison surprisingly removed barriers to the gospel rather than being a barrier.

A. *The blessing of the spread of the gospel (1:13).* The imperial guard, Rome's finest military men, were hearing the gospel in Paul's prison. The chain that deprived him of freedom gave him opportunity to reach those whom he never could have reached any other way.

There is a message in this for you. If you are in a rest home or a hospital, on a difficult job, in an unchristian neighborhood, or in some other tough situation, perhaps God has placed you there for a divine purpose. People are there whom we never could touch otherwise. In your difficult place, the blessedness that can surprise is the spread of the gospel.

B. *The blessing of strengthening other Christians (1:14).* Paul's hardship was just what other Christians needed to witness in order to find courage to speak the Word without fear.

That hard place in your life may become a means of strengthening some other Christian. The way you face the death of a loved one, the ridicule of an unbeliever, the reversal of finances, the loss of position, or the heartache of family problems may be the greatest opportunity you will ever have to strengthen a fellow Christian. Your courage may be just the medicine he needs to pull through his own personal crisis. This is a blessedness that can surprise!

C. *The blessing of personal Christian growth (1:19).* The word "salvation" here means Christian growth, spiritual development, and well-being. Paul was imprisoned not only for the spread of the gospel and the strengthening of other Christians but for his own Christian growth as well.

Are there qualities lacking in your Christian life? There are in most of us. Some of the qualities can be developed within us only when God puts us in a difficult place that is desperately lonely, where fears and doubts almost drown us and where resentment and self-pity threaten to destroy us. But that is the place that will work for the good of our salvation. Sometimes when God is going to work a miracle in us, he cannot do it anywhere else but in the flames of adversity, so he puts us right in the middle of the fire. And life's hard place becomes the very means of our own Christian growth. This is a blessedness that can surprise!

III. A boldness that can sing (1:18, 20–26).

"And I therein do rejoice, yea, and will rejoice" (v. 18). When all is well, we find it delightful to sing. But when hardships come and the rain begins to fall into our lives, we have no song and a smile is replaced with a frown.

A young missionary whose husband had just died received a cablegram from her saintly mother with only two words in it—not sympathy, not regret, not pity, but "Be brave!" This is the boldness that can sing, the boldness we must have today even when the way is dreary and the future uncertain.

A. *Because of a concern for Christ's glory we can know a boldness that can sing.* "But that with all boldness, as always, so now also Christ shall be magnified in my body" (v. 20).

Completely unconcerned about himself, the apostle's concern is for Christ's glory, that Christ be magnified. He was not concerned that Paul be honored or applauded but that his Lord be lifted up so that people might be attracted to him.

Are you more concerned for Christ's glory than you are for your own image, your own ministry, your own success and future? If so, you will know a boldness that can sing no matter where God's will may place you. If not, you will be unhappy even though he places you in a most honored position of life.

B. *Because of a contempt for your own comfort, you can know a boldness that can sing (vv. 20c–21).* "Whether it be by life, or by death. For me to live is Christ, and to die is gain."

Your place, like Paul's, may be not only difficult but also dangerous. The fear of uncertainty and the threat of destruction may hang over you. Death may become as much a possibility as life—you must be ready for either.

When you hold your own comfort in contempt, you too will gain a boldness that can sing, even in the face of life's most difficult hours. You are Christ's no matter what happens, be it life or death!

C. *Because of an abiding confidence in God's control, a boldness that can sing becomes yours (vv. 25–26).* "And having this confidence, I know that I shall abide" (v. 25).

My own godly mother-in-law knew that she had cancer and that all indications were that she had only a few months to live. As a young preacher, I was amazed how confidently and fearlessly she faced the future. Then one day she shared the secret of her peace with me.

"We go through life making mountains out of molehills," she said, "and then one day a real mountain comes along." She paused, and as a smile swept across her radiant face, she added, "But that's all right; God gives us grace and strength for the real mountains too."

Even in the face of death, hers was a boldness that could sing because she had confidence in her Lord's control.

In verse 23 Paul said, "I am in a strait betwixt two. . . ." This portrays a rock wall on both sides that so hems us in that we can only go straight ahead. The apostle had no alternative—he must do God's bidding. And so with confidence in God's control, he boldly marched on.

Conclusion

Are you hard pressed, in a "strait betwixt two," and do not know which way to turn? Does the place you are in bring fears, doubts, a nameless dread? Then claim that boldness that comes only from absolute confidence in God's control. When you do, you will begin to live a life of Christian joy no matter what place you are in!

SUNDAY EVENING, OCTOBER 9

Title: Laying Up Treasures

Text: "Lay not up for yourselves treasures upon earth, where moth and rust doth corrupt, and where thieves break through and steal: But lay up for yourselves treasures in heaven, where neither moth nor rust doth corrupt, and where thieves do not break through nor steal: For where your treasure is, there will your heart be also" (**Matt. 6:19–21**).

Scripture Reading: Matthew 6:19–24

Introduction

A father in Little Rock, Arkansas, got up early one morning to fix breakfast for his family. He fixed the only thing he knew how to fix well—oatmeal.

Finally, the first member of the family made it to the breakfast table. The father turned to his three-year-old son and asked whether he wanted honey, sugar, cream, or butter on his oatmeal. To each of these, the boy said, "Yes."

The father topped the oatmeal with all the condiments the boy requested, but the boy stared at the oatmeal a moment and then turned away. The father said, "You've got everything you want on it; why don't you eat it?"

"I don't like oatmeal," was the boy's reply.

In our affluent society, we Americans probably need our Lord's teachings on earthly and heavenly treasures more than any people of any age have ever needed them.

A treasure is anything in which one finds his main satisfaction, enjoyment, and fulfillment in this life. It is not wrong to possess material things, but it is wrong to find our only satisfaction in them.

I. What is a treasure?

A treasure is anything in which a person trusts. One can check his treasures by asking himself some questions: What one thing in my life would be missed most if it were taken away? Could I be happy if my bank account, house, clothes, friends, status, and other things were eliminated? Could I do without my faith in God through Christ?

A. *Earthly treasures.* Money is an earthly treasure. The Bible teaches that "the love of money is the root of all evil" (1 Tim. 6:10).

Possessions become treasures for some. The Bible plainly teaches, however, that "a man's life does not consist in the abundance of his possessions" (Luke 12:15 NIV).

Someone has well said, "It is impossible to keep up with the Joneses, because just as soon as you think you have caught them, they have refinanced and gone again."

For some people, status is an earthly treasure for which they will literally give their souls. Someone has said, "We Americans spend money that we do not have to buy things that we do not need to keep up with people we do not like." We are reminded, however, that we must "seek first the kingdom of God, and his righteousness" (Matt. 6:33).

The family is an earthly treasure for others. This is why our Lord said, "He that loveth father or mother ... son or daughter more than me is not worthy of me" (Matt. 10:37).

Some people bow down to their business each day as though it were their god. Someday our Lord will say, "This night thy soul shall be required of thee: then whose shall these things be, which thou hast provided?" (Luke 12:20).

B. *Heavenly treasures.* Salvation is a heavenly treasure (Phil. 1:6). To invest our time, talents, and money in God's work on earth are ways of laying up heavenly treasures.

To dedicate all of our possessions to the glory of God must certainly be a part of our heavenly treasures. The Bible says, "But godliness with contentment is great gain. For we brought nothing into this world, and it is certain we can carry nothing out" (1 Tim. 6:6–7). The apostle Paul said, "I have learned to be content whatever the circumstances. I know what it is to be in need, and I know what it is to have plenty. I have learned the secret of being content in any and every situation, whether well fed or hungry, whether living in plenty or in want" (Phil. 4:11–12 NIV).

II. Some are possessed by their possessions.

How sad it is to see a person who is possessed by possessions. Some are so pre-occupied with earthly treasures that they know little about the rest of the world.

A. *Illustrations.* After a doctor had examined his banker friend, the banker asked, "Well, how am I?"

The doctor said, "You are as sound as a dollar." The banker fainted!

A man was hit by a bus and dragged three hundred feet on a street in New York. Seriously injured, he was rushed to the hospital for emergency treatment. A few days later he awoke with both legs bandaged and his arms in splints.

A nurse asked, "Are you comfortable?"

He replied, "Well, I make a living."

In *Collier's Magazine* some years ago there was a striking confession by a rich man. He said, "Sometimes it seems to me that I have worked all these years just to gain hardening of the arteries and a few houses I don't want to live in. I am no more at home in my garden than I am in Central Park. And one of these days I shall die, and all that will be left of me will be an estate for someone to spend or quarrel over."

B. *Earthly treasures are corruptible.* Just as moth and rust destroyed the trea-sures of Jesus' day, there is a destroyer for every earthly treasure. Just as thieves broke in and stole earthly treasures in Jesus' day, there is a thief for every earthly treasure. The thief of time causes us to lose our joy in things. The thief of illness reminds us that no earthly treasure is worth losing our health to gain. The thief of circumstances teaches us the futil-ity of trusting in material things.

The thief of war causes us to see how quickly earthly treasures can vanish. In the novel *Alas, Babylon*, Pat Frank imagines what it would be like if Florida were under a nuclear attack. Electricity goes off. The gas supply is exhausted. Finally, Floridians find themselves trading expensive cars for hens and boats for shakers of salt.

Earthly treasures have a way of controlling our affections (Matt. 6:21) and our conscience (vv. 22–23). Finally, earthly treasures will control our will (v. 24).

J. Paul Getty, who was one of the world's richest men, wrote in the *Saturday Evening Post* many years ago, "The world is mean to millionaires." He said that he received an average of two hundred letters a day asking for an average of five hundred dollars each.

Charles M. Schwab was a millionaire who died in 1939. Before his death he said, "The happiest days of my life were when I had a modest income and lived with my good wife in a cottage with restful comfort. Now we have many houses, even mansions. But we don't own them—they own us."

Conclusion

While some are possessed by their possessions, others are possessed by their profession in Jesus Christ as the Lord of their lives.

In December 1969 the University of Arkansas and the University of Texas played a decisive football game. Many commentators said that the result of the game would determine the nation's number one team for 1969. Prior to the game, H. D. McCarty, pastor of University Baptist Church in Fayetteville, Arkansas, asked four of the first-string Razorbacks to give their testimonies—win or lose—on the Sunday morning after the Saturday afternoon game. Arkansas lost the game by one point. Bill Burnett said in his testimony: "You see, the game of life is the most important game of all, the one you want to win. If we had won the game with Texas, then we would have been Southwest Conference and national champions. This was a very important goal for our team, but it is only temporary, while the game of life is eternal. Through Jesus Christ, I can always have the victory in the game of life."

Cliff Powell said, "God just doesn't do 'His thing' on a part-time basis." He concluded his testimony with these words: "Texas won the game and is number one, but that will fade with the years. The victory I've gained through Jesus Christ will last for eternity."

WEDNESDAY EVENING, OCTOBER 12

Title: Improving Our Acquaintance with God

Text: " ... increasing in the knowledge of God" **(Col. 1:10)**.

Scripture Reading: Colossians 1:1–17

Introduction

Paul stated that he prayed for the brethren in the faith at Colosse daily. He was eager for them to grow toward maturity and to develop spiritual competency as the servants of God (Col. 1:9–10).

Paul shared this deep concern for the saints and faithful brethren in Colosse with Epaphras, who was their faithful minister (Col. 1:7). Later Paul made reference to the fact that Epaphras was "labouring fervently for you in prayers, that ye may stand perfect and complete in all the will of God" (4:12).

It is no accident that Paul prayed for the Colossians that they might have the experience of "increasing in the knowledge of God." The will of God must not be thought of as being separate from the character and nature of God. A vital, personal, experiential knowledge of the nature and character of God is necessary if one is to know the will of God and "stand perfect and complete in all of the will of God."

It was a lack of this perfect knowledge of God, not mere information about him, that caused Israel to go astray (Hos. 4:1). It was the lack of knowledge of his moral nature and character that led to their disobedience to his moral demands (vv. 2, 6–7). God declared through Hosea that the giving of sacrifices and the observance of ritual were not sufficient to obtain his approval (6:6).

I. We must know Christ as Savior and Lord.

The only way by which we can come to know God in person is through Jesus Christ, who is the truth of God, the only way to God, and the source of the very life of God (John 14:6). Jesus defines eternal life in terms of coming to know the true God (John 17:3). Paul tells of his personal knowledge of God: "I know whom I have believed, and am persuaded that he is able to keep that which I have committed unto him against that day" (2 Tim. 1:12). In Philippians 3:10 he speaks of his desire for an ever-increasing knowledge of the Lord Jesus Christ. Paul was not satisfied merely to be acquainted with God. He wanted to deepen that acquaintance as time went by.

II. We must respond to Jesus Christ as heaven's infallible Teacher (Matt. 5:1–2).

The Sermon on the Mount is the lecture of heaven's infallible Teacher to his disciples. He reveals God's will concerning our inner spirit, the influence that we are to have, our superior conduct, our motives, our trust, and so on. If we want to increase our acquaintance with Jesus Christ, we must not only sit at his feet and listen to what he has to say, we must also heed what he has to say.

III. We must be receptive to the guidance of the Holy Spirit (John 16:13–14).

The Holy Spirit came to dwell in the heart of every believer at the time of conversion. He seeks to reveal the nature and character of God as well as the plans of God to those who are responsive to his guidance (1 Cor. 2:9–11).

Conclusion

The better our acquaintance with God is, the more nearly we will be able both to discover and to delight in the doing of his will. He is open and receptive to developing this mutual acquaintance of Creator with creature, of Father with child.

298

SUNDAY MORNING, OCTOBER 16

Title: Joy and the People I'm With

Text: "Only let your conversation be as it becometh the gospel of Christ: that whether I come and see you, or else be absent, I may hear of your affairs, that ye stand fast in one spirit, with one mind striving together for the faith of the gospel" (**Phil. 1:27**).

Scripture Reading: Philippians 1:27–2:30

Hymns: "Take Time to Be Holy," Longstaff

"Let Others See Jesus in You," McKinney

"We're Marching to Zion," Watts

Offertory Prayer: Our Father, who has brought us in safety to the beginning of a new week, we pause in your presence to invoke your blessing and guidance in the days ahead. Save us from the paralysis of fears that are unworthy of your people, for we are mindful that we are surrounded by a great cloud of witnesses. May we dread nothing but the severing of our lives from you and the loss of the joy found only in the fellowship of your children. In all we do in your sanctuary this day, be near us to direct, within us to refresh, around us to protect, above us to bless, and beneath us to uphold us in your everlasting arms. We ask this all in the name of Jesus Christ. Amen.

Introduction

The life of Christian joy. Do you know this kind of life? Some don't because of the people they are with. Or to be more accurate, because of their attitude toward the people they are with. Such a person is quite convinced that the only problem with society is other people.

It came as quite a shock to me to discover that, on the mission field, the main problem is that of conflicts in personal relationships between missionaries. The biggest difficulty is not the indifference of the local nationals, learning the language, or adjusting to a different climate and diet; the main problem is conflicts between missionaries.

But this is not limited to the mission field. It is a potential problem with every Christian. Do you have problems with other Christians in your own church? Do you have problems with other Christians where you work?

The thing that often takes the melody from our hearts and keeps us from living the life of Christian joy is that we are not living in right relationships with other people. There is a maladjustment, and like a dislocated bone, as long as it remains dislocated, there is no ease, no comfort, no joy.

Paul is acutely aware that the life of Christian joy and our attitudes toward people are vitally related. Because he is concerned that personal relationships should never disrupt the life of Christian joy, Paul gets down to the matter of "joy and the people I'm with."

299

I. The stresses that disturb often enter in and disrupt our fellowship and destroy our joy.

Philippians 1:27–30 and 2:3 warn us of two of these disturbing stresses.

A. *Opposition from without, "your adversaries," frequently brings ceaseless pressure to bear against both the Christian and his church (1:27b–30).* Since the church is the "cause of Christian joy," the fellowship of believers, which Satan wants to destroy, he will see to it that a continuous attack is made on the church.

   1. Our duty is to defeat this opposition from without—but how? Here is how: "Stand fast in one spirit, with one mind striving together for the faith of the gospel" (1:27). A spirit of division and defeat brings more confusion and disorder into Christian fellowship than perhaps anything else. One of the basic tactics of military science is to divide and conquer—disrupt the unity then make the most of the disunity.

      The apostle is saying, "When faced with opposition from without, don't give ground; stand fast! It is your duty to defeat Satan in his effort to divide you!"

   2. Our privilege is to face opposition from without, "to suffer for his sake" (1:29). Why do Christians retreat in the face of opposition? Why do they give ground or conceal their faith? Because they do not want to suffer! They don't want people to laugh at them, they can't take criticism and ridicule, so they just fold and give up. This verse says, "Remember, it is part of your privilege, when faced with opposition, to suffer in the behalf of Christ. Believing is part of being a Christian, but so is suffering."

      If there is a disturbing power in the opposition from without, there is even a greater threat in the:

B. *Corruption from within (2:3).* If cowardly retreat disturbs our fellowship, then selfish advancement disturbs it even more. Although this had not actually happened at Philippi, Paul feared that it might, so he warned against it.

   In the face of these stresses that disturb, is there an answer? Yes. It is found in the:

II. Secrets that explain how unity and spiritual progress may be realized (Phil. 1:27; 2:1–2, 5–11).

A. *The presence of a life is one secret the apostle shares with us.* "Let your pattern of life be one that reflects well on the gospel of Christ" (1:27, paraphrased). In 2:2 we are told to share the same love. Where there is this common life and love there is the life of Christian joy.

B. *The second secret is the absence of a limit (2:5–8).* The "mind" that was in Christ was one that set no limit on the amount of suffering that he was willing to experience. Christ never said, "Father, I will go only so far and no further." Our Lord could not have gone further than he went, he could not have suffered more, he could not have been more rejected or shamed or insulted than he was. Yet he, who, being in the form of God, had the right to all the adoration and obedience of all people, took their hatred and rebellion—he took it *all*, and with no limits!

"Let this mind be in you, which was also in Christ Jesus" (2:5). When your insults and injuries exceed those of your Lord, then perhaps you will have the right to call a halt to your forgiveness, but not until then.

One thing causes a break in Christian fellowship—an unwillingness to forgive, the setting of a limit on how much wrong you are willing to suffer from another. The moment you set a limit, the moment you refuse to forgive, you die within, and the life of Christian joy fades.

Have you ever said, "I'll forgive, but I don't want to have anything else to do with him"? Jesus said that we should pray, "Forgive us our debts as we forgive our debtors"—*as* we forgive.

If you prayed, "O, Lord, I am so very sorry I committed that sin," and God answered, "I'll forgive you, but I don't want to have anything else to do with you," you would say, "Why that's no forgiveness at all!" And it isn't. Neither is yours forgiveness if you have set a limit. The life of Christian joy cannot be yours within the confines of a limit.

III. The sequel that should follow is spelled out in Philippians 2:12–16.

A. *A continuing progress is the first sequel with which Paul is so concerned in the life of Christian joy.* "Don't be arrested in your Christian progress. Work it out to its completion," the apostle is saying in verse 12—"Work out your own salvation."

Few things bring our spiritual progress to a halt quite like severed relations with other Christians.

Have you come to a halt? Has your spiritual progress been arrested? Are you bogged down? Perhaps you have not grown for weeks, months, or years. Perhaps you have come to a halt because you fell out with someone, someone insulted you, someone was unkind to you, someone did not thank you, you were not put on a committee, you were criticized by a deacon, or the Sunday school superintendent was not very appreciative. And because of a breakdown in relationships with other Christians, you have come to a spiritual standstill. Paul is much concerned about continuing progress in the salvation of the soul.

"Your own salvation." There is something unique about the experience of God's grace that God is wanting to work in you. Your experience of Christ is quite different from anyone else's. You have something to offer that no one else can give. If you do not offer it, if your growth and development become arrested, the church is going to suffer.

B. *A convincing witness should follow (2:14–16).*
1. Your witness, in order to be convincing, must be supported by your attitude. Don't gripe! "Do all things without murmurings and

disputings" (2:14). Christians who murmur and dispute, like flies, attract each other. You see them attracted to each other on the street corner or in the church. You know exactly what is taking place. They are having a delightfully good gripe. Something has gone all wrong, and they are feasting on it. "The pastor did not visit me in the hospital." "Mrs. So-and-So walked right by me and didn't say a word." In such an attitude there is no testimony, no convincing witness.

2. A convincing witness is strengthened by your fellowship. Some actually believe that not to be a part of the fellowship and harmony with other Christians is a mark of great sanctity. Such a person is not a better Christian. He is dishonoring Christ, grieving the Holy Spirit, and disrupting the unity of the faith. For your witness to be convincing, you must be a part of a Christian fellowship.

IV. Samples that portray the life of Christian joy are seen in the lives of Timothy and Epaphroditus (2:19–30).

As the apostle thinks of "joy and the people I'm with," two men who portray his point come to mind.

A. *Unselfish concern is portrayed in the life of Timothy (2:19–23).* In verse 20 Paul says, "Here is one who will genuinely [naturally] care for you" (my paraphrase). Many were preoccupied with concern for their own interests and the attainment of their own ambitions, but Timothy portrays an unselfish concern for others that brings him a life of Christian joy.

B. *Unceasing service is a sample of the life of Christian joy seen in Epaphroditus (2:25–30).* This man nearly died for the work of Christ, risking life itself. He had become ill because of his service for his Lord. His was a life of unceasing service.

Conclusion

If you are going to live the life of Christian joy, you must have in your heart a right relation with other people. You will not be able to rejoice as long as you have a dislocation, whether it is in your elbow, your finger, or your heart. Get right with others, for you will never sing until you do! But when you do, you too will know the life of Christian joy!

SUNDAY EVENING, OCTOBER 16

Title: Worry—What Is It?

Text: "Therefore I say unto you, Take no thought for your life" (**Matt. 6:25**).

Scripture Reading: Matthew 6:25–30

Introduction

In *Papyrus Ebers*, a medical book written in Egypt about 1552 BC, we are told that people who lived more than three thousand years ago worried about some of the same things we worry about today.

In this medical book is a remedy to prevent hair from turning gray. It suggests that one anoint his hair with the blood of a black calf that has been boiled in oil or the fat of a rattlesnake. To keep from losing hair, this book suggests that one apply a mixture of six fats to his hair, namely, those of the horse, hippopotamus, crocodile, cat, snake, and ibex.

I. An increase in worry.

A. *Drugs.* From every indication, however, we are worrying more now than ever before. At least one out of every six Americans takes some kind of pill to change his or her mental attitude. We've become a nation of pill takers.

B. *Mental disorders.* The number of persons in mental institutions has increased over recent decades at an alarming rate, and thousands more with mental problems cannot or do not get the treatment they need.

C. *Alcohol consumption and drug abuse.* Although attempts have been made on a national basis to curb alcohol and drug abuse, people are still abusing these substances in an attempt to temporarily escape their problems. The abuse of prescription drugs is at an all-time high.

II. What is worry?

The Bible says, "A double-minded man [is] unstable in all he does" (James 1:8 NIV).

A. *Dividing the mind.* The word *worry* comes from two Greek words: *meridzo* means "to divide," and *nous* means the "mind." When one's mind is divided between the material and the spiritual, it affects his allegiance. When one's allegiance is divided between God's will and man's will, he is caused to worry.

B. *Trusting in things.* It is interesting to notice that our Lord discusses worry within the context of a discussion of material things. Could it be that one learns to worry when he puts more trust in things than he does in God?

When our Lord says, "O you of little faith" (Matt. 6:30 NIV), our minds are quickly drawn to an incident in which our Lord and the disciples were tossed about in a ship on the Sea of Galilee.

When the disciples cried out for their lives and indicated their fear of drowning, our Lord said to them, "O you of little faith." Why? Because their faith was in the boat and not in Christ. The boat was a material object. Anytime we place too much faith in things and too little faith in Christ, we, too, will worry about survival—and a hundred other things.

C. *Distracted by things.* Mary sat with Jesus while Martha fixed supper. When Martha complained that Mary was not helping her, Jesus said, "Martha,

Martha, you are worried and upset about many things" (Luke 10:41 NIV). When we are distracted by things, we learn to worry.

Conclusion

What causes worry? Most of our worries can be traced to something material.

Francis C. Ellis tells about a businessman who drew up what he called a "worry chart" in which he kept a record of his worries. He discovered that 40 percent of them were about things that probably would never happen, 30 percent concerned past decisions that he could not now unmake, 12 percent dealt with other people's criticism of him, and 10 percent were worries about his health. He concluded that only 8 percent of them were really legitimate.

WEDNESDAY EVENING, OCTOBER 19

Title: Finding the Will of God

Text: "Do not conform any longer to the pattern of this world, but be transformed by the renewing of your mind. Then you will be able to test and approve what God's will is—his good, pleasing and perfect will" **(Rom. 12:2 NIV)**.

Scripture Reading: Romans 12

Introduction

In our text the apostle Paul declares that if the Christian will refuse to let the world squeeze him into its mold and if he will let the mind of Jesus Christ rule his thoughts, he will be able to present to the world a laboratory demonstration that the will of God is delightful.

Henry Drummond was a Scottish evangelical writer and lecturer of the nineteenth century who proved to be a great blessing not only to his own generation but also to those that have followed. He is famous today for his message based on 1 Corinthians 13 entitled "The Greatest Thing in the World." Following his death, George Adam Smith, his biographer, discovered what might be the secret of his spiritual success. Drummond sought to live by the will of God. Inscribed on the flyleaf of Drummond's Bible were the following eight suggestions concerning discovering and doing the will of God.

I. Pray.

II. Think.

III. Talk to wise people, but don't regard their decision as final.

IV. Beware of the bias of your own will, but don't be too much afraid of it.

God never necessarily thwarts a man's nature and likings, and it is a mistake to think that his will is in the line of the disagreeable.

V. Meanwhile do the next thing.

Doing God's will in small things is the best preparation for doing it in the great things.

VI. When the time of decision comes, act in light of the knowledge at hand.

VII. Never reconsider the decision once it is acted upon.

VIII. You may not find out until afterward that you have been led in it all.

Conclusion

Henry Drummond was a man who found the way into the throne room of God. He discovered and rejoiced in the fact that God is a God of love and would have his people to live in the context and climate of love. Perhaps his suggestions concerning finding and doing the will of God can be helpful to each of us.

SUNDAY MORNING, OCTOBER 23

Title: Joy and the Person I Am

Text: "But what things were gain to me, those I counted loss for Christ. Yea doubtless, and I count all things but loss for the excellency of the knowledge of Christ Jesus my Lord: for whom I have suffered the loss of all things, and do count them but dung, that I may win Christ, and be found in him, not having mine own righteousness, which is of the law, but that which is through the faith of Christ, the righteousness which is of God by faith" **(Phil. 3:7–9)**.

Scripture Reading: Philippians 3

Hymns: "I Would Be True," Walter

          "Come, Thou Fount of Every Blessing," Robinson

          "Open My Eyes That I May See," Scott

Offertory Prayer: Our heavenly Father, you have placed in our souls a love for truth, goodness, and beauty. May your truth make us free — free from prejudice and pride, free from the childish sins that so easily beset us. May your beauty lift us out of the mud and mire of mere things to the heights of the excellent and the lovely. Grant, O God, that we may be the persons you would have us be so that we may do what you would have us do. May we realize that far more important than what "I do" is what "I am" and that only when I am what I ought to be will I live the life of Christian joy. In our Savior's name we pray. Amen.

Introduction

That your life be a life of Christian joy is God's intention for you. If you are not a joyful Christian, you are something less than God wants you to be.

Having clearly shown that the cause of Christian joy is our fellowship with other Christians, the apostle goes on to point out that the life of Christian joy can be lived regardless of the place we are in or the people we are with.

In Philippians 3 a disturbing fact is set forth—that the person I am has a tremendous bearing on my living the life of Christian joy. Paul even suggests that the reason I am not living the life of Christian joy may well be explained by the person I am!

Some Christians will never live the life of Christian joy simply because of the level on which they are content to live their Christian lives. The plain truth is this: if you are to live the life of Christian joy, you must be a certain kind of person.

Three words suggested in Philippians 3 must characterize my attitude toward the person I am if I am to live the life of Christian joy. The first is a rather unexpected word—*bankruptcy*.

I. Bankruptcy (Phil. 3:1–19).

The apostle contends that bankruptcy in the spiritual sense is one of the prerequisites for happiness. "But what things were gain to me, those I counted loss for Christ" (3:7).

As Paul reviews his rich traditions and the triumphs that characterized his Christian service, he declares that they are of no value. He sees himself as bankrupt in the presence of his Lord. He seems to be saying, "If you and I are going to be truly happy, we must acknowledge that we have nothing and that we are nothing apart from Christ." Our Savior said something close to this: "Happy are the *poor* in spirit, for theirs is the kingdom of heaven" (see Matt. 5:3).

A. *We must admit our spiritual bankruptcy regardless of our cultural, social, or religious heritage.* Paul recalls how he was part of all that was best in the heritage of the Jewish faith. But after knowing Jesus, he considers all his rich heritage as worthless and himself as bankrupt (Phil. 3:1–8).

Like this apostle, you must no longer rely on your unimpeachable character, your family background, or even your religious affiliation. They are of no value at all in making things right between you and your God. You must humbly receive salvation as a free gift from God, not as just payment for your works or your heritage.

B. *Regardless of the victories in your Christian service, you must see yourself as bankrupt (3:13).*

Paul's victories had been amazing. He had established churches, traveled scores of miles, suffered much for Christ, won men and women to his Lord, and gained a vast knowledge of Christian doctrine. Yet as he looked back, he said, "I count not myself to have apprehended [arrived]" (3:13).

A real danger for us is that we will rely on our past victories to satisfy us for today—and we go stale. We strive to get the fun and sparkle of the Christian life by living on stale grace.

Is your Christian experience stale? Is it moldy like old bread? We are called to walk in "newness of life," and to do this we must have new victories and new experiences with Christ each day.

C. *Regardless of the hypocrisy that is prevalent, you must remain undisturbed by it and continue to see yourself as bankrupt.* Do not give up and give in by joining those who so twist the truth that it leads them into a life of hypocrisy, indulgence, and shame (3:18–19).

Paul says that you won't find any real joy in that kind of life. To live that way is to become an enemy of the cross, and no enemy of the cross ever lives the life of Christian joy.

If we must admit our bankruptcy, we must also experience a blessed intimacy.

II. Intimacy (3:10).

The word translated "know" is not the "know" of the intellect; it is the "know" of intimacy. We see the intimacy of this word in its usage in Matthew 1:25, where it is said of Joseph that he "knew [Mary] not till she had brought forth her first-born son." Here as in other places this word "know" is used to describe marital relations. This verb indicates the closest and the most intimate and the most personal knowledge of another person. So then, it is not Paul's aim "to know facts about Christ" but personally "to *know*" Christ.

A. *You must share an intimacy with the person of Jesus Christ*— "*That I may know him.*" How often we get things out of order. Sometimes we put power first; sometimes we put blessings first; sometimes we put success first; and sometimes we put the fullness of the Spirit first. But if we put any of these first we are wrong! "That I may know *him*." This is a corrective we can apply to much of our thinking and to much of our praying.

If you have your spiritual priorities out of order, then get them straightened out and put the person of Christ first, for this is the way to "the life of Christian joy."

B. *Yours should be an intimacy with the power of the Lord*— "*That I may know . . . the power of his resurrection.*"

The Reverend L. F. Wilkinson of England told of a Frenchman who became an Englishman because he so admired the British way of life. He had lived in England for so long that he decided to take out his papers and become an Englishman. Someone asked him what difference it made. "Well," he said, "among other things, I find that now instead of losing the battle of Waterloo I've won it!" He had stepped into the heritage of all that Britain had fought for and all that Britain had won, and it was now his. When you and I step into Christ, we step into a new power, a resurrection life; and all that Christ has achieved and won becomes ours if we care to use it.

C. *An intimate knowledge of the sacrificial love of your Lord is part of the secret to the life of Christian joy.* "That I may know . . . the fellowship of his sufferings."

What does the fellowship of the sufferings of Christ mean? He bore the sins of the world, and you and I will never come to know him unless we get under the burden of our world's need. That is why some Christians do not know Christ intimately. It is not that they do not know their Bible, for they know their Bible well enough. But they do not know their Lord in the fellowship of his sufferings. They never will know the joy of Christian living until they know the sacrificial love of Jesus Christ.

In the life of Christian joy, if there is a bankruptcy and an intimacy, there also must be an expectancy.

III. Expectancy (3:12, 14, 20–21).

Some Christians are not expectant. But Paul was. There is always a tomorrow; there is always something new and exciting. This is why he was always rejoicing. In this joyous expectancy, three things play an important part.

A. *"The high calling of God in Christ Jesus" (3:14).* This is the voice of God, and that is all that really mattered to Paul. The one voice that kept on calling him to scale the heights was the "high calling of God in Christ."

Scores of voices call you today—the voices of friends, foe, society, self. But only as you give heed to the voice of God alone will you know the happy expectancy that the life of Christian joy can bring.

B. *The dream that God has for his child (3:12).* Most parents have a dream for their child, and God has a dream for you. You must press on, or you will disappoint Christ and cause his dream for you to go unrealized.

C. *The prize to be won and our anticipation of gaining it.* "I press toward the mark for the *prize* of the high calling of God in Christ Jesus" (3:14).

What is this "prize" that held Paul in such expectancy? It is certainly not an earthly prize. It is the thrill of hearing our Lord say, "Well done, thou good and faithful servant." Whether I hear these words and win the prize that crowns the life of Christian joy depends on the person I am.

Conclusion

My work for the day is almost through;
Was it all as in His sight?
Would Jesus be able to say, "Well done!"
Supposing He came tonight?
There's a tiny sin on my soul today,
And I can't make my face look bright.
Would Jesus ask, "Aren't you glad I've come?"
Supposing He came tonight?
Lord Jesus, I want more grace each day,
To help me walk aright,
So that my heart may gladly welcome You
Supposing You came tonight.

—Author Unknown

SUNDAY EVENING, OCTOBER 23

Title: Worry—How to Overcome It

Text: "Take therefore no thought for the morrow: for the morrow shall take thought for the things of itself. Sufficient unto the day is the evil thereof" **(Matt. 6:34).**

Scripture Reading: Matthew 6:31–34

Introduction

Worry is like a rocking chair. It is something to do, but it never gets you anywhere. A visitor from the Middle East returned to his homeland to describe life in America with three words: "Hurry, worry, and bury." Most of us are aware that we worry. The question is, How can we overcome our worry?

I. Realize how much it hurts.

A. *Worry hurts us spiritually.* When we worry, we call God a liar. The Bible teaches, "Anyone who does not believe God has made him out to be a liar" (1 John 5:10 NIV).

God's Word has made some great promises that are denied by worry: "I will never leave thee, nor forsake thee" (Heb. 13:5); "He careth for you" (1 Peter 5:7); "He hath done all things well" (Mark 7:37); "My God shall supply all your need according to his riches in glory by Christ Jesus" (Phil. 4:19); "I can do all things through Christ which strengtheneth me" (Phil. 4:13); and many more.

If we do not believe these promises from God's Book, we are, in essence, calling God a liar. This certainly hurts our relationship with God and, in the final analysis, our spiritual life as a whole.

B. *Worry hurts us physically.* Our physical body is the temple of the Holy Spirit (1 Cor. 3:16; 6:19; Gal. 4:6).

The Mayo Clinic has reported that fear, worry, hate, selfishness, and the inability to adjust to the world of reality are the main causes of stomach illness and stomach ulcers. Doctors have also concluded that worry affects the heartbeat and blood circulation and makes one a ripe candidate for 219 diseases and 642 complications known to the medical profession.

Dr. Mayo once said that he had never seen a man die of overwork, but had seen many die from doubt. A past president of the American Rheumatism Association claimed that a woman once came to him with gall bladder trouble. She said, "I am going to die." The gall bladder operation was a success, but she died. The autopsy revealed that she just "worried herself to death."

II. Realize how useless worry is.

A. *When we worry we forget our individual worth.* God takes care of the birds. In the sight of God, our value far exceeds that of the birds (Matt. 6:26). We are human beings made in the image of God. Why should we worry?

B. *No one ever became taller by worrying (v. 27).* Actually, nothing has ever been accomplished by worry.

C. *Worrying blinds us to the blessings of God (vv. 28–30).* When we worry we trample the beauties of the earth under our feet and forget that the same God who makes the lily beautiful can also make our lives beautiful and meaningful.

D. *Worry is sinful.* When our Lord said, "After all these things do the Gentiles seek" (v. 32), he was equating the Gentiles with unbelievers. He indicated that one of the marks of an unbeliever is worry. We can call our worry "nerves," "emotional troubles," and a hundred different things, but it makes worry no less sinful.

III. Make the will of God the supreme good in your life.

As indicated in the Lord's Prayer, the kingdom of God and the will of God are synonymous. When people put the will of God above everything else in their lives, they learn to trust instead of worry. How does one find the will of God?

A. *By earnest prayer (Rom. 8:26–27).*

B. *By following the leadership of the Holy Spirit (v. 13).*

C. *By having faith that God will cause everything to fit together in one's life (v. 28).* Whether we realize it or not, we are living in the presence of a God who cares for us and loves us. If we could practice his presence, it would eliminate much of our worry and anxiety.

IV. Live a day at a time in the will of God.

The English author Jonathan Swift was fond of saying, "May you live all the days of your life." Many of us do not live all the days of our lives because we live in yesterday or in tomorrow.

A. *Do not live in tomorrow.* An enterprising service station manager erected this sign on one of his gas pumps: "Free gasoline tomorrow." Of course, this notice meant nothing. Neither does a religion mean anything when it offers happiness tomorrow. The New Testament places the emphasis on *now* (John 16:31; 2 Cor. 6:2; 1 John 3:2).

A widow who had raised six children without the help of a husband was asked, "How did you do it?" Her reply was simply, "I'm in a partnership. One day long ago I said, 'Lord, I will do the work and you do the worrying.' I haven't had a worry since."

The Christian cannot live in tomorrow. Today is the watchword for those who will do the will of God (Heb. 4:7).

B. *Don't live in yesterday.* The Christian cannot live in yesterday. We cannot live with yesterday's sorrows. The parents of a deceased child left his room just as it was when he was alive. They went into his room each day to mourn his passing and denied their two daughters a normal life because they mourned over yesterday's sorrows.

The Christian cannot live with yesterday's sins. We are promised that if we confess our sins, God will forgive (1 John 1:9). We are promised that God will remove our sins "as far as the east is from the west" (Ps. 103:12).

The Christian cannot live with yesterday's success. If we spend today merely recounting the successes of yesterday, we are kept from the success of today.

Harvey Firestone Jr. said in an interview for *Nation's Business*, "My favorite slogan is 'Today is the first day of the rest of your life.' So it's no use fussing about the past because you can't do anything about it. But you have today, and today is when everything that's going to happen from now on begins."

Conclusion

Henry Ward Beecher once said, "When we fill our hours with regrets over the failures of yesterday and with worries over problems of tomorrow, we have no today in which to be thankful."

WEDNESDAY EVENING, OCTOBER 26

Title: "Teach Me to Do Thy Will"

Text: "Teach me to do thy will; for thou art my God: thy spirit is good; lead me into the land of uprightness" **(Ps. 143:10)**.

Scripture Reading: Psalm 143

Introduction

Dr. T. B. Maston wrote a splendid book entitled *God's Will for Your Life* (Nashville: Broadman, 1964), primarily for the benefit of Christian youth seeking to discover the will of God for their lives. Maston believed that God was creatively active in every area of human interest and concern. He declared that God "is no idle spectator. He is on the move in achieving His purposes in the world" (p. 5).

The psalmist believed that God had a will, a plan, a purpose in which he should be involved. He offers a prayer that God will teach him not only to know but to do the divine will.

In Maston's counsel to young people he made certain great affirmations concerning the will of God that both young and old can profit from hearing and heeding.

I. God's will applies to everyone and to all things.

II. God's will is always best.

While doing God's will may not appear to be that which is best at first, those who give themselves faithfully to the doing of his will discover that in the divine will they find fulfillment, freedom, power, peace, and satisfaction.

III. God's will is a continuing experience.

A. *The Lord wants to bestow the gift of salvation within the heart of everyone.*
B. *The Lord desires to assist every young person in choosing his or her life's work.*
C. *The Lord wishes to assist each young person in choosing his or her life companion.*
D. *The Lord is eager to provide guidance for the making of daily decisions along the journey of life.*

IV. God's will can be known.

Maston encouraged his readers to believe that they could find the will of God for their lives if they were willing to seek it sincerely.

A. *One must be willing to use personal resources.*
B. *One can very profitably seek the counsel of others who are knowledgeable, wise, and good.*
C. *A reverent and responsive study of the Bible can provide invaluable aid.*
D. *Time spent in the closet of prayer will give God an opportunity to speak counsel to the believer's heart.*
E. *A cooperative response to the leadership of the Holy Spirit is vital.*
F. *A willing, surrendered heart is absolutely essential.*
G. *One must have the faith to look beyond the problems to a better day.* Doing the will of God is a combination of consenting to the will of God and cooperating with his will as we understand it.

Conclusion

Instead of fighting the will of God, we would be wise to seek his will. Instead of fleeing from the will of God, we should fasten our minds, hearts, and souls to his will and have the spirit of our Lord when he prayed, "Not my will, but thine, be done."

SUNDAY MORNING, OCTOBER 30

Title: Joy and the Good It Does

Text: "Rejoice in the Lord always. I will say it again: Rejoice! Let your gentleness be evident to all. The Lord is near" **(Phil. 4:4–5 NIV)**.

Scripture Reading: Philippians 4

Hymns: "There's a Glad New Song," Fisher

"We're Marching to Zion," Watts

"Let Others See Jesus in You," McKinney

Offertory Prayer: Most merciful God, as we face the duties of the new week, we pray that you will steady our spirits and inspire us to new praise. May we find in each relation with you and with your children a cause for joy. Knowing that out of the travail of difficult times your providence and protection will see us through, help us to live lives of radiant Christian joy that people might be attracted to you. In the name of Jesus Christ, our Savior, we pray. Amen.

Introduction

"The life of Christian joy." Is this life worth the effort it takes to live? What good does it do? Why should I constantly watch my life so as never to disturb the fellowship and thus the joy of which I am a part?

What have I to lose by going my own way, living my own life, and asserting my own will? What have I to gain by living in fellowship with God and his children?

These questions find their answer in Philippians 4. Here Paul speaks of "joy and the good it does." If we have the joy, all the good it does becomes our own.

I. A life of Christian joy makes Christ attractive to others (Phil. 4:1–9).

When Paul spoke of his Lord, that which made Christ so attractive to others was neither Paul's physical appearance nor his eloquence; it was the joy in which he spoke and lived. If your life of Christian joy does nothing more than make Christ attractive to others, it is worth it all! But at Philippi two influential leaders had lost their joy, were not on speaking terms with each other, and were making Christ quite unattractive to others. Nothing makes Christ less appealing to others than sour-puss Christians! This was the situation Paul found necessary to address.

A. *A problem is raised in Philippians 4:2–3.* Two women who had worked with Paul, Euodias and Syntyche, were not speaking to each other. So here in the Philippian church the situation was far from good. These two who once were such a blessing to the church had now become a problem in the church.

1. Notice the prominence of those involved. Paul refers to them as "those women which laboured with me in the gospel" (4:3). These were women of prominence and influence, but they would not speak to one another! They certainly were not "of the same mind in the Lord." They were the source of anxiety and division in the church, and Paul is saying, "This must be dealt with!"

   Strange as it may seem, Christians even on the executive level can become hostile, peevish, and little. When such people become prominent, their hostilities become widely known. Damage is done to the work of Christ, and our Lord is made unattractive to others.

2. "Let your moderation be known" (4:5) seems to indicate that the problem had persisted for quite some time. The apostle is pleading, "Let your yieldedness be known." Because neither Syntyche nor Euodias was willing to yield, the problem persisted. The prominence of the women and the persistence of the problem made Christ most unattractive to those outside the church.

The good that the life of Christian joy can do in a situation like this is to reverse the whole process and make Christ attractive to others. The delight of Christian joy, not the division of Christian people, makes Christ winsome to others.

B. *A presence is recalled when Paul says, "The Lord is at hand" (4:5).* Rather than referring to the return of our Lord, this phrase refers to the nearness of our Lord: "The Lord is near."

In this church where these women's differences were the daily topic of gossip, Paul reminds them that not only is there a problem, but there is also a presence. The Lord is near, and his presence reminds us of two important facts.

1. The value of prayer had been ignored in all their hostilities (4:6). In more pointed language, the apostle admonishes the church to "stop worrying about anything and start praying about everything."

    In all your arguments, in all your self-justification, in all your Christian conversation, remember that the Lord is near. When you leave that class meeting, that business session, that committee meeting, that heated exchange of words with another, and you sit in your car and talk for a little while, remember that although there are only two of you talking, there is a Third. If you and I prayed more about this kind of problem and talked less, we would find a quicker and simpler solution.

2. The virtue of praise so often goes unnoticed when divisions arise in the church. "With thanksgiving [praise] let your requests be made known unto God" (4:6). There is healing power in praise. You can praise God in a time of trouble because you trust him to bring good out of it. You can praise your Lord because you know he will answer your prayer.

    The Christians at Philippi could have praised God because of the past labors of Syntyche and Euodias, labors to which they believed God would restore them in the future. There is virtue in praise, and may we never forget it!

C. *A practice is recommended in verse 8.* Paul is a Christian pragmatist. He realizes that prayer must be coupled with practice. This disruptive matter could not be solved by prayer alone. These people had to quit thinking the nasty thoughts that come so easily when problems arise in the church. And you would do well not to stare at every mud hole and pick at every sore you see. Some Christians will not gossip to another but will allow all kinds of untrue, unfair, and impure thoughts to circulate in their minds until all the joy of Christian living is driven right out of their lives. We are to look for something good in life—whatever is holy, just, pure, lovely, and of a good report.

II. A life of Christian joy imparts grace to cope with life's problems (4:10–19).

Some Christians just do not have the grace to cope with life's problems. They make mountains out of molehills, and when a real mountain confronts them, they fall apart at the seams! They get mad at God, lose faith, crumble beneath the load, or handle their problem in such a way as to cause others to lose confidence in them.

Paul had more problems than any two of us shall ever know, but his life of Christian joy supplied him ample grace to cope with each problem in such a manner as to bring honor—not shame—to his Lord.

A. *Such grace is encouraged by the fellowship of the church (4:10, 14–18).* There are times when we cannot bear our burdens alone. In times like these, if it were not for the fellowship of the church, we would surely break beneath the load! The generosity of the church at Philippi thrilled Paul and encouraged a grace to bear burdens that no mortal man could bear alone. This is why we have a church: We *need* each other and can draw encouragement and grace in those difficult hours of life.

B. *This strengthening grace allows one to be content apart from externals (4:11–12).* "I have learned, in whatsoever state I am, therewith to be content" (v. 11).

I don't know which is more difficult—to have too little or to have too much. We need the grace of God to handle each situation. How often we are deceived by thinking that contentment is found in what one has. "If only I had this or that, I would be happy—I would find contentment!" Then the day comes when we can afford this or that, but when we have obtained it, we discover that it does not bring joy or happiness. Then we become disillusioned, anxious, and frustrated because we have learned that contentment is not dependent on externals—however lavish they may be.

But the life of Christian joy imparts a grace that is content apart from externals. Whether we have much or little, we have Christ, and he is the one who brings contentment, joy, and happiness!

C. *The secret of grace to cope with life's problems is found in Christ (4:13, 19).* What is the secret to the grace that Paul had in the face of his problems? The secret is not found in himself, his friends, or his circumstances, but in the sufficiency of Jesus Christ! In verse 11 Paul uses a word for "contentment" that the pagan Stoics often used. For the Stoic contentment was a human achievement, but for Paul it was a divine gift. The Stoic was self-sufficient, but Paul was Christ-sufficient. Paul could face anything. He could have everything or he could have nothing. It made no difference, because in any situation he had Jesus Christ. The man who walks with Christ and lives in Christ finds grace to cope with anything!

III. A life of Christian joy instills new zest in the church (4:20–23).

Take a church that is half dead and whose work laboriously is being carried on by spiritually anemic souls, inject into its collapsed veins the stimulus of Christian joy, and in a few months you will hardly recognize it as the same church.

It is a sad day when the work of the church is carried on by "TOMs" (Tired Old Men) and "WOWs" (Weary Overworked Women). If we feel that we have "tired blood," then we need the zest that Christian joy alone can bring. It will revive and revolutionize our church. It will give the church a bright and happy spirit that will attract and inspire others.

A. *This new zest expresses love.* "Salute every saint in Christ Jesus. The brethren which are with me greet you. All the saints salute you, chiefly they that are of Caesar's household" (4:21–22).

The Christians at Philippi were interested in the Christians at Rome, and the Christians at Rome were interested in the Christians at Philippi. Paul unashamedly expresses their love and his love to them. We should never hesitate to tell others that we love them and care for them. Our joy in Christian living should overflow in love to others. Yet how often have we said, "If only I had told him how much I loved him!" "If only I had taken time to tell her just what she meant to me!" "If only, if only, if only...." Let your life of Christian joy overflow in praise for and thanksgiving to others so that you will never again have to say, "If only...." This will put new zest in your church and in your life.

B. *The new zest that the life of Christian joy instills in the church exalts our Lord.* "Now unto God and our Father be glory for ever and ever. Amen" (4:20).

The new zest and enthusiasm that Christian joy imparts will not allow us to remain mute concerning our Lord. We must sing his praises! We must exalt his name! We must share his story! We must spread his joy!

Conclusion

For the "life of Christian joy" to do any real good, it must be shared with others. There is a world out there that wonders if Christ really makes a difference. Your life of Christian joy can convince this world of the tremendous difference that our Lord can make in any person's life.

SUNDAY EVENING, OCTOBER 30

Title: "Judge Not"—What It Means

Text: "Judge not ..." (**Matt. 7:1**).

Scripture Reading: Romans 14:1–15

Introduction

A Swiss boy stood on one side of a valley. He shouted, "Hello," and the "Hello" returned. Could there be another boy on the other side?

Soon he became excited and shouted, "You had better not say that anymore," and the same phrase echoed back.

The boy said, "Here I am standing in the sunlight; show yourself." The same challenge rushed back to him.

"Would you like to fight?" he shouted. The repetitious reply mocked him.

By now the boy was angry beyond reason. He rushed home to his mother and relayed the challenging incident. His kind mother listened with interest and smiled. "Why don't you go back where you were," she said, "and shout, 'I like you very much!'" He did this, and the thoughtful reply returned to him on the wind. He hurried home to tell his mother that he had found a new friend in the boy across the valley.

Our lives are usually reflected in what we have to say. Voters must judge between candidates and platforms. A judge on a bench must judge the innocence or guilt of an accused man. We must all participate in some kind of judgment. What then does our Lord mean when he says, "Judge not"?

I. Did Jesus prohibit discernment?

A. *Our Lord is not teaching that the Christian should never express his opinion of others.* He indicates that the Christian must be able to discern between those classified as "dogs" and "hogs" (Matt. 7:6).

B. *He also indicates that the Christian should be able to discriminate between a false and a true prophet (Matt. 7:15).*

C. *The Christian should be able to discriminate between true and false teachings (Gal. 1:8).*

D. *The Christian should be able to detect error (2 Tim. 2:16–18).*

E. *The Christian should detect and eliminate heresy (Titus 3:10).*

II. Marks of the critical person.

Christians should not delight in the censorious criticism and condemnation of others. One of the most unlovely traits in many Christians' lives is a critical spirit. The Bible teaches, "If anyone considers himself religious and yet does not keep a tight rein on his tongue, he deceives himself and his religion is worthless" (James 1:26 NIV). The gossiping Christian is spinning his wheels in Christian service. He may think that he is doing good, but he is doing more harm than good.

A. *The critical person usually criticizes others to cover up his own faults.* Those who gripe the most at work, at home, or at church usually do the least. They gripe to cover up their laziness, unfaithfulness, sin, backsliding, and mistakes.

B. *The critical person criticizes personalities and disregards principles.* For fifteen minutes three women at a restaurant table criticized one of their acquaintances. Finally, there was a few seconds of silence as they rested their jaws.

Then one of them sighed and said, "I tell you, she is a real menace. You don't know that woman like I do."

"Oh yes I do," countered another. "I know her every bit as well as you do."

"Oh," snorted the first woman, "how could you possibly know her as well as I do? I am her best friend."

The critical person never bothers to look behind another's actions but criticizes that person's personality without any thought whatsoever of principles involved.

C. *The critical person expresses his opinion without knowing all of the facts.*

It has been said that a faultfinder is never a good fact finder.

After running a picture of new United States senators taking the oath of office, a newspaper received a sarcastic letter.

The writer complained that "the senator from Hawaii doesn't know his right hand from his left."

The writer observed correctly. Senator Inouye took the oath of office with his left hand. After the Japanese bombed Pearl Harbor, Don Inouye enlisted in the army. He fought in Italy and won the Purple Heart with clusters, the Bronze Star, and the Distinguished Service Cross.

Yes, he took the oath of office with his left hand—because he lost his right arm fighting for his country in Italy.

A Nigerian Christian put it this way: "There may be a hundred things you know about a person—all of them bad. But there may be just one thing you don't know, which if you did know, would completely change your opinion."

D. *The critical person pronounces final judgments.* He does not give people a chance to change. He interprets certain patterns in people's behavior and refuses to change his opinion of them.

Conclusion

A professor at a well-known institute of real estate management recommends that landlords keep at least one scandalous couple in each apartment building to keep tenants happy. He claims that the presence of such a pair will give other tenants something to gossip about and subconsciously, therefore, make them happy.

But Jesus taught that real happiness is found by those who refuse to be critical of others.

NOVEMBER

■ **Sunday Mornings**

"Total Stewardship" is the theme for the Sunday morning messages. A Thanksgiving message is also included. On the last Sunday of the month, begin a series titled "The Meaning of His Name" for the weeks leading up to Christmas. These messages are based on Isaiah's prophecy of the Messiah who was to come. They reveal the adequacy of the Lord Jesus Christ to meet the deepest needs of our lives.

■ **Sunday Evenings**

Continue the series on the Sermon on the Mount.

■ **Wednesday Evenings**

The theme for the Wednesday evening messages is "Gratitude and Stewardship." These messages should encourage church leaders as they lead church members to a greater financial commitment to God's kingdom activities. On the last Wednesday evening of the month, begin a series of messages with a devotional nature. Their purpose is to create a reverent and worshipful observance of the Christmas season.

WEDNESDAY EVENING, NOVEMBER 2

Title: Living in Time for Eternity

Text: "Then Lot chose him all the plain of Jordan; and Lot journeyed east: and they separated themselves the one from the other" (**Gen. 13:11**).

Scripture Reading: Genesis 13

Introduction

Time is but a gap in eternity. Eternity was before time began. Eternity will continue when time is no more. Life at its best is a life lived in time with eternity in mind.

Abraham, the father of the faithful, lived in time successfully with the values of eternity in mind. Lot lived in time as if time were everything and eternity did not even exist. Let us look at the man who lived in time alone and failed to live for eternity. Perhaps we can avoid making the same mistake.

The secret of Lot's failure, as far as eternity is concerned, can be traced to his love for and his loyalty to material values. He lived as if there were no eternity.

For some the secret of their failure is found in alcoholism. Others may fail because of laziness. Still others fail, as far as eternity is concerned, because they live only for the present. Are you living only for the present? Are you living only for security on the rainy day? By examining the destiny of Lot, may you determine to live in time with eternity in mind.

I. Lot had a materialistic scale of values.

He looked at everything with dollar marks on his eyeballs.

A. *He did not seek God's guidance.*
B. *He permitted covetousness to capture the citadel of his heart (Gen. 13:10).*
C. *He did not count the cost of making wealth.*
D. *He deliberately chose to give his life to the pursuit of mammon.*

II. Lot achieved success in time.

A. *He acquired property.*
B. *He acquired popularity.*
C. *He occupied a position of prominence (Gen. 19:1).*

III. Eternity declared Lot to be a failure.

A. *He missed the peace and contentment that result from walking with God.*
B. *He had the humiliating experience of being considered "off his rocker" in a moment of critical danger (Gen. 19:14).*
C. *He had the sad experience of seeing his property going up in smoke and down in ashes.*
D. *He failed to lay up treasures in heaven because he put profit before purity and selfish desires before spiritual service.*
E. *He failed to gain the smile of God's approval because he sought to achieve his selfish desires.*

Conclusion

There is still hope for those who have followed Lot into the city of Sodom if they are willing to learn some lessons from Lot today. The angels warned Lot to flee. Lot warned his relatives. The Bible tells us that this world is going to burn someday and that he who lives for this world only will suffer the loss of all that he has accumulated.

Let us determine to live each day in time with the values of eternity in mind.

SUNDAY MORNING, NOVEMBER 6

Title: Where Is Your Heart?

Text: "Where your treasure is, there will your heart be also" (**Matt. 6:21**).

Scripture Reading: Matthew 6:19–21

Hymns: "God of Our Fathers," Roberts

         "He Leadeth Me," Gilmore

         "I Surrender All," Van de Venter

Offertory Prayer: Our Father, we thank you not only for your gifts to us but also for the privilege of bringing our gifts of love to you. Behind our offering we commit anew to you our hearts. Protect us from covetousness, which is idolatry. Deposit for us these treasures in heaven, even as we invest them in your people and in your work on the earth. In Jesus' name. Amen.

Introduction

Back in 1951, in a campaign to increase circulation, the *St. Petersburg Times* buried a treasure of two hundred dollars in the area. Each day they presented clues, but the spot eluded the public. On the final day, the last clue was printed. Two thousand people gathered in front of the newspaper plant to get the first edition to come off the presses. Within twenty-five minutes the treasure was found.

But in the mad scramble of that final day, several fainted in the mob scene in front of the *Times* building, six people were injured in traffic accidents, and four others were bogged in waist deep mud and had to be dragged out. One building site had to be resurveyed because the crowd ripped up the stakes that had been laid out. All for a mere two hundred dollars!

This is a symbol of the popular mind today. The lure of gold is an irresistible siren call. The effort to get something for nothing is a national pastime. The search for treasure leads people into situations that are sometimes ridiculous and often tragic.

Jesus knew this basic weakness in the human makeup. He saw people losing their souls in the search for fleeting treasures and elusive pleasures. He saw hearts that were committed to the wrong kind of treasures. So, in loving compassion, he gave us some sound advice: "Lay not up for yourselves treasures upon earth ... but lay up for yourselves treasures in heaven."

There is a difference between our treasures and our possessions. Our treasure is something that we love supremely. It is that to which we give our affection, our heart, our whole being.

Religion is a heart affair. The relationship a Christian bears with Christ is a heartfelt experience. Our heart is either in this world or it is in God. "You cannot serve both God and mammon," Jesus says. We lay up our treasure in one of two places. Either our heart is centered in this world or it is centered in treasures that are spiritual and eternal. This is our choice; there is no third alternative. Both worlds are bidding for our hearts. Jesus was not discouraging savings accounts. He encourages prudence and thrift, and he commends our consideration for the needs of tomorrow, particularly for our family.

But how can we lay up treasures in heaven? I once heard a businessman say, "All my life I have heard preachers tell me to lay up treasures in heaven, but they never told me how to do it. I couldn't figure out how I could get the treasure from here to heaven. Then the thought occurred to me that if I was going to get my treasures to heaven, I would have to invest in those who are going there!"

That perceptive layman had the answer. We must invest in people — people

321

for whom Christ died. We invest in missionaries, in Christian schools, in benevolent institutions, in buildings and programs of worship and instruction. When we invest in God's kingdom, we are laying up treasures in heaven. When we lay up treasures, we ask ourselves:

I. Is there a great risk of loss?

If you lay up treasures for yourself on earth, Jesus guarantees that you will lose them. The corruptible treasures of his day were the prey of moths and rust and thieves. Clothing and tapestries and carpets were subject to the ravages of moths. Utensils, jewelry, and all metal objects could rust. Every precious treasure was coveted by thieves who broke through the mud walls to take what they could. In the final analysis, even if one's treasures survived these perils, the possessor could not take them to heaven with him.

Christ guarantees us that treasures dedicated to God are beyond the reach of moths or rust or robbers. Anything that can be taken from us, or anything we cannot take with us, is really not ours in the first place. Paul said, "I know whom I have believed, and am persuaded that he is able to keep that which I have committed unto him against that day" (2 Tim. 1:12). When we lay up treasures we ask ourselves:

II. Is there abiding joy and satisfaction?

A rich young ruler came to Jesus to inquire the way to eternal life. Jesus, seeing that the ruler loved his treasures more than he loved God, asked him to part with his possessions. "And thou shalt have treasures in heaven," Jesus promised. Finally, the young man went away sorrowful. Sorrowful! He was rich, but he asked, "What lack I yet?" He recognized a lack in his life that earthly treasures could not supply.

To commit ourselves and our treasures to God is to have joy and peace in this life as well as treasures in heaven. We have our needs met not only for eternity but also in the here and now. When a wonderful Christian woman died, someone said, "It is not difficult to think of her being in a spiritual world, since everything she greatly cared for could be so easily transferred."

During the depths of the Depression, a layman spoke to a Texas congregation on the stewardship of giving. He had been a wealthy cotton broker in the 1920s. His office was high in the cotton exchange building across the street from his church. He had been generous in giving to the support of his church, to its gigantic building program, to Baylor University, to Buckner Children's Home, and to a multitude of other Christian causes. In the crash of 1929, he was literally wiped out financially. He told of colleagues opening windows in their offices and leaping out to death in the streets below. He told of walking to the window of his office and of looking down on the buildings of his church below and saying to himself and to God, "All I have left is what I have given to my church and the causes dear to my church and my Lord."

Conclusion

What Jesus is saying to us contradicts the old saying, "You can't take it with you." He says, "You can take it with you by sending it on ahead to where you are going for eternity." "The world passeth away, and the lust thereof: but he that doeth the will of God abideth for ever" (1 John 2:17).

SUNDAY EVENING, NOVEMBER 6

Title: Judging — How to Stop It

Text: "Judge not, that ye be not judged" **(Matt. 7:1)**.

Scripture Reading: Matthew 7:1–5

Introduction

In Ballybay, Ireland, in 1966, Cyril Morrison, a young lad, was involved in an unusual accident that involved Farmer McQuade's tractor. It seems that Mr. McQuade's tractor pinned young Morrison's tongue to a wall.

Cyril's tongue was severed at the root. He was rushed to a hospital and was later fitted with an artificial tongue. The Dublin High Court awarded young Morrison more than sixteen thousand dollars for damages.

As far as anyone is able to tell, this is the first time a value in dollars and cents has been placed on the tongue. Perhaps sixteen thousand dollars is underselling the value of the human tongue. The Bible says that this little boneless organ of the human body can be one of the most destructive instruments known to humankind. It is small, but it can kindle a flame that can burn into a roaring fire. It weighs little, but some strong men cannot hold it. How do we overcome the sin of using the tongue to judge others?

I. Become judgment conscious.

Our Lord said we are not to judge others because we are going to be judged ourselves some day. Of course, one's destiny is decided when he decides what to do with Christ on earth. However, it is certainly true that we are judged and punished for some of our sins right here on earth. Sickness and even death could well be the punishment for some sins (1 Cor. 11:30; 2 Cor. 1:4–5).

    A. *The Bible teaches that all of us shall pass through some sort of judgment.* The Judgment Day will affect one's eternal rewards or punishments.

        1. We shall all give an account of our lives to God (Rom. 14:10–12; Gal. 6:5).

        2. The Judgment Day will be a time in which God will test our works (1 Cor. 3:13–15).

        3. Since Christians will go through some sort of judgment, it should encourage us to witness more for Christ (2 Cor. 5:10–11).

        4. For many, the Judgment Day will be a day of shame (1 John 2:28).

5. Since we are all going to be judged some day by God, it behooves us to refrain from judging our fellow humans.

A woman confessed to Francis of Assisi that she had gossiped about her friends. He instructed her to pluck the feathers of a goose and lay a feather on the doorstep of every person against whom she had sinned.

When she returned, he told her to gather up each feather. Later she returned in tears, explaining that the wind had scattered the feathers and made their recovery impossible.

B. *Our Lord taught that we are judged by our own criticism.* When we criticize another we are setting the standard for our own judgment. Whenever we take the seat of judgment on another person's life, we are always expected to be better than the one whom we judged.

1. One of the principles of life is, "To whom men have committed much, of him they will ask the more" (Luke 12:48).
2. When we judge other people, we may be condemning ourselves (Rom. 2:1).
3. When we live in the light of the judgment, it encourages us to be Christlike in the things we say about other people (James 3:1).

II. Realize that no one is capable of judging.

When our Lord spoke of the "mote and the beam," he was indicating how ridiculous it is for one human being to judge another.

A woman rushed into an office and said, "Doctor, tell me frankly what is wrong with me."

"Well," he said, "first, you are too fat. Second, your clothes are too loud. Third, your makeup is all wrong. Fourth, I am a photographer—the doctor's office is one floor up."

The Sioux Indians had a prayer that said, "O Great Spirit, help me never to judge another until I have walked two weeks in his moccasins."

A little girl cried for several hours on board a train with her father. An irritated passenger said to the father, "Why don't you give that child to her mother?"

The father replied, "I'm sorry, but I can't. Her mother is in the baggage car in a casket."

III. Some practical pointers.

A. *When you are tempted to criticize someone, think of the good things about that person.* Comedian Red Skelton claimed that when someone irritated him, he and his wife would "go out into our tea house, have some iced tea, and think of five things we like about the person."

B. *When tempted to criticize someone, let your heart be the graveyard for gossip.* Never repeat criticism. Bury it in the love of God in your own heart. Before saying anything about anyone, ask: Is it kind? Is it necessary? Is it true?

C. *When you are tempted to criticize someone, try to understand him.* Someone said, "We can't stand others because we don't understand others."

D. *Make Christ the Lord of your life. Our Lord prayed for those who crucified him.* There is never any record that he resorted to criticism of anyone for any purpose.

E. *Speak for Christ.* Witness on every occasion. If one would witness on every occasion, he would find himself less and less critical. Those who refuse to "gossip" the gospel usually spend much of their time gossiping.

Conclusion

A Mexican businessman decided that he would sell Mexican burros by mail and ship them into the United States. He tied a personal identification tag around each burro's neck and placed them in lots of fifty in railroad cattle cars for his first shipment to America.

Several days later he began to get excited telegrams from the Chicago Railway Express Agency asking what to do with the burros that had reached Chicago. The Mexican reported, "Each burro has its own individual identification and shipping tag hanging on his neck."

He was quite disappointed when he learned that the burros had systematically eaten each other's identification tags. The Mexican merchant quickly satisfied everyone by issuing a new identification to each burro—sealed inside a tin can, tied around the burro's neck.

When Christian people nibble at each other's spiritual identity, they usually end up discrediting all of Christendom before a lost world.

WEDNESDAY EVENING, NOVEMBER 9

Title: The Language of the Treasury

Text: "For if willingness is there, the gift is acceptable according to what one has, not according to what he does not have" **(2 Cor. 8:12 NIV)**.

Scripture Reading: Mark 12:41–44

Introduction

"Money talks" is a common truism. It talks concerning the seller and the buyer. It talks concerning the giver and the receiver. It talks with a powerful voice, and most people listen to the language of the dollar.

In Mark's account of the widow who gave her two mites, we can learn that money talks even when given to God. Jesus observed and commented on what the widow's gift said concerning her spiritual commitment and involvement.

I. Her gift was a part of her worship.

A. *The poor widow considered the privilege of giving as something to be taken seriously — "even all her living."*

B. *The poor widow really believed in giving.*

C. *The poor widow believed that her giving could best be done in God's house.*

1. A place where God's honor dwelt.
2. A place where human honesty should dwell.

II. Her giving was an expression of her love.

She gave "all that she had."
A. *Love always gives its best.*
B. *Love always gives in the best way possible.*

III. Her giving revealed her character.

What you give gives you away.
A. *She gave more for others than she kept for herself.*
B. *She gave more to God than she kept for herself.*

IV. Her giving was known to God.

Jesus sat over against the treasury.
A. *Pretenders will be recognized.*
B. *Stinginess will be recorded.*
C. *God measures the heart rather than the amount of the gift.*

Conclusion

F. C. Wellman has written a poem about the account of Jesus' thoughts on the widow's contribution. He makes some thought-provoking observations and raises some disturbing questions.

Listen to his words and then evaluate your own giving habits.

Over Against the Treasury

Unnoted He sat by the temple gate
While the rich and the poor passed by;
And He read their hearts as they dropped their gifts
'Neath the gaze of His searching eye.

Each gift He weighed in a subtle scale
As it dropped in the temple store—
And the pain it cost, and the sacrifice,
And the burden of love it bore.

But the piercing eye of the watching Christ
Looked not at the proffered gold;
Not "What did he give?" was His searching test,
But "How much did he withhold?"

By that standard stern the rich man's tithe
Was shamed by the widow's mite;
For she gave her all—while he kept his wealth
As he passed from the Master's sight.

By the gates of the treasury still He sits,
And watches the gifts we bring—
And He measures the gold that we give to Him
By the gold to which we cling.

How much to revive a starving world?
How much for our pampered plates?
How much to extend the King's frontiers?
How much for our own estates?

How much have you sent to the mission field
To invest in the souls of men?
How much to your broker for stocks and bonds
To return to yourself again?

Is it Mammon or God who holds the key
To the vault where your treasure lies?
There's a curse or a blessing locked within
That will follow beyond the skies.

For the hour will come when the wealth of earth
Recedes from our slackened grasp;
And the gold and the goods we have given away
Are all that our hands can clasp.

Oh, Master of men, spur our lagging zeal
Till we answer the Kingdom's call,
And lay on the altar a worthy gift,
Ourselves and our gold, and all.

—From *Meeting House* magazine

SUNDAY MORNING, NOVEMBER 13

Title: Let's Think about Money

Text: "For the love of money is the root of all evil" (**1 Tim. 6:10**).

Scripture Reading: 1 Timothy 6:6–12

Hymns: "This Is My Father's World," Babcock

"All Things Are Thine," Whittier

"Take My Life and Let It Be," Havergal

Offertory Prayer: O heavenly Father, we are aware that the money we call our own is really not ours but yours. We marvel at your trust in us that we might be stewards of your wealth. Give us wisdom to be worthy in our response to the needs of your church and your kingdom. Give us satisfaction in the privilege of partnership with you. Give us joy in the grace of giving. In Jesus' name. Amen.

Introduction

Many of us grew up in churches where money was the last subject to be preached from the pulpit. When the minister felt that the occasion demanded a sermon on giving, he nullified the positive effect of his message by beginning his discourse in an apologetic vein.

Such a preacher does not get his example from our Lord. Over one-third of our Lord's parables deal with the relationship between a person and his material possessions. Jesus had more to say about money than he did about the church, missions, baptism, or heaven and hell.

Jesus seemed utterly indifferent to money for his own use, but he recognized both its virtues and its vices. Money can build churches, support missionaries, feed and clothe orphans, educate our young people, erect hospitals, construct schools, and broadcast the gospel. A lack of money can breed poverty and crime, create ghettos and slums, promote bitterness, and corrupt public officials.

Money can buy many things, but it is limited. It can purchase the finest bed, but it cannot buy peaceful sleep. It can secure the most delicious food, but it cannot cure an ulcer. It can provide a dream vacation, but it cannot get us away from our accusing self. It can pay college tuition, but it cannot guarantee learning. It can avail one of the best medical help in the world, but it cannot buy good health.

There are many things that money cannot buy. It cannot buy love, friendship, happiness, or salvation. We are bought with a price. God has provided the purchase price in the free gift of his own Son.

Money is neither good nor evil. The Bible does not say that money is evil. It says that the *love* of money is the root of "all [kinds] of evil." Money is neutral. Money can build a church or a tavern, a school or a casino. It can send missionaries or missiles abroad.

Money can be either a servant or a master. It is a wonderful servant but a terrible master. Some people think they have money when actually their money has them. Frank Boreham has written:

> *Dug from the mountainside, washed in the glen,*
> *Servant am I or the master of men!*
> *Earn me, I bless you, steal me, I curse you!*
> *Hold me and grasp me, a fiend will possess you!*
> *Live for me, die for me, covet me, take me,*
> *Angel or demon, I am what you make me!*

Jesus is concerned about our attitude toward money.

I. How we earn our money.

Our ethics in the business world will be determined by our attitude toward money. The Lord's work is not dependent on the fast buck. The greed that grows out of a love for money will corrupt the life of the Christian. As the love of money is the root of all kinds of evil, so the love of God is the root of all kinds of good. Far more important than *How much did we make?* is *How did we make it?*

The second principle that concerns Jesus is:

II. How we spend our money.

Our decisions concerning the disposal of our money will grow out of our sense of divine stewardship of our material possessions. The poster that pictures one dime for God and nine for self teaches a false doctrine. All ten tenths belong to God. A minimum of one-tenth belongs to his work through the church, but we are just as responsible in how we spend what remains after our offering. You cannot give God one-tenth and give the Devil a part of the rest. You cannot buy off God with the tithe.

Actually, the practice of tithing will help you to honor God with the other nine-tenths, just as keeping the Lord's Day holy will help you to honor God the other six days of the week.

This brings us to the third principle that concerns Jesus:

III. How we give our money.

We need to realize that our money is actually a coinage of our life. If I hold in my hand my paycheck, I actually hold the money that was given me for forty or fifty hours of life itself. I exchanged the precious commodity of time for my salary. Here is the work of my brain, my muscles, my very life. Here is a week's worth of myself.

Now, if I am not my own, if I belong to God, then this paycheck belongs to him. Dr. J. B. Gambrell had a famous stewardship sermon titled "Who Owns the Wool?" His thesis was "If a farmer owns a sheep, doesn't he own the wool that grows on that sheep?" If God owns you, doesn't he also own your increase?

William Allen White, a distinguished newspaper editor from Emporia, Kansas, spent his last years giving away the modest estate he had accumulated. When he presented his beloved community with fifty acres of land for a park, he was asked to respond to the tribute paid him by his friends.

"This is the last of a fistful of dollars I am giving away today. I have always tried to teach that there are three kicks in every dollar. One is when you make it. The second is when you have it. The third is when you give it way. And I have learned that the biggest kick is in the third."

Conclusion

How gracious and generous is our loving heavenly Father to provide so many material blessings for our lives. But let us never forget that we are responsible to God for our stewardship of his provisions. This is not optional; it is required in stewards "that they be found faithful" (1 Cor. 4:2).

SUNDAY EVENING, NOVEMBER 13

Title: Casting Pearls before Swine

Text: "Give not that which is holy unto the dogs, neither cast ye your pearls before swine, lest they trample them under their feet, and turn again and rend you" **(Matt. 7:6)**.

Scripture Reading: James 3

Introduction

A man by the name of Theodore Rinking faced execution in 1646 because he had offended King Christian IV of Denmark by some things he had said in a book. King Christian offered him two alternatives—"eat your book or be executed." Rinking tore the book into shreds, soaked it in soup, and started munching away until he had devoured the whole book.

Most of us are not able to eat our words as successfully as Theodore Rinking ate his.

I. An explanation of terms.

A. *Dogs.* In Jesus' day dogs were not domesticated as they are today. Many packs of wild dogs roamed the Galilean hills attacking flocks of sheep. They were despised by the Jews. They were the scavengers of the city. They were not kept in houses as they are today.

B. *Swine.* To the Jew, the pig was the most unclean animal of all. One Roman ruler, wanting to make the Jews angry, spread the broth of a hog over the temple. When our Lord indicated that the prodigal son had stooped to feeding swine, he was saying that this Jew had stooped to the lowest task.

C. *Holy things.* When our Lord spoke of the holy things cast before dogs, no doubt he was thinking of those things dedicated to the worship and glory of God. At any rate, he was speaking of letting holy things become commonplace.

D. *Pearls.* Perhaps pearls stand for the good name of Christianity. As the Christian gossips and criticizes, it hurts the name of Christ and Christianity in general. It is like casting pearls before swine. In a general sense, the pearls could be the truth of the gospel of Jesus Christ. Our Lord said that the kingdom of heaven is "like unto a merchant man, seeking goodly pearls" (Matt. 13:45).

II. What this verse does not teach.

A. *The gospel of Jesus Christ is to be withheld from some people.*

Some people interpret this verse to mean that we are giving holy things to dogs and casting pearls before swine when we take the gospel of Jesus Christ to the man on the street. There are some who use this verse to oppose rescue missions, the distribution of tracts and Bibles, street services, jail services, and the sending of missionaries to foreign fields. They contend that some people are just not ready for the gospel, and therefore we are wasting our time proclaiming Christ to them.

B. *The gospel must be changed for some people.* Some people interpret this verse to mean that those classified as dogs and swine cannot receive the demands of discipleship in the gospel of Jesus Christ. Therefore the gospel must be "watered down" to match one's station in life or his spiritual growth.

One need look no further than Mel Trotter to see how unreasonable these interpretations really are. Mel Trotter's father was a saloon keeper and a drunkard. Mel often tended the bar for his father. At age nineteen Mel started drinking and gambling. He lost his job. After several bouts with drinking, he was finally sent to a hospital. He was given treatment for alcoholism, discharged, and handed a medical kit. Fifteen minutes later, he traded the kit for three drinks of whiskey.

Even after the birth of his son, Trotter continued to drink. On returning from a ten-day drinking spree, he found his son dead in the arms of his wife. "I will never take another drop," he promised his wife as the hot tears streamed down his face. But two hours after the baby's funeral, Trotter staggered home—drunk again.

On a cold January night, Trotter staggered through the streets of Chicago with the intention of ending his life in the icy waters of Lake Michigan. Aimlessly he wandered through the doors of the Pacific Garden Mission. There he heard the gospel of Christ proclaimed as a man said, "Jesus loves you."

The speaker looked squarely at Mel Trotter and said, "Make room in your heart for him tonight."

Mel Trotter made room in his heart for Christ that night, and his life was changed. Three years after his conversion, he was appointed superintendent of a rescue mission in Grand Rapids, Michigan. He spent more than forty years there telling others the good news of the gospel of Christ. During that time he used the large Grand Rapids mission as a base to start sixty-six other gospel missions in America—all designed to proclaim the simple gospel of Jesus Christ in a rescue mission just as it is proclaimed in the grandest sanctuary.

III. What this verse does teach.

A. *The awful effects of sin upon one's life.* Sin and rebellion lead some to respond to Christ as though they were dogs and hogs.

As the gospel of Jesus Christ is proclaimed, some fall into the category of dogs and swine as far as their reception of the gospel is concerned. Paul said, "Watch out for those dogs, whose men who do evil, those mutilators of the flesh" (Phil. 3:2 NIV). We are told that "dogs, those who practice magic arts, the sexually immoral, the murderers, the idolaters and everyone who loves and practices falsehood" do not dwell in heaven (Rev. 22:15 NIV).

B. *We must know how to share Christ with people of all backgrounds.* Even though the gospel of Jesus Christ never changes and should never be "watered down," we should use different approaches for different people.

Nicodemus was approached on an intellectual level. Our Lord talked to the Samaritan woman in simple parables. Zacchaeus, the demanding Jewish merchant, would understand the words "Come down from the tree."

Some people, like the Pharisees, need the direct approach, such as, "Ye hypocrites, whitewashed sepulchres." The woman taken in sin understood our Lord when he said, "Go and sin no more."

The morally blind, insensitive, intellectually proud, the cynic who mocks, and the hardened sinner all need the simple gospel of Jesus Christ. However, this same gospel is shared in many different ways.

C. *Holy things must not become commonplace.* It is possible for Christian people to preach Christian truth lightly and without a sense of urgency. Whenever one Christian criticizes another Christian, it is like throwing holy things out to the dogs and pearls before swine.

Conclusion

For the sake of souls, the Christian cannot afford to be critical. His critical spirit may well have a part in sending souls to hell.

WEDNESDAY EVENING, NOVEMBER 16

Title: A Pastor's Tithing Testimony

Text: "Bring ye all the tithes into the storehouse, that there may be meat in mine house, and prove me now herewith, saith the LORD of hosts, if I will not open you the windows of heaven, and pour you out a blessing, that there shall not be room enough to receive it" (**Mal. 3:10**).

Scripture Reading: Malachi 3

Introduction

My message tonight takes the form of a personal testimony. I hope that this message will be informative, inspirational, and challenging to all of the children of God and that it will be unpleasant to no one. Let me say that I have no apology to make to those to whom this subject is unpleasant, for I feel that God has called me to preach all of his Word to all of his people. God does not want me to preach just a portion of the Bible; he wants me to preach all of the Bible. I am convinced that the Bible gives definite information concerning what God desires from his children in a financial way for the expansion of his kingdom work here on earth. God will hold me responsible for the attention that I give to this portion of the Bible just as he will hold me responsible for my preaching of John 3:16.

For more than thirty years I have been bringing my tithe plus an offering into the storehouse of God each Sunday that his work might go forward. Tonight I want to give my testimony as to why I continue to bring the tithe and offering to God.

Let me say from the negative viewpoint that it is not because I have a surplus. It is not because I am out of debt. It is not because I fear that I will go to hell if I don't. It is not primarily because of a sense of duty, although I feel that I have a responsibility of love that requires that I give a tithe as a minimum.

I. I pay the tithe to God through the church in order to acknowledge the divine ownership of all things that I am and have.

I believe with the psalmist that "the earth is the LORD's, and the fulness thereof; the world, and they that dwell therein" (Ps. 24:1). The Lord is our Creator and Sustainer, and he has a right to an increase from that which belongs to him. In Leviticus 27:30 he states what his minimum share shall be: "All the tithe of the land, whether of the seed of the land, or of the fruit of the tree, is the LORD's: it is holy unto the LORD." He defines the tithe: "Concerning the tithe of the herd, or of the flock, even of whatsoever passeth under the rod, the tenth shall be holy unto the LORD" (v. 32).

The prophet Malachi is even plainer in the words of our text in stating the amount that belongs to God. We must beware lest we labor under the impression that if we give the tithe that we have met our financial obligation to God. Malachi 3:8 reads, "Will a man rob God? Yet ye have robbed me, but ye say, Wherein have we robbed thee? In tithes and offerings." Malachi believed that the man who had been blessed with an abundance was obligated to give to God not only a tithe but also offerings over and above the tithe. He is to do this as a recognition of the divine ownership and as an acceptance of his stewardship.

II. I pay the tithe to God through the church because I believe that tithing is God's method for financing the advancing of his kingdom.

A. *Our Lord gave to his church a commission that is worldwide in its significance (Matt. 28:18–20).*

B. *In writing to the church at Corinth, Paul made specific reference to the fact that their offerings should be proportionate (1 Cor. 16:2).* In no verse of Scripture is it ever suggested that God's people should give less than 10 percent of their increase for the Lord's work.

C. *Jesus taught that it was more blessed to give than to receive, and by giving we lay up treasures in heaven (Matt. 6:19–21; Acts 20:35).*

III. I pay a tithe to God through the church because I want to be honest.

A. *I want to be honest in all of my business relationships.*

B. *I want to be honest in all of my family relationships.*

C. *Most of all I want to be honest with God.* If the tithe belongs to God, I want him to have every cent of it. I do not believe that I can prosper by withholding from God that which belongs to him.

333

IV. I pay the tithe to God through the church because it helps me to be more Christlike.

A. *The law of heaven is love—"God is love."* My giving to God is an expression of my love to God, who so loved me that he gave his Son to die for me.

B. *The law of the earth is selfishness.* All of us have an inward inclination to selfishness. We are taught to get all that we can and to can all that we get. It is easy to believe that a man's life consists of the abundance of the things that he possesses. The world would encourage us to measure success in terms of the things that we acquire. God measures us in terms of what we give and the manner in which we serve.

V. I pay the tithe to God through the church because I desire the blessings that God has promised the tither (Mal. 3:10).

A. *By tithing I believe that I can experience the joy of being a soul winner through the ministries of mercy that are rendered by means of the tithe.*

B. *By tithing I have more assurance that I will have treasures in heaven, where moth and rust do not corrupt.*

C. *A part of God's great blessing to the tither comes in a satisfied conscience.*

D. *A part of the blessing of God to the tither is the sense of partnership that comes as we work with God to bring salvation to the hearts and lives of others.*

VI. I pay the tithe to God through the church because it is the best possible investment that I can make.

A. *Most of us believe that when we invest in a home we have made a good investment.*

B. *Some believe that their investment in the form of taxes that they pay to the government is one of the best investments that they make.* Some who have lived where freedom was unknown have expressed a joy as a result of the privilege of being able to pay an income tax.

C. *Most of us believe that the cost of an education is an excellent investment.*

VII. I pay a tithe and bring an offering to the church to demonstrate my love and gratitude to God.

God is love. God proved his love by the gift of his Son for us. You and I can prove our love by giving of our substance to God. Our substance is a portion of our life, for it represents our time, talents, energy, and training.

We can be grateful that we can prove our love by means of a tithe and an offering in the work that is dear to the heart of God. As a pastor I have never known anyone yet who found himself in financial difficulty for the lack of the tithe he gave to the Lord. Many have been the testimonies given to me by people who were faithful tithers to the effect that they found it easier to meet their financial obligations after they had begun to tithe than they did before.

When one decides to become a joyful and regular giver or investor in the work of God, it does something for his spirit. It deepens his love. It increases his interest. It adds to his joy. It makes worship more vital. I encourage each of you to be a tither for the joy that will come into your own heart and life.

SUNDAY MORNING, NOVEMBER 20

Title: Giving Thanks to God

Text: "What shall I render unto the LORD for all his benefits toward me?" (**Ps. 116:12**).

Scripture Reading: Psalm 116:12–16

Hymns: "Come, Ye Thankful People, Come," Alford

"For All the Blessings of the Year," Hutchinson

"Just As I Am, Thine Own to Be," Hearn

Offertory Prayer: O God, on this Thanksgiving Sunday, help us to be truly thankful for all your benefits to us. We wish to make our offering today a thank offering, thanking you for your many gifts to us. Most of all we thank you for the gift of your Son. In his name we give. In response to his love we express our love. Use our gifts to tell others of your great gift. In Jesus' name. Amen.

Introduction

The observance of Thanksgiving Day is a distinctively American tradition. Its practice began 390 years ago, in 1621, on American shores, as grateful Pilgrims gave thanks for a modest harvest on a twenty-acre plot that promised to carry them through another hard winter. For almost 150 years the United States has observed this festive day by presidential decree.

Thanksgiving Day is a distinctively religious observance. It was set aside as a day of prayer and praise. In 1863 President Lincoln set aside the last Thursday in November "as a day of Thanksgiving and praise for our beneficent Father who dwelleth in the heavens." Reinhold Niebuhr expressed concern that our Thanksgiving Day emphasis had departed from this religious purpose. He said, "The Thanksgiving proclamations of the American presidents for the last two decades have increasingly departed from the original rather purely religious spirit of Thanksgiving, and they have increasingly become congratulations to God for having such wonderful children in America."

Thanksgiving Day is not set aside that we might concentrate all our gratitude within the day and take God's gifts for granted the rest of the year. Someone has suggested that we change Thanksgiving Day into a day of grumbling and complaint and spend the other 364 days of the year in thanksgiving.

Benjamin Franklin recalled a childhood experience that brought a sharp rebuke from his father. Situated near the table was an old pork barrel from which the father would daily draw meat for the day's need. Then his father would always pray the prayer, "We thank thee, Father, for the meat thou hast set before us."

One day young Ben suggested: "Father, why not say one prayer over the whole barrel and get it done with? Then we won't have to thank the Lord every meal for every piece of meat we eat." Isn't this often what we do?

We flip a switch on our wall and expect light. We forget the linemen who keep the electricity flowing. We are hardly moved when we read of the electrocution of a worker atop a pole.

We turn the faucet in our kitchen and water flows. In the book *Wind, Sand, and Stars,* written by a pilot of the French Sahara line during World War II, we read of three Moors from the desert who had never seen a tree, a rose, or a flowing river in their native land. After the War they were guests in Europe. They were shown a waterfall in the French Alps. Now, to them, water was worth its weight in gold. This extravagance was overwhelming.

The guide was ready to move on, but they insisted on waiting. "Why?" he asked. Their amazing reply was, "We are waiting for the falls to come to an end." It was simply beyond their comprehension that God should so madly supply water. This water had been running ceaselessly for thousands of years. When they returned to their homeland, they said very little about the waterfalls. No one would believe them anyway.

The psalmist, in a time when his heart sang in praise in an awareness of God's gracious gifts, asked himself, "What shall I render unto the LORD for all his benefits toward me?" (Ps. 116:12). He answered with three responses:

I. I will take the cup of salvation (Ps. 116:13).

This is the first step. The greatest gift of God to humanity is the gift of his Son. "The wages of sin is death; but the gift of God is eternal life through Jesus Christ our Lord" (Rom. 6:23). We cannot sincerely say, "God, we thank you for sending your Son to die for our sins," and not accept that Son as our own Savior. To reject God's Son and his claims on our life is to say, "So far as I am concerned, he might as well not have come to the earth." The first response of gratitude is to "take the cup of salvation, and call upon the name of the Lord." What a blessed promise is the declaration, "Whosoever shall call upon the name of the Lord shall be saved" (Rom. 10:13).

II. I will pay my vows (Ps. 116:14).

"I will pay them," the psalmist suggests, "in the presence of all [God's] people." These are public vows. They begin with a public profession of faith. We declare our allegiance to Christ and his church. Like the public vows of marriage made by two people deeply in love, the public vows of the Christian put us on record and under obligation to be consistent and faithful to our vows to Christ and his church. Think back today on all the vows you have made since that first one. Think of the high emotional experience when your baby was born and you held in your arms a life of your own flesh. Think of that revival meeting, that camp experience, that time of great sorrow or great joy when God was so close and you vowed to love him more devotedly and to follow his will. Thanksgiving Day is a wonderful time to pay our vows to the Lord in the presence of all his people.

III. I will assume the role of the servant (Ps. 116:16).

"O LORD, truly I am thy servant," the psalmist writes. When we assume the role of the servant, we are most like our Lord. The word *minister* means "servant." The word *deacon* means "servant." The New Testament declares that all Christians are called to be "ministers," "servants," in the sense that we are to be concerned with ministering to the needs of others rather than being concerned with being served by others. Jesus said of his coming, "The Son of man came not to be ministered unto, but to minister." Let us follow his example. Let us translate our "thanksgiving" into "thanksliving."

Conclusion

When Jesus addressed Peter with the question, "Do you love me?" He followed Peter's declaration with the words, "Feed my sheep." In other words, if you love, do something about it! Thanksgiving must not be mere words. The Pharisee started his prayer with the words, "God, I thank thee," but followed those words with a bigoted, self-centered eulogy about his own self-righteousness. How does God know we love him? By our doing something about it. This begins with receiving his blessed Son as our Savior.

SUNDAY EVENING, NOVEMBER 20

Title: Ask, Seek, and Knock

Text: "Ask, and it shall be given you; seek, and ye shall find; knock, and it shall be opened unto you" **(Matt. 7:7)**.

Scripture Reading: Matthew 7:7–11

Introduction

Our Lord is still discussing the critical spirit in his Sermon on the Mount. He deplores the censorious spirit that is so akin to the lost and the unredeemed. After he tells us why we should not be critical, he indicates the harm the critical spirit causes outside the church.

How can one maintain a Christlike attitude at all times? Someone has said, "If Christians would pray as much as they grumble, they wouldn't have anything to grumble about." Our Lord inserts a discussion of prayer in this section of the Sermon on the Mount as though to say, "If you want to conquer the critical spirit, you must pray."

I. What is prayer?

A. *What it is not.*

1. Prayer is not a speech to God. One man, praying at a political rally, reminded God that Columbus discovered America in 1492.
2. Prayer is not a speech to man. Many preachers preach a sermon in their prayers as though to say, "I don't have the nerve to say this face-to-face, but I will say it to you through God."
3. Prayer is not necessarily the repetition of certain words. Even when one quotes the Lord's Prayer, he may not be praying.
4. Prayer is not a substitute for work. Some believe that the more religious one is, the more he will pray and the less he will do. Our Lord retreated to prayer on several occasions, but he returned from his place of prayer to a world of service.

B. *Some definitions.* The following are definitions of prayer: "Breathing the breath of God"; "The dove returning home"; "The flight of one alone to the only One"; "The soul's sincere desire—uttered or unuttered"; "Need finding a voice"; "Embarrassment seeking relief"; "Friend in search of a Friend"; "Reaching out in the darkness."

A poet described prayer like this:

> *Prayer is the simplest form of speech*
> *That infant lips can try;*
> *Prayer is the sublimest strains that reach*
> *The majesty on high.*

Phillips Brooks once said, "Prayer, in its simplest definition, is merely a wish turned God-ward."

II. What prayer involves.

The elements of true prayer involve the following:

A. *Repentance of sin.* Before we pray for others, we must ask God's forgiveness of our own sin. The psalmist said, "If I regard iniquity in my heart, the LORD will not hear me" (Ps. 66:18).

B. *Thanksgiving.* True prayer involves a thankful spirit.

C. *Supplication.* We ask God to supply our personal needs. Someone has said, "Prayer is not a method of using God; rather, it is a means of reporting for duty to God."

"Be careful for nothing; but in everything by prayer and supplication with thanksgiving let your requests be made known unto God" (Phil. 4:6).

D. *Persistence.* Our Lord spoke of persistence in prayer. On one occasion he advocated being as persistent as a man who kept coming to his neighbor's door late at night and knocking (Luke 11:8).

All three of these verbs—"Ask," "seek," and "knock"—are in the present imperative mood, indicating that we must keep on asking, seeking, and knocking.

III. Hindrances to prayer.

    A. *Unconfessed sin (Ps. 139:23–24; Isa. 59:1–2).*
    B. *The unforgiving spirit (Matt. 6:14–15; Mark 11:25).*
    C. *Unbelief (James 1:5–7).*
    D. *Selfishness (James 4:3).*
    E. *Unsolved family problems (1 Peter 3:7).*

Conclusion

Robert G. Lee told the story of a young man who called his parents to the side of his bed just before he died.

"Father," he said, "I am going to die. I heard the doctor say so, and you know it and I know it. I want you to promise me one thing."

The young man continued his request: "When I die, do not take me to the cemetery to bury me. Bury me right by the lot gate where you keep the mules. Every day—early in the morning when you go after the mules, back in and out at noon, back in that night after the day's work—I want you to stop by my grave and say out loud: 'There lies a boy who died and went to hell and never heard his father pray.'"

WEDNESDAY EVENING, NOVEMBER 23

Title: A Miracle of God's Grace

Text: "But by the grace of God I am what I am: and his grace which was bestowed upon me was not in vain; but I laboured more abundantly than they all: yet not I, but the grace of God which was with me" (**1 Cor. 15:10**).

Scripture Reading: 1 Corinthians 15:1–10

Introduction

Repeatedly the apostle Paul expressed praise and gratitude to God for the great mercy that had been extended to him. God had interrupted his mad career of persecution with an offer of grace, forgiveness, and guidance.

Paul responded with an attitude of gratitude and surrender to the divine initiative. As time went by, he gave God all of the credit for being responsible for the miracle that had taken place in his life.

In our text Paul thanks God for his grace. God's grace is something more than one of his characteristics. It is his love, mercy, and kindness all wrapped up in one word. God's grace is God in action toward those who do not deserve his grace and mercy.

I. By the grace of God, Paul was not what he had once been.

    A. *He had been a legalistic Pharisee who depended much on and perhaps even boasted of his achievements at the point of keeping the law of God.*
    B. *He had been a cruel persecutor of the church.*

II. By the grace of God, Paul was what he did not deserve to be.

Man finds it exceedingly difficult to accept and to understand the grace of God. Man is naturally proud and independent and wants to depend on his own merit and achievement. Paul, by the grace of God, had experienced a miraculous change.

A. *His sins had been forgiven.*
B. *His heart had been changed.*
C. *The gift of sonship had been bestowed upon him.*
D. *The Spirit of God had come to dwell in his heart.*

III. By the grace of God, Paul was what he never expected to be.

A. *Paul did not expect to become converted to the cause that he was persecuting.*
B. *Paul never dreamed that he would one day become the great missionary apostle, a cosmopolitan and international messenger of the gospel.*
C. *Paul never dreamed that he would be used by the Holy Spirit as the author of Holy Scripture.*

IV. What God by his grace did for Paul, he can do for us.

A. *Paul was a demonstration of the length, breadth, height, and depth of God's grace to humans (1 Tim. 1:16).*
B. *God's grace had prepared him for life in the here and now.*
C. *God's grace had prepared him for life beyond.*

God wants to demonstrate his grace, mercy, love, and power in the life of each of us.

Conclusion

John Newton said, "I am not what I ought to be; I am not what I wish to be; I am not what I hope to be; but by the grace of God, I am not what I was once." God has a wonderful plan for the life of each of us. By his grace God's dream for us can become a reality if we will cooperate with him and work with his grace, which is at work in our hearts.

SUNDAY MORNING, NOVEMBER 27

Title: "His Name . . . Wonderful"

Text: "For unto us a child is born, unto us a son is given: and the government shall be upon his shoulder: and his name shall be called Wonderful, Counsellor, The mighty God, The everlasting Father, The Prince of Peace" **(Isa. 9:6)**.

Scripture Reading: Psalm 8

Hymns: "All Hail the Power," Perronet

         "Blessed Be the Name," Clark

         "Fairest Lord Jesus," Unknown

Offertory Prayer: Our Father in heaven, you have provided all things necessary for our eternal good. As we receive these bounties at your hand, make us mindful of our stewardship of life and possessions. We bring to you our offerings now. Accept them and empower them to bless people everywhere. In Jesus' name. Amen.

Introduction

Isaiah lived in perilous and troubled times. All about him there were gathering clouds of darkness. Within a generation his beloved nation would be taken into captivity. The land would lie idle and wasted. The cities would be torn down and their gates burned with fire. The vineyards would be uprooted and the olive groves hewn down. Only a remnant of the old and weak would be left in the land.

But far away Isaiah saw a bright spot. In the midst of all the prophecy of destruction, the Lord said, "The people that walked in darkness have seen a great light: they that dwell in the land of the shadow of death, upon them hath the light shined" (Isa. 9:2). What was the light that would shine in the darkness? Verse 6 gives the answer: "For unto us a child is born, unto us a Son is given: and the government shall be upon his shoulder: and his name shall be called Wonderful, Counsellor, The mighty God, The everlasting Father, The Prince of Peace." The light that was to be sent was the Bethlehem star, the manger child, the Christ of that first Christmas. John says it this way: "[Jesus] was the true Light, which lighteth every man that cometh into the world" (John 1:9).

The world needs this bright Star. We need the Christ of the first Christmas to shine again in our darkness. His name is Wonderful.

I. The meaning of names.

There are many people in this world who are called by names that do not fit them. Alfred means "justice," but I have known some Alfreds who used a short stick for measure and pressed their thumbs on the scale. Allen means "harmony," but I meet Allens who disrupt every fellowship they join. Paula means "little and demure," but I have seen some Paulas who were large, loud-mouthed women. Nancy means "graceful," but there are Nancys walking about with drooping shoulders and slovenly steps. Not all persons are true to their names. Many are called by titles their lives do not earn. Not so Jesus! He is wonderful! God has given him that name because it describes him.

II. The meaning of his name—Wonderful.

The Old Testament word for "wonderful" is *pele*. The lexicon bears two or three translations of this word. One is "miraculous"; and another possible translation is "lovely." It may also have a cognate meaning, "distinguished" or "apart from the rest." But we will be content to keep to the old translation of "wonderful." The word carries with it the meaning of awe, astonishment, and reverence. It is used in Isaiah's prophecy as a proper name; hence it means "The Wonderful One." Now let's follow this word in the life of our Lord.

A. *His wonderful birth.* The word of our text is first used in the New Testament in Luke 2:18: "and all they that heard it *marvelled* at those things which were told them by the shepherds." Wonderment was the first emotion expressed by mortals when they saw the infant Jesus. Then again in Luke 2:33: "Joseph and his mother *wondered* at those things which were spoken of him" (emphasis added). There is a mystery in what happened at Bethlehem. One of the great mysteries of God is the incarnation. What is this we see at the manger? A world of wonders! The Eternal of the Ages becomes an infant of days. God the Almighty is cradled at a woman's breast. The very God becomes a man—an infant! He is the child of a day yet the monarch of eternity. See God in Him! Omnipotence in a tiny baby's hands. Omniscience in a baby's eye. The voice of Jehovah God in a baby's cry. Wonderful is Jesus' birth!

B. *His wonderful life.* Now follow the word of my text further. Luke 5:26 says, "They were all amazed, and glorified God, and were filled with fear, saying, We have seen strange things today." What had happened? The night before, the disciples had fished and caught nothing. Then at morning light Jesus commanded them to let down their nets for a catch. When they obeyed, the nets were filled with fish! Later that day Jesus healed a leper, and at nightfall he made a paralytic whole. No wonder these men said they had seen strange and wonderful things!

1. Wonderful miracles. Wonderful were the miracles of the Master! Mark 6 records the voyage of Jesus and his disciples across the sea. A sudden storm caught them, and their little vessel was in danger of sinking. Jesus stood and rebuked the wind and the waves. Then verse 51 says, "The wind ceased: and they were sore amazed in themselves beyond measure, and *wondered*" (emphasis added). It is he of whom Isaiah said, "His name shall be called Wonderful."

2. Wonderful teachings. Luke 4:22 says, "[They] all bare him witness, and *wondered* at the gracious words" (emphasis added). And again in John 7:15: "The Jews were *amazed* and asked, 'How did this man get such learning without having studied?'" (NIV, emphasis added). You and I are struck with like amazement. After reading the Sermon on the Mount, we shake our heads in wonderment, for "he taught them as one having authority, and not as the scribes" (Matt. 7:29). He made a lily speak of God's beauty. He let a sparrow teach God's love and care. He let a farmer sowing seed teach how the hearts of people receive the gospel. He let a shepherd's search for one lost sheep represent God's search for one lost man. He took common bread and made it signify the uncommon, life-giving Word of God. Wonderful teachings!

C. *His wonderful death.* I mean no sacrilege to call Jesus' death wonderful. The apostle Paul also speaks of glorying in the cross of Christ. In holy amazement, come with me to Pilate's court. To satisfy the blood thirst of the mob, Pilate had Christ scourged. Bloodied and thorn-crowned,

342

Jesus stood again before Pilate. When Jesus was questioned, the Scripture says, "Jesus made no reply, not even to a single charge—to the great amazement of the governor" (Matt. 27:14 NIV). Pilate was not alone is his wonderment. Jesus' atoning death is the riddle without answer. He was manifest in the flesh and crucified among men. The first is hard enough to think of; but that he was crucified at the hands of sinful men is beyond comprehension. On that cross he pardoned, paid the penalty of, and cleansed sinners.

D. *His wonderful resurrection.* I will not leave you at Calvary. On the third day after Jesus' crucifixion, some of Jesus' female followers came to the tomb. They were prepared to anoint a dead body; they were not prepared for what they saw and heard. They saw an empty tomb. They heard the angel say, "He is not here ... he is risen." After the women reported these strange things to the disciples, two of the men ran to the graveyard. When Peter arrived at the tomb, "stooping down, he beheld the linen clothes laid by themselves, and departed, *wondering* in himself at that which was come to pass" (Luke 24:12). Poor Peter! It is all too amazing—too wonderful! An empty tomb!

Conclusion

The whole world joins the apostle in wonderment. Death we know well enough, but what is this about resurrection? Dare we hope for life beyond the grave? In triumph the apostle Paul says, "Now is Christ risen from the dead, and become the firstfruits of them that slept" (1 Cor. 15:20). Wonderful! Death without a victory. The grave without a victim. Who is this who has become the firstfruits of immortality? Who has mocked corruption? Who has brought life and immortality to light? He of whom the prophet Isaiah spoke twenty-seven centuries ago: "His name shall be called *Wonderful.*"

Is he wonderful to you? Yes, my Jesus, yes!

SUNDAY EVENING, NOVEMBER 27

Title: The Golden Rule

Text: "Therefore all things whatsoever ye would that men should do to you, do ye even so to them: for this is the law and the prophets" **(Matt. 7:12).**

Scripture Reading: Ephesians 4:25–32

Introduction

The Christian's wisdom for exercising moral discrimination while avoiding censorious judgment can be acquired by persistent prayer (Matt. 7:7–11). As he prays for such wisdom, he is assured that God will give him that which he needs. Even though the Christian may not be fully aware of his needs at this point, he can trust God, as a child trusts his father, to supply the need. The relationship of

Christian conduct to the treatment of others is summarized in the Golden Rule (Matt. 7:12).

The Golden Rule has been called "the Everest of ethics," "the capstone of theology," and "the kernel of Christian conduct." In 1750 John Wesley said that the Golden Rule is the "royal law, that golden rule of mercy as well as justice, which even the heathen emperor caused to be written over the gate of his palace."

J. Edgar Hoover, former FBI director, said in an Independence Day speech, "The American ideal has its roots in religion. Without religious inspiration, the American ideal would die. It is the American precept that people shall live as equals under a government of law, which is embodied in the greatest of all laws: 'Whatsoever ye would that men....'"

I. The Golden Rule is different.

A. *It is different from any Jewish writing before or since Jesus.* Hillel and Shammai, the rabbis of the two famous Jewish schools of religion, presented no parallels to the Golden Rule. A young heathen came to each saying, "I will accept your religion if you teach me the whole Law while I am standing on one leg."

Shammai drove him off with a ruler. Hillel said, "What is hateful to yourself, do to no other."

Tobit taught his son all that was necessary in one command: "What thou thyself hatest, to no man do" (Tobit 4:16).

B. *The Golden Rule is different from any rule of its kind found in pagan religions.*

When Tsze-Kung asked Confucius, "Is there one word that may serve as a rule of practice for one's life?" Confucius replied, "What you do not want done to yourself, do not do to others."

These words recur in a Buddhist hymnal: "Kill not nor cause to kill."

C. *The Greeks and the Romans had similar rules, but none like the Golden Rule.*

Socrates said, "What stirs your anger when done to you by others, that do not to others."

Epictetus condemned slavery with "What you avoid suffering yourself, seek not to inflict upon others."

The Stoics said, "What you do not wish to be done to you, do not do to anyone else."

Philo said, "One must not himself do what he hates to have done to him."

D. *All similar teachings are passive, while the Golden Rule is active.* You can keep the rules of Judaism, Confucius, Buddha, the Romans, and the Greeks by merely being passive. But Jesus demands action.

Ultimately, the Christian life is where the action is. Certainly we must not hurt our fellow humans. But what have we given to them? Let's not kill our fellow humans. But what have we done to help them live? The Golden Rule is not passively indifferent. It is actively concerned!

E. *The rules of men are negative, while the Golden Rule is positive.* Christians are

344

not merely negatively good. They are also positively good for something and good for someone. Others may say, "Don't do this," but the Golden Rule says, "Do this."

Edwin M. Stanton once described Abraham Lincoln as a "great ignoramus from Illinois, a baboon who doesn't have brains enough to be the President." But Lincoln was not vindictive. He did not remove Stanton from the office of Secretary of War, for he looked beyond Stanton's faults and saw his true abilities. Eventually Stanton did the same for Lincoln. It was Stanton who wrote the epitaph that appears on Lincoln's tomb: "Now he belongs to the ages."

II. The Golden Rule is difficult.

When an Indian chief first heard the Golden Rule from the lips of a missionary, he said, "It is impossible. If the Great Spirit who made man would give him a new heart, he might do as you say."

A. *The Golden Rule demands a new birth.* One cannot expect to live by the Golden Rule until he has been born again (1 Cor. 2:14).

B. *Many people say, "My religion is living by the Golden Rule."* These people do not realize what they are really saying. The motivation for living by the Golden Rule comes from the inner person through the new birth. One is not saved by keeping the Golden Rule, because no one keeps it perfectly. We are saved by God's grace through our faith in Jesus Christ (Eph. 2:8–9).

III. The Golden Rule is dynamic.

A. *There is power in the Golden Rule to change one's home.* When we can overlook each other's faults and learn to forgive each other's failures, our homes will be much happier. Every person wants to be liked and loved by others. Will Rogers was fond of saying, "I never met a man I didn't like." And Will Rogers was one of the best-liked men in history.

B. *There is power in the Golden Rule to change society.* Years ago Billy Graham said concerning the racial crisis in America, "In my opinion, the racial tension and misunderstanding can only be resolved by exercising the Golden Rule, and the Golden Rule can only be practiced when its Author lives in our hearts."

C. *There is power in the Golden Rule to change the ministry of the church.* If every member of a local church really practiced the Golden Rule in stewardship, witnessing, and dedication, it would change the complexion of the church's ministry.

D. *There is power in the Golden Rule to change the eternal destiny of lost people.* If you were lost and bound for hell, wouldn't you want someone to tell you about Jesus Christ? The Golden Rule will not let us keep silent. Because we live by the Golden Rule, we cannot pass up opportunities to share our faith in Jesus Christ.

Conclusion

The editor of an Illinois newspaper wrote: "The Golden Rule is old, but it is as good as ever. It hasn't been used often enough to result in any appreciable wear." The version of the Golden Rule from the Talmud says, "Love thy neighbor; *he* is thyself."

WEDNESDAY EVENING, NOVEMBER 30

Title: O Come, Let Us Worship

Text: "O come, let us worship and bow down: let us kneel before the LORD our maker" **(Ps. 95:6)**.

Scripture Reading: Psalm 95

Introduction

Matthew reports in his gospel that the magi followed the gleam of the star with exceeding great joy. "And when they were come into the house, they saw the young child with Mary his mother, and fell down, and worshipped him: and when they had opened their treasures, they presented unto him gifts; gold, and frankincense, and myrrh" (Matt. 2:11). If we would properly enter into the true spirit of Christmas, we could well afford to follow the pattern set by the wise men who worshiped the Christ child.

I. O come, let us worship that we may discover who rules our world.

The psalmist says, "For he is our God; and we are the people of his pasture" (Ps. 95:7).

    A. *Bowing down and worshiping before the throne of the Lord of Lords can dispel our fear and replace it with a great faith.*

    B. *To see the Lord on the throne, as Isaiah did, is to find courage and confidence for the living of life during difficult days (Isa. 6:3).* If we do not worship the Christ child who later became the Lord of Lords, we will have a tendency to sentimentalize Christmas without recognizing the significance of the coming of the Son of God to dwell with humans.

II. O come, let us worship that we might be reminded that we are made in the image of God.

    A. *People are more than just intelligent animals.* They are the crown of God's creative activity. They are made in the image and likeness of God. They are the only part of the creation that can have fellowship with the Creator. If we neglect worship, we deny our uniqueness as the crowning act of God's creative activity.

    B. *People were not made to live by bread alone.* We feed our souls on ashes when we neglect to feed our souls on the Bread of Life in continuous experiences of worship.

III. O come, let us worship that we might be delivered from the tyranny of material things.

A. *The world is too much with us.* We are constantly tempted to live as if we are creatures of earth alone.

B. *Many worship material things as gods.* The competitive system has a tendency to measure success only in terms of a large cash balance at the end of the year. The natural acquisitive instinct of people always sees greater goals to reach. Material values can usurp the place that belongs only to God unless one repeatedly goes into the presence of God to maintain a proper balance between material and spiritual values.

IV. O come, let us worship that we might find strength for the responsibilities of life.

"He giveth power to the faint; and to them that have no might he increaseth strength. Even the youths shall faint and be weary, and the young men shall utterly fall: But they that wait upon the LORD shall renew their strength; they shall mount up with wings as eagles; they shall run, and not be weary; and they shall walk, and not faint" (Isa. 40:29–31).

Conclusion

The wise men worshiped the Christ because of the uniqueness of his person and because of the mysterious circumstances surrounding his birth. We will be exceedingly wise if we give ourselves to worship, because by so doing we can experience life as God meant for it to be and as our heart hungers for it to be.

DECEMBER

■ **Sunday Mornings**

Continue the series "The Meaning of His Name" throughout the Christmas season.

■ **Sunday Evenings**

Conclude the series on the Sermon on the Mount.

■ **Wednesday Evenings**

Continue the devotional series to create a reverent and worshipful observance of the Christmas season.

SUNDAY MORNING, DECEMBER 4

Title: "His Name . . . Counsellor"

Text: "For unto us a child is born, unto us a son is given: and the government shall be upon his shoulder: and his name shall be called Wonderful, Counsellor, The mighty God, The everlasting Father, The Prince of Peace" (**Isa. 9:6**).

Scripture Reading: Psalm 139

Hymns: "Guide Me, O Thou Great Jehovah," Williams

         "He Leadeth Me," Gilmore

         "O God, Our Help in Ages Past," Watts

Offertory Prayer: Our Father, we bring to you a living sacrifice in our offerings today. We have expended life in the earning of this money. The gift represents us. May it also represent a measure of our love for you and your kingdom. In Jesus' name. Amen.

Introduction

Names are important. They often reveal something of a person's nature and character. This is true of the names given to Jesus by the prophet Isaiah. Nearly eight hundred years before Christ was born, Isaiah called him "Wonderful, Counsellor, The mighty God, The everlasting Father, The Prince of Peace." These names for our Lord are worthy of our respectful study and careful consideration. Now consider Jesus as Counselor.

I. His name ". . . Counsellor."

Some interpreters prefer to link the first two names of the text together and make the verse read, "His name shall be called Wonderful Counsellor." I do not object to this. He is that. The Hebrew word for "counselor" is *yaats*, and it means to give counsel, to advise, to direct, or to guide. By a counselor our world fell into sin and disobedience. Satan advised Eve in deceit and lies. He questioned God's word: "Yea, hath God said? . . . Ye shall not surely die: For God doth know that in the day ye eat thereof, then your eyes will be opened, and ye shall be as gods, knowing good and evil" (Gen. 3:1, 4–5). So Satan, masked in the beauty of the beast, advised our first mother to disobey the command of God. This was counseling to sin. By an evil counselor sin came into our world. Is it not, then, fitting that by a righteous counselor our world should be restored? But restoration takes more than good advice. It is easy enough to counsel mischief, but how difficult it is to counsel wisely! It took a divine Counselor to restore order to obedience, to sweep away evil, to forgive sin. Who could be this kind of counselor? Our Lord Jesus—he is the Wonderful Counselor.

II. Wonderful Counselor in the past.

    A. *Before the beginning.* Before the worlds were brought into existence, Christ was Counselor with the Father. Before the worlds were fashioned, a divine council was held in the chambers of heaven. Why was this heavenly conclave held? Not for deficiency of knowledge. God is omniscient; he has all wisdom and knowledge. Nor did God need a season for deliberation. People may take weeks or even months to make up their minds, but not so God. Nor was the council held for satisfaction of agreement. A man seeks the counsel and advice of his fellow men in order to hear them say, "Yes, I think you are on the right track. Go ahead." But God needs no such confirmation for his edicts. Why, then, was the heavenly council held? To show the unity and work of the Godhead. The divine Trinity of Father, Son, and Holy Spirit is one. God did not say, "I will make man," but he did say, "Let *us* make man."

    B. *In creation.* Christ was Counselor with the Father and Holy Spirit in matters of creation. John 1:3 says, "All things were made by him [Christ, the Incarnate Word]; and without him was not anything made that was made." And again in Hebrews 1:10: "Thou, Lord, in the beginning hast laid the foundation of the earth; and the heavens are the works of thine hands." Christ was Counselor with the Father when the mountains were weighed, when the limits were fixed for the seas, and when the sun was called forth out of its chamber in the east. By sovereign counsel the stars were hung in space by their invisible threads. All things, small and great, were determined together in heavenly counsel, and Christ was there.

III. Wonderful Counselor in the present.

    A. *In providence.* Jesus is Counselor in matters of providence. God does not act toward the world as a man who winds a watch and then sets it aside to run down. He does not leave the world to itself. We may still sing with truth, "This is my Father's world."

How strange the providences of God may seem to us! Our path often looks like the zigzag mark of a cattle trail across a field. First it goes onward, then backward, then to the right and then to the left. So must the providential hand of God have seemed to Jacob. His beloved son Joseph was taken from him and reported dead. Instead, Joseph had been sold as a slave to Potiphar in Egypt. How could this be God's will? Then came a time of great drought. The pastures dried up and the waters ran dry. Could this be God's will? On an errand to purchase grain in Egypt, Jacob's sons were accused of stealing and his "baby boy" Benjamin was held for ransom. Could this be of God? What Jacob did not know was that God was preparing in Egypt a secure place for his house. There his children would grow and flourish. There they would become a great nation, and after four centuries they would be delivered to return to their homeland again. Jacob cried, "All things work together against me." But the Bible says, "All things work together for good to them that love God" (Rom. 8:28).

Let us learn to leave the mysteries of providence in the hand of our Wonderful Counselor. He will ordain for us only that which is for our good. The writer to the Hebrews declares, "He is able also to save them to the uttermost that come unto God by him, seeing he ever liveth to make intercession for them" (7:25). The last book of the Bible pictures Satan as the accuser of the brethren — still the counselor of lie and deceit. But fear not, Jesus, our Counselor, is intercessor for us. He is our Moses who will safely guide us through the wilderness to the Promised Land.

B. *In grace.* Zechariah says in a messianic passage, "And the counsel of peace shall be between them" (Zech. 6:13). By what agreement did the Trinity decide humankind's salvation? God the Father would satisfy sin by the gift of his Son. Christ would give his life as a ransom. The Holy Spirit would call and convict the hearts of people on the basis of Christ's sacrifice. It was agreed that salvation would be the gift of God to all who would come to Christ in repentance and faith. The cross was no accident in history. It was agreed upon by divine counsel before the worlds were brought forth. The apostle Peter wrote: "Ye were not redeemed with corruptible things, as silver and gold.... But with the precious blood of Christ, as of a lamb without blemish and without spot: Who verily was foreordained before the foundation of the world" (1 Peter 1:18–20). Have you accepted this heavenly counseled grace to the saving of your soul? To you, then, he is the Wonderful Counselor.

C. *In life.* Is Christ your Guide? None ever sought his advice in vain. None ever repented of following his counsel. Today in homes everywhere his living presence is felt. What he was in the days of his flesh he is now. Was he compassionate? Was he kind? Was he the friend of sinners? Did he love children? Was he forgiving? So today!

350

Conclusion

Who among us feels the need of God? Who hungers after righteousness? Who desires to drink of the Living Water? Come, then, to him of whom the prophet said, "His name shall be called Wonderful, Counsellor."

SUNDAY EVENING, DECEMBER 4

Title: Two Gates and Two Roadways

Text: "Enter ye in at the strait gate: for wide is the gate, and broad is the way, that leadeth to destruction, and many there be which go in thereat: Because strait is the gate, and narrow is the way, which leadeth unto life, and few there be that find it" (**Matt. 7:13–14**).

Scripture Reading: Psalm 1

Introduction

Jesus was long on giving invitations. In fact, the entire section of the Sermon on the Mount in Matthew 7:13–27 constitutes an invitation. Jesus closes the Sermon on the Mount with a striking comparison between four sets of pairs.

1. There is a pair of gates leading to a pair of roadways. The narrow gate of self-denial leads to the narrow way of the Christian life, and the broad gate of self-indulgence leads to the broad way of hell.
2. There is a pair of trees producing two kinds of fruit. Self-deception is the fruit of false prophets, and assurance in Christ is the fruit of the true prophets.
3. There is a pair of men. One is wise, and one is foolish.
4. There is a pair of houses. One is built on the rock, and one is built on the sand.

I. Jesus Christ was narrow.

A. *He lived in a narrow area.* The area of Palestine is a long, narrow country no larger than the state of Connecticut. Jesus never traveled more than a hundred miles from the place of his birth.
B. *He had a narrow goal in life — the cross.* Satan tempted him to bypass the cross. People tried to draw his attention away from the narrow path that led to the cross.

II. Jesus demands narrowness.

A. *To be broad-minded is the order of the day.* The "in" crowd talks of "casual sex," "no-fault divorce," "crack," and the "new age."
B. *Self-indulgence is the order of the day.* No one likes to talk about self-denial. We often joke about the person who was so narrow-minded that a flea could sit on his nose and kick out both eyes. Yet the greatest Man who ever

351

walked this earth was quite narrow-minded and taught that the real secret of enjoying life is not self-indulgence but self-denial.

C. *Entrance into the Christian life is narrow.* Cities in Jesus' day were off the beaten path. One entered ancient cities by a gate that led to a narrow passageway before going into the city. Jesus compares entrance into the kingdom of God to entrance into a city gate. This gate lets one in at a time. We do not come to Christ as families, couples, or groups. We come to Jesus Christ as individuals in a personal encounter.

D. *When we come to Christ, we must leave some things behind.* As one enters the narrow gate of the Christian life, he cannot carry excess baggage. Jesus challenged one man to bid his company farewell and follow him without compromise. He said to another, "Let the dead bury the dead. Come and follow me." He challenged James and John to leave their ship and their father and follow him. "Follow me, and I will make you fishers of men," he said to Peter and Andrew.

E. *The way of the Christian life is narrow.* The gate was narrow and the way that led into the city was also narrow. It is a radical experience to follow Jesus Christ. The Christian is challenged to take up his cross daily and follow Christ. He is engaged in a continual battle with the Devil, and he must put on the whole armor of God daily to withstand (Eph. 6:12–19).

The great violinist Fritz Kreisler once said, "Narrow is the road that leads to the life of a violinist. Hour after hour, day after day, and week after week, for years, I lived with my violin. There were so many things that I wanted to do that I had to leave undone; there were so many places I wanted to go that I had to miss if I was to master the violin. The road that I traveled was a narrow road and the way was hard." Just as Kreisler found fulfillment in his self-denial, the Christian finds fulfillment in life by denying himself and taking up the cross of Christ daily.

III. Jesus invites all to enter the narrow way.

Jesus calls us not to admire or consider him but to follow him. He calls us not to look at the narrow gate and the narrow way but to enter.

A. *Recognize your need of Christ.* Jesus opened the blind eyes of Bartimaeus because he recognized his need. He gave the water of life to the Samaritan woman when she said, "Give me this water, that I thirst not." He lifted Simon Peter from the waters of the Sea of Galilee when he cried, "Lord, save me."

The first step toward entering the narrow gate of the Christian life is that of recognizing your need of Christ (Rom. 3:23).

B. *Understand the cross.* No one fully understands the cross. Theologians have argued for generations about the various theories of the atonement. But if one opens his heart to an understanding of the cross, he has taken another step toward the narrow gate.

A young reporter in Scotland was asked what Billy Graham was preaching at a crusade in Glasgow. When he tried to explain the gospel, he said, "You see, it's this way—Christ died for me; Christ died for my sins and rose again." When he said this, he suddenly realized that he was speaking the truth and trusted Christ as his own personal Savior.

C. *Count the cost.* Before one ventures into the narrow gate of salvation, he should count the cost and be sure that he can pay that price (Luke 14:28).

D. *Take that definite step.* Every person is intellect, emotion, and will. We can accept Christ intellectually and emotionally, but we are not saved until we surrender our will to Jesus Christ (Matt. 6:33).

E. *Allow God to change your life.* When one has taken that definite step of commitment, he must allow God to change his life. Then he commits his life to walk the narrow road of self-denial instead of the broad road of self-indulgence.

Conclusion

In 1967 the driving laws changed in Sweden. At five o'clock one September morning, drivers switched from driving on the left to the right side of the street.

Some radical changes took place for the two million cars and the thousands of bicycles and motorcycles in Sweden. More than a quarter million traffic signs on sixty thousand miles of roads had to be changed. Ramps designed for low-speed exits from superhighways became high-speed entrance ramps, and the entrance ramps became exit ramps. Doors on buses and trolleys that once let passengers out at the curb now let them out in the center of traffic.

Likewise, when Christ calls one to enter the narrow gate and walk the narrow road, it may be an upsetting experience to that person and to those about him.

WEDNESDAY EVENING, DECEMBER 7

Title: "Oh, That Men Would Praise the Lord"

Text: "Oh that men would praise the LORD for his goodness, and for his wonderful works to the children of men!" (**Ps. 107:8, 15, 21, 31**).

Scripture Reading: Psalm 107:1–31

Introduction

The heart of the psalmist was filled to overflowing with joy and praise. If we would properly observe this Christmas season, we must let the joy the psalmist felt fill our hearts to the extent that it loosens our tongues so that we can give voice to praises to the Lord for his wonderful works for the children of men.

I. Giving voice to praise should be very natural.

A. *We do not hesitate to voice praise for a good mother.*

B. *We do not hesitate to voice praise for a good community in which to live.*
C. *In the same natural manner, we should praise God for all of his wonderful works and gifts to us.* The greatest of these is the gift of his Son, whose birth we celebrate at this season.

II. Giving voice to praise is beneficial to us personally.

A. *Many of us have discovered that when we praise God for his wonderful works, we come to a new appreciation of what God has done.* We even discover that God has done far more than we recognized.
B. *To praise God for past blessings strengthens our faith for the facing of the future.* When we recognize how good God has been in the past, we are encouraged to believe that he will continue to be the same kind of God in the future.
C. *Giving voice to praise creates an attitude of gratitude and makes life more joyful as we face the routine duties, disappointments, and responsibilities.*

III. Giving voice to praise is most helpful to others.

A. *Our praises of the Lord make it possible for those who have no faith to recognize his goodness and to respond to him with the faith that brings the forgiveness of sin and the gift of eternal life (Rom. 10:14–17).*
B. *The divine plan for the redemption of the lost world is associated with our praising the Lord.* "Sing unto the LORD, bless his name; shew forth his salvation from day to day. Declare his glory among the heathen, his wonders among all people. For the LORD is great, and greatly to be praised: he is to be feared above all gods" (Ps. 96:2–4).
C. *If we remain silent when we should voice the praise of our Lord, we are depriving others of values more precious than gold.* Humankind's greatest need is for a genuine faith in the God who has revealed himself in the Christ child who later was crucified and then rose from death.

Conclusion

During this period of the year when many concentrate on frivolous things, let us determine to concentrate on giving praise to our Lord. Let us join with David, who said, "Every day will I bless thee; and I will praise thy name for ever and ever. Great is the LORD, and greatly to be praised; and his greatness is unsearchable. One generation shall praise thy works to another, and shall declare thy mighty acts" (Ps. 145:2–4). Let us contemplate what the results would be if each of us would respond to the challenge of the text, "Oh that men would praise the LORD for his goodness, and for his wonderful works to the children of men!"

SUNDAY MORNING, DECEMBER 11

Title: "His Name ... Mighty God"

Text: "For unto us a child is born, unto us a son is given: and the government shall be upon his shoulder: and his name shall be called Wonderful, Counsellor, The mighty God, The everlasting Father, The Prince of Peace" **(Isa. 9:6)**.

Scripture Reading: Psalm 27

Hymns: "God of Our Fathers," Roberts

"A Mighty Fortress Is Our God," Luther

"Come, Thou Almighty King," Anonymous

Offertory Prayer: Our Father, we pray, "Thy Kingdom come, thy will be done, on earth as it is in heaven." Now help us to make our prayers answered as we bring our offerings to your altar. We thank you that by this dedication we can have a share in the extension of your kingdom around the world. In Jesus' name. Amen.

Introduction

Isaiah the prophet, nearly eight hundred years before the birth of Christ, declared by some divine theophany the names of our Lord. He is called "Wonderful, Counsellor, The mighty God, The everlasting Father, The Prince of Peace." These names contain revealing characteristics of the Lord. Though certainly not comprehending all that these titles mean, Isaiah recognized the Messiah as "The mighty God."

I. Meaning of the name—"Mighty God."

The words "mighty God" are translated by others as "the Illustrious One" or "the Shining One." But the Hebrew word for God is *El* and has as its root meaning "strength." When the word is a proper name, it is translated "the Strong One." The other word of the title is *gibbor* and also means strength or might. When the two words are put together, they mean "The Mighty Strong One." In the prophecy of Isaiah, the word *El* refers to deity in the absolute sense. It is never used of men but only of divinity. It is never used metaphorically. So the Hebrew title *Gibbor El* means "The Mighty God."

II. Christ is the mighty God.

The text says, "Unto us a child is born, unto us a son is given." Jesus is the Son of God. The text also says, "His name shall be called ... Mighty God." These words declare Jesus' deity. Jesus is not only the Son of God; he is God himself. What the Messiah came to do could be done by none but God himself. Only God can redeem people from his sin; only God can vanquish death; only God can triumph over Satan; and none but God can make atonement. In this work of reconciliation, the prophets recognized the Messiah as more than a man. He must

355

be also partaker of the divine nature; he must be God. The angel said to Joseph of the yet unborn Jesus, "Call his name Emmanuel, which being interpreted is, God with us" (Matt. 1:23). The prophets did not comprehend our doctrine of the Trinity, yet they believed that some day God would robe himself in human flesh and enter into humankind's world. Jesus is this God-in-the-flesh. He is the mighty God.

A. *Some deny his deity.* They say he is not the mighty God. He is a good man but not the God-man. The New Testament has strong words of condemnation about the person who denies our Lord is very God. "Who is the liar? It is the man who denies that Jesus is the Christ. Such a man is the antichrist—he denies the Father and the Son. No one who denies the Son has the Father; whoever acknowledges the Son has the Father also" (1 John 2:22–23 NIV).

If Jesus is not the mighty God, then we all are idolaters. We worship him who is not God. The first command of the Decalogue is "Thou shalt have no other Gods before me." If we worship a Christ who is not God, we sin.

If Christ is not the mighty God, he was a blasphemer and was worthy of death. He claimed to be God. He said, "He that hath seen me hath seen the Father.... I am in the Father, and the Father in me" (John 14:9–10).

Paul declares in 1 Corinthians 15:12–20 that, if Christ is not the mighty God, then all of our preaching is in vain and our faith is also in vain. If Christ is not the mighty God, then they who are asleep in Christ have perished. Their hope of glory in eternal life is so much grasping after straw! But it is true—Christ is God! He is coequal and coeternal with the Father.

B. *The Bible declares his deity.*

1. Jesus claimed it for himself. "And the high priest answered and said unto him, I adjure thee by the living God, that thou tell us whether thou be the Christ, the Son of God. Jesus saith unto him, Thou hast said: ... Hereafter shall ye see the Son of man sitting on the right hand of power, and coming in the clouds of heaven." The high priest understood that Jesus claimed deity because at these words he tore his clothes and said, "He hath spoken blasphemy" (Matt. 26:63–65).

2. John the Baptist thought Jesus was God. He cried out, "Prepare ye the way of the Lord," and then pointing to Jesus, he said, "Behold the Lamb of God, which taketh away the sin of the world" (John 1:29).

3. John the apostle believed Jesus was God. He begins his gospel thus: "In the beginning was the Word, and the Word was with God, and the Word was God" and "The Word was made flesh, and dwelt among us" (John 1:1, 14). The absence of the article before the second use of "God" (*theos*) in the Greek of verse 1 shows that "God" is the predicate noun and precedes the verb "was" for emphasis. This absence of an article does not, however—as some have argued—indicate that "the Word was *a* God." To the Jewish ear, this would have been abominable. In verse 18 of this same chapter, John writes, "The only begotten Son,

which is in the bosom of the Father, he hath declared him." These words establish beyond any question the deity of Christ.

4. Peter believed Jesus was God. He so declared him on the road to Philippi: "Thou art the Christ" (Matt. 16:16).

5. The apostle Paul believed Jesus was God. In Romans 9:5 he says, "Of whom as concerning the flesh Christ came, who is over all, God blessed for ever." In Colossians 2:9, "For in him dwelleth all the fulness of the Godhead bodily." And in Philippians 2:6, Christ was "in the form of God." The Greek word translated "form" is *morphe*. It means the sum of those qualities that make a thing precisely what it is. How would you describe the "form" of a spoon? It is metal, but so is a shovel. It has a handle, but so has the shovel. "Form" means more than size and shape. It means the genesis of being, the purpose of being, and of the same. Christ is more than "like" God; he is precisely and specifically God. The Bible presses its point—Jesus is the mighty God.

C. *History proclaims Jesus as the mighty God.* How else will you explain his mark on history? Nearly twenty centuries ago he was born contrary to all the laws of human reproduction. He lived in poverty and was reared in obscurity. As an infant he was exiled to Egypt to escape the wrath of a jealous king. His hometown of Nazareth was synonymous with that which is little and least. He seldom moved outside an area no larger than our county. Yet today millions call him "Lord."

As a lad of twelve, Jesus startled the professors of his day with his knowledge. In his manhood he ruled the course of nature, walked on the surface of the sea, and stilled the tempest. The least that was said about him was, "He went about doing good." He never wrote a book, but volumes have been written to explain his contribution to civilization. He never attended an academy, yet scholars recognize his greatness. He never commanded an army, but no commander had more volunteers than he. He is the peer of history. He is the unfathomed mystery of the ages. Explain all this if he is not the mighty God.

Sam Hadley was one of the meanest men in all New York. He was a slave to drink, and he cheated, lied, and stole. He deserted friends and family. He would do anything to get enough money for one more drink. One Christmas Eve, after his wife and little girl were asleep, Sam crept into the house and stole the Christmas presents and hocked them for booze. That is how mean he was.

One day he stumbled into the Bowery Mission. There he heard how Jesus, the Son of God, came to this earth to die on the cross for sinners. That day Sam Hadley repented of his sins and gave his heart to Christ. The glory part of the story is that Sam became a changed man, a good husband and father, and a sober citizen. Later he became a director of that very mission where he met the Savior. Explain Sam Hadley if Christ is not the mighty God.

Conclusion

Some day everyone will confess that Christ is the mighty God. When he comes in the glory of the angels to judge the nations, every eye will see him. Then every knee shall bow and every tongue will confess that Jesus is Lord, to the glory of the Father. But it will be too late for some then. In that day it will be a confession out of fear on the part of those who have neglected to make him their mighty God. It will be a confession unto condemnation and not unto salvation. Do not wait for the day of vengeance.

Now is the day of salvation. Now is the acceptable time. Confess Christ today as the mighty God who came in love to be your Savior.

SUNDAY EVENING, DECEMBER 11

Title: False Prophets

Text: "Beware of false prophets, which come to you in sheep's clothing, but inwardly they are ravening wolves. Ye shall know them by their fruits. Do men gather grapes of thorns, or figs of thistles? Even so every good tree bringeth forth good fruit; but a corrupt tree bringeth forth evil fruit. A good tree cannot bring forth evil fruit, neither can a corrupt tree bring forth good fruit. Every tree that bringeth not forth good fruit is hewn down, and cast into the fire. Wherefore by their fruits ye shall know them" (**Matt. 7:15–20**).

Scripture Reading: Jude

Introduction

The Sermon on the Mount is now ended. Our Lord is giving the invitation. He bids us enter the narrow gate of salvation and walk the narrow way of the Christian life.

Salvation Army founder William Booth said, "I am of the opinion that the chief dangers which confront the coming century will be religion without the Holy Spirit, Christianity without Christ, forgiveness without repentance, salvation without regeneration, and heaven without hell!"

Booth's prophecy is becoming a reality more every day. But why? The answer is simple: there are many false prophets preaching a false religion. Carlyle once asked, "Can there be a more horrible object in existence than an eloquent man not speaking the truth?"

A man changing a road sign may cause inconvenience to drivers. One who labels poison as cough syrup may be responsible for murder. But one who alters religious truth can lead others to eternal doom!

I. Description of false prophets.

A. *Our Lord describes the false prophets as those who wear sheep's clothing—they are deceptive.* Shepherds wore sheepskins with the skin on the outside and the fleece on the inside. The sheep were accustomed to the presence of the shepherd and could spot him by his sheepskin coat. But if a wolf could wear sheepskin, this would be the height of deception.

B. *Our Lord said that false prophets are like wolves—they are destructive.* Ezekiel speaks of false prophets as "wolves ravening the prey, to shed blood, and to destroy souls" (22:27).

Zephaniah describes false prophets as "evening wolves" which "gnaw not the bones till the morrow" (3:3).

The apostle Paul said that "grievous wolves [would] enter in among you, not sparing the flock" (Acts 20:29).

II. Beware of false prophets!

A. *Beware of false prophets who preach an easy religion.* Jeremiah speaks of false prophets who speak of "Peace, peace; when there is no peace" (Jer. 6:14). The followers of false prophets are satisfied. They feel that their church is fulfilling its purpose if it is acting as a social outlet or a cultural center or as a boost to its members' businesses.

The followers of a false prophet are comfortable. The false prophet preaches for self-gain, prestige, and self-satisfaction. He finds out what will be popular and preaches it. The true prophet is never popular with everyone. His preaching may border on offensive to some.

B. *Beware of false prophets who push Jesus Christ into the background.* The false prophet preaches a social gospel. He is bent on saving society, but he is not too interested in saving souls.

Liberal theologians deny that people are lost. What is left for them to preach? They look about them and observe social needs. They cry, "Social structures must be changed!" Thus they overlook the individual whom Christ came to save, and they spend their time trying to save society. False prophets deplore evangelicals, saying, "You are not interested in the whole man; you are interested only in his soul." They denounce evangelism and classify all professional evangelists as modern-day Elmer Gantrys. They forget that in Christ "dwelleth all the fulness of the Godhead bodily" (Col. 2:9). They are never caught proclaiming that "God was in Christ reconciling the world unto himself" (2 Cor. 5:19).

A Mexican carrying a large basket of bread on his head cried to the crowd, "Bread! Bread!"

"What kind of bread do you have?" a woman asked.

"I have bread that costs money and bread that is free," said the Christian merchant. He took his Bible and read the words of Jesus Christ, "I am the bread of life: he that cometh to me shall never hunger; and he that believeth on me shall never thirst" (John 6:35). Those who preach only a social gospel of bread for the body are false prophets if they do not also proclaim that Christ is the bread for the soul.

C. *Beware of false prophets who cast doubts upon the Bible.* The Christian should beware of any false prophet who makes little reference to the Bible. Some have no text for what they say—just philosophical discourses. The Christian should beware of any false prophet who quotes Scripture out of context to make it say what he wants it to say.

The Christian should beware of any false prophet who accepts the Bible as only a piece of great literature or who accepts a part of the Bible and rejects other parts of it.

III. The fruits of false prophets.

Flowers may or may not be beautiful, but what really counts is the fruit of a plant. There are many fruits of false prophets, the most notable a "secondhand religion." What is secondhand religion?

A. *It is thinking that being born into a Christian home makes one a Christian.* It is leaving religion to the wife and kids. It is joining a church without being born again.

It is letting the church mean less than a fishing trip, washing the car, a football game, or visiting relatives.

B. *The fruits of false prophets are seen in the multitudes of church members who have just enough religion to make them miserable.*

C. *Somewhere down the line we have forgotten that one cannot be a practicing sinner and a practicing saint at the same time.* The Scriptures say, "He who does what is sinful is of the devil.... No one who is born of God will continue to sin, because God's seed remains in him; he cannot go on sinning, because he has been born of God. This is how we know who the children of God are and who the children of the devil are: Anyone who does not do what is right is not a child of God; nor is anyone who does not love his brother" (1 John 3:8–10 NIV).

Conclusion

Socrates said, "The surest way to live with honor in the world is to be, in reality, what we would appear to be."

WEDNESDAY EVENING, DECEMBER 14

Title: "O Come, Let Us Sing unto the Lord"

Text: "O come, let us sing unto the LORD: let us make a joyful noise to the rock of our salvation. Let us come before his presence with thanksgiving, and make a joyful noise unto him with psalms" **(Ps. 95:1–2).**

Scripture Reading: Psalm 100

Introduction

Christmas is a time of joyous singing. From all directions we can hear

Christmas songs and carols. Most of these are secular in nature and give voice to the festive spirit associated with the season. Many of these carols are sacred in nature and proclaim the praises of the Christ who was born in Bethlehem to be our King.

I. The angelic host sang a song of praise.

Christ came to put a song in the hearts of the people. The angelic choir announced his birth with psalms of praise. They sang, "Glory to God in the highest, and on earth peace, good will toward men" (Luke 2:14).

A. *They sang to the Lord.*
B. *They sang for the Lord.* Our singing for the Lord should be singing to the Lord as well as for the people. Our songs can be the testimony of our hearts. They can be a real blessing to others if we let them give expression to our faith, our gratitude, and our love for our Lord. Christianity is a singing religion.

II. Our Lord led his disciples in singing praises.

"When they had sung a hymn, they went out to the Mount of Olives" (Matt. 26:30 NIV). Even as our Lord faced the cross, he could still give voice to joyous praises to God.

III. The early church sang the praises of God.

"Every day they continued to meet together in the temple courts. They broke bread in their homes and ate together with glad and sincere hearts, praising God and enjoying the favor of all the people" (Acts 2:46–47 NIV).

A. *They could sing about the new discovery of the greatness of the love of God that had been revealed in the sacrificial death of God's Son on the cross.*
B. *They could sing about the glad consciousness of forgiven sin.*
C. *They could sing of their assurance that death was a defeated foe and that the grave had lost its power.*
D. *They could sing concerning the continuing companionship of the living Lord who made himself near to them and became dearer to them as time went by.*
E. *They could sing of their assurance of an eternal home where there will be no more sin, suffering, or sorrow, and where fellowship with God will be unhindered and unending.*

Conclusion

Only a faith that sings can make a real impact on the unbelieving. Such was the case during the first century of the Christian era, and such continues to be the case in our day.

It was the prayers and songs of praise by Paul and Silas in the Philippian jail at midnight that produced a powerful spiritual impact on both the prisoners and the jailer.

Not only during this Christmas season but throughout the coming year let us join with the psalmist and with the saints of all ages in singing the praises of our Lord. Let us determine with the psalmist, "I will sing unto the LORD as long as I live: I will sing praise to my God while I have my being" (Ps. 104:33).

SUNDAY MORNING, DECEMBER 18

Title: "His Name . . . Everlasting Father"

Text: "For unto us a child is born, unto us a son is given: and the government shall be upon his shoulder: and his name shall be called Wonderful, Counsellor, The mighty God, The everlasting Father, The Prince of Peace" **(Isa. 9:6)**.

Scripture Reading: Luke 2:1–8

Hymns: "Joy to the World," Watts

"All Creatures of Our God and King," Francis of Assisi

"O Little Town of Bethlehem," Brooks

Offertory Prayer: Our Father in heaven, in response to your great love for us, we bring our tithes and love gifts to you. May our faithful stewardship of our possessions make possible the sharing of the true Christmas tidings to all the world. In Jesus' name. Amen.

Introduction

The Old Testament reveals little of the doctrine of the fatherhood of God. References to God as Father are few indeed. When the word "father" is used, the passage is redemptive in character. "Thou art my father, my God, and the rock of my salvation" (Ps. 89:26). "Thou, O LORD, art our father, our redeemer; thy name is from everlasting" (Isa. 63:16). And, our text, Isaiah 9:6, "His name shall be called . . . everlasting Father." In the Old Testament there is only a dim conception of any relationship of personal sonship to God.

I. The nature of God.

Much is said in the Old Testament of God's majesty, power, might, and awesomeness, but little is said of his fatherhood. The most vivid picture of God is that of Jehovah of Sinai. He is the God who speaks in lightning, earthquake, and fire; he is unapproachable. God as a Father who loves and cares for his children is almost wholly a New Testament doctrine. Nearly eight hundred years before the birth of Jesus, Isaiah used one of the most astonishing names for our Lord in all the Bible. The words "everlasting Father" are among the shortest in the Hebrew language. The word "father" is *ab*, and "everlasting" is *ad*. Literally the words mean "father of eternity." It is most amazing that Christ is given this title in the Old Testament. The Son is the everlasting Father. Though it seems impossible, it is true. Jesus declared that he and the Father are one. There is a holy unity to the divine Trinity. Christ is the child born, yet he is also the everlasting Father.

II. The nature of Christ.

Christ came into our world to reveal the nature of God. How would he make himself known to man? Would he take the form of an angel or cherub? No, he would take the form of man. The Bible says, "Verily he took not on him the nature of angels; but he took on him the seed of Abraham" (Heb. 2:16). Christ was born of a woman; he became flesh and was made in the likeness of men. Men are persons, whether kings or peasants, whether bond or free. But what form of man would the Messiah take?

A. *King.* Was Christ a king? Yes, he was of royal lineage and had claim to the throne of David. The wise men came to Jerusalem asking, "Where is he that is born king of the Jews?" Matthew 21:5 declares that Christ's royal entry into Jerusalem on Palm Sunday was a fulfillment of the prophecy of Zechariah that said, "See, your king comes to you, righteous and having salvation, gentle and riding on a donkey" (Zech. 9:9 NIV). Above his dying body on the cross was his title, "Jesus ... King of the Jews." Yes, he came to this earth as a king.

Yet Jesus came not to claim an earthly kingdom. I am glad he did not claim an earthly crown. Many of us are stirred deeply by the sight or sound of royalty. A sovereign is someone to be feared, reverenced, obeyed, and served. He is one to whom tribute is paid and obeisance is done. But he is not really "one of us." If he is loved at all, it is a patriotic sort of thing and not a personal affection of heart and spirit. History records few kings who were really loved by all their subjects. If not an earthly king, what sort of man did Christ come to be?

B. *Priest.* Was Christ a priest? Yes, the Bible often speaks of his ministry before the altar. The book of Hebrews substantiates his claim to a priesthood after the order of Melchizedek. But he was more than a priest. Even in this enlightened age most people feel a little uneasy around priests. There is sort of a "no man's land" between clergy and laity. Those who have received the hand of ordination have joined the ranks of the untouchables.

Years ago I served as an evangelist in a revival. At the noon hour the pastor and I had the privilege of sharing a meal in the home of one of the members. We had a delightful time of fellowship and food. As we were leaving, the host said, "Preacher, I've found out you fellows are not much different than the rest of us." Few people have made this discovery. Between most people and the priest is a great gulf fixed. God knew this. He sent his Son to earth to do more than the work of a priest.

C. *Prophet.* Was Christ a prophet? Yes, indeed! But this was not the essential revelation of his nature. People may listen to prophets, but they do not universally love them. As Jesus said it, one generation kills the prophets and the next builds monuments to their memory. How then did God reveal himself in Christ?

D. *Father.* Everywhere in our world a father is the ideal of that which is good.

A father loves and protects and provides. Some of our most noble thoughts and dearest memories are associated with the word *father*.

Father is the name Jesus most often used to describe what God is like. He could have used a host of Hebrew names for God. There were "Elohim," "Shaddai," "Adonai," and "Jehovah"; but Jesus kept talking about the Father. The word was repeated often in phrases such as, "Your Father knoweth what things ye have need of"; "Pray to thy Father, ... and thy Father which seeth in secret shall reward thee openly"; and "Our Father, who art in heaven"; and "Your heavenly Father will also forgive you." On most every page of the New Testament God is Father. He is the anxious Father awaiting the return of the wayward son. And he is the Father who forgives, welcomes, and restores. This about God's love and grace we can understand. Have we not all a Father?

III. What fatherhood means.

A. *Family relationship.*

How does God become my Father? How do I become his child? By birth. "Jesus declared, 'I tell you the truth, no one can see the kingdom of God unless he is born again'" (John 3:3 NIV). Many make the mistake of supposing that just because they are born into a "Christian home," they are the children of God. But Jesus said, "Flesh gives birth to flesh, but the Spirit gives birth to spirit. You should not be surprised at my saying, 'You must be born again.'" (John 3:6–7 NIV). Without the second birth, the spiritual birth, it is impossible for God to be your "everlasting Father." Have you a Father? Have you been born again?

B. *The Father's care and provision.* Read the wonderful words from the lips of Jesus as they are found in Matthew 6:25–32. The New Testament teaches that the heavenly Father's care and provision for his children are constant and particular. It includes all his children, and it includes me. We have a Father.

C. *The Father's love.* The everlasting Father not only cares and provides for us, but he also loves us. First John 3:1 says, "Behold, what manner of love the Father hath bestowed upon us, that we should be called the sons of God." The Father's love is not mere amiability; nor is it silly sentimentality. Remember, his is the love of a father, not a grandfather! The Father's love means mercy and forgiveness, acceptance and fellowship; but it also means obedience and discipline. The Bible says, "The Lord disciplines those he loves, and he punishes everyone he accepts as a son" (Heb. 12:6 NIV). Our heavenly Father's concern is not so much that we are happy, but that we are holy. He desires that we grow up to look and act like him. Day by day he tries in love to reproduce in us the image of his Son. Or, as Paul expresses it in Ephesians 4:13–15, "Till we all come ... unto the measure of the stature of the fulness of Christ; that we henceforth be no more children.... But speaking the truth in love, may grow up into him in all things." God wants what any father wants—children who grow up to continue his name, his likeness, and his work.

D. *The Father's home.* At last we shall dwell in the Father's home. My mother and father live in Bradenton, Florida. Dad is a retired preacher. They have a lovely Florida home. My father has already given me his name, his love and care, his protection and provision; but one day, by inheritance, he will give me his home too. The everlasting Father will give us all that he has. "Then shall the King say unto them on his right hand, Come, ye blessed of my Father, inherit the kingdom prepared for you" (Matt. 25:34). "Fear not, little flock; for it is your Father's good pleasure to give you the kingdom" (Luke 12:32). "All things that the Father hath are mine: ... he shall take of mine, and shall shew it unto you" (John 16:15). A wonderful song says: "My Father is rich in houses and lands. / He holdeth the wealth of the world in his hands! / Of rubies and diamonds, of silver and gold, / his coffers are full, he has riches untold."

Are you a child of the King? Do you have a Father?

SUNDAY EVENING, DECEMBER 18

Title: "I Never Knew You"

Text: "Not every one that saith unto me, Lord, Lord, shall enter into the kingdom of heaven; but he that doeth the will of my Father which is in heaven. Many will say to me in that day, Lord, Lord, have we not prophesied in thy name? and in thy name have cast out devils? and in thy name done many wonderful works? And then will I profess unto them, I never knew you: depart from me, ye that work iniquity" **(Matt. 7:21–23).**

Scripture Reading: Luke 13:22–33

Introduction

D. Martyn Lloyd-Jones concluded that our text contains "the most solemn and solemnizing words ever uttered in this world, not only by any man, but even by the Son of God Himself."

I. Words without deeds.

A. *Jesus once said, "Well done."* He did not say, "Well said," "Well planned," "Well thought," or "Well intended," but he said, "Well *done.*" The emphasis is on *doing* in the kingdom of God. Of course, one must *be* something before he enters the kingdom of God. He must be born again. After one has been born into the kingdom of God, he is supposed to do something for God.

B. *We are not saved by good works, but good works reveal that we have been saved (James 2:20).*

365

We are encouraged to be doers of the Word and not hearers only (James 1:22). Horace Mann said, "I have never heard anything about the resolutions of the apostles, but a great deal about their acts."

George Washington was fond of saying, "Actions, not words, are the true characteristic marks of the attachment of friends." There are two types that always seem to have misfortune — those who did it and never thought and those who thought and never did it.

C. *When one is a Christian, he should do something about it.* During a bitter debate in his cabinet, President Abraham Lincoln stopped and asked what seemed to be a foolish question: "How many legs would a sheep have if you say that the tail is a leg?"

"If you say that the tail is a leg," replied one of the cabinet members, "then the sheep would have five legs."

"No," explained Lincoln, "just to say the tail is a leg does not make it so." To say that one is a Christian is not enough; we must do something about it.

II. Many are self-deceived.

A. *If we are merely hearers of the word and not doers, we deceive ourselves (James 1:22).* Many have deceived themselves into thinking that they are Christians.

B. *How many church members are actually lost in their self-deception?* No one really knows. Some pastors have estimated that as high as 85 percent of their church membership is probably unredeemed.

In the parable of the ten virgins, our Lord indicated that exactly half of them were self-deceived in thinking that they were ready for the bridegroom (Matt. 25).

C. *Some are self-deceived because they misunderstand salvation.* Some surmise that since "once saved always saved," the Christian can "live like the Devil." They are ignorant of the Bible teaching, "If any man be in Christ, he is a new creature" (2 Cor. 5:17).

D. *Many are self-deceived because they have misunderstood the place of good works in the Christian life.*

"I am trying to do enough good works to balance out my sins," said one well-meaning church member. Some people throw themselves into the activities of their church to salve their conscience while they live in adultery or cheat in their business. Some never darken the door of a church but come running to the pastor when their wives discover their double life. Many pastors have testified that wayward men have joined their churches as somewhat of a concession to their wives. But when all things are rosy at home again, these men seldom return to the church.

E. *The self-deceived person fails to realize that what really counts is his relationship to Jesus Christ.* California was leading Georgia Tech by a score of 7–6 in a Rose Bowl game many years ago. Roy Riegels, a linebacker, grabbed the football and started running. The crowd in the stands stood to their feet and cheered. But alas! He was running in the wrong direction. When he crossed the wrong goal, it gave Georgia Tech two points and the victory. It makes no difference how hard one is running in the religious race. If Jesus Christ is not running with him, he is going in the wrong direction. When all is said and done, the saddest words ever spoken to any human being will be the words of Jesus Christ when he says, "I never knew you."

III. There will be a day of reckoning.

A. *On the judgment day, Jesus will reveal why we have done what we have done.* We claim to do many things in Jesus' name, but the Judgment will reveal our motives.

B. *"Depart from me" indicates that the hypocrite will be eternally separated from God in hell.* Hell is described as "separation from the presence of the Lord."

In the latter part of 1967, *Mariner 5* discovered that Venus is a "hell hole with fiery storms raging in a metal-melting atmosphere so dense that light can't escape."

Scientists say that Venus glows eerily and that light cannot escape from this planet. They claim that the temperature on the surface of Venus is 860 degrees Fahrenheit. With knowledge such as this about a distant planet, why is it so difficult to believe that there is such a place as hell and that the worst thing about hell is not the fire but the separation from God?

Conclusion

The four saddest words that you can ever hear are these: (1) "I"—listen the Son of God is speaking; (2) "never"—no relationship to Jesus Christ has ever existed, for there is no such thing as knowing him awhile and then ceasing to know him; (3) "knew"—you can know a lot about Jesus Christ, but the important thing is for him to know you; (4) "you"—salvation is personal; whether or not one has had a personal encounter with Jesus Christ is what really matters in this life and in the life to come.

WEDNESDAY EVENING, DECEMBER 21

Title: "O Come, Let Us Adore Him"

Text: "And when they were come into the house, they saw the young child with Mary his mother, and fell down, and worshipped him: and when they had opened their treasures, they presented unto him gifts; gold, and frankincense, and myrrh" **(Matt. 2:11).**

Scripture Reading: Matthew 2:1–12

Introduction

Sometime, somewhere there lived a talented and devoted servant of God who continues to live and speak a gracious word to those who will listen. His name is unknown to us; he may have been a monk in the thirteenth century; he may have lived in England in the eighteenth century. Yet the devotion of his heart and the work of his mind still invite a world to come to the Savior. I refer to the unknown author of the Latin hymn "Adeste Fideles"—the Christmas hymn later translated into English as "O Come, All Ye Faithful."

> *O come, all ye faithful, joyful and triumphant,*
> *Come ye, O come ye to Bethlehem;*
> *Come and behold Him, born the King of angels:*
> *O come, let us adore Him; O come, let us adore Him;*
> *O come, let us adore Him, Christ, the Lord!*

In our modern secular society, we have almost completely commercialized Christmas. We are confronted with the real peril of letting Santa Claus and all that he represents take the place in our thoughts that should be given to Jesus Christ, whose birth we celebrate. Let us respond positively to the request of the chorus of the unknown poet who has been with God for several centuries.

I. Come, let us adore him because of who he is.

A. *He was and is the fulfillment of prophecy.*
B. *He was God, the Eternal, the Creator, the Almighty clothed in human flesh.*

II. Come, let us adore him because of what he dared to do.

A. *He clothed himself in human flesh (John 1:14).*
B. *He really loved the unlovely and gave himself to render ministries of mercy to them.*
  1. The publicans.
  2. The sick.
  3. The lepers.
  4. The prostitutes.
  5. The outcasts.
  6. The Gentiles.
C. *He took upon himself the burden of guilt and the sin of a wayward race (2 Cor. 5:21).*
D. *He entered the chamber of death itself for us (Heb. 2:9).*

III. Come, let us adore him because of what he has accomplished.

A. *He conquered death (Rev. 1:18).*
B. *He revealed the reality of immortality (2 Tim. 1:10).*
C. *He humanized man.*
D. *He dignified womanhood.*
E. *He set the captives free.*
F. *He has been and continues to be involved in every movement that serves as a lift to the human spirit.* He is unalterably opposed to every effort or system that would degrade or dehumanize people.

Conclusion

Jesus is worthy of our adoration, our loyalty, and our trust—our best. As the wise men of old fell down before him in adoration and worship, so let each of us worship him in spirit and in truth.

SUNDAY MORNING, DECEMBER 25

Title: "His Name ... Prince of Peace"

Text: "For unto us a child is born, unto us a son is given: and the government shall be upon his shoulder: and his name shall be called Wonderful, Counsellor, The mighty God, The everlasting Father, The Prince of Peace" (**Isa. 9:6**).

Scripture Reading: Luke 2:8–20

Hymns: "It Came Upon the Midnight Clear," Sears

           "O Come, All Ye Faithful," Wade

           "Silent Night! Holy Night!" Mohr

Offertory Prayer: Our Father, in the true spirit of this festive season, we bring our tithes and offerings to your house. Our gifts are but your own, for all is of your mercy and grace. We give because you have first given to us. Let everywhere the glad tidings be told that Christ is Immanuel, God with us. In Jesus' name. Amen.

Introduction

The five names given to Christ by Isaiah's prophecy are not repetitious. Each one describes a different attribute of his character. As "Wonderful," he is the awesome One, the God-in-the-flesh miracle worker. As "Counsellor," he advises us of all things right and best. We do well to walk in the path he directs. As "mighty God," he is the Divine One, very God of very God. He who knows him knows the Father also. As "everlasting Father," he is a provider, protector, and disciplinarian for his children. Everything a good father is, he is. And now, as "Prince of Peace," he gives his divine calm to those who trust him.

I. The promise of peace.

Our world has known so little real peace. When Isaiah spoke this prophecy twenty-eight hundred years ago, his nation was threatened with destruction. Already the rumblings of war, defeat, and slavery were heard on the horizon. Within a generation the nation would be suffering the bondage of Babylon. Yet Isaiah held out to the people a magnificent hope. He said, "The people that walked in darkness have seen a great light: they that dwell in the land of the shadow of death, upon them hath the light shined" (Isa. 9:2). Where is this light? "Unto us a child is born; unto us a Son is given: and his name shall be called ... Prince of Peace."

The Hebrew word for peace, *shalom*, was known well enough. So common was its usage that it was employed as a greeting of the day. It was used as we would say "Hello" to a friend. But the real meaning of the word had eluded the people for centuries. The promise of peace had been given often, for example, "I will give peace in the land, and ye shall lie down, and none shall make you afraid" (Lev. 26:6), and "The LORD will bless his people with peace" (Ps. 29:11). Then when Isaiah announced the coming of the Messiah, he said his name would be "Prince of Peace." Yet, for all the promises, there was so very little peace. Then, finally, on that first Christmas, peace came.

II. The promise fulfilled.

A. *While shepherds watched.* It was a wintry night in old Judea. The shepherds had built a fire in the crevice of the rocks and huddled together to escape the cold. They were the least to expect that this night the Prince of Peace would come. Because they were shepherds, they were ceremonially unclean. They were not allowed inside the "church." They were the nobodies of their day. They could not be called as witnesses in court, for who could believe the testimony of a shepherd? They were despised, looked down upon, and often hated. The Jewish Talmud says, "Give no help to the heathen or a shepherd." But there is no such prejudice with God. These who were the forgotten among men were not to be forgotten by God. Sometimes we may feel like the shepherds, outcast from the world, alone and lonely, and forbidden the "niceties" that others have. We feel friendless and lost. Our despair increases until we almost wish life would not have a tomorrow. The Scripture says, "He ... giveth grace to the humble" (1 Peter 5:5). It is to that type of person that God most often reveals himself. It was true of the shepherds in Bethlehem's field.

B. *The angel's song.* Suddenly the darkness became as midday. The angel of the Lord appeared and said, "Fear not: for, behold, I bring you good tidings of great joy.... For unto you is born this day in the city of David a Saviour.... And suddenly there was with the angel a multitude of the heavenly host praising God, and saying, Glory to God in the highest, and on earth peace, good will toward men" (Luke 2:10–14). Then, as suddenly as the light had come, it was gone. All the way to the manger those shepherds must have repeated the words of the angels: "Glory to God ... and on earth ... peace ... peace." No more war and hate and killing. No more Roman soldiers in the land. Peace! At the manger they told what the angels had said, and everyone wondered at the things told them by the shepherds.

C. *No peace on earth.* As the months passed, the whole countryside was astir with the promise of peace. Then one day the Roman Legion came to Bethlehem with orders from Herod. While the people were gathered in the village square, the centurion read the edict, "Let all the children of Bethlehem and all the borders thereof two years of age and under, be slain." Matthew's gospel tells the tragic story. "A voice is heard in Ramah, weeping and great mourning, Rachel weeping for her children and refusing to be comforted, because they are no more" (Matt. 2:18 NIV). So from a hundred broken and bleeding hearts came the wail, "The angels lied. There is no peace on earth." Two thousand years have not changed the cry of the earth. Like the poet Longfellow, we say, "And in despair I bowed my head: 'There is no peace on earth,' I said." Did God lie? Did the Messiah come to earth to bring peace or not?

III. Messiah's peace.

Jesus is in truth the Prince of Peace. The peace he came to give is peace that passes the understanding of the world. It is not a political peace, a peace among nations, a peace that outlaws war. It is more than nonaggression treaties. What is the peace Jesus came to give?

A. *A peace with* God. "Therefore being justified by faith, we have peace with God through our Lord Jesus Christ" (Rom. 5:1). Sin separates. It puts a barrier between man and God. This wall of partition destroys peace. Isaiah said, "There is no peace to the wicked." Sin is the great disturber, the constant troubler of the heart. It is the source of all disorder, strife, jealousy, envy, covetousness, hate, war, and killing. Jesus came to restore order to your heart. He came to redress and redeem. In preparing Joseph for Jesus' birth, the angel said, "Call his name Jesus: for he shall save his people from their sins." Do you have this peace with God in the forgiveness of your sins?

B. *The peace of* God. Not only does Jesus give us peace *with* God, but he gives the Christian peace *of* God. Philippians 4:7 says, "And the peace of God, which passeth all understanding, shall keep your hearts and minds through Christ Jesus." When the apostle wrote these words, he was a prisoner in Rome. In that cold and lightless dungeon, Paul relied on the peace of God to keep him. Paul spoke of an inner calm, a serenity of soul, an inward peace born of faith and trust in God.

Christ had this peace. It gave him calm in the midst of a midnight storm when all others were afraid. It was the poise of mind that brought his tormentors to naught when they sought to trap him in his words. It was love that caused him to say on the cross, "Father, forgive them." This is the peace of God.

C. *How can I find this peace?* This peace of God does not come through the world of men. Search as you will, you cannot find this peace in worldly amusements, possessions, or acclaim. Jesus said, "My peace I give unto you: not as the world giveth." The peace of God is a gift. You must accept it in humility and thanksgiving. The Old Testament prophet said, "Thou wilt keep him in perfect peace, whose mind is stayed on thee: because he trusteth in thee" (Isa. 26:3). The last phrase is the important one— "because he trusteth in thee." These words contain the secret to the possession of this peace. The person who trusts his life to God through Jesus Christ has this peace. It is God's gift in response to repentance and faith.

Conclusion

The peace of God is really the gift of himself. Paul wrote to the Ephesians, "For he is our peace" (2:14). The peace of God *is* God. This is the real meaning of the angel's song. Peace on earth means Christmas—God with us.

The fortunes of war had liberated a small village on the western slopes of the mountains of Italy. The men of the American Seventh Army were engaged in securing the town against a counterattack. Through the rubble of a partly destroyed cathedral stepped an American soldier with his gun ready. Then he heard the voice of someone weeping. There at the torn altar an old man knelt. The soldier asked the cause of his weeping. Had he been injured in the fighting? Had he lost a loved one or friend? The old man looked up and said, "No, it's nothing like that. It's just a peace. She is a so good." Yes, my friend, peace is so good. It is Heaven's gift to earth and God's gift to man.

SUNDAY EVENING, DECEMBER 25

Title: How to Build a Life

Text: "Therefore whosoever heareth these sayings of mine, and doeth them, I will liken him unto a wise man" (**Matt. 7:24**).

Scripture Reading: Matthew 7:24–29

Introduction

In the parable that closes the Sermon on the Mount, Jesus draws spiritual truths from a common occurrence of his day. When people in Jesus' day moved to and settled in another place, it was usually in the winter. The hot, sultry days of the summer saw few "moving vans" in the Palestinian countryside. Many people would try to get their belongings moved and their house built before the spring rains came.

It was not uncommon for a man to build his house in a sandy creek bed. No one wanted to build on a rocky mountain or among towering trees. A sandy creek bed usually looked rather inviting to a builder. It would not be difficult to dig into the sand. There were usually a few trees along the creek bank, but they were always well nourished. Of course, the person who built in a dry creek bed did so by mistake. But the mistake was paid for when the spring rains came and the flooding waters filled the dry creek.

Jesus is giving his plan for building a life in the final paragraph of the Sermon on the Mount. But this plan is useless to the person who will not abide by it. Without following this plan, one might find, when the flooding waters of trial cascade around his life, that he has built on an insecure site and an inadequate foundation.

Would you build a life that will stand? Would you find the real meaning of life? Would you make a life instead of a living? Listen, then, to Jesus' advice.

I. Consider the site.

A. *Consider its past.* Before building on a site, the builder wants to know its past. If the foolish builder of the parable had considered the past of the plot of land on which he built, he never would have built there. If he had just asked a neighboring friend, he would have informed him that his proposed site had been a raging creek last spring.

A man sat in a rescue mission in Fort Worth, Texas, with a troubled look on his face. When testimony time came, the man jumped to his feet and began to declare in a disturbed tone with choppy, stammering speech that he was not a Christian and that his life had been ruined by what he thought was pleasure. He had fallen victim to the theory that drinking alcohol in moderation is all right. But now he stood in a shabby rescue mission to say that pleasure is a shaky foundation on which to build a life. The talkative alcoholic became more restless as the speaker brought the sermon. Finally, he charged out of the mission to the nearest tavern. His words echoed in the ears of those present: "Now, I want to quit what I thought was fun, but it has a hold on my life and I can't quit! Please pray for me!"

The same testimonies could be given on the past experiences that others have had with riches, popularity, education, and religion as a building site for a life. When one chooses a site other than Christ on which to build his life, he has chosen the wrong site. He need do no more than consider Christianity's past to find adequate reason for building a life on Christ. All religions except Christianity were founded by mortal men who are now dead. But the Christian serves a living Christ (John 14:1–6). He lives because, in the past, he was buried and arose again.

B. *Consider its future.* If the builder had checked the past, he would have been aware of the future of his site in the dry creek bed. He would have known that you can expect no more in the future of a creek bed than it has been in the past.

Only Christ offers an adequate promise for the future. He promises the Christian future joy while living on the earth. He promises the Christian future life in heaven. He does not, however, promise easy digging—only that those who build their lives on him will never have to worry about their future outcome.

C. *Remember that the easiest place to build is not always the best.* Another reason for the fall of the foolish builder's house was that he built where it was easiest to dig—in the sand. The same is true of the man who builds his life on shaky ground—it is usually the easy life.

Christ never promised that his followers would have it easy. In fact, his commands are difficult to obey. He requires a commitment of every area of one's life. He requires that one take up his cross and follow him. This is not an optional request; it is a requirement (Luke 14:27). Jesus said that if any man would come after him, he had to "take up his cross" (aorist,

373

indicating a definite time of committal), "deny himself" (aorist, indicating a particular time of denial), and "follow me" (continuous action, indicating continuous following) (Matt. 16:24).

To take up the cross of Christ involves many difficult tasks. It means to crucify the old life (Gal. 6:14), to crucify sin in one's life (Rom. 6:6). In short, it is putting all else aside—including self—to follow that which Christ requires. It must be a voluntary experience, for Jesus says that one must "take up his cross." This is not easy digging.

D. *Remember that the most attractive plot is not always the best.* The trees along a creek bank are usually plentiful and healthy looking, even in the winter season. The foolish builder who looked only for outward beauty would not hesitate to build his house where things "look good."

Such was the case in Fort Worth, Texas, not many years ago. Several families built homes in the path of the overflowing Trinity River, which appeared to be a fertile valley. The next spring the homes were flooded and families evacuated. They learned the lesson that the most attractive plot is not always the best.

The same is true in one's choice of "religions." It is not difficult in our day to find an attractive religion. But one must remember that real religion is not in what one gets out of it but in what one gives to it. It must not only be worth dying for but also worth living for. Jesus demands complete commitment of life. He does not promise that one's life will be outwardly attractive, but he does promise that it will be inwardly peaceful. He does not promise an eternal vacation; he demands total dedication of time, talent, money, mind, and attitude.

II. Build on a solid foundation.

One may choose the right site for his building and still build a house that will crumble. One may decide to build his life on Christ and still build a life that will crumble under tension. It is easy to believe Christ and all that he taught with the mind, but it is difficult to commit one's life to him and obey his teachings.

Jesus taught in the Sermon on the Mount that a wise builder is one who not only *hears* his teachings but also *does* them. One can decide that these teachings are wonderful, but he has not planted his life on a solid foundation until he abides by them. The solid foundation of a Christian's life is found in the teachings of the Sermon on the Mount. Jesus gives us no choice—we must *do* them before we can expect our lives to stand in time of trial.

A. *Live the harmonious life (Matt. 5:1–16).*
   1. By living in harmony with God (vv. 3–6, 8).
     a. Be totally dependent on God (vv. 3–5).
     b. Maintain dissatisfaction with self (v. 6).
     c. Maintain private fellowship with God (v. 8).

2. By living in harmony with your fellow humans (vv. 7, 9–12).
   a. Be merciful in treatment of others (v. 7).
   b. Promote friendly relations among people (v. 9).
   c. Face man-made trials with assurance (vv. 10–12).
3. By living in harmony with God's mission for Christians (vv. 13–16).
   a. Preservation (v. 13).
   b. Demonstration (vv. 14–16).

B. *Possess Christian righteousness (5:20–48).*
   1. By correcting inward sin before it is expressed in outward actions (vv. 21–32).
      a. Correct anger before it develops into murder (vv. 21–26).
      b. Correct lust before it develops into adultery and divorce (vv. 29–30).
   2. By controlling outward actions (vv. 33–42).
      a. Be simple and truthful in speech (vv. 33–37).
      b. Bear insult without retaliation (vv. 38–39).
      c. Do more for others than is required (vv. 40–42).
   3. By having unbiased love for the unlovely (vv. 43–47).
   4. By seeking to be perfect (v. 48).

C. *Live a righteous life with a consciousness of the presence of God, not the praise of men (6:1–18).*
   1. When doing good deeds.
   2. When praying.
   3. When fasting.

D. *Let your life be dedicated to the laying up of heavenly treasures (6:19–34).*
   1. By using material possessions wisely (vv. 19–24).
   2. By making God's will the object of your life (v. 33).
   3. By trusting God for material needs (vv. 25–32, 34).

E. *Treat your fellow humans in a Christian manner (7:1–23).*
   1. Do not criticize (vv. 1–5).
   2. Treat the antagonistic lost person with caution and as you would like to be treated (vv. 6–14).
   3. Be aware of false teaching, but let God punish the false teacher (vv. 15–23).

Conclusion

When the storms of life come, we usually do not have time to check the site and be sure that we are resting on a solid foundation. That decision must be made before the storm. When death comes rushing down the dry creek bed of a lost person's life, it does not wait for him to rebuild. If one has committed his life to the Christ of the mount and has verified that committal by obeying the teachings of the Sermon on the Mount, he has built a life—not just a living!

WEDNESDAY EVENING, DECEMBER 28

Title: Emissaries of the Faith

Text: "Now then we are ambassadors for Christ ..." **(2 Cor. 5:20)**.

Scripture Reading: 2 Corinthians 5:16–21

Introduction

Since the new year is quickly approaching, many of us have been thinking about resolutions that we will make for the new year. Let me suggest that you give prayerful consideration to the following:

I. Let us resolve to forget the past and to honor God more in 2012!

"Forgetting those things which are behind and reaching forth unto those things which are before, I press toward the mark for the prize of the high calling of God in Christ Jesus" (Phil. 3:13–14).

II. Let us resolve to live for Christ before the world!

"For me to live is Christ, and to die is gain" (Phil. 1:21).

III. Let us resolve to trust God with a strong faith!

"Now faith is the substance of things hoped for, the evidence of things not seen" (Heb. 11:1).

IV. Let us resolve to be faithful in worship!

"Not forsaking the assembling of ourselves together, as the manner of some is; but exhorting one another: and so much the more, as ye see the day approaching" (Heb. 10:25).

V. Let us resolve to honor God with our income!

"Bring ye all the tithes into the storehouse, that there may be meat in mine house, and prove me now herewith, saith the LORD of hosts, if I will not open you the windows of heaven, and pour you out a blessing, that there shall not be room enough to receive it" (Mal. 3:10).

VI. Let us resolve to bear one another's burdens!

"Bear ye one another's burdens, and so fulfil the law of Christ" (Gal. 6:2).

VII. Let us resolve to faithfully witness to the unsaved!

"They that sow in tears shall reap in joy. He that goeth forth and weepeth, bearing precious seed, shall doubtless come again with rejoicing, bringing his sheaves with him" (Ps. 126:5–6).

Conclusion

Paul said, "I am ready." Paul was ready because of his spiritual indebtedness to God. He felt an obligation to a needy world. He felt an obligation to his own better self. We could well follow his example and say with sincerity and earnestness, "I am ready."

MISCELLANEOUS HELPS

MESSAGES ON THE LORD'S SUPPER

Title: God's Masterpiece

Text: "When they came to the place which is called The Skull, there they crucified him, and the criminals, one on the right and one on the left" **(Luke 23:33 RSV)**.

Scripture Reading: Luke 23:32–38

Introduction

Frequently a person will stand before the world and declare, "This is my masterpiece. It is the fruit of my hands, the work of my life." It may be a painting or a symphony, a book or a building. In any event, it represents his best, his convictions, his dreams.

In like manner, God has a masterpiece. It was not when he spoke the worlds into existence nor when he breathed into man the breath of life. It was not when he delivered the children of Israel from bondage in Egypt nor when he parted the Red Sea.

No, as great and glorious as all of these are, none is God's masterpiece. Turn your eyes to Jerusalem two thousand years ago. The scene is outside the city walls on a hill called Calvary. There you see Jesus as he is crucified. A crown of thorns is placed on his head, and nails are driven into his hands and feet. You hear him pray, "Father forgive them, for they know not what they do." You see him die! This is God's masterpiece.

This a masterpiece? How absurd! The world calls it foolishness. The multitudes call it a blunder and a stumbling block. But to God it is his masterpiece. Here all of his attributes are brought together in one glorious expression. Here his grace is seen pitying, his wisdom is seen planning, his power is seen preparing, and his love is seen providing.

This is God's masterpiece. To understand it one must see:

I. The work of the cross.

A. *The work of the cross is understood when one realizes that it was God doing for people what they could not do for themselves.* Possessed by guilt, overwhelmed by the burden of sin, and condemned by the wickedness of their sin, people stand before God ready to hear the words: "Depart from me, ye that work iniquity" (Matt. 7:23). Then Jesus comes and takes the burden and guilt and condemnation of sin on himself.

B. *It was a voluntary death.* He chose to die. "No man taketh [my life] from me, but I lay it down of myself" (John 10:18).

C. *It was a vicarious death.* He died in our place. "He who knew no sin was made to be sin for us," says the Scripture (2 Cor. 5:21).

D. It was a victorious death. It meant the defeat of Satan, the deliverance from sin and the doom of death.

II. The worth of the cross.

To understand fully the worth of the cross one must see what it means:

A. *To God.* It means that God can be just and at the same time the Justifier of those who believe.

B. *To the individual.* It means to the individual that he is redeemed by God, reconciled to God, and adopted into the family of God.

C. *To the world.* It means to the world that there is hope, there is salvation. "Salvation is found in no one else, for there is no other name under heaven given to men by which we must be saved" (Acts 4:12 NIV).

III. The way of the cross.

The way of the cross is the way to:

A. *Peace.* "Therefore being justified by faith, we have peace" (Rom. 5:1).

B. *Security.* "There is therefore now no condemnation to them which are in Christ Jesus" (Rom. 8:1).

C. *Home.* It may be true that "all roads lead to Rome," but there is only one road home. "I am the way," said Jesus. Because of this we sing, "It is sweet to know, as I onward go — the way of the cross leads home."

Conclusion

God's masterpiece is seen today as we gather about his table. It is for you. Experience it anew as we partake of the bread and the wine!

Title: This Do in Remembrance of Me

Text: "Take, eat: this is my body, which is broken for you: this do in remembrance of me.... This cup is the new testament in my blood: this do ye, as oft as ye drink it, in remembrance of me" (**1 Cor. 11:24–25**).

Scripture Reading: 1 Corinthians 11:23–34

Lord's Supper Prayer Meditation

Heavenly Father, we want to fill our hearts and minds with thoughts of your great love for us as it was demonstrated in the substitutionary sufferings and the sacrificial death of your precious Son, Jesus Christ, whom we have come to know as Savior, Lord, and Friend.

Help us to experience the sacred significance of the event and actions that our Lord ordained to be repeated again and again by his disciples as they met together for worship and fellowship.

Help us to remember Christ in Gethsemane, where he prayed and agonized on behalf of both himself and us.

Help us to remember Christ—his gentleness, kindness, and compassion when he was betrayed by a kiss from Judas. Help us to so relate ourselves to him in love and loyalty that we shall never betray him as Judas did.

Help us to remember Christ and how he looked with compassion, pity, and forgiveness upon Peter when Peter had denied him the third time. Help us to so love him and be loyal to him that we will not deny him either with the words of our mouth or with the conduct of our life.

Help us to remember Christ as they scourged him. The prophet Isaiah said, "By his stripes we are healed." We cannot understand why he would love us so much that he would be willing to die for us. Help us to believe in that love and to respond to that love.

Help us to remember Christ as he wore the crown of thorns. He deserved to wear a crown of gold bedecked with precious stones; instead, Roman soldiers pressed a crown of thorns upon his brow. As we remember the extent of his love for us, help us to crown him as Lord of our lives and help us to begin to love him as he so fully loved us then.

Help us to remember how the nails pierced Christ's hands and feet. It was his love for us and for you that kept him on the cross when he was taunted and invited to come down to prove his Sonship. Help us, Lord, to dedicate our feet to walk in his paths and our hands to do his work in the world today.

Help us to remember Christ's agony on the cross as he suffered isolation and desolation because our sin had been placed on him. Help us to let love and gratitude well up within our hearts. Help us to determine that we shall love him more. Help us to decide now to demonstrate our love for him in ministries of mercy and grace to a needy world that he was willing to die for. Grant to us, O gracious and loving Father, that as we now partake of the elements of this Supper, we may remember that our lives and our salvation have come to us through the Christ who suffered and died on the cross.

Help us as we partake to joyfully pledge our lives, our time, our possessions, and our talents in devoted service to Christ until we have given our lives completely into his service. Amen.

THEMES FOR WEDDING CEREMONIES

Title: Faith, Hope, and Love

Introduction

It is a combination of faith, hope, and love that brings this young couple to this significant point on the road of life.

Genuine faith is an absolute essential for the highest happiness in marriage. Each of you needs a genuine, active faith in God that expresses itself in worship and obedience. You need to have faith in each other. You must conduct yourself in a manner so as to encourage an ever-increasing confidence in you on the part of your companion.

All of you need faith in yourself as individuals. May God help you to believe

380

that you can be a good husband or a good wife and in due time good parents and the builders of a successful home.

Another essential for happiness in marriage is hope. It is because of hope for happiness and fulfillment that you meet together now to be united in holy wedlock. When your hope is built on faith in God, faith in your companion, and faith in yourself, which expresses itself in commitment, then you can be assured that you have a real basis for hope for success in marriage.

It is because of love that you stand here to be united in holy matrimony. Perhaps it was romantic love that first attracted you to one another. If you would achieve true success, you need to combine the practice of Christian love with the expression of romantic love. Paul describes the nature of Christian love in 1 Corinthians 13. Let us read from the Phillips translation, verses 4–8:

> This love of which I speak is slow to lose patience — it looks for a way of being constructive. It is not possessive: It is neither anxious to impress nor does it cherish inflated ideas of its own importance.
>
> Love has good manners and does not pursue selfish advantage. It is not touchy. It does not keep account of evil or gloat over the wickedness of other people. On the contrary, it is glad with all good men when truth prevails.
>
> Love knows no limit to its endurance, no end to its trust, no fading of its hope; it can outlast anything. It is, in fact, the one thing that still stands when all else has fallen.

The Ceremony

If you, then, _____ and _____ , have freely and deliberately chosen each other as partners in this holy estate and know of no just cause why you should not be so united, in token thereof you will please join your right hands.

Groom's Vow

_____ , in taking the woman you hold by the right hand to be your lawful, wedded wife, before God and the witnesses present you must promise to love her; to honor and cherish her in that relation; and leaving all others, cleave only to her and be to her in all things a true and faithful husband as long as you both shall live. Do you so promise? *(I do.)*

Bride's Vow

_____ , in taking the man you hold by the right hand to be your lawful, wedded husband, before God and the witnesses present you must promise to love him; to honor and cherish him in that relation; and leaving all others, cleave only to him and be to him in all things a true and faithful wife as long as you both shall live. Do you so promise? *(I do.)*

Pastor's Response

Then are you each given to the other in advances and reverses, in poverty or in riches, in sickness and in health, to love and to cherish, until death shall part you.

The Ring(s)

For centuries the ring has been used on important occasions. It has reached its loftiest prestige in the symbolic significance it vouches at the marriage altar. It is a perfect circle having no end. It symbolizes your desire, our desire, and God's desire that there be no end to the happiness and success for which your heart hungers. It is thus a symbol of the unending plan and purpose of God for your happiness and well-being.

Do you give these rings to each other as a token of your love for each other? *(We do.)*

Will each of you receive this ring as a token of your companion's wedded love for you, and will you wear it as a token of your love for your companion? *(We will.)*

Closing Proclamation

Here in the presence of your parents, relatives, friends, pastor, and most important, the living God, you have made vows. These vows are binding upon you by the laws of this state and by the law of God. And they are binding upon you by the law of your own love for each other. You have sealed these vows by the giving and receiving of rings. Acting in the authority vested in me as a minister of the gospel by this state, and looking to heaven for divine sanction, I now pronounce you husband and wife. What therefore God hath joined together do not let any man put asunder. Amen.

Title: Submission, Love, and Reverence

Introduction

In Paul's epistle to the Ephesians, he uses the husband-wife relationship to illustrate the mystical union between Christ and his church. In this discussion of the nature of the church, the apostle says much that can be both profitable and practical for a couple entering holy wedlock.

Paul suggests that the husband and the wife adjust themselves to each other in such a manner as to be pleasing to God (Eph. 5:21). Both the husband and wife are responsible to God for the way in which they relate to each other as husband and wife.

The responsibilities of the husband and the wife are emphasized rather than the rights and privileges they hope to enjoy in the marriage relationship.

Two specific suggestions are given to wives. A wife is to submit to her husband as the head of the household. She is to recognize him as the responsible head of the organization or corporation. She is to look to him for leadership as well as for protection and provision (Eph. 5:22–24).

One specific suggestion with a twofold application is given concerning the responsibility of the husband toward the wife. First, the husband is encouraged to love his wife even as Christ loved the church and gave himself for it. Christ gave his life for the church because of his love. The second explanation of this command to love states that a man is to love his wife as he loves his own body. "He that loveth his wife loveth himself. For no man ever yet hated his own flesh; but nourisheth and cherisheth it, even as the Lord the church: For we are members of his body, of his flesh, and of his bones" (Eph. 5:28–30).

The closing suggestion to the wife is to the effect that she is to "reverence her husband." She is to look up to him with reverence and respect.

If you will pledge yourself to continuous cooperation with each other in the will of God, loving each other devotedly, giving reverent respect to the needs and the rights of each other, you have a basis for hoping for real success in this most important of human relationships.

The apostle Paul says, "For this cause shall a man leave his father and mother, and shall be joined unto his wife, and they two shall be one flesh" (Eph. 5:31).

The Marriage Ceremony

Who gives this woman to this man in marriage? *(The person replying may say, "I do," or "Her mother and I do.")*

If you, then, _____ and _____ , after careful consideration and in the fear of God, have deliberately chosen each other as partners in this holy estate and know of no just cause why you should not be so united, in token thereof please join your right hands.

Groom's Vow

_____ , wilt thou have this woman to be thy wedded wife, to live together after God's ordinance in the holy estate of matrimony? Wilt thou love her; comfort her; honor her; and keep her in sickness and in health; and, forsaking all others, keep thee only unto her so long as you both shall live? *(I will.)*

Bride's Vow

_____ , wilt thou have this man to be thy wedded husband, to live together after God's ordinance in the holy estate of matrimony? Wilt thou love him; honor him; and keep him in sickness and in health; and, forsaking all others, keep thee only unto him so long as you both shall live? *(I will.)*

Vows to Each Other

I, _____ (Groom), take thee, _____ (Bride), to be my wedded wife, to have and to hold from this day forward, in prosperity or adversity, in sickness or in health, in advances or reverses, to love and to cherish till death do us part, according to God's holy ordinance, and thereto I pledge thee my faith.

I, _____ (Bride), take thee, _____ (Groom), to be my wedded husband, to have and to hold from this day forward, in prosperity or adversity, in sickness or in health, in advances or reverses, to love and to cherish till death do us part, according to God's holy ordinance, and thereto I pledge thee my faith.

Then are you each given to the other for richer or poorer, for better or worse, in sickness and in health, till death alone shall part you.

The Ring(s)

From time immemorial the ring has been used to seal important covenants. The golden circlet, most prized of jewels, has come to its loftiest prestige in the symbolic significance it vouches at the marriage altar. Its untarnishable material is of the purest gold. Even so may your love for each other be pure, and may it grow brighter and brighter as time goes by. The ring is a circle, thus having no end. Even so may there be no end to the happiness and success that come to you as you unite your lives together.

Do you, _____ (Groom), give this ring to your wedded wife as a token of your love for her? *(I do.)*

Will you, _____ (Bride), receive this ring as a token of your wedded husband's love for you, and will you wear it as a token of your love for him? *(I will.)*

Do you, _____ (Bride), give this ring to your wedded husband as a token of your love for him? *(I do.)*

Will you, _____ (Groom), receive this ring as a token of your wedded wife's love for you, and will you wear it as a token of your love for her? *(I will.)*

Closing Proclamation

Since you have pledged your faith in and love to each other in the sight of God and these assembled witnesses and have sealed your solemn marital vows by the giving and receiving of rings, I now, by the authority vested in me as a minister of the gospel by this state, and looking to heaven for divine sanction, pronounce you husband and wife. What therefore God hath joined together do not let any man put asunder. (Prayer.)

MEDITATIONS FOR FUNERAL SERVICES

Title: Life and Immortality through Jesus Christ

Text: " ... our Saviour Jesus Christ, who hath abolished death, and hath brought life and immortality to light through the gospel" **(2 Tim. 1:10)**.

Scripture Reading: 2 Timothy 1:8–10

Introduction

When death comes and removes a Christian loved one from our midst, many resources are available to comfort the hearts of those who have faith. Comfort comes to the heart by the recalling of fond memories and through the presence and sympathy of friends. The gift of flowers speaks of the beauty of the life of the departed, and their fragrance speaks of the concern of friends for the time of need. But the greatest source of comfort is to be found in the promises of God. The words of Paul to Timothy can communicate God's promises to us in a time like this.

I. Salvation is an accomplished fact.

"Who hath saved us" (2 Tim. 1:9). Salvation of the soul is an accomplished fact when the individual receives Jesus Christ as Lord and Savior. In the miracle of the new birth, the departed loved one became a child of God and thus a member of the family of God. On the basis of this believer's faith and response to the gospel of Jesus Christ, we can believe that he was a child of God and that he has gone to be with his Redeemer.

II. Salvation is by the grace of God.

"Not according to our works, but according to his own purpose and grace" (2 Tim. 1:9). The God of grace never deals with us on the basis of our merit and moral achievement. God deals with us on the basis of his own grace and mercy.

It is unnecessary for you to speculate today concerning whether your departed loved one's good deeds outweigh his bad deeds. It is unnecessary for you to concern yourselves with whether he was worthy of divine favor and has gone to heaven. Our salvation does not come at the end of the way on the basis of good deeds. The truth is, if salvation depended upon human good works and moral excellence, not a single one of us would make it. We would have to have a perfect record in order to go to heaven, and there is not one among us who does not sin.

Salvation comes to us through the channel of our faith on the basis of God's nature of grace and mercy (Eph. 2:8–9). God has demonstrated his love for sinful humanity in the gift of his Son Jesus Christ, who died for our sins on the cross. God dealt with the sin of your departed loved one on the basis that Jesus Christ had paid his sin debt on the cross. Today we can be grateful that your departed loved one saw the need for forgiveness and responded to God's grace by receiving Jesus Christ as Lord and Savior.

III. Salvation is through Jesus Christ.

Paul declares that, for the believer, Jesus Christ has abolished death and has demonstrated the reality of immortality by his resurrection from the dead.

The death that humans have to fear is not the death of the physical organism but rather the death of the soul because of sin. As the separation of life from the body indicates physical death, even so the separation of the soul from God is spiritual death. Jesus died on the cross that he might remove the sin that separates the soul of man from his holy God, and by his death he abolished spiritual death for those who will respond to the gospel and trust him as their Savior.

By his resurrection from the dead Jesus demonstrated that, in the plan of God, physical death ultimately is to be abolished. He said to his disciples, "Because I live, ye shall live also" (John 14:19). Scriptures testify that the day will come when death shall be swallowed up in victory (1 Cor. 15:51–54).

By his resurrection from the dead Jesus Christ gave a demonstration of the reality of immortality. Immortality is not a natural characteristic of the human soul, but rather it is the gift of God's grace and power to the believer when this mortal body puts on immortality.

Conclusion

Today, instead of concentrating on saying good-bye to our loved one, we should concentrate, with appreciation and gratitude to God, on the grace that has made it possible for him to move out of a house that was no longer useful that he might enter into a house not made with hands, eternal in the heavens (2 Cor. 5:1–4).

The wisest action in which any of us can participate is that of making preparation not only to meet God in eternity but also to enter into a living relationship with him now so that we can walk and talk with him during life. To know him in the present by faith and fellowship is to have no fear of him when we approach the time when we will meet him face-to-face.

Title: Let Not Your Heart Be Troubled

Text: "Let not your heart be troubled: ye believe in God, believe also in me" **(John 14:1)**.

Scripture Reading: John 14:1–14

Introduction

Our text has been used by the Holy Spirit of God to bring comfort to the hearts of millions when death has taken away a loved one. May God give you the comfort, strength, and faith that you need this day that you might not be utterly crushed by the grief you are experiencing.

Jesus came with precious promises to his disciples. He insisted that they trust him, and we would be wise to trust him implicitly today.

I. Let not your heart be troubled about the past.

God in his grace and mercy has promised to forgive every sin that would separate our souls from him if we will only come to him with our request for him to do so. God delights in granting forgiveness. We can rejoice that God's grace was not only offered to but also received by your loved one who has gone to be with the Lord.

II. Let not your heart be troubled about the present.

Our Lord has promised, "I will never leave thee, nor forsake thee" (Heb. 13:5). He is present with us today, and he has been present since the moment you became aware that death had come to your dear one. He is present now to provide comfort. To receive comfort is to receive strength and courage and hope.

III. Let not your heart be troubled about the future.

To some degree almost all of us fear the future. We stand in awe before the mystery of tomorrow. We have fear of the unknown.

We must face the future with faith in him who will be with us in all of our tomorrows. Jesus promised, "Lo, I am with you alway, even unto the end of the world" (Matt. 28:20). While we cannot know what tomorrow holds, we can know him who holds tomorrow.

IV. Let not your heart be troubled about eternity.

Jesus sought to dispel the fears of his disciples concerning eternity by declaring, "In my Father's house are many mansions: if it were not so, I would have told you. I go to prepare a place for you. And if I go and prepare a place for you, I will come again, and receive you unto myself; that where I am, there ye may be also" (John 14:2–3). To the dying thief on the cross, Jesus said, "Today shalt thou be with me in paradise" (Luke 23:43). By divine inspiration Paul said to the Corinthians, "We are confident, I say, and willing rather to be absent from the body, and to be present with the Lord" (2 Cor. 5:8). Paul saw death as the experience in which a man moved out of the body and into the presence of the Lord. Where Jesus is, our loved ones in Christ are.

Conclusion

With our face looking to the Lord, we need not be troubled about the past or the present or the future or eternity. By faith, let us look up and face the future in the assurance that our living Lord will be with us each step of the way. "Surely goodness and mercy shall follow me all the days of my life: and I will dwell in the house of the LORD for ever" (Ps. 23:6).

MESSAGES FOR CHILDREN AND YOUNG PEOPLE

Title: The Way to Win in the Game of Life

Text: "Now to him who by the power at work within us is able to do far more abundantly than all that we ask or think" (**Eph. 3:20 RSV**).

Scripture Reading: Ephesians 3

Introduction

Do you love the excitement and thrill of a good contest? We have a desire to win, and anticipation of victory causes the fires of our enthusiasm to burn.

Life is a contest where we win and lose. The Bible often compares the Christian's life to the games people play, with the purpose of showing us the way to win.

I. The secret that is in ourselves.

A. *The importance of the fundamentals.* There is no substitute for learning the fundamentals, for self-discipline and dedicated training. This is true in education and in character building. Jesus refers to this as "building a good foundation" and "counting the cost." We cannot expect to win if we are not willing to pay the price of victory.

B. *The difference between a winner and a loser.* When the favored team loses, we call it an "upset." The momentum swings and turns the tide of victory and defeat. Often this has to do with the "winning spirit" within us. Every coach knows this secret. Bud Wilkinson, former coach at Oklahoma University, once said, "You've got to go into the game believing you can win. Somehow the other team believes you will win too."

This winning spirit comes from the coach who believes in his men and helps them believe in themselves. We can draw no better comparison than the relationship of Christ to his followers. He said, "All things are possible to him that believeth" (Mark 9:23). The greatest champion of the gospel of Christ said, "I am able to do all things through him who strengthens me" (Phil. 4:13 RSV).

II. The characteristics of a champion.

We are ready to offer an answer to the question so important to every young person, "How can I become a winner instead of a loser?"

A. *"You've got to have heart."* The words of a once popular song said, "You've got to have heart." There is no substitute for learning the fundamentals of the game—the self-discipline in conditioning and the dedicated hours of training. But in the final analysis, winning takes heart. The champion is a champion because he never quits. He gets knocked down, but he gets up again. You never really lose the battle until you lose heart. As the aforementioned song goes, "When the odds are saying, 'You'll never win,' that's when the grin should start; man, you've got to have heart."

On the other hand, there are those who, in their own minds and in the opinion of others, are losers. One writer who apparently recognized inevitable defeat as the pattern in his life wrote a song entitled "Born to Lose." This is a tragic resignation, a failure to see the truth that a person brings about his own defeat. Either he is unwilling to pay the price of victory, or he sees himself as unworthy of victory. But no person was born to lose. We all are born to win and must believe that.

B. *You've got to have faith.* "Heart" and "faith" are inseparable qualities. What keeps us from losing heart but a faith that we will win? Of course, our faith must be not in ourselves but in Christ, the one who makes us more than conquerors.

It is important to remember that our real foe is Satan. Paul wrote, "We are not contending against flesh and blood, but against the principalities, against the powers" (Eph. 6:12 RSV). But Satan is a defeated foe, for Christ conquered him. The Son of God took upon himself the form of human flesh and subjected himself to every temptation, yet he never sinned. The great climactic struggle came when he engaged the powers of darkness in his death on the cross and God raised him from the dead. He said, "Be of good cheer; I have overcome the world" (John 16:33).

Our faith, therefore, must be in Christ and not in ourselves. Self-sufficiency is our greatest danger. Every great person in the Bible had to experience personal failure in order to be able to win by the grace of God.

III. Do you have what it takes to win?

A. *"Put on the whole armor of God."* We need to put it all together to win. This is implied in Paul's inventory of the spiritual resources needed by the Christian soldier in Ephesians 6:13–18. There we find the confidence and poise that is not conceit but is the assurance we gain from Christ, who has run the race before us.

B. *Follow the "game plan."* Every coach determines his game plan by calculating the strengths and weaknesses of his opponent. He studies the opponent's methods and teaches his players how to defend against these tactics.

God has a game plan. He has made known to us the devices and cunningness of Satan. He has established his church on earth—a community of the Holy Spirit, the body of Christ. He has instructed us in the way to win, and the gates of hell shall not prevail against us.

Conclusion

You were born to win; with Christ you cannot lose. "Be strong in the Lord and in the strength of his might" (Eph. 6:10 RSV).

Title: How Do You Measure Your Worth?

Text: "It is not the will of your Father which is in heaven, that one of these little ones should perish" **(Matt. 18:14)**.

Scripture Reading: Matthew 18:1–14

Introduction

"Of how much more value is a man than a sheep?" (Matt. 12:12 RSV). "Of how much more value are you than the birds?" (Luke 12:24 RSV). How do you measure the value of an individual's life? In a world where life was cheap, Jesus stressed the infinite worth of the individual. He saw the individual in the crowd (19:5). He heard the cry of the individual above the noise of the crowd (18:40). He felt the touch of the individual in the push of the crowd (8:45).

How do you measure your worth as a young person? Your answer and the implications of that answer to life are the plan and purpose of this sermon.

389

I. Does it matter what I think?

A. *It mattered to Jesus what you think.* He knew that the value one places on his life will determine what he does with it, the care he gives it, and the price he places on it. It would not profit a man "to gain the whole world" if in the process he "lost his life" (Luke 9:25).

B. *Others are concerned about what you think.* Psychologists believe that self-esteem (your feeling of worth) is the "core value" in the growth and development of a healthy personality. Sociologists are interested in your self-image (the way you see yourself in relation to others). They believe a person behaves according to the kind of person he sees himself to be. This is the explanation for much delinquent behavior.

C. *Now what do you think?* The answer is not so simple. For one thing, we have not really been aware of the question. It has been greatly influencing our choices and actions, but we did not realize it. Another reason we hesitate is that we need some standards—some kind of yardstick or scales to use as a measure. This is the place to start.

II. False standards that influence our thinking and feeling about ourselves.

A. *How does society measure a person's worth?* There are things we call "status symbols." If you have them, you are an important person. If not, you are without status.

It is false to measure a person by what he has instead of what he is, by who he knows instead of what he can do. Yet many young people feel inferior to others because they measure themselves by such standards.

How would Jesus measure up in terms of our "status symbols"? He was born to common parents in a stable. He grew up in a small, out-of-the-way place. He learned a trade, never traveled far, was a friend to sinners, and died a criminal's death with two common thieves.

B. *How do we inwardly measure our worth?* Someone once said, "I'm not what I think I am, I'm not what you think I am, I am what I think you think I am." This little thought twister points out the importance of our interpersonal relationships.

To see ourselves as persons of worth, we have to feel that we are worth something to someone else. We need to be loved for ourselves. It does not matter how we measure up in terms of status if it does not seem to matter to anyone what happens to us. The most pathetic of all words are these: "No man cared for my soul" (Ps. 142:4).

C. *One more thing that can distort our sense of self-worth is the experience of life.* It could be some great personal tragedy, some deed done, or some hurt we caused that makes us feel that God cannot forgive us or that we cannot forgive ourselves. A good example is the leper who said to Jesus, "Lord, if you will, you can make me clean" (Mark 1:40 RSV), or "I don't doubt your power, but I doubt if I am worth your trouble." Jesus said, "I will" (Mark 1:41).

III. True standards to measure our worth.

A. *We are the work of God's creation.* We are unique, one of a kind. We have different fingerprints, different voices, different ways of thinking.

This was brought home to me the week that President Kennedy's infant died of a lung condition. I held a graveside service for a baby born out of wedlock who died of the same disease. The whole nation mourned the loss of the president's child, but hardly anyone knew of the other. To God they were equal—a life is a life. God gives each his own worth.

B. *We are the objects of God's love in redemption.* A "homeless" dog followed me home from school one day. We became inseparable friends. By anyone else's standards, he was worthless. To me, he was priceless. I loved him. That gave him his worth.

The greatest measure of our worth to God is revealed in the death of his Son for our sins (John 3:16). This is the gospel we preach, to make known the redemptive love of God in Christ. The purpose of the church is to see all people as persons for whom Christ died. We are the family of God offering loving and caring relationships where each sees himself and others as persons of worth.

Conclusion

How do you measure your worth? If you are a Christian, your status will be measured in terms of your service to others. When you are redeemed by the "precious blood of Christ," always keep in mind that "you are not your own; you were bought with a price" (1 Cor. 6:20 RSV). You are priceless because Christ loved you enough to die for you.

Title: If I Were Young Again

Text: "In all your ways acknowledge him, and he will make straight your paths" **(Prov. 3:6 RSV).**

Scripture Reading: Proverbs 3:1–8

Introduction

A friend of mine, upon his retirement, was asked to speak on the subject "If I had it all to do over again." He stood and said he believed he could sum up his conclusion in two words: "I wouldn't." He went on to share with us from his wealth of experience.

The "good old days" are an illusion. They were not as good as we are inclined to remember them. We forget about how difficult it was to be young, how uncertain and insecure we were at the crossroads, how very much we wanted guidance and a sure sense of direction.

Yet everyone at some time asks, If I had my life to live over again, how would it be different? Knowing what I know now, what principles, what faith would I live by? Lessons learned from experience are what age owes to youth. Young people don't need rules from the "good old days"; they need truths that apply in every generation.

I. I would choose a positive attitude toward life.

A. *This is a choice each of us has.* Many things we could not choose; they were chosen for us. Compared to some, we did not fare so well. But the important thing is the attitude we choose to have about the circumstances and experiences of life.

Resentment, anger, and self-pity are the negative attitudes that poison the whole of our lives and our relationships.

B. *I would accept life as a gift.* What a transformation in outlook and daily living it makes when life is lived as a gift. When something is given, we express the gratitude we feel to the giver. We use it, invest it, enjoy it, and care for it in respect to the one who made it possible.

II. I would get more from life.

A. *I would believe that life can be better, and I would make it so.* If your life is really worthwhile, it is not because you found it that way. Jesus said, "I came that they may have life, and have it abundantly" (John 10:10 RSV). Abundant living means getting more out of life, and Christ said that he came to make this possible. We can give only what we ourselves have received.

B. *I would aim higher than before.* I believe most of us undersell ourselves. For fear of failure, we bury what talent God has given us. We get more from life when we are challenged by a task worthy of our powers. So lift your sights—aim high.

III. I would put more into life.

A. *This is another choice we make.* Each of us decides what he is willing to give to life. "The measure you give will be the measure you get back" (Luke 6:38 RSV). "For whoever would save his life will lose it" (9:24 RSV).

B. "It is more blessed to give than to receive" (Acts 20:35). So I would put all I have at the disposal of God for the needs of others. I would be faithful to God. Jesus said, "If any man would come after me, let him deny himself and take up his cross daily and follow me" (Luke 9:23 RSV). I would "lay up treasure in heaven."

Conclusion

If I were young again and could live my life over, I would change me, not the circumstances of my birth or the gifts God gave me.

Sentence Sermonettes

When life knocks you to your knees, you are in a perfect position to pray.
Only God can redeem the heart.
Christian love is primarily something we do, not something we feel.
Sunshine alone creates a desert.
To go against conscience is neither right nor safe.
The Christian's trademark is obedience.
The good must not be permitted to become a substitute for the best.
Men, like trees, are known by their fruit.
For renewal the church must become a "go" group instead of a "come" group.
Humans, without God, become dehumanized.
Possessions can become idols.
Time is God's creation and God's gift.
God calls us to intelligent and creative obedience.
True religion involves the acts of God and the acts of people.
Courage is fear that has said its prayers.
When a man is average, he is just as close to the bottom as he is to the top.
The soul is the eternal part of a human.
God will be no person's debtor.
Prayer is the occupation of the soul with its needs. Praise is the occupation of
    the soul with its blessings. Worship is the occupation of the soul with God
    himself.
When temptations come, we must guard against entertaining them.
The mind of God has come to earth in the man Jesus.
Jesus Christ was the eternal God clothed in a human body.
A heresy is seldom a complete lie. A heresy usually results when one facet of the
    truth is unduly emphasized.
God has always been like Jesus was. God always will be like Jesus was.
Not all of the darkness in the world can extinguish the littlest flame.
The most valuable people around us have lived largely for others.
We grow only by giving the best of ourselves to something that we believe in
    heart and soul.
No one can be happy who lives only for self.
Supreme happiness comes to those who squander themselves for a noble purpose.
It is possible for one to create his own hell in the present.
Who gossips to you will gossip of you.
Not failure, but taking a low aim, is a crime.
When wealth is lost, nothing is lost; when health is lost, something is lost; when
    character is lost, all is lost.

Subject Index

Index of Scripture Texts

Share Your Thoughts

With the Author: Your comments will be forwarded to the author when you send them to *zauthor@zondervan.com*.

With Zondervan: Submit your review of this book by writing to *zreview@zondervan.com*.

Free Online Resources at
www.zondervan.com

Zondervan AuthorTracker: Be notified whenever your favorite authors publish new books, go on tour, or post an update about what's happening in their lives at www.zondervan.com/authortracker.

Daily Bible Verses and Devotions: Enrich your life with daily Bible verses or devotions that help you start every morning focused on God. Visit www.zondervan.com/newsletters.

Free Email Publications: Sign up for newsletters on Christian living, academic resources, church ministry, fiction, children's resources, and more. Visit www.zondervan.com/newsletters.

Zondervan Bible Search: Find and compare Bible passages in a variety of translations at www.zondervanbiblesearch.com.

Other Benefits: Register yourself to receive online benefits like coupons and special offers, or to participate in research.

■ ZONDERVAN®

ZONDERVAN.com/
AUTHORTRACKER
follow your favorite authors